STUDIENREIHE ROMANIA

Herausgegeben von Martina Drescher, Ingrid Neumann-Holzschuh,
Silke Segler-Meßner und Roland Spiller

Band 40

Expert Cultures and Standardization

Expertenkulturen und Standardisierung

Romance Languages in the Early Modern Period

Romanische Sprachen in der Frühen Neuzeit

Herausgegeben von
Maria Selig und Laura Linzmeier

ERICH SCHMIDT VERLAG

Bibliografische Information der Deutschen Nationalbibliothek

Die Deutsche Nationalbibliothek verzeichnet diese Publikation
in der Deutschen Nationalbibliografie;
detaillierte bibliografische Daten sind im Internet
über http://dnb.d-nb.de abrufbar.

Weitere Informationen zu diesem Titel finden Sie im Internet unter
ESV.info/978-3-503-20913-2

Gedruckt mit freundlicher Unterstützung des
Deutschen Romanistenverbands (DRV).

Gedrucktes Werk: ISBN 978-3-503-20913-2
eBook: ISBN 978-3-503-20914-9

Alle Rechte vorbehalten
© Erich Schmidt Verlag GmbH & Co. KG, Berlin 2023
www.ESV.info

Druck: Hubert & Co., Göttingen

Contents

Maria Selig, Laura Linzmeier
'Doing expertise': linguistic standardization in early modern
Romance expert cultures (Introduction) 7

*Sebastian Lauschus, Guido Mensching, Luca Refrigeri,
Frank Savelsberg*
Medizinisch-botanische Synonymenlisten zu den hebräischen
Übersetzungen von Avicennas Qānūn. Ein Beitrag zur überregionalen
Diffusion romanischer Fachterminologien in Mittelalter und
Früher Neuzeit 23

Christine Paasch-Kaiser
Conventionalization of verb-noun constructions in legal discourse 43

Gabriele Zanello
I linguaggi tecnici nelle carte friulane del tardo Medioevo 65

Lorenzo Tomasin
Più *trasmigratori* che *poeti*. Percorsi non letterari nella storia e nella
lessicografia dell'italiano 89

Tabea Salzmann
Standardisierungsprozesse in der administrativen Schriftlichkeit des
Estado da Índia im 16. Jahrhundert 105

Marina Albers
Knowledge and Writing in the Spanish Colony. The Promotion of
Education and Literacy by the Jesuits and internal epistolary
communication in the eighteenth-century Province of Paraguay 127

Katharina Fezer
„Le parfait négociant" als vollendeter Sprecher?
Wirtschaftsfachsprache und Sprachnormierungsdebatte im
Frankreich des 17. Jahrhunderts 145

Contents

Laura Linzmeier
"Navigating" the visual surface – the writing strategies of French navigational experts in the seventeenth and eighteenth centuries 163

Anne Weber, Daniele Moretti, Vahram Atayan
Ways of wisdom: the transfer of knowledge into German-speaking countries discussed on the basis of the *Heidelberg Bibliography of Translations of Nonfictional Texts* 183

Martin Sinn
Sprachliche Vielfalt und disziplinäre Ausdifferenzierung: Dante in den Akademievorträgen Benedetto Varchis (1543–1547) 205

Franz Meier
Les phrases pseudo-clivées inversées dans la traduction scientifique dans l'Italie de la fin du 18ᵉ siècle 223

Biographies 241

Maria Selig and Laura Linzmeier

'Doing expertise': linguistic standardization in early modern Romance expert cultures

1. Expert cultures and standardization: some preliminary remarks

For more than thirty years, there has been an increasing interest in "alternative language histories" (Elspaß 2021: 94). Rather than concentrating on literary norms or the norms of higher social classes, scholars have tried to conceive language history from a new perspective and have shifted their interest to varieties hitherto seldom taken into consideration: the language of 'ordinary people', not of privileged classes, and the language of informal use – that is, private letters, account books and trial proceedings instead of literary poetry and prose, sacred texts and courtly conversation (cf. Elspaß 2021: 99–102; cf. also Oesterreicher 1997). This shift to a *language history from below* (Elspaß 2005) is meant not only to highlight domains which until now have been eclipsed by traditional narratives; the classic models of standardization, heavily influenced by concepts of national identity and hegemonial, homogeneous national languages, are also at stake. The aim of these new approaches, then, is to show how historical instances of standardization processes have been influenced by dynamics located 'below' the social classes and/or communicative genres believed to be the driving forces behind the selection, elaboration, codification and implementation of standard varieties.

The title of this volume signals our desire to continue this line of thinking. The expert cultures and literate practices rooted in these circles are not the domains that standardization theories presume to be decisive for establishing supra-regional and codified varieties. But, as we will show in section 1.2, the communicative practices of these experts are not 'below' the literary circles, courtly entourages or princely academies that histories of standardization seem to favor. We deliberately avoid any social or cultural hierarchizations, but think rather of 'parallel' or 'different' communicative dynamics, each of which contributes in a specific way to standardizing processes. Or, in the words of Lorenzo Tomasin: we do not conceive expert cultures as an "anecdotal appendix, or at most occasional participant in the [standard's] path of diffusion, expansion, and affirmation", but as one of the "numerous and varied currents" that nurture historical standardization processes.[1]

This, in turn, leads us to question some standard ideas about standardization: in section 1.1, we argue for a model that includes not only the classical top-down processes controlled by language authorities and guided by standard language ideologies, but also invisible-hand processes related to functional-pragmatic aspects of literacy and the domain of communicative distance (cf. Koch/Oesterreicher 2011; 2012). We suggest, therefore, taking a close look at the communicative practices rooted in expert cultures (1.2) and seeing to what degree they contributed to linguistic elaboration, centralization and normalization (1.3).

1.1 'Spontaneous' standardization processes

In standardization theory, there has always been a tension between approaches focused on the functional requirements of (Klossian) *Ausbau* and nation-wide communication on one hand and sociolinguistic interpretations criticizing standard language ideology and interpreting it as a means of repressive social control on the other. Functionalist perspectives can be traced back to the Prague School of structuralism and its ideas on functional stylistics and later, in the sixties and seventies, to sociolinguistic research on language planning, especially in the context of nation-development and the standardization of minority languages (cf. Ayres-Bennett 2021: 29–33). Yet with regard to this functional perspective, a non-normative, descriptive approach has also been developed: Peter Koch and Wulf Oesterreicher's model of "conceptional variation" (Koch/Oesterreicher 2011: 3–20; cf. also Koch/Oesterreicher 2007: 20–42) argues for directly relating the linguistic effects of *Ausbau* and elaboration to the interplay of context and discourse. Their model relies on insights from text/discourse-centered approaches as to the relevance of situational features for the choice of verbalization strategies. It therefore highlights: a) social parameters such as the degree of social and emotional distance between the interlocutors or the variation between more private/more public communication; b) cognitive parameters such as the variation between situationally embedded/non-embedded verbalization; and c) cognitive-interactional parameters such as spontaneous or non-spontaneous turn-taking, the specific possibilities of planning or the varying degrees to

---

[1] Cf. "una sorta di appendice aneddotica, o al più di partecipante occasionale al percorso di diffusione, espansione e affermazione [dello standard]", "sviluppi storici di una lingua che in realtà è stata silenziosamente alimentata da correnti ben più numerose e variegate" (Tomasin, this volume, p. 94–95).

which communication focuses exclusively on one thematic domain (cf. Koch/ Oesterreicher 2011: 6–10; cf. also Selig/Schmidt-Riese 2021: 149–153).

We cannot fully develop the theoretical background and variational aspects of this model.[2] It may suffice here, though, to underline those aspects that are essential for understanding standardization. First, it is important to note that Koch and Oesterreicher's model conceptualizes the varying situational features and corresponding verbalization strategies as a multidimensional continuum, spanning from the pole of "communicative immediacy" (i.e., maximally informal communication) to that of "communicative distance" (i.e., maximally formal communication). The model thus provides a comprehensive vision of the interplay of contextual parameters and verbalization strategies and allows us to grasp linguistic variation along the entire range of communicative practices at a community's disposal (cf. Winter-Froemel 2023). Second, the framework allows for a more analytic approach to functionalist attributes of standard languages, such as *intellectualization* (Garvin 1959), *minimal variation in form* or *maximal variation in function* (Haugen 1966), because it traces them back to the conceptional profile of communicative practices that instantiate conditions of communicative distance. Finally, even if it was originally conceived as independent from media-related aspects, the model allows one to integrate material as well as cognitive and social effects of literacy und to provide an analytic framework able to disentangle the close relationship between literate practices, literate infrastructure and standardization (cf. Grübl et al. 2021; Selig 2017; 2022a). Standardization processes such as linguistic elaboration or normalization can then be rooted anthropologically: They are related to the agency of individual speakers/writers and hearers/readers, interacting in formal contexts of communicative distance and adapting their linguistic choices to the functional – i.e., epistemic and social – needs of these communicative configurations.

From the standpoint of language history, this shift from focusing on explicit, institutionally concentrated top-down-processes to an actor-practice-centered definition is essential. It allows for a better understanding of the impact of major socio-cultural dynamics such as urbanization, the tendency towards juridification and increasing public administration – as well as the rise of vernacular literacy with the dissemination of literate practices in larger social contexts. These changes enlarge the communicative genres at a society's disposal (especially in the domain of communicative distance), while *Ausbau* on the level of text/discourse acts as an incentive towards elaboration processes in the lexical and syntactic domains (cf. Koch/Oester-

---

[2] Cf. Grübl et al. (2021); Schmidt-Riese/Selig (2021); Selig (2017; 2022a). Cf. also the contributions in Winter-Froemel/Octavio de Toledo y Huerta (2023).

reicher 2011: 135–142).³ We may add that urbanization increases the contexts favorable to spontaneous koineizations and that literacy is often related to supra-regional networks which, in turn, favor dialect convergence and the emergence of less local, more "anonymous" (Woolard 2007: 133–135) varieties (cf. Grübl 2014; Selig 2022b). These elaboration dynamics and centralizing tendencies are not planned and their effects may be limited. Nevertheless, from an analytic point of view, these invisible-hand processes are not random but systematic, and they intersect with prototypical instances of standardization processes at more than one point. It seems necessary in standardization theory, then, to focus not only on literary contexts of communicative distance, but also on non-literary ones which are not controlled by rhetorical culture. We therefore suggest taking a closer look at those who, by their expertise, are involved in these non-literary practices of so-called pragmatic literacy.

1.2 Expert groups and expert cultures

In the early modern era, the concepts of 'expertise' and 'expert' are still fuzzy ones. This vagueness stems from the combined interest in both practical and theoretical know-how, that is, in

> a form of knowledge that was not fully rooted in practical, hands-on experience, nor yet in abstract mathematics or a rarified natural philosophy. It was something of a mix, ever in flux, always being negotiated, nameless because the name we now use for it had yet to come into being. (Ash 2019: 74)

Historically speaking, this interest is related to the revaluation of practical fields of action (the *artes mechanicae*) whose practically oriented knowledge initially circulated mainly orally within a small community of skilled workers. After the rise of vernacular literacy and the invention of printing, however, such knowledge could reach wider circles, also thanks to the increasing interest of scholars in experiments and the documentation of technical and practical knowledge. This knowledge includes, among others, the know-how and expertise of craftsmen, those engaged in the healing professions, veterinarians, traders, bankers, etc. (cf. Rankin 2022: 144; Pöckl 1990: 274).

---

³ Whereas Haugen's term 'elaboration' (Haugen 1966) concentrated on language-internal aspects, Kloss (1967) was also interested in external, i.e., practice-related aspects of appropriating text genres of communicative distance when using the term *Ausbau*. Cf. also Koch and Oesterreicher's distinction between *intensiver Ausbau* (i.e., linguistic) and *extensiver Ausbau* (i.e., genre-related) (Koch/Oesterreicher 2011: 136).

The word 'expert' was initially used less as a noun and more as an adjective. The underlying Latin expression *expertus sum* can be translated as "I experienced" or also "I know from experience/from trying it out", indicating participation in an act (whether in the form of observing and assisting or actually performing it) (cf. Rankin 2022: 143). This means that one could be an "expert-by-practice" or an "expert-by-knowledge" (Steven Walton quoted in Ash 2019: 77) or even a combination of both: "seeing, touching, observing, experimenting: doing something" (Rankin 2022: 143).

From the sixteenth century onward, the publication of reference books, manuals and specialized dictionaries increased and the term 'expert' started to appear on the titles of monographs (cf. Füssel 2012: 270). Even though the ideas of what an expert or expertise was were still "hotly contested" (Rankin 2022: 144), the notion of what actually defined an expert was slightly refined in the seventeenth and eighteenth centuries. For example, Füssel (2012: 270, n. 7) points out that Richelet's *Dictionnaire françoise, contenant les mots et les choses* from 1680 contains only a short definition of the term, but that the later edition of 1759 describes much more precisely what characterizes 'experts': "des personnes qui ont acquis par une longue pratique, la connoissance de certaines choses, en sorte que lorsqu'il s'agit de décider des questions de fait, on nomme des Experts pour en dire leur sentiment" (Richelet 1759: 148).

Nevertheless, it still remains unclear who exactly fell under this category and who did not:[4] With reference to Ash (2019), it must be emphasized that if the term 'expert' can be applied simply to anyone who is particularly competent or experienced at something, then the term has been completely overextended. According to Ash (2019: 80–81), it is therefore advisable for researchers on the early modern era not to use the term descriptively, but rather exclusively as a "meta-category" and to have recourse to the concrete professional designations common to the time, such as *surgeon, artisan, alchemist* etc. As long as there were no institutions regulating the understanding of who was an expert and who was not, "the negotiation of expertise was much more vague, contingent, and open to differing interpretations and agendas" (Ash 2019: 83).

We therefore define expertise not simply as 'knowledge' or 'skill', since it combines practical know-how with theoretical underpinning:

---

[4] The French adjective *expert/e* has long remained synonymous with the English term 'experienced' and has therefore been used to refer to different professional groups; cf. Richelet (1759): "Un matelot fort expert" (1759: 605), "L'Ingénieur est un Mathématicien habile, expert & hardi, qui fait l'Art de l'Architecture militaire" (1759: 443), "Les Maréchaux de camp doivent être braves, experts & judicieux" (1759: 592).

It is the nuanced combination(s) of practical ability and a more general, theoretical understanding that makes expertise different from other, related concepts such as 'experience'. Thus, if the early modern knowledge and skills in question were usually encompassed in a straightforward artisanal apprenticeship, they may better be thought of as 'craft knowledge' or 'workshop knowledge', but probably not as 'expertise' per se. (Ash 2019: 81)

The same holds for the concept of 'expert' in the early modern period. Related to the question of standardization, we suggest that this term be restricted to professionals who were equipped with theoretical knowledge (which they might also have used in the execution of practical actions), had to pass through examinations or come before specific authorities in order to qualify as such and had access to literacy (through schooling or other educational practices). In this sense, early modern experts are not only characterized by special knowledge and skills, but are also often associated with higher social positions, a special use of language, competence in handling instruments and tools and the mastery of "precise ritual choreographies of expert action" ("genaue rituelle Choreographien des Expertenhandelns", Rexroth/Schröder-Stapper 2018: 9; cf. also Füssel et al. 2019: 10). In a nutshell: these experts do not necessarily act 'below' – and certainly not apart from – literary, courtly or public authorities.

1.3 'Polymorphic' standardization

What, then, is the role of expert cultures in standardization? Were expert cultures involved at all in this development? According to the idea of bottom-up standardizing processes, related to the specific discourse-pragmatic conditions of communicative distance and to the material and cognitive dispositions of literacy, the answer is clearly yes: Premodern experts, albeit not belonging to elitist literary circles, were involved in standardization. The contributions of Sebastian Lauschus, Guido Mensching, Luca Refrigeri and Frank Savelsberg, Christiane Paasch-Kaiser and Gabriele Zanello show that from the beginnings of the written use of vernaculars by expert groups, we witness the elaboration of technical vocabulary and complex syntax. The question then arises as to whether the standardization processes initiated by these experts took place in an independent way, occurring only locally and at an individual level. Here, the answer is no: These processes, then as now, are never isolated and completely autonomous, but rather are embedded in larger communication networks. This means that even if vernacular, non-literary experts are located outside hegemonial (Latin) literacy and act on a more regional level, they contribute to "supralocalizations" and "supraregionalizations", terms used by Gijsbert Rutten and Rik Vosters for premodern linguistic accommodation and dialect convergence phenomena (Rutten/ Vosters 2021: 67). The same holds for later developments such as the setting up of large administrative systems in the colonial empires, new forms of schooling or the increasing role of the book market after the invention of printing. Here too, non-literary, vernacular expert groups actively participate in building up these structures, and their literate practices and the communication networks they establish continue to contribute to standardizing processes. It is true, however, that the new experts are not 'absorbed' by traditional, Latin-based rhetoric culture. Esthetic norms may dominate in private or public academies in Renaissance Italy, as has been shown by Martin Sinn, but vernacular expert groups do not follow those tendencies for the most part. The contributions of Lorenzo Tomasin, Tabea Salzmann, Marina Albers, Katharina Fezer and Laura Linzmeier, therefore, advocate for a differentiated approach. Indeed, premodern experts take advantage of (Latin) educational infrastructure, adapt politeness patterns developed by ecclesiastical hierarchies and rely on bureaucratic handwriting traditions. Yet, all in all, they continue to align their textual and linguistic strategies towards the functional needs of pragmatic literacy and to adopt a flexible, inclusive concept of linguistic normativity, which tolerates the use of group- or genre-specific varieties. According to the contributions of Anne Weber, Daniel Moretti, Vahram Atayan and Franz Meier, who analyze premodern translational practices in theoretical-pragmatical literature, we may even witness the first signs of a definite shift away from rhetorical to non-rhetorical, i.e., 'functionally' oriented patterns before the rise of modern standardization 'from above' in the mid-eighteenth century (cf. Rutten/Vosters 2021).

The question, then, is not so much whether non-literary experts partake in standardization, but whether expert cultures are in line with general tendencies or are acting 'against' them. Let us first note that premodern experts may be active in written practices situated nearer to the pole of communicative immediacy, such as contextually embedded lists or private correspondence within immediate professional and/or familiar contexts. However, it would be grossly misleading to compare their (pragmatically, not literarily oriented) skills to those of less experienced occasional writers 'below' the prevailing standards of literacy. Analyzing expert cultures is a highly necessary complement to language histories biased by their exclusive focus on literary traditions, but this must be done without subscribing to the tendency to locate everything non-literary 'below' influential social settings. This, in turn, means that we should not advocate for a narrow definition of standardization which necessarily encompasses metalinguistic activities promoting standard language ideology and exclude – on principle – unplanned, bottom-up and not explicitly thematized invisible-hand processes from such a definition. We must certainly take into account the "fundamental breach"

(Rutten/Vosters 2021: 68) that can be observed in European language history around 1750 on the threshold to the modern era. Standardization, at this point of cultural and social evolution, clearly comes 'from above'. It begins to be based on nationalist ideologies and modern concepts of citizenship, such that codification practices are addressed to entire national language communities, extending the normative claims to linguistic practice as such, regardless of contextually motivated variation. However, on the conceptual level, when analytic tools used to describe the processes involved in standardizing are under discussion, it may be more advisable to signal the historical continuity of elaboration and centralization, and to provide the means to mark clearly that without the results of these processes, modern standardization would not have been possible (cf. Elspaß 2021: 97–98).

Following a proposal by Peter Auer (2005: 22), Gisbert Rutten and Rik Vosters characterize the linguistic situation preceding the nineteenth century's standardization 'from above' as "diaglossia with fairly local writing practices on one side of the sociolinguistic continuum, supralocal writing traditions on the other side and a wide spectrum of variation in-between" (Rutten/Vosters 2021: 65).[5] The contributions gathered in this volume are interested in analyzing how this "wide spectrum of variation" and the flexible understanding of written norms came into being in medieval and early modern Romance-speaking areas and to what extent vernacular expert cultures were involved in this process. We think that as a result of these analyses, the interest of a broader vision of language history including research on expert groups is beyond any doubt. The contributions show that premodern standardization is not exclusively related to literary domains, but rather is anchored in more than one *epistemic culture* (Knorr-Cetina 1999). They show that premodern standardization dynamics are mostly driven by communicative practice and by the agency of historical actors, not by institutionalized language authorities. Moreover, they contribute to a differentiated, more complex view of standardizing dynamics by showing that elaboration and convergence processes are not necessarily interrelated and may in fact

---

[5] Rutten and Vosters 'enlarge' the notion of diaglossia and apply it regardless of Auer's original orientation towards the modelling of spoken dialect-standard continua (cf. Auer 2005: 22–24) to written language as well (cf. Rutten/Vosters 2021: 65). This implies that configurations of communicative immediacy, the prototypical domain of dialects in premodern Europe, are mingled with those of communicative distance, which is prototypically associated with written use. It would be necessary to differentiate more clearly media-related and discourse-pragmatic phenomena, but we concentrate here on Rutten and Vosters' idea that premodern literacy should be modelled as a continuum, with varying norms according to genres, groups and regions.

be signs of conflicting tendencies, yet are nevertheless rooted in essentially the same anthropological, functional and social dynamics, i.e., the dynamics of literacy and communicative distance.

We have decided not to include the literate practices of experts and their standardizing effects in dichotomous opposition to the traditionally focused literary cultures. In our understanding, expert cultures do not act 'outside' or 'against' these developments, even if they are not always exactly in line with them. By contrast, we propose conceiving of premodern standardization as 'polymorphic', encompassing processes originating in different contexts, but comparable as to their social and communicative conditions. The outcome of these processes – diaglossia – is certainly much less mandatory then modern standard situations, as it offers flexible norms together with genre- and group-specific solutions. Nevertheless, diaglossia is not ephemeral and purely transitional, but rather a standardization context adapted to the needs of premodern literate societies and their multiple epistemic cultures.

2. The contributions of the present volume

The articles gathered in this volume are clustered into three major thematic areas that focus on the linguistic features (2.1 Specialized/technical languages and terminological elaboration), cultural embeddings (2.2 Expert practices and cultural models) and contact-driven processes (2.3 Knowledge flows, translations and scientific literacy) of premodern expert cultures. The case studies they offer provide insights into historical situations situated not only in Europe, but also in overseas areas of the Romance-speaking world.

2.1 Specialized/technical languages and terminological elaboration

Sebastian Lauschus, Guido Mensching, Luca Refrigeri and **Frank Savelsberg** ("Medizinisch-botanische Synonymenlisten zu den hebräischen Übersetzungen von Avicennas *Qānūn*. Ein Beitrag zur überregionalen Diffusion romanischer Fachterminologien in Mittelalter und Früher Neuzeit") concentrate on the dissemination of Occitan specialized terminology in Jewish medical texts of the fourteenth to sixteenth centuries. They show that this terminology spread to other cultural areas such as the Iberian Peninsula, Northern France and Central Italy, even before the period of premodern globalization. Furthermore, they argue that the Occitan terminology was quasi-standardized either through its use as loan-words or as a kind of model for the creation of local terminologies. The Occitan context and the Jewish community in Southern France can thus be considered as pivotal in the transmission of Arabic medico-botanical knowledge to other European areas, at least until the rise of the humanistic intellectual movements and their tendency towards basing scientific terminologies on Latin or Greek forms in order to mark the passage to a new scholarly paradigm.

Christine Paasch-Kaiser's paper ("Conventionalization of verb-noun constructions in legal discourse") deals with the occurrence, distribution and diachronic development of verb-noun collocations in legal textbooks originating from Normandy in the fourteenth through sixteenth centuries. The study is concerned with examining five verb-noun collocations containing the legal terminological unit *plet*. The author raises the question as to whether these constructions can be characterized as conventionalized patterns that are part of the customary law of Normandy and whether they shape the understanding of an implicit legal norm that was not exclusively tied to that region. The study allows for three of the verb-noun collocations to be identified as conventionalized constructions, whose use was not limited to Normandy. Furthermore, the author highlights the effects of the law reforms in the sixteenth century, which caused the collocations considered here to lose their status as conventionalized forms. There seems, then, to be a clear parallel to the transition to a new knowledge paradigm observed by Sebastian Lauschus and his colleagues in the domain of medico-botanical practices.

Gabriele Zanello's paper ("I linguaggi tecnici nelle carte friulane del tardo Medioevo") offers insights into another important context of vernacular pragmatic literacy, namely that of charters and other administrative texts that closely mirror situations, actions and objects of everyday life. The author analyzes the technical vocabulary of agriculture, craftsmanship and administration in a corpus of Friulian texts from Cividale, Udine and Gemona, covering the period between ca. 1300 and 1400. He shows how these terms reflect the multilingual situation created, for instance, by the presence of groups of Tuscan merchants in the Friulian towns: On the one hand, the technical terms are predominantly of local origin, yet on the other, their morphology is adapted to central varieties and Tuscan features, by adding final vowels or final consonants; Friu. *savolon*, 'sand' (It. *sabbia*), for instance, figures in the texts as *savolone*. Interestingly, the comparison with modern dialect data shows that in the medieval texts, there are many abstract nouns ending in *-ura*, *-arìa* and *-son*, which do not have modern dialect correspondences. This leads to the question as to what extent medieval scribes used word formation techniques to create the complex vocabulary they needed in a more or less *ad hoc* fashion.

2.2 Expert practices and cultural models

Lorenzo Tomasin's article ("Più *trasmigratori* che *poeti*. Percorsi non letterari nella storia e nella lessicografia dell'italiano") underlines the necessity of alternative approaches to standardization history, especially in the case of Italian. He shows how traditional historiography has narrowed its focus on the evolution of literary language and/or Tuscan varieties to the point that *storia della lingua* and *storia della letteratura* seem to be identical. This might be related to the particular historical background of Italian standard language ideology, which, due to secular trends towards regional fragmentation, emerged in Renaissance Italy without any relation to political and/or economic centralization. But as Tomasin convincingly argues, discussions on literary norms must have been paralleled by other non-literary practices to explain the formation of common linguistic and metalinguistic traditions. He therefore proposes analyzing the impact of professional migration contexts and of pragmatically oriented bilingual and multilingual lexicography on premodern standardization processes.

Tabea Salzmann's article ("Standardisierungsprozesse in der administrativen Schriftlichkeit des *Estado da Índia* im 16. Jahrhundert") focuses on the effects of language contact on the pragmatic writing of Portuguese administrators in the sixteenth-century *Estado da Índia*. She shows that the documents display a relatively homogeneous form, even though they originate from numerous different writers. The author therefore suggests an underlying professional practice of writing in addition to a well-organized and stable network between the Portuguese colonies and the European motherland, institutions and individuals and other factors that encouraged the spread and use of standardized forms.

Marina Albers focuses on the epistolary writing practice of Jesuits in the historical province of Paraguay ("Knowledge and Writing in the Spanish Colony. The Promotion of Education and Literacy by the Jesuits and internal epistolary communication in the eighteenth-century Province of Paraguay"). Drawing on the evidence that the Jesuits contributed significantly to the establishment of educational structures and the dissemination of knowledge in the colony, the author uses a discourse-traditional and pragmatic analysis of a corpus of eighteenth-century letters to examine the extent to which Jesuit epistolary culture parallels the European epistolary discourse tradition. The study shows that the writers not only respect traditional strategies of communicative distance of the European epistolary tradition (e.g., structure, address forms and formulaic patterns), but at the same time are open to expanding the understanding of the discourse tradition and to linguistic innovations that emerged during the *primer español moderno* (1675–1825) (e.g., inclusion of short messages, telegram-like style with condensed and elliptical expressions).

Katharina Fezer's contribution ("'Le parfait négociant' als vollendeter Sprecher? Wirtschaftsfachsprache und Sprachnormierungsdebatte im Frankreich des 17. Jahrhunderts") deals with French language of trade in the context of the seventeenth-century language standardization debate in France. After an overview of the different positions on this linguistic variety in metalinguistic treatises – which simultaneously reveal an attitude of rejection as well as toleration towards language of trade – a linguistic-structural analysis of a sample of commercial letters included in manuals for merchants and in letter-writing manuals shows that this form of pragmatic-functional writing uses its own standard forms (e.g., structures of efficiency and condensation such as elliptical constructions) that clearly deviate from codified norms of literary use of the day.

Laura Linzmeier's article ("'Navigating' the visual surface – the writing strategies of French navigational experts in the seventeenth and eighteenth centuries") focuses on the maritime writing practice of French navigators based on an exemplary analysis of a navigational journal from the mid-eighteenth century. The study shows that the writing culture of navigational experts is a clearly individual undertaking when it comes to documenting personal observations, discoveries etc. Navigators of the eighteenth century are aware of their expert role and therefore allow themselves to disregard official guidelines, such as pre-structured tables, by which the authorities intended to force the writers to record navigation-specific information in ever more detail and mathematical form. Maritime writers prefer instead narrative structures with coherence-creating linking strategies and are less interested in the purely numerical documentation of individual nautical details.

2.3 Knowledge flows, translations and scientific literacy

The contribution of **Anne Weber**, **Daniele Moretti** and **Vahram Atayan** ("Ways of wisdom: the transfer of knowledge into German-speaking countries discussed on the basis of the *Heidelberg Bibliography of Translations of Nonfictional Texts*") presents an ongoing bibliographical database project on translations of nonfictional texts from Latin, French, Italian, Spanish, English and Dutch into German from the invention of printing up to 1850. Linguistic historiography has concentrated for a long time on literary genres, and approaches to premodern translations have mostly ignored the large amount of nonfictional texts as source texts. The Heidelberg database (https://hueb.iued.uni-heidelberg.de/de/) is meant to fill this gap and provide a solid basis for research on the dynamics of premodern cultural transfer. The article presents some of the results of quantitative analyses of the metadata that have been collated in the database. By comparing the distribution of subject matters across time periods, languages and/or cultural areas, clear correlations between subjects and languages and/or cultural areas can be seen. Whereas Latin dominates the religious domains till the nineteenth century, French source texts mostly come from the fields of history and geography, while English texts hail from the sciences. Interestingly, the bibliography reveals a large number of translations into German based on already translated versions of the originals. Dutch thus often functions as an intermediary language in the case of English texts, and French seems to be another prestigious intermediary language, due to its supposed *clarté*.

Martin Sinn confronts two important figures in Italian linguistic history, Dante Alighieri and Benedetto Varchi, and analyzes their contribution to the elaboration of the vernacular in the domain of scientific language ("Sprachliche Vielfalt und disziplinäre Ausdifferenzierung: Dante in den Akademievorträgen Benedetto Varchis (1543–1547)"). The author shows that both intellectuals commit themselves explicitly to linguistic elaboration: Dante in the *Convivio* and the *Divina Commedia*; Varchi in his *Lezioni su Dante*, delivered to the *Accademia Fiorentina* between 1543 and 1547. But whereas Dante acts in the framework of medieval *theologia*, where literary and scientific discourse are not yet separated, Varchi distinguishes clearly between Dante the poet and Dante the *philosophus*, ready to differentiate his aesthetic judgement according to the topics Dante discusses. In doing so, Varchi does not adopt Bembo's harsh judgement on Dante's 'mixed' and 'impure' style and accepts the specific cognitive and terminological needs of specialized language. But, with regard to his stylistic ambitions, Varchi prefers the idea of *bello scrivere* even in scientific prose. This clearly indicates that he shares the hierarchical understanding of linguistic and stylistic variation, common in then-contemporary literary circles, and extends the scope of rhetoric and literary esthetics to include technical and scientific discourse as well.

Franz Meier discusses the phenomenon of cross-linguistic influence via translations of scholarly literature in eighteenth-century Italy ("Les phrases pseudo-clivées inversées dans la traduction scientifique dans l'Italie de la fin du 18e siècle"). He analyses the distribution of French and Italian reversed pseudo-cleft sentences in a corpus of 30 non-translated and 60 translated articles, published between 1770 and 1795 in Italian scientific reviews. Whereas in the French source texts, there is not a single attestation of the construction, he observes in the Italian texts (whether translated or not) a regular, though not frequent, use. While this distribution excludes direct code copying, a thorough analysis of the pragmatic and textual features of the Italian examples shows that the reversed pseudo-cleft constructions mostly combine complex noun phrases, resuming anaphoric information on topic subjects, with relative clauses adding new information with a defining or specifying function ("Questa luce, infiammazione, o fuoco, che scappa [...], è ciò che si appella Fuoco Elettrico", this volume, p. 228). The construction, then, appears to be related to the functional needs of scientific texts, with its use being not the result of mechanical copying, but rather a sign of the active appropriation of the verbalization strategies of communicative distance.

References

Ash, E. H. 2019. What is an Early Modern Expert? And why does it matter? In Füssel, M. / Rexroth, F. / Schürmann, I. Eds. *Praktiken und Räume des Wissens: Expertenkulturen in Geschichte und Gegenwart*. Göttingen: Vandenhoeck & Ruprecht, 69–88.

Auer, P. 2005. Europe's sociolinguistic unity, or: a typology of European dialect/standard constellations. In Delbecque, N. / Van der Auwera, J. / Geeraerts, D. Eds. *Perspectives on Variation*. Berlin: Mouton de Gruyter, 7–42.

Ayres-Bennett, W. 2021. Modelling Language Standardization. In Ayres-Bennett, W. / Bellamy, J. Eds. *The Cambridge Handbook of Language Standardization*. Cambridge: Cambridge University Press, 27–64.

Elspaß, S. 2005. *Sprachgeschichte von unten. Untersuchungen zum geschriebenen Alltagsdeutsch im 19. Jahrhundert*. Zugl.: Universität Münster [Habilitationsschrift, 2003]. Berlin: De Gruyter (= Reihe Germanistische Linguistik, 263).

Elspaß, S. 2021. Language Standardization in a View 'from Below'. In Ayres-Bennett, W. / Bellamy, J. Eds. *The Cambridge Handbook of Language Standardization*. Cambridge: Cambridge University Press, 93–114.

Füssel, M. 2012. Die Experten, die Verkehrten? Gelehrtensatire als Expertenkritik in der Frühen Neuzeit. In Reich, B. / Rexroth, F. / Roick, M. Eds. *Wissen, maßgeschneidert. Experten und Expertenkulturen im Europa der Vormoderne*. München: Oldenburg, 269–288.

Füssel, M. / Rexroth, F. / Schürmann, I. 2019. Experten in vormodernen und modernen Kulturen. Zur Einführung. In Füssel, M. / Rexroth, F. / Schürmann, I. Eds. *Praktiken und Räume des Wissens: Expertenkulturen in Geschichte und Gegenwart*. Göttingen: Vandenhoeck & Ruprecht, 7–16.

Garvin, P. 1959. The Standard Language Problem: Concepts and Methods. *Anthropological Linguistics* 1/3, 28–31.

Grübl, K. 2014. *Varietätenkontakt und Standardisierung im mittelalterlichen Französischen. Theorie, Forschungsgeschichte und Untersuchung eines Urkundenkorpus aus Beauvais (1241–1455)*. Tübingen: Narr.

Grübl, K. / Gruber, T. / Scharinger, T. 2021. Was bleibt von kommunikativer Nähe und Distanz? Revisionen eines linguistischen Paradigmas. In Gruber, T. / Grübl, K. / Scharinger, T. Eds. *Was bleibt von kommunikativer Nähe und Distanz? Mediale und konzeptionelle Aspekte sprachlicher Variation*. Tübingen: Narr, 9–56.

Haugen, E. 1966. Dialect, language and nation. *American Anthropologist* 68/4, 922–935.

Kloss, H. 1967. 'Abstandlanguages' and 'Ausbaulanguages'. *Anthropological Linguistics* 9/7, 29–41.

Knorr-Cetina, K. 1999. *Epistemic cultures. How the sciences make knowledge*. Cambridge, Mass.: Harvard University Press.

Koch, P. / Oesterreicher, W. 2007. *Lengua hablada en la Romania: español, francés, italiano*. Madrid: Gredos (= span. translation of Koch/Oesterreicher 1990).

Koch, P. / Oesterreicher, W. 2011 [1990]. *Gesprochene Sprache in der Romania: Französisch – Italienisch – Spanisch*. Berlin / New York: De Gruyter.

Koch, P. / Oesterreicher, W. 2012. Language of immediacy – language of distance. Orality and literacy from the perspective of language theory and linguistic history. In Lange, C. / Weber, B. / Wolf, G. Eds. *Communicative Spaces. Variation, Contact and Change. Papers in Honour of Ursula Schaefer*. Frankfurt a. M.: Peter Lang, 441–473.

Oesterreicher, W. 1997. Types of orality in text. In Bakker, E. / Kahane, A. Eds. *Written voices, spoken signs*. Cambridge, Mass.: Harvard University Press, 190–214.

Pöckl, W. 1990. Französisch: Fachsprachen. Langues de spécialité. In Holtus, G. / Metzeltin, M. / Schmitt, C. Eds. *Lexikon der romanistischen Linguistik*. Band 5/1. Tübingen: Niemeyer, 267–282.

Rankin, A. 2022. How to "Be Expert" in Early Modern Europe. *Historical Studies in the Natural Sciences* 52/1, 143–146.

Rexroth, F. / Schröder-Stapper, T. 2018. Woran man Experten erkennt. Einführende Überlegungen zur performativen Dimension von Sonderwissen während der Vormoderne. In Rexroth, F. / Schröder-Stapper, T. Eds. *Experten, Wissen, Symbole. Performanz und Medialität vormoderner Wissenskulturen*. Berlin / Boston: De Gruyter, 7–26.

Richelet, P. 1680. *Dictionnaire françoise, contenant les mots et les choses*, ... Genève: J.H. Widerhold. https://archive.org/details/dictionnairefra00rich/page/n335/mode/2up?q=expert&view=theater (2023-03-30).

Richelet, P. 1759. *Dictionnaire de la langue Françoise, ancienne et moderne*. vol. 2. Lyon: Pierre Bruyset-Ponthus. https://archive.org/details/dictionnairedela259rich/mode/2up?q=expert (2023-03-30).

Rutten, G. / Vosters, R. 2021. Language Standardization "from Above". In Ayres-Bennett, W. / Bellamy, J. Eds. *The Cambridge Handbook of Language Standardization*. Cambridge: Cambridge University Press, 65–92.

Selig, M. 2017. Plädoyer für einen einheitlichen, aber nicht einförmigen Sprachbegriff: Zur aktuellen Rezeption des Nähe-Distanz-Modells. *Romanistisches Jahrbuch* 68, 114–145.

Selig, M. 2022a. Diamesic Variation. In Ledgeway, A. / Maiden, M. Eds. *The Cambridge Handbook of Romance Linguistics*. Cambridge: Cambridge University Press, 870–897.

Selig, M. 2022b. Standardisierung aus der Akteursperspektive. Überlegungen zu den Ausbau- und Überdachungsprozessen im mittelalterlichen Französischen. In Böhmer, H. / Schmidt-Riese, R. Eds. *Kommunikation, Text und Sprachwandel im romanischen Mittelalter*. Frankfurt a. M.: Peter Lang, 25–89.

Selig, M. / Schmidt-Riese, R. 2021. Noticias sobre inmediatez y distancia: Esbozo de situación, dispositivos mediales y variación concepcional. In Gruber, T. / Grübl, K. / Scharinger, T. Eds. *Was bleibt von kommunikativer Nähe und Distanz? Mediale und konzeptionelle Aspekte sprachlicher Variation*. Tübingen: Narr, 145–169.

Winter-Froemel, E. 2023. Discourse traditions research: foundations, theoretical issues and implications. In Winter-Froemel, E. / Octavio Toledo y Huerta, A. Eds. *Manual of Discourse Traditions in Romance*. Berlin / New York: De Gruyter, 25–58.

Winter-Froemel, E. / Octavio Toledo y Huerta, A. Eds. 2023. *Manual of Discourse Traditions in Romance*. Berlin / New York: De Gruyter.

Woolard, K. 2007. La autoridad lingüística del español y las ideologías de la autenticidad y el anonimato. In Del Valle, J. Ed. *La lengua, ¿patria común?: ideas e ideologías del español*. Madrid / Frankfurt: Iberoamericana / Vervuert, 129–142.

Sebastian Lauschus, Guido Mensching, Luca Refrigeri und Frank Savelsberg

Medizinisch-botanische Synonymenlisten zu den hebräischen Übersetzungen von Avicennas *Qānūn*

Ein Beitrag zur überregionalen Diffusion romanischer Fachterminologien in Mittelalter und Früher Neuzeit

Abstract. This contribution uses an example from the field of Jewish medicine to sketch some tendencies in how Romance specialized terminology spread and became quasi-standardized across regional borders even before the trends of humanistic re-Latinization and early modern globalization. The article focuses on three lists of medico-botanical word correspondences (Arabic–Latin/Romance) in Hebrew characters. These alphabetically ordered lists are based on an index or table of contents originally belonging to a Hebrew version of Avicenna's *Canon of Medicine*, apparently originating from Southern France. In the oldest line of transmission for these lists, the Romance component is written in Old Occitan. We retrace how this Old Occitan terminology in Hebrew garb spread to central Italy, where it was enriched through a multitude of Italo-Romance lexical items. In this process, some Old Occitan terms persisted in the texts, figuring alongside a great number of Italo-Romance forms. In this context, the Occitan linguistic and cultural area can be considered as a kind of center of irradiation, from which medico-botanical knowledge and linguistic forms spread to other geographic and cultural areas, such as the Iberian Peninsula, northern France, and Italy, functioning as a kind of model for the creation of local terminologies. Thus, the synonym lists under consideration elucidate some aspects of transregional diffusion of knowledge in the pre-modern era. In addition, they enhance the documentary basis of Old Italo-Romance, for which the scientific terminology is underrepresented in texts in Latin script (due to the long predominance of Latin in scientific writing), in contrast to the Jewish scientific literature of the same period.

Abstract. Anhand eines Beispiels aus der jüdischen Medizingeschichte werden einige Tendenzen der Diffusion und Quasi-Standardisierung von romanischer Fachterminologie skizziert, die bereits vor dem Einsetzen der humanistischen Relatinisierung und der frühneuzeitlichen Globalisierung über regionale Grenzen hinaus wirkten. Zentraler Untersuchungsgegenstand sind dabei drei in hebräischer Schrift vorliegende alphabetisch geordnete Listen mit medizinisch-botanischen Synonymen (Arabisch–Latein/Romanisch). Diese basieren auf einem Index oder Inhaltsverzeichnis, der bzw. das ursprünglich zu einer wohl in Südfrankreich entstandenen hebräischen Version von Avicennas *Kanon der Medizin* gehörte. In dem Beitrag wird nachgezeichnet, wie die altokzitanische Terminologie, die die volkssprachliche Synonymenschicht des ältesten Überlieferungszweigs dieser Texttradition bildet, in hebräischem Gewand ihren Weg nach Mittelitalien fand und dort mit einer Vielzahl italoromanischer Formen angereichert wurde. Bei diesem Prozess blieb das ursprüngliche altokzitanische Wortgut neben dem neu hinzugefügten italoromanischen teilweise erhalten. Der okzitanische Sprach- und Kulturraum kann in diesem Zusammenhang als ein Zentrum gesehen werden, von dem aus medizinisch-botanisches Wissen sowie die entsprechende altokzitanische Terminologie in andere Areale wie die Iberische Halbinsel, Nordfrankreich und hier Italien ausstrahlte und die Folie zum Ausbau entsprechender lokaler Fachsprachen bildete. Die untersuchten drei Textzeugen geben aber nicht nur Aufschluss über einige Aspekte der vormodernen transregionalen Wissensverbreitung, sondern tragen auch dazu bei, die Dokumentationsbasis der altitaloromanischen Fachsprachlichkeit zu erweitern. Aufgrund der langen Dominanz des Lateinischen ist diese im Vergleich zur jüdischen wissenschaftlichen Literatur im lateinischen Schrifttum zur gleichen Zeit eher spärlich überliefert.

1. Einleitung

Ziel des vorliegenden Artikels ist es, Tendenzen überregionaler Verbreitung und Vereinheitlichung romanischer Fachterminologie in der Phase vor der humanistischen Relatinisierung und vor den frühneuzeitlichen Globalisierungstendenzen anhand eines konkreten Beispiels aus der in romanischsprachigen Ländern praktizierten jüdischen Medizin vorzustellen. Dies erscheint uns deshalb interessant, weil die jüdischen Wissens-, Schreib- und Diskurstraditionen größtenteils unabhängig vom lateinischen Schrifttum waren. Somit muss der volkssprachliche Anteil nicht zwangsläufig auf der Folie lateinischer und romanischer Vorbilder gesehen werden. Der Beitrag verarbeitet erste Ergebnisse aus unserem DFG-Projekt „Eine medizinisch-botanische Synonymenliste in hebräischer Schrift aus Mittelitalien".[1]

Zentraler Forschungsgegenstand des Projekts sind sogenannte Synonymenlisten, eine Weiterentwicklung von Glossen und Glossaren. Nach MacKinney (1938) handelt es sich dabei in der griechisch-lateinischen Tradition um eine aus *glossaria* und *hermeneumata* hervorgegangene Art mehrsprachiger Lexika:

> These appear under the titles *glossaria, hermeneumata, synonyma, vocabularia, index, expositio nominum*, etc., and are usually characterized by the *id est* formula; that is, each entry is followed by *id est* (or a variation thereof) and the explanatory material. Such works are clearly distinguishable from concordances and pharmaceutical handbooks in that their chief purpose was phi-

---

[1] Das Projekt wird von einer Göttinger Arbeitsgruppe, die aus den Autoren dieses Beitrags besteht, in Kooperation mit einer Kölner Arbeitsgruppe um den Judaisten Gerrit Bos durchgeführt. Eine ausführlichere Beschreibung des Projekts ist unter https://gepris.dfg.de/gepris/projekt/430923012 (30.03.2022) zu finden.

lological (i.e., the clarification of word meanings) and not the presentation of purely medical information. (MacKinney 1938: 261–262) In der arabischen Tradition existierten ähnliche Listen (cf. hierzu KaT IX–X). Nach MacKinney entstanden die westlichen Synonymenlisten im engeren Sinne im Rahmen der Rezeption der arabischen medizinischen Schriften durch die Anreicherung griechisch-lateinischer Wortgleichungen mit (latinisierten) arabischen Entsprechungen.[2] Hieran anknüpfend bzw. auf jeden Fall in ähnlicher Weise entstanden auch im jüdischen Fachschrifttum (und insbesondere im Rahmen von Übersetzungen) Glossare und Synonymenlisten, in denen vornehmlich arabische Termini mit lateinischen, romanischen und – seltener – hebräischen Entsprechungen versehen wurden. Im Zentrum unserer Ausführungen stehen Vertreter dieser Gattung in hebräischer Graphie, deren Einträge in der Regel wie anhand von Beispiel (1) illustriert aufgebaut sind:[3]

(1) Ms. Vatikan, Biblioteca Apostolica Vaticana, ebr. 550, fol. 113v, Alef 1:
אכליל אל מלך הוא קורונא ריאל או מלילוט
'KLYL 'L MLK, das ist QWRWN' RY'L oder MLYLWṬ

Wie man im Beispiel (1) sieht, werden medizinische Fachtermini in verschiedenen Sprachen gegenübergestellt, in diesem Falle arabisch *iklīl al-malik*, wörtlich 'Königskrone' für 'Echter Steinklee', Melilotus officinalis (L.) Pall. (cf. KaT Nr. 50 und 995; DT 388–390; ShS 282), und die beiden gleichbedeutenden okzitanischen Entsprechungen *corona re(i)al (DiTMAO s. v. *corona real, dort ausschließlich in gleicher hebräischer Schreibung belegt) und *melilot* (DOMel s. v. *melilot*; DAO Nr. 919 1-1; DiTMAO s. v. *melilot*, dort auch in gleicher hebräischer Schreibung wie hier).

Ausgangssprache ist meistens das Arabische, da diese Listen im Kontext von hebräischen Übersetzungen arabischer Medizinwerke entstanden sind. Bevor sie eigenständig kursierten, waren solche oder ähnliche Listen als Indices, Glossare oder Inhaltsverzeichnisse den Übersetzungen beigefügt. Auch die in unserem Projekt behandelten Listen basieren ursprünglich auf

---

[2] Zur Gattung der mittelalterlichen medizinisch-botanischen Synonymenlisten siehe u.a. MacKinney (1938), Gutiérrez Rodilla (2007), ShS 5–10.

[3] Hier und im weiteren Verlauf dieser Ausführungen folgt der Edition der Beispiele aus dem hebräischen Text eine Eins-zu-eins-Transliteration der hebräischen Konsonantenzeichen, die z. T. auch einen vokalischen Wert haben können. Metasprachliches hebräisches Material in den einzelnen Einträgen wird ins Deutsche übersetzt. Bei der Entzifferung romanischer Wörter in semitischen Schriftsystemen ergeben sich die üblichen Schwierigkeiten, die wir an dieser Stelle jedoch nicht näher erläutern können (diesbezüglich und zum Transkriptionssystem cf. ShS 4–5 sowie Mensching 2015).

einem Index bzw. Inhaltsverzeichnis, in diesem Falle zum zweiten Buch von Avicennas *Qānūn fī l-ṭibb* (im Folgenden *Qānūn*; cf. Steinschneider 1893: 684 und 838–839), in dem die *Materia medica* behandelt wird. Die hier besprochenen Manuskripte gehen auf hebräische Bearbeitungen vom Ende des 13. Jahrhunderts zurück (Shatzmiller 1994: 49), die bereits die arabische Nomenklatur in Listenform beinhalteten (beginnend bei Natan ben Eli'ezer ha-Me'ati und Zeraḥya ben Yiṣḥaq ben Še'alti'el Ḥen).[4] Die genauen Zusammenhänge sind Gegenstand des Projekts.[5] Die auf den folgenden Seiten thematisierten Quellen stellen sich in den Codices als Listen dar, die unabhängig von den *Qānūn*-Bearbeitungen figurieren und somit keinen Indexcharakter mehr haben. In ihnen erscheinen die arabischen Termini in hebräischer Schrift als Lemmata, gefolgt von romanischen und seltener lateinischen Entsprechungen. Die Metasprache für weitere Erklärungen ist hierbei das Hebräische. Im Vordergrund unseres Projekts stehen drei Manuskripte, die sich alle in diese Tradition einordnen lassen:

---

[4] Die primäre Quelle ist also nicht die lateinische Übersetzung von Gerhard von Cremona (12. Jh.), zu der ebenfalls Indices existierten (cf. Mensching 1994: 21). Zumindest in dem weiter unten besprochenen Ms. Florenz, Biblioteca Medicea Laurenziana, Or. 17, erscheinen allerdings einige Termini eingeschachtelt, die offenbar auf die lateinische, auf Gerhard beruhende Tradition zurückgehen. Cf. hierzu Abschnitt 5.

[5] Da die mittelalterliche jüdische Medizin in der Romania ihren Ursprung in Al-Andalus hatte, wo das Arabische ebenfalls von jüdischen Ärzten und Gelehrten als Wissenschaftssprache verwendet wurde, gab es zunächst keine ausgebaute hebräische Medizinterminologie. Eine solche wurde in Südfrankreich maßgeblich von Šem Tov ben Yiṣḥaq aus Tortosa (*1198) in seinem *Sefer ha-Šimmuš* – einer hebräischen Übersetzung von Abulcasis' *Kitāb al-Taṣrīf* – entwickelt (Bos 2011–2022). Dabei griff der Übersetzer von vornherein auch auf die lokale romanische Varietät zurück, nämlich das Okzitanische. In der ersten der beiden Synonymenlisten, die sich im 29. Buch des *Sefer ha-Šimmuš* befinden, wird das Okzitanische umfänglich neben dem Arabischen zur Erklärung der in der Übersetzung neu eingeführten hebräischen Terminologie verwendet, in der zweiten Liste bilden die okzitanischen Lemmata sogar das Ausgangsmaterial für eine Glossierung überwiegend auf Arabisch (cf. ShS 10–31). Diese durch Šem Tov neu eingeführte Terminologie (einschließlich der dort enthaltenen Okzitanismen, cf. hierzu Abschnitt 6) konnte sich fortan etablieren und findet sich nicht zuletzt in den Indices bzw. Inhaltsverzeichnissen der hebräischen *Qānūn*-Übersetzungen von Natan ha-Me'ati und Zeraḥya ben Še'alti'el Ḥen wieder, die die Vorläufer der im Folgenden von uns behandelten Listen bilden. Zu einer frühen Untersuchung dieser Zusammenhänge siehe Steinschneider (1893: 684).

Medizinisch-botanische Synonymenlisten zu Avicennas Qānūn

- Ms. Vatikan, Biblioteca Apostolica Vaticana, ebr. 550
- Ms. München, Bayerische Staatsbibliothek, Cod. hebr. 8
- Ms. Florenz, Biblioteca Medicea Laurenziana, Or. 17

Hieraus leitet sich die Struktur des vorliegenden Beitrags ab, in dem wir jedes Manuskript kurz vorstellen und ausgewählte Beispiele im Hinblick auf die Genese dieser Texttradition und die Stellung und Funktion des romanischen – hier zunächst okzitanischen und italoromanischen – Wortguts besprechen (Abschnitte 2–4). In einem weiteren Punkt (Abschnitt 5) diskutieren wir kurz eine erste Hypothese zur Filiation, bevor in einem letzten Schritt Bezüge zu den Bereichen Fachsprachen, Expertenkulturen und Standardisierung in der Romania des Spätmittelalters und der Frühen Neuzeit hergestellt werden (Abschnitt 6).

2. Ms. Vatikan, Biblioteca Apostolica Vaticana, ebr. 550

Soweit wir dies bisher rekonstruieren konnten, repräsentiert das Manuskript Vatikan, ebr. 550, die älteste Überlieferungslinie der in Abschnitt 1 dargestellten Texttradition. Unsere Liste befindet sich auf den Folios 113v–131r und ist Teil einer medizinischen Sammelhandschrift. Das Manuskript lässt sich nach Richler (2008: 466) auf das frühe 14. Jahrhundert datieren; es ist in einer sephardischen Kursive abgefasst, einer Schriftart, die sowohl unter den Juden der Iberischen Halbinsel als auch im Süden Frankreichs gebräuchlich war (cf. Beit-Arié 1992: 27). Die alphabetisch vollständige Synonymenliste enthält insgesamt 622 Einträge, die in der Regel wie in (2) aufgebaut sind:

(2) Ms. Vatikan, fol. 113v, Alef 3:
אפסנתין הוא איישינץ
'PSNTYN, das ist 'YYŠYNṢ

Das erste Wort, 'PSNTYN, repräsentiert arabisch *afsintīn* mit der Bedeutung 'Wermut', Artemisia absinthium L. (cf. KaT Nr. 14; DT 369–371; ShS 115). Die Entsprechung 'YYŠYNṢ lässt sich recht eindeutig als das gleichbedeutende altokzitanische *ai(s)senz* oder *ei(s)senz* lesen (DOM 6,422a–b; DAO Nr. 1065 1-2; DiTMAO s. v. *ansens*, dort auch dokumentiert in gleicher hebräischer Schreibung wie hier).

Das folgende Beispiel (3) repräsentiert die Myrte, Myrtus communis L., und ist etwas komplexer als (2). Neben dem arabischen Lemma 'S, lies *ās* (cf. KaT Nr. 520; DT 172–173; ShS 377), folgt zunächst die Bedeutung auf Hebräisch (HDS 'Myrte'), welches die Metasprache darstellt. Die romanischen Entsprechungen werden durch die hebräische Abkürzung ב״ל für *be-la'az* eingeleitet, was so viel wie 'in der Volkssprache' bedeutet (cf. EJ² 12,405–406 s. v. *la'az*). Hier werden zwei romanische Termini genannt, nämlich das altokzitanische *nerta* (DOMel s. v. *mirta, murta, nerta*; DAO Nr. 767 1-4; DiTMAO s. v. *nerta*, dort auch in gleicher hebräischer Schreibung wie hier), gefolgt von der Bezeichnung ihrer Beeren, *mirtils* (DAO Nr. 769 1-1).

(3) Ms. Vatikan, fol. 113v, Alef 4:

אס הוא הדס ובי״ל נירטא או מירטילץ

'S, das ist Myrte, in der Volkssprache NYRṬ' oder MYRṬYLṢ

Im Beispiel (4) folgt dem arabischen Lemma *isfānāḫ* 'Spinat', Spinacia oleracea L. (cf. Leclerc 60) wieder nur eine einzige volkssprachliche Entsprechung, die als altokzitanisch *espinarc* (DOMel s. v. *espinarc*; DAO Nr. 826 1-1) gelesen werden kann:

(4) Ms. Vatikan, fol. 114v, Alef 46:

אספאנך הוא אשפינרק

'SP'NK, das ist 'ŠPYNRQ

Insgesamt haben wir in mindestens einem Drittel der 622 Einträge okzitanische Elemente nachweisen können. Die Präsenz des Okzitanischen überrascht hier nicht, da die meisten uns bekannten medizinisch-botanischen Glossare und Synonymenlisten mit romanischen Elementen Okzitanisch enthalten (cf. u.a. Bos/Mensching 2005; 2015). Hintergrund sind einerseits die medizinischen Fakultäten und Schulen in Südfrankreich, andererseits die jahrhundertelange Beschäftigung der südfranzösischen Juden mit arabischer Medizin (cf. u.a. Bos/Hajek/Mensching 2022). Das Okzitanische wurde wahrscheinlich zum einen deshalb verwendet, weil die in der Bibel und im Talmud vorhandenen Fachtermini nicht die Gegebenheiten Südfrankreichs – hier hauptsächlich die Flora – wiedergeben konnten. Zum anderen werden die Synonymenlisten sicher auch einen praktischen Nutzen gehabt haben, damit Ärzte und Apotheker, die nicht des Arabischen mächtig waren, die richtigen Ingredienzien zur Verfügung stellen bzw. verwenden konnten (cf. ShS 7–8).

3. Ms. München, Bayerische Staatsbibliothek, Cod. hebr. 8

Die zweite Liste, die hier vorgestellt werden soll, liegt im Manuskript München, Cod. hebr. 8, vor. Bei dieser handelt es sich um eine wahrscheinlich in Italien entstandene Weiterbearbeitung; die Kopie stammt aus dem 16. Jahrhundert. Die Liste befindet sich auf den Folios 192v–199r und ist ebenfalls Teil einer medizinischen Sammelhandschrift. Im Gegensatz zum Vatikan-

Manuskript ist diese Kopie in einer aschkenasischen Kursive verfasst,[6] die ursprünglich aus Nordfrankreich und dem deutschsprachigen Raum stammt, aber auch in Italien Verwendung fand (cf. Engel 2015: 30). Die Liste ist unvollständig, sie reicht nur bis zum Buchstaben Lamed, ist teilweise schlecht lesbar und umfasst 372 Einträge.

Zunächst fällt auf, dass viele Einträge länger geworden sind, wie hier anhand der Synopse zweier sich entsprechender Einträge zu Wermut aus Ms. Vatikan in (5a) (wiederholt aus (2)) und Ms. München in (5b) gezeigt wird:

(5) a. Ms. Vatikan, fol. 113v, Alef 3:
אפסנתין הוא איישינץ
ʾPSNTYN, das ist ʾYYŠYNṢ

b. Ms. München, fol. 192v, Alef 3:
אִפְּסָנְתִין לעטין אַפְּסִינְתָין לעז אישניץ הוא נשינצו
ʾiPəSiNəTiYN, [...] ʾiPəSiYNəTiYN, Volkssprache ʾYŠNYṢ, das ist NŠYNṢW

Wir erkennen in dem Lemma in (5b) das arabische Wort *afsintīn* wieder, das hier allerdings durch möglicherweise später hinzugefügte Punktierungen für Vokale entstellt erscheint.[7] Bei der folgenden Form handelt es sich wahrscheinlich um eine Variante des arabischen Lemmas oder eine hebräische Entsprechung.[8] Danach sehen wir das bereits bekannte okzitanische Wort *ais(s)enz/eis(s)enz*, wenn auch in der leicht veränderten Form ʾYŠNYṢ. Schließlich befindet sich am Ende der Zusatz NŠYNṢW, der als *nasc(i)enzo* gelesen werden kann. Hierbei handelt es sich recht eindeutig um Italienisch bzw. Italoromanisch (GDLI 11,192; LEI 1,173).

In dem Eintrag in (6b) zur Myrte (arab. *ās*) wurde im Vergleich zur Parallelstelle im Ms. Vatikan (6a) (wiederholt aus (3)) das aramäische Synonym *āsā* (ShS 95) hinzugefügt. Darüber hinaus wurde das okzitanische *nerta* durch das im Manuskript als Latein ausgewiesene *myrta* (Alphita M1; DMLBS 6,1878b) ersetzt und die okzitanische Ergänzung *mirtils* (cf. oben zu (3)) wird – hier in der Variante MYRṬYLYŠ – als die Beeren der Myrte präzisiert:

---

[6] Cf. diesbezüglich Steinschneider (1895: 2). Die Liste aus Ms. München wurde von ihm als „ital. um 1550, sehr incorrect" und als ein „Glossar zum Kanon von Natan ha-M'ati" identifiziert.

[7] Die Punktierungen für Vokale werden den in ShS 4 dargestellten Konventionen folgend in der Transliteration als Kleinbuchstaben wiedergegeben.

[8] Das erste Sprachlabel לעטין scheint verschrieben, es entspricht weder der gängigen Schreibung für Latein (לטין) noch der für die Volkssprache (לעז).

(6) a. Ms. Vatikan, fol. 113v, Alef 4:
אס הוא הדס וב"ל נירטא או מירטיל"ץ
'S, das ist Myrte, in der Volkssprache NYRṬ' oder MYRṬYLṢ

b. Ms. München, fol. 192v, Alef 4:
אס הוא הדס או אסא לטין מִירְטָא וגרגריו מירטיליש
'aS, das ist Myrte oder 'S', Latein MiYRəṬa', ihre Beeren [heißen] MYRṬYLYŠ

Das Beispiel (7b) behält das okzitanische Wort 'ŠPYNRQ für 'Spinat' aus (7a) (cf. oben zu (4)) bei und zeigt ebenfalls einen Zusatz, SPNṢY, am Ende. Dieser lässt sich wieder als Italoromanisch, nämlich *spinaci* oder *spinace* (Ineichen 1966: 210; Mazzeo 2011: 357), lesen:

(7) a. Ms. Vatikan, fol. 114v, Alef 46:
אספאנך הוא אשפינרק
'SP'NK, das ist 'ŠPYNRQ

b. Ms. München, fol. 193v, Alef 55:
אספאנג הוא אשפינרק הם ספנצי
'SP'NG, das ist 'ŠPYNRQ, das ist SPNṢY

Zusammenfassend kann gesagt werden, dass das Manuskript München in vielen Fällen italoromanische Entsprechungen hinzufügt. Die okzitanischen Termini bleiben allerdings als Synonyme erhalten. Ein genauerer Blick auf die italoromanischen Wörter zeigt Folgendes: Während *spinaci/-e* in (7b) in den meisten Varietäten mit Ausnahme Nordwestitaliens weit verbreitet ist (cf. AIS Karte Nr. 1365), lässt sich die Form in (5b) in ein begrenzteres Gebiet einordnen. Es handelt sich hierbei um eine mittel- und süditalienische Form, die beispielsweise in den Abruzzen und auf Sizilien als *nascienzo* (cf. Penzig 1924: 1,49; Rapisarda 2001: 7, §4.12) und in Kampanien als *nascienzio* (cf. Penzig 1924: 1,49) vorkommt.

Neben dem Verfahren der Hinzufügung italoromanischer Entsprechungen zu den okzitanischen lässt sich in anderen Fällen die Ersetzung des okzitanischen Worts durch ein italoromanisches beobachten: Eine solche Ersetzung ist im Manuskript München jedoch nicht allzu häufig. Als Beispiel soll der Eintrag zu arabisch *asṭarak* 'Storax/Styrax', Styrax officinalis L. (cf. KaT Nr. 69; DT 111; ShS 215–216), dienen, welches sowohl den Styraxbaum als auch dessen Harz bezeichnet:

(8) a. Ms. Vatikan, fol. 113v, Alef 17:
אצטורך הוא אצטורק
'ṢṬWRK, das ist 'ṢṬWRQ

b.   Ms. München, fol. 192v, Alef 17:
אצטרך הוא מין משטורצי
'aṢəṬəRaK, das ist eine Art ŠəṬWoRaṢəY

In den Beispielen unter (8) sieht man die Ersetzung des okzitanischen *estorac* in (8a) (DOMel s. v. *storax, storac*; DAO Nr. 570 3-1; DiTMAO s. v. *estorex*, dort in gleicher hebräischer Schreibung wie hier) durch eine italoromanische Form ŠəṬWoRaṢəY in (8b), die *storace* (Glessgen 1996: 2,831; Ineichen 1966: 213) gelesen werden kann.

Ebenso wurde in den folgenden Beispielen unter (9) in dem Eintrag zu arab. *ḥurf* 'Gartenkresse', Lepidium sativum L. (cf. KaT Nr. 361 und 519; DT 301; ShS 503), das okzitanische NŠṬWRŠ, d. i. *nas(i)tors*, in (9a) (DOMel s. v. *nazitort*; DAO Nr. 824 2-1; DiTMAO s. v. *nassitort*, dort in gleicher hebräischer Schreibung wie hier) durch ein italoromanisches Lexem NŠṬRWṢY'W in (9b) ersetzt, welches dem alttoskanischen *nastruzio* (GDLI 11,211) entsprechen könnte (ähnliche metathetische Formen sind allerdings auch für das Veneto und Sizilien belegt; cf. in Abschnitt 4 zu (12)):

(9) a.   Ms. Vatikan, fol. 119v, Ḥet 5:
חרף הוא נשטורש
ḤRP, das ist NŠṬWRŠ

b.   Ms. München, fol. 198r, Ḥet 5:
חרף הוא נשטרוציאו ויש ממנו שני מינים
ḤRP, das ist NŠṬRWṢY'W, und es gibt davon zwei Arten

4. Ms. Florenz, Biblioteca Medicea Laurenziana, Or. 17

Im Gegensatz zu den in den Abschnitten 2 und 3 besprochenen beiden Listen liefert die im Folgenden vorgestellte Handschrift aus Florenz genauere Angaben zu ihrer Entstehung: Sie ist auf das Jahr 1464 datiert und als Entstehungsort wird Anagni (Frosinone, Latium) genannt. Ferner ist der Name Abraham ben Daniel „der Arzt" als Verfasser bzw. Kopist vermerkt (siehe den Kolophon auf Folio 67v; cf. Steinschneider 1868: 101). Die Synonymenliste befindet sich auf den Folios 68r–92v als Teil einer medizinischen Sammelhandschrift, die in einer italienischen Kursive abgefasst ist (cf. Steinschneider 1893: 839). Die Liste ist von den dreien die weitaus umfangreichste und umfasst 1753 Einträge (eine erste Einordnung des volkssprachlichen Materials dieser Liste liegt in Bos/Mensching 2014 vor).

Die beiden Manuskripte München und Florenz teilen bestimmte Eigenschaften, worauf noch zurückzukommen ist. Auch im Manuskript Florenz zeigen sich auf der einen Seite Fälle, in denen das okzitanische Wort beibehalten und durch ein italoromanisches ergänzt wird. Als Beispiel soll hier der 'Spinat'-Eintrag in (10a–c) dienen:

(10) a.   Ms. Vatikan, fol. 114v, Alef 46:
אספאנך הוא אשפינרק
'SP'NK, das ist 'ŠPYNRQ

      b.   Ms. München, fol. 193v, Alef 55:
אספאנג הוא אשפינרק הם ספנצי
'SP'NG, das ist 'ŠPYNRQ, das ist SPNṢY

      c.   Ms. Florenz, fol. 68v, Alef 54:
[...] אספנג או אספינאך הוא אספינאק הוא ספינצי
'SPNG, oder 'SPYN'K, das ist 'SPYN'Q, das ist SPYNṢY [...]

Die arabischen Formen mit auslautendem Gimel – 'SP'NG in (10b) und 'SPNG in (10c) – Varianten zu klassisch-arabisch *isfānāḫ* in (4) – bestätigen einen engen Kopierzusammenhang zwischen den Handschriften München und Florenz. Das fehlende Resch in der ersten romanischen Form 'SPYN'Q in (10c) kann auf einen Kopistenfehler zurückgehen oder auf eine entsprechende katalanische Form *espinac* (DCVB 5,431a; DECLC 3,648a).

Auf der anderen Seite kommt es auch im Manuskript Florenz zu Ersetzungen des okzitanischen Wortguts durch italoromanisches, was am folgenden Beispiel (11) deutlich wird, wo die Einträge aus Ms. München in (11b) und Ms. Florenz in (11c) sehr ähnlich sind und beiden der okzitanischen Terminus *estorac* fehlt:

(11) a.   Ms. Vatikan, fol. 113v, Alef 17:
אצטורך הוא אצטורק
'ṢṬWRK, das ist 'ṢṬWRQ

      b.   Ms. München, fol. 192v, Alef 17:
אַצְטָרך הוא מין מִשְׁטוֹרצִי
'aṢəṬəRaK, das ist eine Art ŠəṬWoRaṢəY

      c.   Ms. Florenz, fol. 68r, Alef 17:
אצטרך הוא מיץ שְׁטוֹרָצִי
'ṢṬRK, das ist Saft (Harz) von ŠəṬWoRaṢiY

Gleiches gilt für den Eintrag zur Gartenkresse (arab. *ḥurf*, s. o. zu (9)), wobei das Manuskript Florenz hier offenbar eine Pluralform NŠṬRWṢY, *nastrozzi*, zeigt (für den Singular cf. Penzig 1924: 1,267; VocSic 3,21; VocVen 215a).

(12) a. Ms. Vatikan, fol. 119v, Ḥet 5:
חרף הוא נשטורש
ḤRP, das ist NŠṬWRŠ

b. Ms. München, fol. 198r, Ḥet 5:
חרף הוא נשטרוציאו ויש ממנו שני מינים
ḤRP, das ist NŠṬRWṢY'W, und es gibt davon zwei Arten

c. Ms. Florenz, fol. 78r, Ḥet 5:
חרף הוא נשטרוצי ונמ' שני מינים
ḤRP, das ist NŠṬRWṢY, und es gibt davon zwei Arten

Bei dem folgenden Eintrag zu arab. *zinğār* 'Grünspan' (cf. Käs 2010, 2,669–674) in Beispiel (13) zeigt sich hingegen, dass das okzitanische Wort *verdet* (DOMel s. v. *verdet*; DAO Nr. 375 1-1; DiTMAO s. v. *verdet*, dort in gleicher hebräischer Schreibung wie hier) im Laufe der Textüberlieferung unterdrückt wurde: In den Manuskripten Vatikan (13a) und München (13b) ist es vorhanden, wohingegen in der Florentiner Handschrift lediglich die italoromanische Entsprechung WYRDY R'MY (13c) figuriert, d. i. *verde rame* (Glessgen 1996: 870f.;[9] GDLI 21,767; LEI 1,1108 s. v. *aeramen*; in Ms. München ohne Alef WYRDY RMY). Solche und weitere Indizien lassen uns vermuten, dass das Manuskript Florenz eine spätere Bearbeitungsstufe repräsentiert als das Manuskript München:

(13) a. Ms. Vatikan, fol. 119r, Zayin 16:
זנגאר הוא וירדיט
ZNG'R, das ist WYRDYṬ

b. Ms. München, fol. 197v, Zayin 15:
זנגואר הוא וירדיט הוא וירדי רמי
ZNGW'R, das ist WYRDYṬ, das ist WYRDY RMY

c. Ms. Florenz, fol. 77r, Zayin 12:
זנגואר הוא וירדי ראמי
ZNGW'R, das ist WYRDY R'MY

Einen interessanten Fall bildet das folgende Beispiel (14), bei dem zwei verschiedene italoromanische Dialektformen als Entsprechungen für das arabische Lemma *mišmiš* 'Aprikose', Prunus Armeniaca L. (DT 177–178; ShS 111), angegeben sind:

---

[9] Glessgen (1996: 871): *verderame* bzw. *verde rame* ist „systematisch eindeutig und variantenarm im Ait. bekannt".

(14) Ms. Florenz, fol. 83r, Mem 35:
מַשְׁמַשׁ הם אמוניאצי הם גריסומולי ה' ברקוק
MaŠəMaŠ, das sind 'MWNY'ṢY, das sind GRYSWMWLY, das ist BRQWQ[10]

Das erste Synonym 'MWNY'ṢY ist norditaloromanisch *ammuniaci (von lat. *armeniacus*; REW 654; LEI 3,1293–1303: I.1.b.β südl. Marken *amunaci*, I.1.a paduanisch *aumuniaco*), bei dem zweiten, GRYSWMWLY, handelt es sich um *grisomole/grisomule* (cf. Piro 2011: 267, 341, 673, 809; aufgefunden mit Hilfe des OVI-Korpus), eine italoromanische Variante, die (heute) in ähnlichen Formen in süditalienischen Varietäten vorkommt, im Mittelalter aber ebenfalls für Norditalien belegt ist (von gr. χρυσόμηλον, LEI 3,1302; für kalabresisch *grisuommulu*, Velletri *grasiommoľo* cf. REW 1891, siehe auch Bos/Mensching 2014: 17; für *grisoməlľ*ᵃ cf. AIS Karte Nr. 1276, Punkt 637 Capestrano [AQ]). Dies spricht dafür, dass bei den Glossaren tatsächlich der praktische Nutzen im Vordergrund stand, die Pflanze an verschiedenen Orten in Italien beschaffen zu können.

5. Erste Hypothese zur Filiation

Der Gesamtbefund zum Manuskript Florenz deutet darauf hin, dass dieses – obwohl es früher kopiert wurde als das Manuskript München – einen späteren Bearbeitungszustand darstellt. In Verbindung mit den bisher im Rahmen unseres Projekts gesammelten Informationen ermöglicht uns dieser Befund, das Stemma in Fig. 1 zu postulieren.

Wir haben das Stemma in zwei Abschnitte unterteilt, um die beiden Gebiete zu verdeutlichen, aus denen die Manuskripte stammen. Der Ursprung der Tradition kann ohne Weiteres in den okzitanischen Raum verortet werden, auch wenn dies hier nicht genauer ausgeführt werden kann. Dort entstand aller Wahrscheinlichkeit nach aus einer hebräischen Übersetzung von Avicennas *Qānūn* (Ω) eine erste Liste (ω). Auch V, dessen sprachliche Eigenschaften wir in Abschnitt 2 vorgestellt haben, stammt aus diesem Gebiet.

---

[10] Bei dem dritten Äquivalent BRQWQ handelt es sich um katalanisch *bercoc* 'Aprikose' (DCVB 1,428a–429a) oder um sein Etymon, arab. *barqūq*, welches eigentlich die Pflaume (Prunus domestica L.) im Maghreb bezeichnet (Meyerhof 1940: 10–11), aber anderen Quellen zufolge ebenfalls als Synonym für die Aprikose verwendet wird (DT 177).

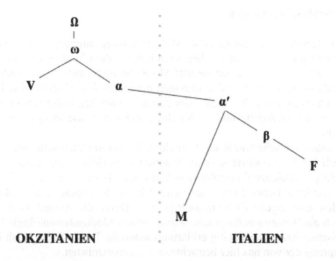

Fig. 1. Vorläufige Einordnung der Manuskripte Vatikan (V), München (M) und Florenz (F) in ein Stemma.

Eine ähnliche Liste – hier α genannt – lieferte die Grundlage für die erste, in Italien entstandene Kopie α'. Von dieser ersten „italienischen" Version stammen sowohl M als auch F ab, allerdings auf unterschiedliche Art und Weise: Denn M, obwohl später entstanden und somit zeitlich gesehen weiter entfernt von α' als F, scheint einen älteren Bearbeitungsstand abzubilden. F hingegen, wenngleich ungefähr ein Jahrhundert älter als M, zeigt Spuren einer komplexeren Entwicklung, die über eine noch unbestimmte Anzahl an Zwischenschritten – hier abgebildet als β – erfolgt sein muss. Die in F sichtbaren Veränderungen und Neuerungen gegenüber dem „Original" gründen unter anderem auf einer Kontamination mit anderen, ähnlichen Listen von *synonyma*. Darunter befinden sich wahrscheinlich berühmte mittelalterliche Kompilationen wie die anonyme *Alphita* (erste Hälfte des 13. Jh.) oder die *Clavis sanationis*, das medizinische Lexikon von Simon von Genua (13. Jh.; Editio princeps: Mailand 1473).[11] Einige Einträge ähneln stark den Indices zu Gerhards von Cremona lateinischer Übersetzung von Avicennas *Qānūn*.[12]

---

[11] Zu einem Überblick über dieses Werk und seinen Autor cf. Bouras-Vallianatos (2013).

[12] Cf. hierzu Vercellin (1991) sowie insbesondere Mensching (1994: 21–22 und 39).

6. Schlussfolgerungen

Im Folgenden seien einige Schlussfolgerungen zusammengetragen: Die Juden entwickelten im lateinischen Mittelalter in ihrer Funktion als kulturelle „Dolmetscher" – um einen Begriff Moritz Steinschneiders zu bemühen[13] – gerade im Rahmen ihrer Aufarbeitung der arabischen Medizin eine Expertenkultur aus, die sich jenseits oder zumindest am Rande der scholastischen Universität ansiedelte und in der das Lateinische eine marginalere Rolle spielte.

Das Arabische wurde im Zuge der Übersetzung klassischer und mittelalterlicher Medizintexte aus dem Arabischen ins Hebräische zunehmend unwichtiger. Gleichzeitig etablierte sich das Hebräische – auch durch die Übersetzung lateinischer Texte – als neue Wissenschaftssprache der Juden und bildete eine eigene Fachterminologie aus. Durch die Abkehr vom Arabischen als Wissenschaftssprache wurde dessen Medizinterminologie für die jüdischen Ärzte gleichzeitig erklärungsbedürftig. Dieser Sachverhalt ist der Ursprung der von uns hier betrachteten Synonymenlisten.

Neben der neuen sich etwa ab der zweiten Hälfte des 13. Jahrhunderts herausbildenden Wissenschaftssprache Hebräisch spielten bei den Juden die lokalen romanischen Volkssprachen im westlichen Mittelmeerraum eine wichtige Rolle bei der Benennung der *Materia medica*.[14] Dies ist zum einen durch die regionale Flora und Fauna bedingt, die teilweise von der des östlichen Mittelmeerraums abweicht, sieht sich aber auch in der medizinisch-pharmakologischen Praxis begründet im Umgang mit nichtjüdischen Apothekern und Patienten vor Ort (cf. ShS 7).

Von dem hohen Stellenwert der lokalen romanischen Varietäten geben die Übersetzungen selbst Zeugnis, in denen die Fachterminologie der übersetzten Sprachen teilweise durch romanische Äquivalente ersetzt wurde, die sich nahtlos in die ansonsten hebräische Metasprache einfügten (Beispiele hierfür sind u.a. in Bos/Mensching 2000, Mensching/Zwink 2014 sowie Bos/Hajek/Mensching 2022 zu finden).

Südfrankreich bildete im Spätmittelalter eine Schnittstelle zwischen dem sephardischen Judentum im Westen und dem aschkenasischen Judentum in der Mitte Europas sowie das Epizentrum des Wissenstransfers im Bereich der Medizin. Somit war die lokale romanische Varietät, die primär in die hier vorgestellten Übersetzungen und Synonymenlisten Einzug hielt, das Okzitanische.

---

[13] Cf. sein Werk *Die hebräischen Übersetzungen des Mittelalters und die Juden als Dolmetscher* (Steinschneider 1893).

[14] Cf. insbesondere Bos (2011–2022) sowie Bos (2019) zur hebräischen Medizinterminologie.

Medizinisch-botanische Synonymenlisten zu Avicennas Qānūn

Was wir im vorliegenden Beitrag zeigen wollten, ist, dass die medizinische Expertenkultur, die sich unter den Juden Südfrankreichs ausgebildet hatte, in andere Gebiete ausstrahlte; im Falle der von uns vorgestellten Listen wären hier die Rezeption und Weiterverarbeitung derselben in Italien zu nennen. Überraschend dabei ist, dass das okzitanische Wortgut bei diesem Überlieferungsprozess zu einem nicht unerheblichen Anteil erhalten blieb. Dies könnte man dahingehend interpretieren, dass okzitanische medizinisch-botanische Fachtermini auch außerhalb Südfrankreichs von den Juden als terminologisch wahrgenommen wurden. Zumindest für das Verständnis der in Südfrankreich entstandenen Übersetzungen war die Kenntnis dieser Termini grundlegend auch außerhalb dieses Gebiets; ansonsten mussten die Texte unverständlich bleiben.

Dieses Argument widerspricht einem Verständnis der okzitanischen Elemente in derartigen Listen als reine, bis ins 16. Jahrhundert tradierte Reliktwörter. Vielmehr scheint es sich bei der okzitanischen Terminologie zumindest über einen gewissen Zeitraum hinweg um eine Art Standardterminologie gehandelt zu haben, neben der sich in einem ersten Schritt lokale italoromanische Varianten allmählich etablierten, die dann ihrerseits – wie im Fall des Florenz-Manuskripts – das Okzitanische verdrängen konnten. Inwieweit diese annähernde Standardterminologie des Okzitanischen bei den Juden eine Modellfunktion für den Ausbau der lokalen italoromanischen Varietäten einnahm, muss zukünftig noch untersucht werden.

In der Florentiner Handschrift lassen sich bezüglich des italoromanischen Wortguts an einigen wenigen Stellen Charakteristika des sogenannten Judenitalienisch ausmachen (cf. u.a. Rubin 2016: 320; Ryzhik im Erscheinen). Hierzu gehört der Erhalt von lateinisch L in Clustern nach Konsonant:

(15) a. פינוקלו (PYNWQLW): *fenocclo* < FENUCULUM (cf. ital. *finocchio*)
 b. נוקלי (NWQLY): *noccle*, Pl. zu *noccla* < NUCULA (cf. ital. *nocchia*)
 c. פורקקלי (PWRQQLY): *porcaccle*, Pl. zu *porcaccla* < *portacula* < PORTULACA (cf. ital. *porcacchia*)

In der Forschung zur mittelalterlichen und frühneuzeitlichen judenitalienischen Textproduktion herrscht die Meinung vor, dass bis zu den Vertreibungen der Juden aus den zur Krone Aragon gehörenden Gebieten im Süden der Apenninenhalbinsel süditalienische Varietäten die Basis einer jüdischen italoromanischen Koiné bildeten. Nach der Vertreibung und seit der Bildung der Ghettos in den norditalienischen Städten wurde diese Koiné durch lokale norditalienische Varietäten bei den Juden Italiens abgelöst (cf. u.a. Sermoneta 1976 sowie Cuomo 1983). Letztere entwickelten allerdings keine Schriftkultur.

Die zwei hier vorgestellten Manuskripte mit italoromanischen Elementen siedeln sich zeitlich an dieser Bruchkante an (Ms. Florenz 1464, Ms.

München im 16. Jahrhundert) und weisen somit vorrangig mittel- und süditalienische Züge auf. Unser Befund zeigt allerdings auch, dass für die medizinische Wissenschaftsterminologie nicht von einer solchen süditalienischen Koiné auszugehen ist, wie sie für andere jüdische Diskurstraditionen postuliert wird, die sich des Italoromanischen bedienen. Vielmehr handelt es sich um lokale Varianten, die in unseren Listen zuweilen sogar parallel nebeneinander erscheinen und vereinzelt auch gar nicht aus Mittel- oder Süditalien stammen, sondern norditalienische Varietäten widerspiegeln.

Zusammenfassend und ausblickend können wir somit zwei gegensätzliche Tendenzen feststellen: zum einen die Konservierung okzitanischen Wortguts in der jüdischen Medizin als eine Art vormoderner Standard, zum anderen die Verwendung lokal relativ begrenzter italoromanischer Formen, die dem bereits genannten praktischen Nutzen geschuldet sind, nämlich die Pflanzen und Substanzen exakt zu identifizieren. Die hier nachgezeichneten Tendenzen eines terminologischen Gebrauchs der romanischen Sprachen bei den Juden scheinen dem fachsprachlichen Ausbau in der christlichen Expertenkultur zeitlich vorgelagert, nahmen bei der Standardisierung des Romanischen gesonderte Wege und hatten mit anderen Schwierigkeiten bei der Etablierung einer Fachterminologie zu kämpfen.

Literatur

AIS = Jaberg, K. / Jud, J. 1928–1942. *Sprachatlas Italiens und der Südschweiz.* 8 Bde. Zofingen: Ringier.

Alphita = García-González, A. Ed. 2007. *Alphita.* Florenz: SISMEL – Edizioni del Galluzzo.

Beit-Arié, M. 1992. *Hebrew manuscripts of East and West. Towards a comparative codicology.* London: The British Library.

Bos, G. 2011–2022. *Novel medical and general Hebrew terminology.* 5 Bde. Oxford: Oxford University Press (Bde. 1–3), Leiden / Boston: Brill (Bde. 4–5).

Bos. G. 2019. *A concise dictionary of novel medical and general Hebrew terminology from the Middle Ages.* Leiden / Boston: Brill.

Bos, G. / Mensching, G. 2000. Macer Floridus: A Middle Hebrew fragment with Romance elements. *The Jewish Quarterly Review* 91, 17–51.

Bos, G. / Mensching, G. 2005. The literature of Hebrew medical synonyms: Romance and Latin terms and their identification. *Aleph* 5, 169–211.

Bos, G. / Mensching, G. 2014. A medico-botanical glossary in Hebrew characters of Italian origin. *Iberia Judaica* 6, 11–21.

Bos, G. / Mensching, G. 2015. Arabic-Romance medico-botanical glossaries in Hebrew manuscripts from the Iberian Peninsula and Italy. *Aleph* 15, 9–61.

Bos, G. / Hajek, S. / Mensching, G. 2022. A fragment of Abraham Avigdor's translation of Gerard de Solo's *Practica* from the Cairo Genizah: edition and analysis with special regard to the Old Occitan elements. *Aleph* 21, 309–357.

Bouras-Vallianatos, P. 2013. Simon of Genoa's *Clavis sanationis*: a study of thirteenth-century Latin pharmacological lexicography. In Zipser, B. Ed. *Simon of Genoa's medical lexicon*. London: Versita, 31–47.

Cuomo, L. 1983. Il giudeo italiano e le vicende linguistiche degli ebrei in Italia. In Ministero per i beni culturali e ambientali Ed. *Italia Judaica. Atti del I Convegno internazionale Bari 18–22 maggio 1981*, Rom: Multigrafica editrice, 427–454.

DAO = Baldinger, K. et al. 1975–2007. *Dictionnaire onomasiologique de l'ancien occitan*. 10 Fasz., Tübingen: Niemeyer.

DCVB = Alcover, A. M. / Moll, F. de B. 1980–1985. *Diccionari català-valencià-balear*. 10 Bde. Palma de Mallorca: Moll.

DECLC = Coromines, J. 1980–2001. *Diccionari etimològic i complementari de la llengua catalana*. 10 Bde. Barcelona: Curial.

DiTMAO = Bos, G. / Corradini, M. S. / Mensching, G. Eds. In Vorbereitung. *Dictionnaire des termes médico-botaniques de l'ancien occitan*. Elektronische Ressource.

DMLBS = Latham, R. E. et al. 1975–2013. *Dictionary of medieval Latin from British sources*. 13 Fasz., London: Oxford Universitary Press.

DOM = Stimm, H. / Stempel, W.-D. 1996–2013. *Dictionnaire de l'occitan médiéval*. 7 Faszikel und 1 Supplementband. Berlin: De Gruyter / Tübingen: Niemeyer.

DOMel = Selig, M. / Stimm, H. / Stempel, W.-D. 2014–. *DOM en ligne. Dictionnaire de l'occitan médiéval*. Elektronische Ressource. München: Bayerische Akademie der Wissenschaften. http://www.dom-en-ligne.de/index.html (23.03.2022).

DT = Dietrich, A. 1988. *Dioscurides Triumphans. Ein anonymer arabischer Kommentar (Ende 12. Jahrh. n. Chr.) zur Materia medica*. 2 Bde. Göttingen: Vandenhoeck & Ruprecht.

EJ[2] = Berenbaum, M. / Skolnik, F. 2007. *Encyclopedia Judaica*. 2. Auflage. Detroit: Macmillan.

Engel, E. 2015. Immigrant scribes' handwriting in Northern Italy from the late thirteenth to the mid-sixteenth century: Sephardi and Ashkenazi attitudes toward the Italian script. In del Barco, J. Ed. *The late medieval Hebrew book in the Western Mediterranean. Hebrew manuscripts and incunabula in context*. Leiden / Boston: Brill, 28–45.

GDLI = Battaglia, S. et al. 1961–2002. *Grande dizionario della lingua italiana*. 21 Bde. Turin: UTET.

Glessgen, M.-D. 1996. *Die Falkenheilkunde des 'Moamin' im Spiegel ihrer volgarizzamenti*. 2 Bde. Tübingen: Niemeyer.

S. *Lauschus, G. Mensching, L. Refrigeri, F. Savelsberg*

Gutiérrez Rodilla, B. 2007. *La esforzada reelaboración del saber*. Repertorios médicos de interés lexicográfico anteriores a la imprenta. San Millán de la Cogolla: Cilengua.

Ineichen, G. 1962–1966. *El libro agregà de Serapiom – volgarizzamento di Frater Jacobus Philippus de Padua*. 2 Bde. Venedig: Istituto per la collaborazione culturale.

Käs, F. 2010. *Die Mineralien in der arabischen Pharmakognosie. Eine Konkordanz zur mineralischen Materia medica der klassischen arabischen Heilmittelkunde nebst überlieferungsgeschichtlichen Studien*. 2 Bde. Wiesbaden: Harrassowitz.

KaT = Bos, G. / Käs, F. / Lübke, M. / Mensching G. Eds. 2020. *Marwān ibn Janāḥ: On the nomenclature of medicinal drugs (Kitāb al-Talkhīṣ). Edition, translation, and commentary, with special reference to the Ibero-Romance terminology*. 2 Bde. Leiden / Boston: Brill.

Leclerc = Ibn al-Bayṭār. 1877. *Traité des simples*, traduction par Lucien Leclerc. 3 Bde. Paris: Imprimerie nationale. (Nachdruck Paris 1987).

LEI = Pfister, M. et al. 1979–. *Lessico Etimologico Italiano*. Bisher 14 Bde. Wiesbaden: Reichert Verlag.

MacKinney, L. C. 1938. Medieval medical dictionaries and glossaries. In Cate, J. L. / Anderson, E. N. Eds. *Medieval and historiographical essays in honor of James Westfall Thompson*. Chicago: University of Chicago Press, 240–268.

Mazzeo, M. 2011. *Trattato di igiene e dietetica, Anonimo Tarantino (cod. XII E 7 Biblioteca Nazionale di Napoli)*. Dissertation. Rom: «Sapienza», Università di Roma.

Mensching, G. 1994. *La sinonima delos nonbres delas medeçinas griegos e latynos e arauigos. Estudio y edición crítica*. Madrid: Arco Libros.

Mensching, G. 2015. Éléments lexicaux et textes occitans en caractères hébreux. In Trotter, D. Ed. *Manuel de la philologie de l'édition*. Berlin: De Gruyter, 237–266.

Mensching, G. / Zwink, J. 2014. L'ancien occitan en tant que langage scientifique de la médecine. Termes vernaculaires dans la traduction hébraïque du *Zād almusāfir wa-qūt al-ḥādir* (XIIIe siècle). In Alén Garabato, C. / Torreilles, C. / Verny, M.-J. Eds. *Los que fan viure e treslusir l'occitan. Actes du Xe congrès de l'AIEO, Béziers, 12–19 juin 2011*. Limoges: Lambert-Lucas, 226–236.

Meyerhof, M. Ed. 1940. *L'explication des noms de drogues. Un glossaire de matière médicale composé par Maïmonide (Sharḥ asmā' al-'uqqār)*. Kairo: Impr. de l'Institut Français.

OVI = *Opera del vocabolario italiano. Corpus testuale del Tesoro della Lingua Italiana delle Origini*. Florenz: Opera del vocabolario italiano. http://gattoweb.ovi.cnr.it/ (30.03.2022).

Penzig, O. 1924. *Flora popolare italiana*. 2 Bde. Genua: Orto Botanico della R.[a] Università (Nachdruck Bologna 1972).

Piro, R. Ed. 2011. *L'Almansore. Volgarizzamento fiorentino del XIV secolo. Edizione critica*. Florenz: SISMEL – Edizioni del Galluzzo.

Rapisarda, S. 2001. *Il "Thesaurus pauperum" in volgare siciliano*. Palermo: Centro di studi filologici e linguistici siciliani.

REW = Meyer-Lübke, W. 1935. *Romanisches Etymologisches Wörterbuch*. 3. Auflage. Heidelberg: Winter.

Richler, B. 2008. *Hebrew manuscripts in the Vatican library*. Vatikanstadt: Biblioteca Apostolica Vaticana.

Rubin, A. D. 2016. Judeo-Italian. In Kahn, L. / Rubin, A. Eds. *Handbook of Jewish languages*. Leiden / Boston: Brill, 297–364.

Ryzhik, M. im Erscheinen. Italo-Romance. In Mensching, G. / Savelsberg, F. Eds. *Manual of Judaeo-Romance linguistics and philology*. Berlin / Boston: De Gruyter.

Sermoneta, G. 1976. Considerazioni frammentarie sul giudeo-italiano. *Italia* 1, 1–29.

Shatzmiller, J. 1994. *Jews, medicine, and medieval society*. Berkeley / Los Angeles: University of California Press.

ShS = Bos, G. / Hussein, M. / Mensching, G. / Savelsberg, F. 2011. *Medical synonym lists from medieval Provence: Shem Tov ben Isaac of Tortosa, Sefer ha-Shimmush, Book 29, Part 1: Edition and commentary of List 1 (Hebrew – Arabic – Romance/Latin)*. Leiden / Boston: Brill.

Steinschneider, M. 1867–1868. Donnolo. Pharmakologische Fragmente aus dem X. Jahrhundert, nebst Beiträgen zur Literatur der Salernitaner hauptsächlich nach handschriftlichen hebräischen Quellen. *Virchow's Archiv für Pathologische Anatomie* 38 [1867], 65–91; 39 [1867], 296–336; 40 [1867], 80–124; 42 [1868], 51–112.

Steinschneider, M. 1893. *Die hebräischen Übersetzungen des Mittelalters und die Juden als Dolmetscher*. Berlin: Kommissionsverlag des Bibliographischen Bureaus.

Steinschneider, M. 1895. *Die hebräischen Handschriften der königlichen Hof- und Staatsbibliothek in München*. 2. Auflage. München: Palm.

Vercellin, G. Ed. 1991. *Il Canone di Avicenna fra Europa e Oriente nel primo Cinquecento: l'Interpretatio Arabicorum nominum di Andrea Alpago*. Torino: UTET.

VocSic = Piccitto, G. / Tropea, G. / Trovato, S. 1977–2002. *Vocabolario siciliano*. 5 Bde. Palermo: Centro di studi filologici e linguistici siciliani.

VocVen = Patriarchi, G. 1775. *Vocabolario veneziano e padovano co'termini e modi corrispondenti toscani*. Padua: Conzatti.

Christine Paasch-Kaiser

Conventionalization of verb-noun constructions in legal discourse

Abstract. Phraseological units and especially verb-noun constructions are a key element of legal texts. However, their diachronic development and their entrenchment in historical French legal discourse have rarely been studied. In this paper, the presence and diachronic development of five verb-noun collocations whose nucleus is the legal terminological unit *plet* will be examined exemplarily on the basis of legal text books from Normandy or texts related to them. Most of them are part of the RIN ConDÉ-Corpus and were written or printed between the 14th and the 16th century. The aim of this paper is to examine whether these verb-noun collocations are conventionalized legal phraseological units of the customary law of Normandy and beyond the limits of this region.

1. Introduction

Until recently, the language used in the French customary law and texts related to it have received little attention. While terminological units (TU) of the French customary law seem to have been conventionalized – they appear in a series of dictionaries such as the DEAFél, the FEW, the DMF or the AND, and also in glossaries such as those of Ragueau / Laurière (1882 [1704]) or Hoüard (1780–83) – and their use has been investigated at least since the 1950s (cf. among others Baldinger 1951) still little is known about the legal phraseological units (LPU) in which these TU appear, although LPUs and especially verb-noun constructions (VNC) constitute an important means for the production of legally effective and valid legal texts.[1]

The aim of this paper is to fill this gap analyzing whether, between the 14th and the 16th century, a kind of commonly used phraseological stock already existed. In the present paper, I study, exemplarily, the presence, distribution and diachronic development of five verb-noun collocations in texts from legal experts in the field of the customary law of Normandy. The conceptual nucleus of the examined verb-noun collocations is the legal TU *plet*.[2]

---

[1] The situation is different with regard to proverbs (cf. e.g. Cornu 2005 [1990]).

[2] I choose the most frequent form as lemma as there is no uniformity in the consulted texts. The TU derived from lat. PLACĬTUM (FEW, s. v. *placĭtum*, 2b).

The aim of this paper is to examine whether these verb-noun collocations are conventionalized VNCs. According to Ewald (2013), *conventionalization* is the uncoordinated selection processes that language users, in our case the producers of written texts, undertake unconsciously, e.g. the selection of particular verb-noun collocations to convey a specialized (legal) meaning. These selection processes lead to an entrenchment of certain features and, in a later stage, to the establishment and consolidation of norms. Thus, conventionalization processes occur first and foremost in the stages preceding the formal codification of norms.

While the use of forms or constructions in texts about the customary law of Normandy does not permit to draw conclusions on a general use throughout the Gallo-Roman territory, their study permits to visualize the existence and/or development of implicit – tacit, undiscussed and unwritten – usage-based norms. Not aiming at tracing the process of conventionalization in particular, a former analysis of VNCs (Paasch-Kaiser 2022) based on the TU *record*[3] shows that some VNCs were frequently used between the 13th and the 16th century by experts in the field of customary law of Normandy. These VNCs seem to have been the normal, usual and thus conventional LPUs to transmit a certain specialized knowledge. Later, however, these VNCs mostly disappeared from use. Consequently, the study of verb-noun collocations built upon a legal TU permits to detect conventionalized LPUs that have become the implicit norm for experts in the field.

The paper is structured as follows: In section 2, I will outline the characteristics of VNCs as one particular type of LPU. In section 3, I will briefly describe my corpus. My methodological approach and the results of my analysis will be presented in section 4. Finally, in section 5, I will summarize my findings.

2. Verb-noun constructions

In specialized phraseology, the verb-noun construction (VNC) is considered the most frequently used type of phraseological unit (PU) (cf. Gläser 2007).

Its legal meaning dates back to the Merovingians: "Aus der bed. 'gerichtsverhandlung' (a) entsteht dann mit leichtigkeit die bed. 'prozess, streitfall' (b)".

[3] Old Fr. *record* is a TU that denominates an (oral) "testimony of fact, declaration (as a witness)" (AND, s. v. *record* 2) in court, or as the author of the GC says: "[...] record est racontement en court de la chose qui a este faite et ramenee amemoire" (Ms. Ham 192, II: 35b).

This also applies for the legal domain (cf. Tabares Plasencia 2012).[4] Legal phraseological units (LPU) are "key elements in understanding and producing law texts adequate to the linguistic conventions in a language at a specific point in time and in a particular legal system" (Hourani Martín/Tabares Plasencia 2020: 115). According to Tabares Plasencia (2012: 321), a LPU is

> [a] chain of lexical and/or grammatical words, that usually but not essentially includes a (mono- or pluriverbal) term and has a degree of fixation, conventionality and usage in such a way that it is prototypic and specific, that is, recognisable as specialised knowledge unit in the different text types of legal discourse (translated by Hourani Martín/Tabares Plasencia 2020: 115).

Tabares Plasencia's (2012) definition of LPUs is based on two criteria proposed by Gouadec (1994): *prototypicality* and *specificity*. Prototypicality refers to the fact that LPUs are recognized easily as such by experts in the field, because they are conventionalized elements. By specificity, Tabares Plasencia (2012) understands that the PUs transmit specialized (legal) knowledge different from general knowledge. Consequently, in legal contexts the LPUs transmit a concept that they do not transmit in other contexts. These characteristics convert them into units of specialized knowledge. Conventionalized LPUs can be identified by consulting a legal expert.[5] They appear in different genres of legal texts,[6] and have to be used in particular contexts to reach a certain legal effect because of the ritual character of the legal language.[7] In historical contexts it is much more difficult to identify conventionalized LPUs because of the missing living experts, in our case, active producers and users of customary law texts. Hence, a combination of qualitative and quantitative criteria is necessary. The frequency of occurrence could serve as indicator. However, this is not an absolute criterion because in a particular co- and context some combinations do not occur as often as others. According to Tabares Plasencia (2020: 76), in addition different sources need to be analyzed such as reference corpora or (if they exist) terminographic or lexicographic sources to identify the status of a verb-noun collocation. These sources can serve as a base of comparison to verify the LPU's status. The

---

[4] Tabares Plasencia (2012) distinguishes 3 types of LPUs: 1. VNC; 2. Grammatical chains with prepositional function and formulaic adverb phrases; and 3. formulaic texts (cf. Hourani Martín/Tabares Plasencia 2020: 115).

[5] This is the procedure Hourani Martín (2017) uses to identify VNCs in the area of environmental law.

[6] Tabares Plasencia (2020: 76) calls it *institutionalization in the juridical discourse*.

[7] Cf. Brunner (1868) on this subject in a study on formulae in medieval legal French texts.

consultation of different text genres might also be helpful as LPUs (can) occur in different genres of legal texts.

According to Tabares Plasencia (2012), LPUs have two linguistic characteristics.[8] They consist of two or more elements, one of which can be a TU. Monoverbal enunciations with legal effect, such as Sp. *¡protesto!* represent an exception (cf. Tabares Plasencia 2018). In the case of the VNCs we are interested in, a verb is accompanied by a terminological unit (TU). As Tabares Plasencia (2012) states, the TU can be a simple – or monolexical – TU, such as Old Fr. *recort*, or a polylexical – or multi-word – one, such as Old Fr. *recort deschiquier* (cf. Paasch-Kaiser 2022).[9] The TU is the conceptual nucleus of the PU (cf. Bevilacqua 2004: 16–17). It constitutes the subject or the complement (direct or prepositional object) of the verb. The verb of the VNC is a phraseological verb. It expresses an action, process or state. Light verbs are considered among the phraseological verbs, too. The meaning of phraseological verbs does not necessarily differ from that in non-specialized contexts, but in cooccurrence with a TU the verbs acquire a specialized meaning (cf. Lorente Casafont 2002, Tabares Plasencia 2012: 321–322). The VNC's function is to transmit the specialized knowledge relative to a specialized field of knowledge (cf. Bevilacqua 2004: 16–17). I assume that, especially in the case of early written legal French texts, certain verb-noun collocations acquire the status of legal VNCs in this context, even though they also might appear in the same way in nonspecialized discourse. Nevertheless, they are necessary to express a determined action, etc. that is not (or still cannot be) expressed in a different way. I believe that this is due to the fact that, on the one hand, legal language still needed to be accessible, i.e. understandable for everybody that got in touch with law (cf. Schmidt-Wiegand 1998: 280–282 on early legal German). On the other hand, the authors probably still lacked of more "professional solutions" because the French legal language was still developing during the 13th and the 16th cen-

---

[8] Tabares Plasencia (2012) rejects *idiomaticity* understood as metaphorical meaning, i.e. opacity, as a criterion to identify LPUs arguing that, wherever possible, ambiguities are avoided in legal discourse. Therefore, I suppose that a VNC's meaning is not necessarily compositional.

[9] Tabares Plasencia's (2012) approach differs from that of other scholars, such as Gläser (2007: 490–493). While Tabares Plasencia (2012) rejects to include polylexical TUs such Sp. *derecho civil* (Engl. *civil law*) among the LPUs, Gläser (2007) considers them phraseological units and denominates them *Nominationen*.

tury, and hence it was still closely related to the general language (cf. Biu 2009: 460–461, Tardif 1903).[10]

The second linguistic characteristic is that VNCs are not fully lexicalized, i.e. paradigmatic and syntagmatic transformations of VNCs are still possible and quite common in legal discourse. For example, the nominalization of a verb forms part of a VNC like Sp. *celebrar* in *celebrar matrimonio*, 'to marry', that appears as *celebración del matrimonio*. The meaning conveyed by the nominalized form is still that of the VNC. In my opinion, the fact that the users perform transformations and even form new verb-noun collocations, e.g. out of a nominalized VNC, serves as a further hint to identify which verb-noun collocation constitutes a conventionalized pattern that is entrenched in the user's mental grammar.[11]

3. The text corpus

The present paper is based on several texts that belong to the RIN ConDÉ corpus (Larrivée/Goux 2021)[12] and on a copy of the officially elaborated customary law of Normandy, the *Coutume du Pais de Normandie* (CPN), that is available online.[13] The thoroughly searched texts taken from the RIN ConDÉ corpus are listed in Table 1.[14] The manuscript of the *Grand Coutumier* of Normandy (GC 1300, HLS MS 91) contains glosses on the page margin. They have been added at a later, but until now not precisely defined point in time, which is why I differentiate between the verb-noun collocations that appear in the text and those that belong to the gloss. In the case of

---

[10] Cf. also Sinner (2012: 629–633) who describes a similar situation for the emerging Portuguese specialized language of botany.

[11] In her study on VNCs in the emerging domain of environmental law, Hourani Martín (2017) found out that nominalization was the most frequent paradigmatic transformation, whereas passivization was the most frequent syntagmatic one in her corpus.

[12] The RIN ConDÉ corpus assembles ten texts in French from the 13th to the 19th century, i.e. manuscripts and books of the customary law of Normandy elaborated before the invention of the printing press, and printed legal commentaries on the customary law of Normandy (cf. Goux/Decoux/Pica to appear).

[13] The CPN was elaborated between 1578 and 1583 (cf. Yver 1986).

[14] The author (and the translator?) of the GC as well as the commentators were not university scholars but men working in the everyday legal practice. However, they seem to have received an institutional education in law (cf. Besnier 1935).

the commentaries of Le Rouille (1539) and Terrien (1578)[15], I only considered those tokens that do not belong to the version of the GC they include. The commentary of Terrien (1578) further contains several other texts: the *Style de procéder*[16], different documents from the *Echequier de Normandy* (Engl. 'Exchequer of Normandy') and from several French kings. These supplementary texts extend the corpus and permit to show whether a verb-noun collocation has been used in other texts from other points in time, too.

Texts	Date of the main text	Source
GC[17]	1300	RIN ConDÉ
Instructions et ensaignemens	1386–1390	RIN ConDÉ
Le Rouille	1539	RIN ConDÉ
Terrien	1578	RIN ConDÉ
CPN	1586	Google books

Tab. 1. Text corpus of the present study.

4. Methodology and corpus analysis

4.1 Methodology

Among different options, in this paper, I focus on those verb-noun collocations whose nucleus is the TU *plet*. The consulted dictionaries show that the TU was widely accepted and used throughout the Gallo-Roman domain, i.e. it was an entrenched TU. According to the TLFi (2022, s. v. *plaid*1), the TU *plet* has been lost, i.e. it is no longer used in modern, contemporary French in any kind of ((non-) specialized) discourse with a legal meaning. It is a TU that occurs in all texts of my corpus but with several meanings. In the study, I only take into account those cases in which the TU *plet* appears with the

---

[15] Terrien's (1578) text seems to have been considered an authority text, also after the elaboration of the official customary law of Normandy (Reulos 1976, fn. 32).

[16] It is also called *Stille de proceder en Normendie* and dates back to the end of the 15th or beginning of the 16th century (cf. https://portail.biblissima.fr/en/ark:/43093/edatadc130d7c4bc7e0dd1e88591fb38df09c0a3502ff; October 2021).

[17] The GC dates back to the second third of the 13th century and has initially been written in Latin (cf. Tardif 1903; Neveux 2011). It represents a kind of reference text to which the commentaries of Le Rouille (1539) and Terrien (1578) refer.

meaning 'procès, instance, action en justice' (Engl. 'action at law, plea, suit', cf. AND s. v. *plet*).[18] I further limit the number of verb-noun collocations examined in this paper to the most frequent cases in which the TU constitutes the direct object of the verb and in which the verb is a phraseological verb in the sense of Lorente Casafont (2002). For the extraction of the occurrences, I used the platforms of the RIN ConDÉ corpus and the tool *sketchengine*[19] where I integrated the text of the CPN.

My analysis focusses on three aspects that I consider to be decisive for the question whether a verb-noun collocation is a conventionalized VNC: 1) the presence of a verb-noun collocation including its paradigmatic and syntagmatic transformations in several texts of my corpus and its frequency of occurrence, 2) its occurrence in other French customary laws, 3) the documentation of the collocation in dictionaries and glossaries.

The use and the frequency of occurrences of the verb-noun collocations vary considerable between the texts. The individual frequency shows the authors preferences while a collocation's occurrence in various texts permits to determine its status as VNC. This way it is possible to verify whether a VNC forms part of the bigger legal discourse on customary law of Normandy and hence its conventionalization. However, a low frequency of occurrence *per se* does not mean that this construction has not been conventionalized. Instead, it might be an indicator for a diachronic change. Nevertheless, if a certain collocation appears only in one text it is impossible to distinguish between the author's individual preference or style and a not frequent VNC. Further texts then need to be consulted. Consequently, other customary law texts from other regions will be analyzed at to find out which the verb-noun collocations' scope was.[20] Finally, the verb-noun collocations' presence in dictionaries and glossaries such as the AND, DMF, DEAF, FEW, NDHL,

---

[18] It has been stated that from the 14th to the 16th century, the legal French language was still not as fixed as it is nowadays (cf. Biu 2009). Therefore, several competing TUs with *plet*, such as *cause* or *proces*, as well as VNCs containing that TU might have existed. This does not, however, mean that verb-noun collocations based on the TU *plet* could not have become VNCs. The conditions for the use of one or the other collocation cannot, for the sake of space, be studied in the present article.

[19] https://www.sketchengine.eu/ (October 2021).

[20] This comparison has been done in a rather rough way consulting the digitaled versions of the *Nouveau coutumier général* (NCG, Bourdot de Richebourg 1724) and a version of the *Coutumes du Beauvaisis* (CB) (Philippe de Beaumanoir, 13th century) on the gallica website of the French National Library (https://gallica.bnf.fr; October 2021) where I searched for the term *plet* and its spelling variants.

the glossary of Rageau and Laurière (1882 [1704]) and that of Hoüard (1780–1783) need to be checked to determine their conventionalization.

The following Table 2 provides an overview on the frequency and distribution of the analyzed verb-noun collocations. The occurrences in texts included within other texts such as glosses or copied texts, except those of the copies of the GC, are indicated in parentheses:

	GC 1300	*Instructions et ensaignemens* 1386–1390	Le Rouille 1539	Terrien 1578	CPN 1586
aloigner le plet	3	–	3	–	–
commencer le plet	4	–	1	–	–
delaier le plet	5	–	6	3	–
finer le plet	15 (+ 1)	–	2	(2)	–
mouvoir le plet	8	–	–	–	–
porloigner le plet	5	–	4	–	–

Tab. 2. Frequency and distribution of the analyzed verb-noun collocations.

4.2 Analysis of the verb-noun collocations

4.2.1 *finer le plet*

The verb-noun collocation *finer le plet* 'to close/to settle an action at law/suit' is the most frequent of the analyzed collocations in the GC (1300), were it occurs 15 times:[21]

(1)   ℂ Et si doit l en savoir que se le plet n est fine dedens vi mois puis que liglise est escheue. l evesque du lieu qui doit porvoier des yglises de son dyocese la porra donner a qui que il voudra. (GC, De patronage d iglises. Cviii.)

The collocation also occurs in several other texts of the corpus although the frequency of occurrence in these texts is by far not as high as in the GC (1300). In (2), (3) and (4) examples are given from the gloss of the GC, the

---

[21]   The examples are taken from the website of the RIN ConDÉ corpus. I did not manipulate the offered transcription, although it might have contained transcription errors. The text is formatted as justified text. The blans between graphemes – often due to missing apostrophes or after initials – appear in the current version (May/September 2022). I have underlined the important sequences to highlight them.

commentary of Le Rouille (1539) and in the *Style de proceder* included in the Terrien (1578):

(2) Davoir conseil asavoir mon se es causes de marchie de bourse le premier achateour de qui le marchie est demande demandant le plait pendant entre les pluz prouchainz ara le marchie ou il atendra tant que le plet soit fine entre les pluz prouchainz. (Gloss GC, De ra pel de ter par borse. cx iv, commentary 20, MS HLS, seq. 259)

(3) C Item aussi on doibt auoir letres du bailly. ainsi que le texte met adrecantz au prelat que il ne recoiue desormais aulcun a ladicte eglise / iusques a ce que le plet soit fine / (Le Rouille, La seconde partie, 2, commentary 312)

(4) Et à la fin desdits plets ou assises se passent les encheres, si pour quelque cause raisonnable, ou du consentement des parties, icelles encheres n'estoient differees. (Terrien, LIVRE DIXIEME, Chap. X, Au Style de proceder)

In the case of the gloss (2), *finer le plet* occurs on a page of the GC where the construction is not used. The two occurrences in the Le Rouille (1539) appear in a part of the commentary in which the TU *plet* is used; in the case of (3), it is even *finer le plet* that appears in the part of the GC the commentary refers to. However, in none of the two occurrences it is a direct commentary, i.e. there is no direct relation to the construction of the GC. The collocation seems to be an accepted and valid option that Le Rouille (1539) (still) uses without fearing that his message would not be understood. The cases cited in the Terrien (1578) proceed from the *Style* and date thus from the end of the 15th or beginning of the 16th century. The construction seems to have been an accepted VNC until the middle of the 16th century.[22]

The VNC is, however, not completely lexicalized; several paradigmatic and syntagmatic transformations occur in the texts. The most frequent are passive constructions, among them two modalized passive constructions with the modal verbs *souloir* and *devoir*, as in (1) and (2), and nominalizations as in (4). It also occurs as infinitive phrase. In all but one cases, the TU appears with a definite article. In the GC (1300), the nominalized form *la fin des plet* even forms part of another verb-noun collocation *porloigner la fin des ples* 'to delay the closing of an action at law/a suit' (5):

---

[22] In Berault's (1614) commentary I still found one occurrence of a syntagmatic transformation of the VNC (participalization): "[...] quand mesme ils n'en seroyent requisy pour apres les plés finis faire lesdites informations [...]" (TITRE DE JURISDICTION, Article X, note 29). In the text, the author refers to, only the TU *plet* appears but not the entire VNC, and the verb *finer* or *finir* does not occur in the co- or context what I consider a proof for the conventionalization of the VNC even if its use is rare at this time.

(5) L angor <u>porloigne la fin des ples</u>. (GC, De langor. xxxviii)

In my opinion, this use confirms the collocation's status of *finer le plet* as VNC.

Besides these occurrences, the collocation does not appear in any of the consulted lexicographical sources. The search of the CB (13th century) revealed that there the verb-noun collocation is used (8 occ.) with the same meaning, as can be seen in (6). It is the normal LPU to express that a suit is or will be settled/closed what I consider further proof for the status of the collocation as VNC, i.e. as a conventionalized LPU:[23]

(6) : si que<u>, quant li ples est fines,</u> soit à perte soit à gaaing, qu'on suce li quel poent perdre et gaaigner à plet (CB, Chap. IV, 17, Des Procureurs, 81)

It needs to be mentioned that no alternative collocation, such as *clore le plet* or *terminer le plet* appears in the texts.[24]

---

[23] In the MLLM (2002, s. v. *placitum*) appears an example from Latin conveying the same meaning: "Sic namque inter nos <u>finitum est placitum</u> et deliberatum" (emphasis CPK). However, a search in a NCG (1724) did not reveal further examples of this construction.

[24] However, in the *Très Ancien Coutumier* of Normandy (TAC; 1250–1300) the verb-noun collocation *terminer le plet* occurs conveying the same meaning. In Basnage's (1678) commentary on the customary law of Normandy, the TU *plet* does not appear anymore. Instead, a different verb-noun collocation conveying the same meaning appears: *terminer le procez*. A first search in this text shows that the verb-noun collocation *terminer le procez* occurs four times with the meaning 'to close/to settle an action at law/a suit', i.e. that of *finer le plet* and *terminer le plet*. In Merville's (1731) text, I also found two occurrences of *terminer le procès*, both cases of participalization and coordinated structures with the verb *juger* 'to judge' in "le procès jugé & terminée" (Titre 5, Art. LXXII). The collocation *terminer le procès* can also be observed in Bérault's (1614) commentary on the CPN. In Terrien's (1578) text, however, the collocation *clore un procez* occurs. I also observed *terminer le proces* in the NCG (1724) where it appears in a coordinated structure with *décider* 'to decide' "terminer & decider les causes & procès" (T2, 2, 1234, Chap. III, Statuts et ancienne coutumes de la comté et barronie de Bueil), "procès decidez & terminez" (T3, 618, Proces verbal des Coutumes d'Auxerre) and with *régler* 'to resolve/to settle' "&leurs differends & procès reiglez & terminez" (T3, 619, Proces verbal des Coutumes d'Auxerre). Consequently, *terminer le procès* might be a "modern" variant of *finer le plet*, a hypothesis that needs further proof.

4.2.2 *aloigner le plet*

Another verb-noun collocation that appears repeatedly, but only in the GC (1300) and the Le Rouille (1539), is *aloigner le plet / al(l)onger le plait* 'to prolong/extend (in time) an action at law/a suit'. In (7) and (8), it forms part of a general proposition on the possibility to extend the duration of a suit by the nomination of a warrantor (Fr. *garant*):

(7) C Cestes ueues ont la maniere de nouele dessesine. Mes que garant ipoet estre uouchie. et celui qui est uouchie a garant poet uouchier 1 autre. et 1 autre le tiers. Mes le tiers qui est uouchie ne poet uouchier le quart. quer issi aloignereit trop le plait (GC, De brief de mariage encombré iiii xx et xviii.)

(8) C Item 1 'en doibt noter que se aulcun vouche garant / ou comme defenseur ou comme ainsne de fief au quel il s arreste a garantie absolute : il peut alonger le plet tant qu il ait par trois defaultz mis sa partie en amende par iugement (Le Rouille, quarte distinction, Chap. l., note 69)

In Le Rouille's (1539) text, the verb-noun collocation occurs in those parts of the commentary that refer to the GC in which the same collocation is present. Again, the occurrences are no direct repetitions of the GC. Instead, they seem to be an acceptable option for the author to address the extension of an action at law or a suit. The GC does not contain syntagmatic or paradigmatic transformations of the collocation. In Le Rouille's (1539) text, however, three occurrences of the collocation appear, one of it being the nominalization *alongement de plet* that does not form part of the included GC. The low verb-noun collocation's frequency of occurrence in the texts and the fact that it is only used in two texts does not permit to consider it a conventionalized VNC on the basis of the examined corpus. However, in the CB (13th century) this verb-noun collocation (3 occ.) occurs, too, conveying the same meaning, as in (9):

(9) Mais se cil qui requiert le recort, le fet par malice, por alongier le plet de ce c'on li demande, il ne doit pas estre soufert ; ou s'il a el païs aucun de cex qui furent à le besongoe par les quix li recors pot estre fes, si comme deus personnes ou plus, on ne doit pas le plet alongier, ne atargier outre l'espasse de deus assises, en lieu de deus productions qui doivent estre douées à cix qui ont à prover, por les autres recordeurs atendre ; car aucun ples en porroit estre atargiés par malice (CB, T1, 119).

The search of the NCG (1724) revealed one case in the local custom of Berry and Lorris (from the end of the 13th century, 1260/1275, NCG T3, 2, 1008), but the collocation is not mentioned in the consulted lexicographical sources. To sum up, its occurrence in texts from Normandy and other regions seems to be an argument in favor of its qualifications as VNC. However, the question requires further research as the number of texts in which it occurs is small as well as the frequency of occurrence within these texts.

Interestingly, in the GC (1300) *aloigner le plet/al(l)onger le plait* competes with another verb-noun collocation *porloigner le plet* that conveys the same meaning, as in (10). It also occurs in Le Rouille's (1539) text, but always in the form of a nominalization as in (11), referring in all cases to parts of the GC. However, only in the case of the chapter on widowhood (Fr. *veufuete*) the construction appears in the text of the cited piece of the custom:

(10) C Ceste essoigne poet estre cassee sele a este fete autre fois de cele querele quer une soule fois en poet aucun estre essoignie en une querele ne le plet n en puet plus estre porloignie. (GC, De essoigne. xxxvii.)

(11) De gesine de femmes. ch. xli. fo. lxiiij.
C Cy est traicte que gesine de femme est prolongement de plet iusques a quarante iours : et qui veult contredire telle exoine il doibt estre receu. De veufuete de femmes. cha. xlii. fo. eodem. (Le Rouille, Matière liminaire 3)

The DMF (s. v. *aloigner*) explains the meaning of *aloigner* with "Prolonger [dans le temps]" 'prolong/lenghten (in time)'. For the author of the GC (1300), *aloigner le plet* and *porloigner le plet* seem to be synonymous verb-noun collocations. As concerns the transformation of the latter, passivization (1 occ.) as well as a combination of passivization and modalization (*devoir, pouvoir*) of *porloigner the plet* occur. However, as *porloigner le plet* cannot be found in other texts, except in Le Rouille's (1539), it might be an idiolectal particularity.[25]

4.2.3 *delaier le plet*

Another verb-noun collocation observed in the GC (1300) (12) as well as in Le Rouille's (1539) (13) and Terrien's (1578) (14) texts is *delaier/delayer le plet* that in all cases convey the meaning 'to delay an action at law/a suit':

(12) S e aucun a receu semonse de diuers iuges destre en diuers lieus a un meisme ior il doit aler a la cort au plus haut qui par ses letres pendans le porra deliurer de la defaute de cel ior et fere le plet delaier iusqu a i autre terme. ceste escusation poet estre fete une soule fois par un iuge (GC, D escusement par iustise. xliiii.)

---

[25] In the GC (~1300), the TU *querelle* also appears in collocations with *aloigner* and *porloigner*. This similarity seems to be an indicator for the exchangeability of the two verbs and the collocations' synonymy.

Conventionalization of verb-noun constructions in legal discourse

(13) C car aultrement il pourroit <u>delayer le plet</u> luy qui est partie / tant que l eglise cherroit en elaps de temps (Le Rouille, La charte au roy Philippe. cx., commentary 4)

(14) Sommation de garant.
Pour laquelle <u>le plet ne sera delayé</u>, si le demandeur ne veut. (Terrien, LIVRE NEVFIEME, Chap. XXIII, note 6)

Several transformations of the collocation can be observed in the corpus: It is used in a causative construction with the verb *fere* 'to make' as in (12) and in passive constructions as in (14). Cases of nominalization occur, too. The nominalization of the verb leads to two different nouns: *delai de plet* and *delaiement de plet* conveying both the verb-noun collocation's meaning. The last one can be found once in Le Rouille's (1539) and in Terrien's (1578) text. However, in Terrien's text (LIVRE NEVFIEME, Chap. VIII, note) its use is a clear repetition of a part of the included customary law text. The frequency of occurrence of the collocation, its presence in several texts and the existence of syntagmatic and paradigmatic transformations seem to be solid arguments to consider *delaier/delayer le plet* a VNC.

Further proof of this assumption comes from the CB (13th century), where *delaier le plet* (7 occ.) appears with the same meaning, too. However, neither the AND nor the DMF or any consulted glossary states this collocation, but the DMF (s. v. *delaier*) indicates *delaier une cause* 'Différer un procès' ('to delay/to defer a suit'), which appears in Le Rouille (1539), Terrien (1578) and Berault (1614). In the AND (s. v. *delaier*), the verb *delaier* is marked as *legal* with the meaning 'to postpone'. Although it does not seem to be very frequent and widely distributed, I consider *delayer le plet* a conventionalized VNC that is a valid means for the users from Normandy and nearby while a temporal (and spatial) restriction might exist.

4.2.4 *commencer le plet*

The verb-noun collocation *commencer le plet* 'to open an action at law/a suit' is not very frequent and occurs only in the GC (1300) (15) and in Rouille's (1539) (16) text:

(15) L a ueouete des femmes qui nont pere ne filx ne neuous qui soit en aage ne qui latiegne en sa main ne qui ait o lie possession de fieu ne de moeble. porloigne la fin des ples. et il ont terme de querre conseil iusques a i an et i jor quant cel terme sera passe ele se doit offrir pardeuant la iustise amener <u>le plet qui a este commencie</u>. (GC, De weouete de femmes. xl.)

(16) C Apres ensuit eu texte.
 C Aulcun ne se peut plaindre que ses seurs ayent desaduenant mariage. etc. Par ce texte appert que s aulcun veult rappeller aulcun don de mariage comme desaduenant il conuient qu <u>il en commence le plet</u> dedens l an et iour de la mort du donneur / ou en l an et iour qu ' il est venu en aage / s il estoit soubzaage. [...] (Le Rouille, La seconde partie, De brief de mariage encombre. Chap. c, commentary 283)

Besides the < verb + TU (direct object) > structure, only syntagmatic transformations, i.e. passivization and relativization of the verb-noun collocation can be observed in the GC (1300). Other cases in Le Rouille's (1539) text are part of the included GC. Interestingly, no other collocation such as *ouvrir le plet* 'to open a suit' occurs in the texts.

The collocation does not occur in the NCG (1724), but in the CB (13th century) there are several cases (8 occ.) and transformations, besides the < verb + TU > form, such as of modalization and nominalization e.g. *commenc(h)ement du plet*.[26] The low frequency of occurrence of this collocation in the texts does not permit to consider *commencer le plet* as a VNC without further proof.

4.2.5 *mouvoir le plet*

The last verb-noun collocation, *mouuoir le plet*, is well documented in lexicographical works. In the AND (s. v. *plai*1, *mover* and *moveir*) it is marked as legal construction, having the meaning 'to initiate an action or plea'. The AND indicates two forms *mover plai* and *moveir plai*. The DMF (s. v. *plaid* II, B) also states *mouvoir (le) plaid* 'Intenter une action en justice' ('to initiate an action at law'). Due to this fact, I consider it a VNC.

In our corpus, the VNC occurs with this meaning in the GC (1300, 8 occ.) and in the *Charte au Roy Philippe* included in the GC and in Le Rouille's (1539) and Terrien's (1578) text:

(17) et pardesus ce nos volon que se celui qui dit que le patronage de l iglise apartient a lui et <u>n en muet plet</u> dedens vi mois apres ce que ele est escheue. l arcevesque ou l evesque aient franche poeste de donner la a qui que il voudra (GC, De Phelipe roy de Franche. Cxj.)

---

[26] In the TAC (1250–1300), I also found an occurrence of this collocation. In Le Rouille's (1539) text as well as in Basnage's (1678) commentary there are several occurrences (and transformations) of the verb-noun collocation *commencer le proces* what could be regarded as a further developed variant of *commencer le plet*, a hypothesis that needs further proof.

This VNC only shows syntagmatic transformation in the corpus, i.e. passivization and relativization together with passivization. Besides the occurrences in the *Charte*, the Le Rouille (1539) and the Terrien (1578) do not use this verb-noun collocation.[27] Nevertheless, I consider *mouvoir le plet* a VNC due to its presence in other legal texts mentioned in the dictionaries as well as in the CB (13th c., 5 occ.) where it occurs in modalized constructions or without transformation.

5. Conclusions

With this study, a step has been taken to identify conventionalized LPUs used commonly by experts in the field of the customary law of Normandy. In my paper the occurrence, distribution and development of five verb-noun collocations in the legal discourse of the customary law of Normandy represented in texts from between the 14th to the 16th century were traced. The aim of the paper was to determine whether these verb-noun collocations can be considered conventionalized legal VNCs and thus elements of an implicit regional usage-based norm in legal discourse.

In order to detect these conventionalized VNCs, I have examined three criteria: first, the presence and the absolute frequency of occurrence of a verb-noun-collocation in different texts belonging to a text corpus consisting of texts from the domain of the customary law in a particular region – in my case Normandy – including the presence of syntagmatic and paradigmatic transformations of these verb-noun-collocations; second, the collocation's occurrence in customary law texts from other regions; and third, their inclusion in lexicographic sources.

The examination of these verb-noun collocations permits to conclude that three out of five verb-noun collocations, *finer le plet*, *delaier le plet* and *mouuoir le plet* are conventionalized VNCs. The scope of all three is larger than the limits of Normandy: they also appear in the customary law texts from other regions. The VNCs differ by the fact that *delaier le plet* is more common also in later stages than *finer le plet* (cf. table 2) and *mouuoir le plet*. The legal TU *plet* has been lost, which is probably the reason why none

---

[27] This VNC is already present in the TAC (1250–1300) (4 occ.) and is mentioned as VNC in Tardif's glossary (1903, s. v. plez1). In the Berault's (1614), Basnage's (1678) and Merville's (1731) texts I state the verb-noun collocation *mouvoir le procès*, but further research has to clarify whether it has the same meaning in all contexts.

of the VNCs appears anymore in texts published after 1539.[28] Instead of *plet*, the TU *proces/procez* occurs in combination with the verbs *finer* (and *terminer*) and *mouuoir*. These verb-noun collocations might be considered innovative variants of the VNC *finer le plet* and *mouuoir le plet* while the older ones disappear, a hypothesis that needs further proof. In the case of *delaier le plet*, no such innovative construction could be found in the consulted texts. The fact that *delaier le plet* and *finer le plet* are used by experts in the field from different epochs and different regions are clear indicators for a conventionalization similar to that of *mouvoir le plet*, a VNC that has been described in several dictionaries.

The remaining two cases, *aloigner le plet* and *commencer le plet*, are the least common collocations. Each of them only occurs in two texts of the corpus. *Aloigner le plet* further appears in texts from outside of Normandy, what could be taken as an indicator for its status as conventionalized VNC. However, as its frequency in the texts is low, such a conclusion needs further proof from other texts from the legal domain. Besides, it was shown that in the GC (1300) *aloigner le plet* competes with a synonymic construction *porloigner le plet*. Possibly, its use is due to a still ongoing development of the legal language between the 13th and the 16th century or to an idiolectal preference. The collocation *commencer le plet* only occurs in two texts related to the customary law of Normandy, and in one case, its frequency is extremely low. However, it also appears in a French version of the TAC of Normandy and in the CB. Further research needs to be done to clarify the collocation's status in legal discourse given the different frequency of occurrence in the texts. It is possible that the collocations in questions early fell into disuse and were subsequently replaced by others.

Finally, the last important aspect to be mentioned is the fact that none of the studied constructions occurs in the CPN (1586). As Grinberg (2006) highlights, the reformation process of the customary law also served to renew the wording. Even if some verb-noun collocations could be identified as conventionalized VNCs, their total lack in the official customary law seems to indicate their functional loss in that period and thus their status as conventionalized VNCs.

---

[28] Perhaps its loss is due to the increasing integration of notions from the Roman law in the French legal language (cf. Biu 2009: 460). Another reason could have been the polysemy of the TU.

References

AND = Aberystwyth University, Arts and Humanities Research Council. 2022. *Anglo-Norman Dictionary*. https://anglo-norman.net (2022-09-15).

Anonyme. 1250–1300. Très Ancien Coutumier. Bibliothèque Sainte-Geneviève, ms 1743. (ed. A. Marnier). In Larrivée, P. / Goux, M. Dir. 2021. *Corpus ConDÉ*, version Beta 1.0, Caen, CRISCO (EA 4255) et PDN (MRSH) de l'Université de Caen. https://www.unicaen.fr/coutumiers/conde/sommaire/tac_lighter.html (2022-09-15).

Anonyme. 1403. *Grand Coutumier de Normandie* (Staatsbibliothek zu Berlin, Ms. Ham 192, I–II).

Baldinger, K. 1951. Die Coutumes und ihre Bedeutung für die Geschichte des französischen Wortschatzes. *Zeitschrift für romanische Philologie* 67, 3–48.

Basnage, H. 1678. La coutume réformée du païs et duché de Normandie ..., 2 Vols. Rouen. In Larrivée, P. / Goux, M. Dir. 2021. *Corpus ConDÉ*, version Beta 1.0, Caen, CRISCO (EA 4255) et PDN (MRSH) de l'Université de Caen. https://www.unicaen.fr/coutumiers/conde/sommaire/basnage_lighter.html (2022-09-15).

Berault, J. 1614. La coustume réformée du pays et duché de Normandie ..., seconde édition, Rouen. Exemplaire conservé à la Bibliothèque nationale de France. In Larrivée, P. / Goux, M. Dir. 2021. *Corpus ConDÉ*, version Beta 1.0, Caen, CRISCO (EA 4255) et PDN (MRSH) de l'Université de Caen. https://www.unicaen.fr/coutumiers/conde/sommaire/berault_lighter.html (2022-09-15).

Besnier, R. 1935. *La Coutume de Normandie. Histoire externe.* Paris: Librairie du Recueil, Sirey.

Bevilacqua, C. R. 2004. *Unidades fraseológicas especializadas eventivas: descripción y reglas de formación en el ámbito de la energía solar*. PhD Thesis in pdf. Barcelona: Institut Universitari de Lingüística Aplicada, Universitat Pompeu Fabra. http://hdl.handle.net/10803/7515 (2022-11-29).

Biu, H. 2009. La Somme Acé : prolégomènes à une étude de la traduction française de la « Summa Azonis » d'après le manuscrit Bibl. Vat., Reg. lat. 1063. *Bibliothèque de l'école des chartes* 167/2, 417–464. https://doi.org/10.3406/bec.2009.463968 (2022-11-29).

Brunner, H. 1868. *Wort und Form im altfranzösischen Process*. Akademie der Wissenschaften. Wien: Gerold in Komm. 655–780. https://www.digitale-sammlungen.de/de/view/bsb10548453?page=4,5 (2022-11-29).

CB = Beaumanoir, P. de. 13th century. *Les Coutumes du Beauvaisis*. Ed. by Beugnot, Auguste-Arthur (1842). 2 Vols. Paris: J. Renouard. https://catalogue.bnf.fr/ark:/12148/cb35719794r (2022-09-15).

Cornu, G. 2005 [1990]. *Linguistique juridique*. 3e édition. Paris: Montchrestien.

CPN = Anonyme. 1586. *Coustume du Pais de Normandie. Anciens ressors, et enclaves d'iceluy*. Paris: Iaques du Puit. https://books.google.de/books?id =wCdkAAAAcAAJ&hl=de&pg=PP5#v=ononepa&q&f=false (2022-11-29).

DEAFél = Heidelberger Akademie der Wissenschaften. Eds. 2010–2021. *Dictionnaire étymologique de l'ancien français électronique*. https://www.hadw-bw.de/deaf (2022-11-29).

Di Stefano, G. 2015. *Nouveau Dictionnaire Historique des Locutions. Ancien Français, Moyen Français, Renaissance* (NDHL). 2 Vols. A-K, L-Z. Turnhout: Brepols.

DMF = ATILF-CNRS / Université de Lorraine. Laboratoire Analyse et traitement informatique de la langue française. 2020. *Dictionnaire du Moyen Français* (online). http://www.atilf.fr/dmf (2022-11-29).

Ewald, P. 2013. Konventionalisierung. In Schierholz, S. J. Ed. *Wörterbücher zur Sprach- und Kommunikationswissenschaft* (WSK) *Online*. Berlin / Boston: De Gruyter. https://www.degruyter.com/database/WSK/entry/wsk_id_wsk_artikel _artikel_14057/html (2022-11-29).

FEW = Wartburg, W. von et al. 1928–2002. *Französisches etymologisches Wörterbuch: eine Darstellung des galloromanischen Sprachschatzes*. Bonn / Basel / Leipzig: Helbing & Lichtenhahn, Klopp, Teubner, Zbinden. https://lecteur-few.atilf.fr/index.php/page/view (2022-11-29).

GC = Anonym. 1300. *Grand Coutumier de Normandie*. In Violette, C. / Bretthauer, I. / Goux, M. / Étienne, B. / Viel, J.-B. / Barré, É. / Paasch-Kaiser, C. / Pica, M. / Picard, M. Eds. *Transcription of HLS MS 91. Harvard Law School Library*. https://nrs.lib.harvard.edu/urn-3:hls.libr:2395903. In Larrivée, P. / Goux, M. Dir. 2021. *Corpus ConDÉ*, version Beta 1.0, Caen, CRISCO (EA 4255) et PDN (MRSH) de l'Université de Caen. https://www.unicaen.fr/ coutumiers/conde/sommaire/gc_lighter.html (2022-09-15).

Gläser, R. 2007 [2008]. Fachphraseologie. In Burger, H. / Dobrovol'skij, D. / Kühn, P. / Norrick, N. R. Eds. *Phraseologie / Phraseology. Ein internationales Handbuch zeitgenössischer Forschung / An International Handbook of Contemporary Research*. Berlin / Boston: De Gruyter Mouton, 482–505. https://doi.org/ 10.1515/9783110197136-045 (2022-11-29).

Gouadec, D. 1994. Nature et traitement des entités phraséologiques. Terminologie et phraséologie. In Gouadec, D. Ed. *Terminologie et phraséologie. Acteurs et aménageurs. Actes du deuxième Université d'Automne en Terminologie*. Paris: La Maison du dictionnaire, 167–193.

Goux, M. / Decoux, P. / Pica, M. to appear. Le corpus ConDÉ : bilans, leçons, perspectives. In Hesselbach, R. / Rohl T. Eds. *Approches numériques des corpus historiques des langues de France*. München: AVM.

Grinberg, M. 2006. *Ecrire Les Coutumes: Les droits seigneuriaux en France, 16e–18e siècle*. Paris: PUF.

Hoüard, D. 1780–1783. *Dictionnaire analytique historique étymologique critique et interprétative de la Coutume de Normandie*. 4 Vols. Rouen: Le Boucher. http://catalogue.bnf.fr/ark:/12148/bpt6k94053c, http://catalogue.bnf.fr/ark:/12148/bpt6k94054q, http://catalogue.bnf.fr/ark:/12148/bpt6k940552, http://catalogue.bnf.fr/ark:/12148/bpt6k914365 (2022-11-29).

Hourani Martín, D. 2017. *Unidades fraseológicas especializadas en un corpus de derecho ambiental sobre la protección frente al cambio climático (alemán-español)*. Universidad de Granada (PhD Thesis). http://hdl.handle.net/10481/48151 (2022-11-29).

Hourani Martín, D. / Tabares Plasencia, E. 2020. Morphosyntactic and semantic behaviour of legal phraseological units: A case study in Spanish verb-noun constructions about money laundering. *Terminology. International journal of theoretical and applied issues in specialized communication* 26, 108–131.

Instrucions et ensaignemens = Besnier, G. / Génestal, R. Eds. 1912. *Instrucions et ensaignemens* [Texte imprimé] : style de procéder d'une justice seigneuriale normande (1386–90). Caen, 27–67. In Larrivée, P. / Goux, M. Dir. 2021. *Corpus ConDÉ*, version Beta 1.0, Caen, CRISCO (EA 4255) et PDN (MRSH) de l'Université de Caen. https://www.unicaen.fr/coutumiers/conde/sommaire/instructions_lighter.html (2022-09-15).

Larrivée, P. / Goux, M. Eds. 2021. *Corpus ConDÉ*, version Beta 1.0, Caen, CRISCO (EA 4255) et PDN (MRSH) de l'Université de Caen. https://www.unicaen.fr/coutumiers/conde/accueil.html (2022-09-15).

Le Rouille, G. 1539. Le grand coustumier du pays et duché de Normandie …, Rouen. Exemplaire conservé à la Bibliothèque nationale de France. In Larrivée, P. / Goux, M. Dir. 2021. *Corpus ConDÉ*, version Beta 1.0, Caen, CRISCO (EA 4255) et PDN (MRSH) de l'Université de Caen. https://www.unicaen.fr/coutumiers/conde/sommaire/rouille_lighter.html (2022-09-15).

Lorente Casafont, M. 2002. Terminología y fraseología especializada: del léxico a la sintaxis. In Guerrero Ramos, G. / Pérez Lagos, M. F. Eds. *Panorama Actual de la Terminología*. Granada: Editorial Comares, 159–179.

Merville, P. B. 1731. Décisions sur chaque article de la coutume de Normandie …, Paris. In Larrivée, P. / Goux, M. Dir. 2021. *Corpus ConDÉ*, version Beta 1.0, Caen, CRISCO (EA 4255) et PDN (MRSH) de l'Université de Caen. https://www.unicaen.fr/coutumiers/conde/sommaire/merville_lighter.html (2022-09-15).

MLLM = Niermeyer, J. F. / van de Kieft, C. 2002. *Mediae latinitatis lexicon minus*. 2 Vols. Vol. 1 A–L, Vol. 2 M–Z. Darmstadt: Wiss. Buchgesellschaft.

NCG = Bourdot de Richebourg, C. A. Ed. 1724. *Nouveau Coutumier General ou Corps de Coutumes générales et particulières de France et des provinces connues sous le nom de Gaules*. 8 Vols. Paris: Michel Brunet. https://catalogue.bnf.fr/ark:/12148/cb33332762w (2022-11-29).

Neveux, F. 2011. Le contexte historique de la rédaction des coutumiers normands. *Annales de Normandie* 2 (61ᵉ année), 11–22. https://doi.org/10.3917/annor.612.0011%20(2022-11-29).

Paasch-Kaiser, C. 2022. Sur la phraséologie juridique de la Coutume de Normandie. *Studia linguistica romanica* 8. Numéro thématique: *Le long temps : l'évolution du français dans un corpus textuel calibré. Le témoignage de la coutume de Normandie* (Mathieu Goux (ed.)), 87–115. https://doi.org/10.25364/19.2022.8.5 (2022-11-29).

Ragueau, F. / de Laurière, E. 1882 [1704]. *Glossaire du droit françois.* Niort: Favre. http://catalogue.bnf.fr/ark:/12148/bpt6k508455 (2022-11-29).

Reulos, M. 1976. Les juristes humanistes et la coutume de Normandie. In *Droit privé et Institutions régionales : Études offertes à Jean Yver* [en ligne]. Mont-Saint-Aignan: Presses universitaires de Rouen et du Havre. https://doi.org/10.4000/books.purh.12578 (2022-11-29).

Schmidt-Wiegand, R. 1998 [2008]. Anwendungsmöglichkeiten und bisherige Anwendung von philologisch-historischen Methoden bei der Erforschung der älteren Rechtssprache. In Hoffmann, L. / Kalverkämper, H. / Wiegand, H. E. Eds. *Fachsprachen / Languages for Special Purposes. Ein internationales Handbuch der Fachsprachenforschung und Terminologiewissenschaft / An international Handbook of Special-Language and Terminology Research.* Vol. II. Berlin / New York: De Gruyter, 277–283. https://doi.org/10.1515/9783110203271-005 (2022-11-29).

Sinner, C. 2012. *Wissenschaftliches Schreiben in Portugal zum Ende des* Antigo Regime *(1779–1821): Die Memórias económicas der Academia das Ciências de Lisboa.* Berlin: Frank & Timme.

Tabares Plasencia, E. 2012. Analyse und Abgrenzung rechtssprachlicher phraseologischer Einheiten im Spanischen und Deutschen und ihre Bedeutung für die Übersetzung. *Lebende Sprachen* 57/2, 314–328. https://doi.org/ 10.1515/les-2012-0024 (2022-11-29).

Tabares Plasencia, E. 2018. La fraseología jurídica en el Libro de Buen Amor. *Estudis romànics* 40, 59–88. https://doi.org/10.2436/20.2500.01.237 (2022-11-29).

Tabares Plasencia, E. 2020. Fraseología jurídica en un corpus diacrónico de textos literarios españoles y su representación fraseográfica. *CLAC* 82, 69–92. https://doi.org/10.5209/clac.68964 (2022-11-29).

Tardif, J. E. 1903. *Coutumiers de Normandie. Textes critiques.* Vol. I, 2: *Le Très Ancien Coutumier de Normandie. Textes français et normand.* Rouen / Paris: A. Lestringant, A. Picard et Fils. http://catalogue.bnf.fr/ark:/12148/bpt6k5502865x (2022-11-29).

Terrien, G. 1578. Commentaires du droict civil tant public que privé observé au pays et duché de Normandie, Paris. In Larrivée, P. / Goux, M. Dir. 2021. *Corpus ConDÉ*, version Beta 1.0, Caen, CRISCO (EA 4255) et PDN (MRSH) de l'Université de Caen. https://www.unicaen.fr/coutumiers/conde/sommaire/terrien_lighter.html (2022-09-15).

TLFi = *Trésor de la Langue Française informatisé.* 2022. http://stella.atilf.fr/ (2022-11-29).

Yver, J. 1986. La rédaction officielle de la coutume de Normandie (Rouen, 1583). Son esprit. *Annales de Normandie* 1986, 1 (36e année). *Identités normandes*, 3–36. https://doi.org/10.3406/annor.1986.1716 (2022-11-29).

Gabriele Zanello

I linguaggi tecnici nelle carte friulane del tardo Medioevo

Abstract. Between 1250 and 1420, in the age of the decline of the Friulian patriarchal state, a city life began to develop in Friuli animated by new social forces and professional groups. This social and economic process, accompanied by the diffusion of writing and reading skills, also had significant repercussions on the level of language: Once the previous linguistic and social fracture between the German-speaking ruling class and the Romance-speaking popular class had been overcome, Friulian began to be adopted as an administrative language by all those people who, in addition to usually using it in oral form, needed to use it even in writing. An important project of transcription and publication of the materials preserved in various collections of the Region has been dedicated to the phenomenon of the usual Friulian *scripta* between the 14th and 15th centuries: the edition of a substantial number of ancient manuscripts now makes it possible to carry out specific surveys on the lexicographical sector. In particular, it becomes possible to collect the examples of technical language that emerge from the documents and examine them, from various points of view, with different objectives: an illustration of the professional fields present in three urban centers; an in-depth study on the origin of the technical terms and a parallel assessment of the patrimonial lexemes and of the incidence of loans; an evaluation of the phenomena of conservation and innovation, examining the persistence of technicalities in the Friulian of the following centuries. Ultimately, a survey of this kind, albeit limited, collects useful data to define the influence of new professional groups on linguistic development and to determine more precisely the role of functional writing in the standardization process (both from an intralinguistic point of view, i.e. in the Friulian, and inter-linguistic, in relation to the progressive diffusion of Tuscan-Venetian models).

Abstract. Tra il 1250 e il 1420, nell'età del declino dello stato patriarcale friulano, incominciò a svilupparsi in Friuli una vita cittadina animata da nuove forze sociali e gruppi professionali. Questo processo sociale ed economico, accompagnato dalla diffusione delle competenze di scrittura e di lettura, ha avuto significative ripercussioni anche sul piano della lingua: archiviata la precedente frattura linguistica e sociale tra la classe dominante germanofona e quella popolare romanzofona, il friulano iniziò a essere con funzione di linguaggio amministrativo da parte di tutte quelle persone che, oltre a servirsene abitualmente in forma orale, avevano la necessità di adoperarlo anche nella scrittura. Al fenomeno della *scripta* usuale friulana tra XIV e XV secolo è dedicato ormai da diversi anni un importante progetto di segnalazione, trascrizione e pubblicazione dei materiali conservati in vari fondi del Friuli: l'edizione di un consistente numero di manoscritti antichi permette ora di svolgere specifiche indagini sul settore della lessicografia. Diventa possibile, in particolare, raccogliere gli esempi di linguaggio tecnico che emergono dalle carte ed esaminarli sotto vari punti di vista, proponendosi diversi obiettivi: un'illustrazione degli ambiti professionali presenti in tre centri urbani; un approfondimento sulla provenienza dei tecnicismi e una parallela valutazione della patrimonialità dei lessemi e dell'incidenza dei prestiti; uno studio dei fenomeni di conservazione e innovazione, vagliando la persistenza dei tecnicismi nel friulano dei secoli successivi. In definitiva, un'indagine di questo genere, seppur limitata, raccoglie dati utili a definire l'influenza di nuovi gruppi professionali sullo sviluppo linguistico e a determinare con maggiore precisione il ruolo della scrittura funzionale nel processo di standardizzazione (sia in ottica intralinguistica, cioè nel friulano, sia interlinguistica, in rapporto alla progressiva diffusione di modelli tosco-veneti).

1. Introduzione

Tra il 1250 e il 1420, nell'età del declino politico dello stato patriarcale friulano, in un contesto segnato per un verso dal progressivo allontanamento dei patriarchi di Aquileia dall'orbita imperiale, per un altro dalla crescente antitesi tra il Friuli e Venezia, incomincia a svilupparsi nella regione una vita cittadina animata da nuove forze sociali costituite da artigiani, notai, mercanti, maestri di scuola e altri gruppi professionali. E mentre si espande velocemente il centro di Udine, che in breve soppianterà Cividale anche quale sede del patriarca, si vanno rapidamente trasformando anche altre realtà urbane, come Gemona, San Daniele e Sacile. Le modifiche che le riguardano, e che le conducono ad assumere nuove funzioni, sono strettamente connesse con l'emergere e il profilarsi di un ceto mercantile e borghese, che risulta dallo sforzo di elevazione degli strati popolari e rurali; nel corso del tempo, tale ceto diventa sempre più indipendente da quello nobiliare, rivolgendosi con rinnovata intraprendenza allo svolgimento delle proprie attività.

Questo processo sociale ed economico, accompagnato dalla diffusione delle capacità di scrittura e lettura, ha notevoli ricadute anche sul piano della lingua: archiviata la precedente frattura linguistica e sociale tra classe dominante germanofona e classe popolare romanzofona, il friulano inizia ad essere adottato con funzione di linguaggio amministrativo da parte di tutte quelle persone che, oltre a servirsene abitualmente in forma orale, hanno la necessità di usarlo anche nella scrittura: accade dunque che atti amministrativi, rendiconti, elenchi, lettere e altri simili documenti, che incominciano a essere numerosi a partire dal Trecento, siano redatti parzialmente o interamente in friulano. Il fenomeno non è lineare e istantaneo, ma ammette co-occorrenze e concorrenze: in una prima fase con il latino, più tardi con veneto e italiano (cf. Francescato/Salimbeni 1977: 139–162). Ad ogni modo queste carte pratiche, che guadagnano al friulano ambiti d'uso amministrativi e talvolta formali, registrano per la prima volta non soltanto una quantità ragguardevole di tecnicismi, ma anche alcuni cultismi.

I linguaggi tecnici nelle carte friulane del tardo Medioevo

Attraverso l'edizione di un consistente numero di manoscritti antichi[1], molti interessanti materiali conservati in vari fondi del Friuli sono stati proposti all'attenzione degli studiosi che si occupano della *scripta* usuale friulana tra XIV e XV secolo, rendendo possibili specifiche indagini sul settore della lessicografia. Poiché dai repertori lessicali realizzati a partire da queste carte è stato possibile raccogliere numerosi saggi di linguaggio settoriale, il presente contributo si propone di offrire qualche primo materiale utile al raggiungimento di questi obiettivi:

- illustrare gli ambiti professionali (attività agricole, artigianali, amministrative...) coperti in tre diversi centri urbani, dei quali vengono sommariamente illustrate le caratteristiche in riferimento allo sviluppo politico ed economico;
- valutare il tasso di patrimonialità dei lessemi e l'incidenza dei prestiti ipotizzando la provenienza dei tecnicismi, mostrando peraltro come in molti casi sia arduo stabilirla in modo univoco;
- indagare i fenomeni di conservazione e innovazione vagliando la persistenza di questi termini nel friulano dei secoli successivi.

Com'è facilmente prevedibile, anche per il friulano antico ci si deve confrontare con la scarsa regolarità e sistematicità degli usi grafici, e non soltanto all'interno della stessa serie di carte, ma anche in uno stesso documento (cf. Vicario 1998: 55). La causa di questa situazione deve essere ricondotta non tanto all'assenza di una varietà friulana di riferimento, quanto alla maggiore confidenza con la scrittura del latino e alla pressione esercitata dai codici di maggiore peso «politico» (prima il tedesco e poi il tosco-veneto; cf. Cadorini 2015).

2. Le città di provenienza dei documenti e gli ambiti professionali rappresentati

Anche nel basso medioevo il Friuli è rimasto estraneo all'azione esercitata altrove dalle città: l'unità regionale, infatti, non è emersa come aggregazione territoriale intorno a un unico centro urbano, ma si è costituita come spazio

---

[1] Al fenomeno è dedicato ormai da diversi anni un progetto di segnalazione, trascrizione e pubblicazione dei principali testimoni: avviato nel 1998 e ancora in corso, ha già messo a disposizione almeno due repertori complessivi (riguardanti i quaderni gemonesi del Trecento e i manoscritti tardomedievali della Biblioteca Civica «V. Joppi» di Udine) ed è rivolto alla redazione di un *Dizionario storico friulano* già consultabile online (https://www.dizionariofriulano.it/; aprile 2023).

ampio e abbastanza omogeneo intorno all'autorità centrale dei patriarchi di Aquileia. Ciò non significa che nel patriarcato le comunità cittadine non si siano sviluppate anche fortemente, condensando al proprio interno le attività che connotavano gli altri centri urbani; quello che a esse mancò, piuttosto, è il controllo giurisdizionale e politico sul territorio circostante (cf. Degrassi 1988: 355).

I tre repertori che ho consultato per preparare questo intervento riguardano proprio tre centri urbani e rappresentano una fonte imprescindibile per indagare l'influenza dei nuovi gruppi professionali sullo sviluppo linguistico e per determinare in modo più preciso il ruolo della scrittura funzionale e dei linguaggi settoriali nel processo di standardizzazione (sia in ottica intralinguistica, cioè nel friulano, sia interlinguistica, per la progressiva diffusione di modelli tosco-veneti).

2.1 Cividale

La prima realtà di cui ci occuperemo è Cividale. La città che per i longobardi era diventata il centro della regione friulana e che in epoca carolingia era stata riconosciuta come capitale della marca di confine, poté in seguito giovarsi del fatto di essere il luogo principale (benché non esclusivo) di residenza dei patriarchi di Aquileia. Lo sviluppo economico e la concentrazione delle attività commerciali furono permessi dalla posizione cruciale lungo la via che raccordava la costa con le regioni alpine, dal gettito fiscale garantito dalla *muda* e dalla concessione del mercato permanente avvenuta nel XII secolo.

Dalla metà del Duecento i parametri economici accelerarono fortemente grazie all'arrivo di emigranti benestanti e qualificati, prevalentemente toscani e lombardi. Dalla fine di quel secolo ruoli amministrativi pubblici di particolare importanza vennero affidati ai lombardi, mentre erano toscane le principali compagnie d'affari: i senesi erano attivi già verso la metà del secolo, mentre nell'ultimo quarto si fece più forte l'afflusso dei fiorentini. Notevole anche la presenza di ebrei, che condividevano con i toscani l'attività di prestatori di denaro, mentre non è molto significativa quella dei veneziani. Era ancora molto presente, invece, il gruppo germanico. Come si può facilmente intuire, nella Cividale del Due e Trecento si registra non soltanto la disponibilità di moltissimi prodotti dell'artigianato, ma anche una vita sociale, culturale e religiosa molto intensa. All'inizio del XIV secolo venne addirittura aperto uno *studium generale* di livello universitario, ma ormai in quella fase il vigore della città iniziava ad avviarsi verso il declino: essa, infatti, si era trovata decentrata rispetto all'omogeneità acquistata dal territorio regionale grazie all'opera dei patriarchi, e fu dunque destinata a perdere forza a favore di Udine.[2]

Il documento da cui sono ricavati i materiali lessicali è un quaderno vergato in friulano dal notaio Odorlico intorno al 1360: conservato presso l'Archivio di Stato di Udine[3] ed edito un paio di decenni fa da Federico Vicario (1998) in un volume dotato di un cospicuo glossario, è caratterizzato da coerenza, razionalità e regolarità, ed è reso ancor più prezioso dal fatto che fra le sue carte compaiono i nomi di numerosi personaggi di rilievo storico. Certamente su questa impressione di regolarità influisce il fatto che questo documento è opera di una sola mano. Tuttavia anche altri documenti coevi portano a ipotizzare che la diffusione della scrittura in friulano negli ambienti notarili cividalesi abbia condotto alla formulazione di un sistema grafico piuttosto omogeneo e quindi a una sorta di «codificazione» del friulano abbastanza elaborata e stabile (cf. Vicario 1998: 56–58).[4]

Il lessico di queste carte può apparire piuttosto ripetitivo e comunque non molto vario, «di buona qualità ma di scarsa quantità» (Vicario 1998: 123). D'altra parte esso riguarda prevalentemente incarichi di lavoro, pagamenti e riscossioni, ma ci aiuta ugualmente ad abbozzare il quadro delle attività economiche più comuni e a ricostruire i relativi lessici.

Per quanto riguarda Odorlico da Cividale, si possono ascrivere ai linguaggi settoriali poco più di 150 parole, circa l'11 % delle quali si riferiscono all'agricoltura; una percentuale simile – circa il 37–38 % – è relativa per un verso all'artigianato, per un altro al «terziario» (Fig. 1).

2.2 Udine

L'evidente declino al quale Cividale andò incontro nel Trecento è parallelo all'ascesa del suo immediato concorrente, il centro urbano di Udine. Crescita demografica e sviluppo economico lo avviarono al ruolo direzionale che in precedenza era appartenuto alla città sul Natisone. La preminenza di Udine nel XII secolo è quella di centro di un territorio agricolo molto vasto; lì, infatti, si trovava la *canipa* alla quale venivano convogliati i censi dei massari

---

[2] Sull'economia di Cividale nel medioevo, con particolare attenzione all'afflusso di forestieri, cf. Figliuolo (2012); cf. anche Degrassi (1988: 358–362).
[3] Archivio di Stato di Udine, Archivio notarile antico, b. (689).
[4] Sui documenti del cividalese antico cf. Vicario (2006; 2012a). Con il termine *codificazione* non si intende, naturalmente, un vero e proprio processo volto al raggiungimento di una norma linguistica, ma una sorta di «standardizzazione dal basso» non immune da incertezze, oscillazioni e incoerenze grafiche; un fenomeno che si può comunque rilevare in queste tre località anche a fronte della variazione diatopica.

delle terre patriarcali. Se nella metà del XII secolo era ancora poco più ampia dell'insediamento militare posto sul colle, entro la fine del secolo successivo l'espansione abitativa rese necessaria la costruzione di due ulteriori cerchie murarie, alle quali, entro la fine del Quattrocento, se ne sarebbero aggiunte altre due. Il costante flusso migratorio proveniente dal contado e il conseguente incremento demico furono accompagnati dalla costruzione di case, magazzini, botteghe per attività commerciali e artigianali, ma anche chiese, monasteri e conventi.[5]

Anche per la città di Udine sono state messe a disposizione negli ultimi anni le edizioni di numerosi manoscritti in volgare friulano delle origini; un volume riunisce i materiali lessicali – circa 2.000 voci – accanto a quelli antroponomici e toponomastici. In questo caso, rispetto al caso di Odorlico, è più ampio il lasso temporale sul quale si distribuiscono le carte, anche se il secolo più rappresentato è il Quattrocento. Ma è importante soprattutto osservare come i volumi pubblicati nella collana della Biblioteca «Joppi» riguardino anche alcune carte provenienti da altre località, come Cividale, Tricesimo e Venzone, anche se la maggior parte dei documenti è comunque riferibile a istituzioni udinesi.

Un quarto delle 350 parole raccolte nel glossario relativo a Udine pertiene all'agricoltura e all'allevamento (Fig. 2): è il valore più alto fra le tre realtà (26 %), a scapito del «terziario», che qui presenta il valore più basso (28 %); l'artigianato si assesta su valori simili a Cividale (39 %), ma di molto inferiori a Gemona.

Notevole la presenza di nomi di diverse specie ittiche, completamente assenti negli altri due centri considerati. Nell'artigianato si segnala, per un numero di lemmi superiore alla media, il lessico dei calzolai[6], ma spiccano anche quelli della lavorazione del legno e della tessitura.

2.3 Gemona

Anche se non poteva ambire all'importanza rivestita da Cividale e ormai destinata a passare a Udine, quella di Gemona era, dal punto di vista economico, la realtà più dinamica di tutto l'alto Friuli. La sua crescita e la fioritura di una vita cittadina (benché difficilmente paragonabile a quella degli altri due centri) furono connesse al costante flusso di merci e di persone lungo l'itinerario che collegava la pianura alle regioni alpine e transalpine. L'apice dello sviluppo, sia sul piano economico che su quello demografico, si può collo-

---

[5] Sull'economia di Udine nel medioevo cf. Degrassi (1988: 362–369).
[6] Verosimilmente perché tra i materiali pubblicati ci sono appunto i rotoli della Fraterna dei Calzolai.

care tra la fine del XII e la prima metà del XIII secolo (è del 1184 la concessione di un mercato settimanale), mentre la successiva interruzione dell'ampliamento urbanistico è il segnale di difficoltà e dell'inizio di un lento declino rispetto al quale non è estraneo l'emergere di un nuovo nucleo urbano, quello di Venzone, posto poco più a monte lungo il percorso transalpino. Ma Gemona si era ormai arricchita grazie alla corrente commerciale, alla disponibilità di materie prime, alle numerose attività artigianali, alla consuetudine della sosta necessaria per caricare le merci dai carri più grossi a quelli più piccoli. A tale pratica era legato il diritto di riscuotere il *Niederlech*, che nel XIII secolo il patriarca concesse alla comunità cittadina (cf. Degrassi 1988: 308). La complessità della vita economica cittadina emerge in modo chiaro dagli statuti che Gemona decise di darsi nel 1381 al fine di regolare i rapporti istituzionali, civili e commerciali (cf. Londero et al. 2020).[7]

Il materiale riferibile alla terza realtà urbana qui considerata è decisamente più abbondante; in questo caso, come per quello di Udine, in quanto il repertorio lessicale che conclude la serie dei *Quaderni gemonesi del Trecento*, che consta di circa 2.000 voci, attinge alle numerosissime carte in volgare appartenenti alle tre serie della Pieve di Santa Maria, dell'Ospedale di San Michele e dei Massari del Comune di Gemona del Friuli. I cinquantatré quaderni pubblicati coprono un arco temporale che va dal 1311 all'anno 1400, anche se la maggior parte di essi risale alla seconda metà del secolo, e in particolare all'ultimo quarto (cf. Vicario 2013: 13–16). Benché opera di mani diverse, sono caratterizzati da una certa omogeneità formale.

Lo spoglio del repertorio relativo a Gemona ha permesso di isolare quasi 400 lemmi. Quasi la metà di questi riguardano l'artigianato, circa il 16 % l'agricoltura, circa il 30 % il «terziario» (Fig. 3).

A Gemona è ricchissimo il lessico dell'edilizia, ma in generale sono molte anche le parole ascrivibili all'artigianato in generale (e che dunque è difficile attribuire all'uno o all'altro settore specialistico). Nello specifico, inoltre, le carte della pieve di Santa Maria ci trasmettono un buon numero di termini riferibili all'artigianato librario e alla scrittura.

---

[7] Sull'economia di Gemona nel medioevo cf. Degrassi (1988: 374–375).

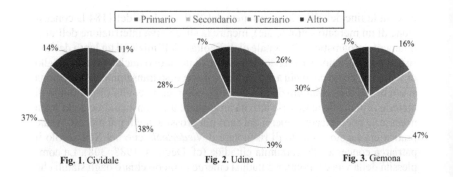

Fig. 1. Cividale   Fig. 2. Udine   Fig. 3. Gemona

3. I tecnicismi e la loro provenienza etimologica

Nelle carte usuali di area friulana del Tre e del Quattrocento non è particolarmente cospicua la presenza di parole che denuncino una specifica e costante volontà di differenziazione o distanziamento consapevole dal linguaggio di tutti i giorni; questo sarebbe dovuto principalmente alla natura di queste carte: il loro argomento pratico, infatti, non richiede vocaboli aulici o ricercati (se non nella forma di prestiti di necessità da varietà sovraregionali più elaborate e ricche sul piano lessicale). Esige più frequentemente, invece, il ricorso a tecnicismi, cioè a termini settoriali il cui uso si rende necessario al fine di indicare in modo più puntuale funzioni, contratti, azioni, ma anche – per esempio – gli oggetti dei diversi settori artigianali (cf. Vicario 2009b: 139)[8], benché non sia facile distinguere chiaramente – tantomeno a distanza di secoli – tra voci tecniche e voci più generiche, o fra *termini* e *vocaboli comuni* (cf. Vicario 2009b: 142–145).

Dal punto di vista della provenienza dei tecnicismi su un piano strettamente etimologico è assolutamente evidente come nella stragrande maggioranza dei casi si tratti di voci di matrice neolatina; per il momento non mi inoltro nell'indagine con ragguagli ulteriori (che, come vedremo, saranno necessari). Mi limito a osservare che, se raffrontato all'insieme, il numero delle voci individuabili come prestiti da lingue non neolatine è piuttosto scarso; esso riguarda soprattutto le lingue germaniche, che nei tre repertori esaminati sono rappresentate da poco più di una cinquantina di voci. Appaiono trascurabili gli apporti dalle lingue slave, mentre il periodo al quale si rivolge l'attenzione del nostro discorso permette di tralasciare i celtismi e i grecismi, quasi sempre mediati dal latino.

---

[8]   Sulle attività artigianali del Friuli medievale: cf. Degrassi (1988: 389–417).

3.1 I germanismi

Naturalmente i repertori che offrono il numero più ampio di germanismi – oltre trenta – sono quello relativo ai documenti della Biblioteca Civica di Udine e quello delle carte gemonesi. Sono una quindicina le voci comuni a due repertori, e alcune sono attestate in tutti e tre. Si tratta per lo più di voci non esclusive del friulano, e comunque caratterizzate da una certa tendenza alla conservazione (infatti, per buona parte, risultano tuttora in uso). Esse provengono dal gotico, dal longobardo, dal francone, dal tedesco carinziano o da quello bavarese.[9]

Come si può osservare da questo elenco[10], i germanismi riguardano prevalentemente l'ambito della cultura materiale: *araclis* 'frasche, rami secchi'; *arinchis* 'anelli, ganci'; *banch* 'banco, desco, panca'; *baril* 'barile, botte'; *baris* 'bare'; *bindis* 'bende, garze, fasce'; *blaf* 'tessuto azzurro'; *blancheta* 'casacca, camiciola bianca'; *blegon, bleon* 'lenzuolo'; *bre(g)a, breie* 'tavola'; *bredul* 'sgabello, predellina di legno'; *brotula* 'garzuolo, manipolo di lino pettinato e netto'; *ceche* 'federa (di cuscino)'; *cevre, çevra* 'cestone, corba di vimini'; *comat* 'collare del cavallo'; *confanon* 'gonfalone, bandiera, vessillo'; *daspa* 'aspo, guindolo'; *lata* 'pertica, steccone'; *lataroli* 'chiodi da pertica'; *masanch* 'roncola, pennato'; *planchuz* 'panchetta'; *rincho* 'anello'; *rosta* 'diga costruita nei torrenti'; *slosy* 'serrature, chiudende'; *spanga* 'barra, asta, stanga'; *spangar* 'mettere le stanghe'; *stafa* 'staffa'; *stanga* 'stanga, pertica'; *stuc* 'stucco'; *taponedor* 'tappo, chiusura'; *taponar* 'turare, chiudere, tappare'; *tapons* 'tappi'; *tasa* 'catasta'; *uadia* 'anello, fede matrimoniale'.

Alcune voci concernono edifici o loro parti: *balc(h)on* 'finestra'; *bastia* 'bastia, costruzione bassa'; *garit* 'garitto, tipo di imposta'; *gater* 'grata, inferriata'. Altre, invece, indicano pertinenze dell'abitazione o del villaggio: *baiarz, bayarç* 'podere, appezzamento, campo'; *borch* 'borgo, borgata, strada'; *braide, braida* (e *braidera, braiduça*) 'poderetto chiuso'. Non sono molte quelle che indicano mestieri o attività: *cramar* 'merciaio ambulante' (e cfr. *cramarga*); *snaider* 'sarto'; *taschar* 'artigiano che fa tasche o borse'; *trombeta* 'suonatore di tromba'; *uarda* 'guardia, sentinella' e *uardian* 'guardiano, custode'. Nell'ambito di consuetudini e norme si incontrano: *lic(h)of* (o *licouf, licovo*) 'merenda, festa per la conclusione del lavoro'; *morgingraç*

---

[9] In alcuni casi le annotazioni etimologiche rinviano genericamente all'alto tedesco antico e all'alto tedesco medio.

[10] Grazie all'ordinamento alfabetico, le singole voci citate in questo paragrafo possono essere facilmente reperite in Vicario (2012c; 2013); alcune sono presenti anche in Vicario (1998).

'dono del mattino, dono nuziale dello sposo alla sposa'; *uadia* 'pegno, cauzione giudiziaria, multa'; e anche *bant* 'multa, imposta'.

Una delle voci più degne di nota riguarda una istituzione risalente al periodo longobardo, la *gastaldia* o castalderia, in friulano *giastaldio*. In questo vocabolo, attestato per la prima volta in friulano nel quaderno di Odorlico di Cividale, va segnalata la presenza della palatalizzazione, probabile indizio dell'antichità del prestito.

In tutti i repertori esaminati sono presenti infine due germanismi che riguardano l'ambito della circolazione monetaria: i *fortons* 'fortoni (moneta)' e la *marcha* (o *marchie*, pl. *marchis*). Anche in questo caso si tratta di una presenza del tutto marginale rispetto alle altre monete o valute, le denominazioni delle quali appaiono riferibili all'ambito romanzo: *dinar*, *duc(h)at*, *flurin*, *grues*, *pavès*, *piçulg*, *solç*, *vornès* (oltre ai generici *moneda* e *solt*).

Sembra essere pressoché privo di germanismi il settore delle coltivazioni, nel quale si registra soltanto *blava* 'biada (nome generico delle granaglie)'; così come quello dell'alimentazione, presente con *broado* 'brovada, pietanza a base di rape inacetite'.

Mancano quasi completamente, fra i prestiti germanici, termini astratti.

3.2 Tra latino e tosco-veneto

Si è già accennato al fatto che l'etimologia della grande maggioranza dei tecnicismi individuati nei tre repertori deve essere ricercata nel vocabolario latino (classico, volgare e medievale). È peraltro evidente che il friulano ha mutuato diverse voci non dal latino per derivazione ereditaria, bensì dalle varietà italiane settentrionali, soprattutto dal veneto, se non addirittura dal toscano. Il fenomeno dei tecnicismi si intreccia qui con quella dei cultismi: sul piano diafasico, la marcatezza per sottocodice si associa in queste voci a una marcatezza di registro.

Benché la questione sia indubbiamente complessa (e probabilmente, per molti casi, irrisolvibile)[11], non deve tuttavia essere considerata oziosa ai fini dell'argomento qui discusso. Leggendo le carte medievali, infatti, ci si chiede inevitabilmente se quel volgare friulano, prima di cedere il passo a una

---

[11] Anche alcuni degli autori che hanno redatto le singole voci del *Dizionario etimologico storico friulano* (DESF), completato purtroppo soltanto fino alla lettera E, tendono a considerare prestiti dall'italiano o dal veneto molte delle voci tecniche o culte che dal punto di vista fonologico potrebbero anche rappresentare esiti regolari dal latino attraverso mutamenti fonetici tardivi o ripescaggi seriori. Come si può osservare anche da alcuni degli esempi qui addotti, la pubblicazione dei documenti obbliga a ripensare alcune delle soluzioni prospettate dal DESF ormai più di trent'anni fa.

norma sovra-regionale di circolazione più ampia, fosse già in grado almeno di aspirare, per maturità e per esaustività, al rango di lingua amministrativa.[12] Bisogna comunque tenere presente che i repertori consultati attingono i loro materiali da documenti molto diversificati, la lingua dei quali può essere più o meno influenzata dai modelli tosco-veneti; in genere sono le carte più recenti a risentire di tali modelli in modo più sensibile. Normalmente possono essere riconosciuti con una certa sicurezza come venetismi (o, in altri casi, come generici italianismi) quei termini che mostrano di non rispettare le regole di mutamento tipiche del friulano (per esempio la palatalizzazione di CA- e GA- iniziali o postconsonantici, o il dileguo delle velari intervocaliche), o che non conservano il nesso di *muta cum liquida*. Tuttavia l'osservazione di alcuni di questi dati può essere offuscata dalle irregolarità grafiche che caratterizzano la prassi di scrittura di molti camerari, notai e cancellieri.

Nel quaderno dell'Ospedale udinese di Santa Maria Maddalena, per esempio, l'occlusiva palatale sorda [c] è resa con ‹ch› o ‹c›, mentre [ɟ] è resa con ‹g› (es. *caliar* 'calzolaio', *carn* 'carne', *casis* 'case', *champ* 'campo'; *galine* 'gallina'). Sul grafema ‹c› grava un considerevole carico funzionale, in quanto esso è utilizzato, accanto a ‹ç›, per le affricate alveolari o postalveolari sia sorde che sonore ([ts], [dz], [tʃ] e [dʒ]), oltre che per la velare sorda [k]. Odorlico da Cividale, invece, per le occlusive palatali sorde e sonore adotta rispettivamente ‹chi› e ‹gi› (es. *chiamp* 'campo', *chiaval* 'cavallo'; *gial* 'gallo').

È evidente come, soprattutto nella prima situazione, legittimi dubbi di lettura riguardino proprio i sospetti italianismi (cf. Vicario 1999: 126–131), anche perché si può neppure fare affidamento pieno sulla pronuncia del friulano attuale. Infatti in uno dei quaderni udinesi troviamo *chiariole* (accanto a *cariole* e *chariole*), con evidente palatalizzazione (e dunque la pronuncia [car'jɔle]), anche se nel friulano attuale al termine è stata restituita, su pressione di veneto e italiano, la precedente velare (cf. Vicario 2012c: 75). Nei quaderni di Gemona per 'carro' o 'carretto' troviamo le forme *car*, *charuç* e

---

[12] Se lo chiede, peraltro, anche Vicario: «Al di là di una più attenta disamina del complesso dei documenti e dei singoli casi, con le necessarie integrazioni, resta sullo sfondo una prospettiva di ricerca che parte dalla discussione del valore e del numero di queste voci per arrivare ad una più ampia considerazione sulla qualità della *scripta* volgare dell'epoca. Si tratta, insomma, prendendo a prestito termini della sociolinguistica, di passare da un esame del *corpus* ad una valutazione dello *status* del friulano del tardo Medioevo, andando a verificare se e in quale misura poteva considerarsi avviato, o magari concluso, quel processo che porta una lingua ad assurgere, nello scritto, a ruoli ufficiali o co-ufficiali» (Vicario 2009b: 148).

chiaruz, da pronunciarsi verosimilmente tutte con [c]; e inoltre *galina* 'gallina' ma anche *giambi* 'cambio', entrambe con [ɟ].[13]

Ad ogni modo si possono riconoscere come italianismi certi[14]:

> *legat, lechat, leghat* 'legato': per il mancato dileguo della velare sonora intervocalica (che invece si osserva in *realia* 'regalia, dono');
> *libri* 'libro': per la mancata sonorizzazione (o addirittura dileguo) della bilabiale nel nesso -*br*- (come invece in *lavri, luvri, lire, fiere, fari...*);
> *nota, note* 'nota': per la mancata sonorizzazione dell'alveodentale sorda intervocalica e il mancato dittongamento della mediobassa lat. ŏ;
> *plubichà* 'pubblicare, rendere pubblico; convocare come testimone': per il mancato dileguo della velare sorda intervocalica;
> *salt* 'saldo, pagamento residuo': per l'affinità con l'italiano (dove deriva dal lat. *solidum* incrociato con *validum*).

Una mediazione veneta o italiana dovrà essere ipotizzata per alcuni esotismi, in particolare arabismi come *ambra* 'ambra', *çupa* 'giubba, farsetto', *çupirel* 'giubbetto', *richamat* 'ricamato', *tanburlin* 'tamburino'; ma anche per voci che l'italiano ha mutuato da lingue più vicine: *conpremès* 'compromesso, accordo' (franc. *compromis*), *inbasadò, inbasador* 'ambasciatore', *inbasaria* 'ambasceria' (provenz. *Ambaissador, ambaisar*), *meresal* 'maresciallo' (franc. *maréchal*, dal francone MARHSKALK).

Rimangono immuni dai mutamenti della trafila popolare i nomi specifici di certi tessuti, tele o stoffe di provenienza per lo più orientale, e che in alcuni casi avevano ricevuto anche una denominazione latina tarda:

> *baratin* 'berrettino, tela grossa e cruda, di scarso valore': probabilmente dall'ar. BĀRUTĪ (DESF: 205, s.v. *beretìn*);
> *berc(h)ant* 'capo di biancheria o di vestiario (di lino o di cotone)', *berchant* 'barracano, tessuto forte': dall'ar. BARRAKAN attraverso il lat. BERCANDUM (DESF: 204, s.v. *bercandus*);

---

[13] Oggi presentano la velare (e non l'occlusiva) voci come *cançilir, cantor, caretat, cavalaria*, ma anche *chanovaç, chapele, chasela, chavalir* etc. Invece, a parità di grafia, vengono oggi pronunciate con l'occlusiva *carpint, caldera* (che compare accanto a *chialdiruzo, calderuça, chalderis*), *canaipa, carador*, e *chaniva, chastenar, chaluni, charpin* etc. (cf. Vicario 2012c, 2013: *passim*). Il problema della velare o occlusiva si pone anche in corpo di parola. Nei quaderni gemonesi troviamo *incantar, inchantar* 'mettere all'incanto', e *incanto, incanti, inchant* 'incanto' («per incantar e per far scrivi lu incanti di Miculùs e di Çuan del Savi», Vicario 2013: 99); ma in Odorlico da Cividale è chiarissimo *inchiantarin* 'diedero all'incanto' (Vicario 1998: 162), così come, nei quaderni udinesi, *inchiant, inchiantà* (Vicario 2012c: 150).

[14] Anche queste voci sono tratte da Vicario (2012c; 2013); più sporadicamente da Vicario (1998).

blaf 'tessuto azzurro': dal francone BLAO attraverso il lat. BLAVUS (DESF: 229-230, s.v. *blâf*);
bochasin 'sorta di stoffa': dal turco BOGASÝ, poi nel lat. BOCASSINUS; qui probabilmente attraverso il veneziano (DESF: 236, s.v. *bochasìn*);
*brotula 'garzuolo, manipolo di lino pettinato e netto': secondo il DESF 271, (s.v. *bròtule*) probabilmente dal got. **BRUT;
cendal 'zendado alla veneziana': forse dal gr. SINDÔN 'tessuto sottile', col suff. veneto *-ado* (invece di *-ato*);
samit 'sciamito, tessuto simile al velluto': dal gr. tardo (HE)KSÁMITOS;
scharlatin 'scarlattino, drappo scarlatto': dal lat. mediev. SCARLATUS, e questo dall'ar. SAQIRLĀṬ.

Le difficoltà interpretative diventano tangibili nei casi in cui, per ragioni di volta in volta diverse, sia legittimo dubitare di un'influenza del tosco-veneto, o quantomeno non si possa escludere una derivazione, naturalmente di indole dotta, direttamente dal latino:

chunpliment, conpliment e *cumpliment* 'compimento, fine, saldo, pagamento': il DESF (455, s.v. *complimènt*), considerandola soltanto nell'accezione di 'espressione d'affetto o elogio', la ritiene voce letteraria dall'it. *complimento* (a sua volta dallo spagnolo); qui tuttavia viene usata nel significato di 'termine, fine' (per es. di un contratto), quindi propenderei per un deverbale dal verbo *cumplì* 'compiere', attestato nel cividalese antico (DESF: 554, s.v. *cumplì*), con un suffisso astrattivo non insolito nel friulano (*-ment*);
clausola 'clausola': per il DESF (417, s.v. *clàusule*) è «Voce dotta. Dal lat. *clausula*, possibilmente attraverso l'italiano dove essa è un latinismo»; mi limito a osservare che comunque il dittongo *au* solitamente si conserva in friulano, anche quando non è tonico;
coleta 'colletta': per il DESF (437, s.v. *colète*[2]) è italianismo da *colletta*; bisogna peraltro aggiungere che sembra coesistere con *colta* 'colletta, raccolta di denaro, imposta straordinaria', voce che Vicario (2012c: 89) riferisce al lat. COLLECTAM, mentre il DESF (441, s.v. *còlt*[3]) la confronta con l'it. *còlta* 'raccolta di denaro o di prodotti, incetta, colletta';
chustion 'questione': va sicuramente confrontato anche con il veneto *custion*, ma Vicario (2012c: 82) non esita a riferirlo al lat. QUAESTIONEM;
daci 'dazio': Vicario (2012c: 106) lo riferisce al lat. DATIO, -ONIS, ma mantenuto al nominativo, mentre il DESF (577, s.v. *dàzi*) lo considera senz'altro un italianismo;
dipuesit, dupuesit 'deposito': non sembra essere un «adattamento dell'it. *deposito*» come sostiene il DESF (597, s.v. *dipuésit*), in quanto presenta regolare dittongo *-ue-* per la medio-bassa lat. (cf. Vicario 2012b: 489).

Spesso nei documenti si osservano coppie di forme della stessa voce (o anche di voci affini), una delle quali appare influenzata, in modo più o meno vistoso, dal tosco-veneto, mentre l'altra presenta i tratti del lessico ereditario del friulano (cf. 4.2)[15]:

alimosina (ed *elimosina*) 'elemosina', ma anche, con regolare dittongo, *elmuesine*, *almuesine*, *almuesina* (nonché *almusine*);
quader(n), ma anche, con riduzione della labiovelare, *choder*;
deliberation e *diliberacion* 'deliberazione', ma anche, con spirantizzazione, *diliverà* 'deliberare, stabilire' e *dilivrat* 'stabilito';
lago 'lascito' (riferibile alla forma settentrionale *lagar*, per la quale è stata ipotizzata una derivazione dal lat. *LACARE: cf. soprattutto Meyer-Lübke 1894: 269, § 235, e REW: 402–403, n. 4955; e DEI: 2150, s.v. *lagare*[1], che rinvia a un lat. regionale *LAGARE), ma anche *las* (con lo stesso significato, ma dal lat. LAXĀRE: cf. ancora REW: 402–403, n. 4955, DEI: 2173, s.v. *lassare*[2]);
sicurador 'garante, fideiussore, mallevadore', ma anche, con dileguo della velare, *siuritat* 'assicurazione, promessa, garanzia, malleveria'.

Il passaggio graduale a una *scripta* sempre più orientata verso modelli tosco-veneti ha prodotto peraltro anche fenomeni di italianizzazione di voci friulane. Nei quaderni gemonesi leggiamo:

(1) *ll. dy sol. c per l-achordeson dal Bilious inchontra Donat chamerar* (Vicario 2013: 19)
(2) *per la chordeson dal vino dalis mesis dy Nadal prosim chi ven* (Vicario 2013: 61)
(3) *spendey a ser pre Nichollut lo plavan per una chordeson dal vino* (Vicario 2013: 61)
(4) *sol. xx per jᵃ cordesone daly aredy Tribòs* (Vicario 2013: 71)

dove la forma *cordesone* di (4) sembra appunto ricevere la vocale finale per una volontà di adeguamento al modello toscano. E ancora:

(5) *spendey per j draço di draçar lu savalon* (Vicario 2013: 82)
(6) *sol. vj chi diey alla temesarie per j° draçut chi io comperay di gliè per temesà savalon* (Vicario 2012c: 120)

Il frammento (5), tratto da un quaderno gemonese, è morfologicamente orientato verso il tosco-veneto, come si deduce dalla vocale finale *-o* in *draço* e dalla vibrante nell'infinito verbale *draçar*. Tuttavia, benché il termine *draço* (*draç*), che il DESF (643, s.v. *draz*) fa derivare dalla «voce latino-celtica» *DRAGIU, sia «presente in varie aree dell'Italia sett., specialmente venete, trentine e lombarde», in questo caso è difficile non interpretarlo come una italianizzazione del vocabolo *draç* – assai comune in friulano – che com-

---

[15] Per stabilire, di volta in volta, se si tratti di vere e proprie allotropie sarebbero necessari prelievi più sistematici.

pare, nella forma diminutiva *draçut*, anche nell'esempio (6), tratto da un quaderno della Fabbrica del duomo di Udine. Lo stesso si può dire per *devorenti* 'travetti (del tetto), correntini', rielaborato sul frl. *diurint* (< lat. DE + CURRENTE; gli Statuti di Udine del XIV sec. testimoniano la forma *devorendus*; cf. DESF: 628 s.v. *dïurìnt*) più che sul ven. *degorént* (ma Piccini 2006: 206–207 attesta anche *degurentus*); o anche, infine, per *savolono* 'sabbia' (< lat. SABULONUM; Vicario 2006: 492).

4. Fenomeni di conservazione e innovazione

Un raffronto tra il lessico tecnico (e talvolta anche colto) ancora in uso e quello che osserviamo nelle carte medievali ci permette di isolare almeno alcuni fenomeni di conservazione e di innovazione. Un ulteriore termine di confronto può essere fornito dal *Nuovo Pirona*, il vocabolario ripubblicato nel 1935 da Ercole Carletti e Giovan Battista Corgnali sulla base del rifacimento a cui Giulio Andrea Pirona aveva sottoposto il primo vocabolario friulano edito da suo zio Jacopo nel 1871. Proprio il *Nuovo Pirona* – nel quale confluiscono alcune voci dei documenti antichi eventualmente indicate come arcaiche, rare o non più in uso – può soccorrere nei casi in cui si voglia tentare di circoscrivere l'epoca in cui si è verificata la perdita dell'uso di una determinata parola.

4.1 Casi di caduta dall'uso

Il caso più comune è, naturalmente, quello delle parole cadute dall'uso a causa della scomparsa degli oggetti, delle azioni o delle realtà (anche astratte) cui si riferivano. È scomparso, per esempio, il termine *morgingraç* perché è venuta meno l'usanza del dono nuziale che al mattino lo sposo porgeva alla sposa, ma è sopravvissuta quella del *lic(h)of*, il piccolo rinfresco che viene offerto al compimento di lavoro o attività, e che viene segnalato attraverso una frasca innalzata sul punto più alto dell'edificio.

Tra i nomi delle valute e delle monete sono sopravvissuti soltanto quelli generici o più comuni, come *duc(h)at* 'ducato' (pl. *duchaç*), *flurin* 'fiorino', *monede* 'moneta, soldo'; a *dina(r)s* 'denari' e *solç* 'soldi' si preferisce oggi nel Friuli centrale il collettivo *bêçs* 'soldi, denaro', a meno che gli altri due termini non debbano essere usati per indicare in modo specifico una unità monetaria del passato. Sono scomparsi *fortons* 'fortoni, fertoni', *marchie* 'marca (aquileiese), unità di denaro', *grues* o *gros* 'grosso, moneta' (ma sopravvive come semplice aggettivo), *pavès* 'pavese, grosso scudo', *piçul* 'piccolo, moneta di modesto valore, divisione del denaro' (pl. *piçulg*; anche in questo caso persiste l'aggettivo), *vornès* 'veronese, soldo, moneta'.

Tra i nomi indicanti unità di misura (e spesso i rispettivi recipienti) ne sopravvivono alcuni ma ormai quasi completamente privati del preciso valore da essi rivestito in epoca medievale. È il caso di *lira* (ant. anche *livra*) 'libbra, unità di peso; moneta di conto', *onça* 'oncia, dodicesima parte della libbra', *paret* 'parete, misura di lunghezza e di superficie per tessuti', *pas* 'passo, misura lineare di cinque piedi'. Sono ormai rari, in quanto usati con il significato antico, *orna* 'orna, misura di capacità, principalmente per vino e olio, corrispondente a sei secchie', *pesonal* 'pesinale, antica unità di misura' (ma dotata anche di un significato traslato di cui si dirà), *quarte* 'quarta, misura di capacità per grani, quarta parte dello staio o del sacco', *setor* 'misura per i prati', *spana* 'spanna, misura di lunghezza', *star* 'staio, antica unità di misura per granaglie'. Sono invece caduti *maça* 'massa, misura lineare corrispondente a due piedi', *magerli* 'secchiello', misura di capacità, *quartarola* 'quartarolo, misura di capacità per grani', *miçina* 'mezzina, misura per il grano', *mieri* (e *miedri*) 'miero, misura da olio', *scata* 'misura frumentaria per calcolare la molenda (il macinato)', *scif* 'schiffo, misura frumentaria', *virlin* 'misura di capacità per granaglie'.

Per quanto riguarda l'artigianato si può osservare innanzitutto come nel tempo siano radicalmente mutate le figure professionali[16], e di conseguenza siano cadute in disuso le voci con le quali venivano indicate quelle ora scomparse, al punto che in alcuni casi è addirittura difficile individuare un significato plausibile. Vicario (2013: 28), per esempio, traduce *arçador* con 'artigiano che costruisce o vende casse o bare', ma mi pare invece di poter confermare un legame con il verbo *arzare* 'battere la lana', 'cardare' e quindi pensare a un 'cardatore' (oggi *sgarzadôr* < lat. *(EX)CARDIĀRE).[17] Ma anche per *mitridor* Vicario (2013: 124) può soltanto ipotizzare 'misuratore'. L'elenco è dunque ampio: *agoselar* e *goselar* 'agoraio, che fabbrica o vende aghi'; *balistir* 'balestriere, colui che costruisce o vende le balestre'; *barbir* 'barbiere' ma anche 'cerusico, chirurgo'; *cartar* 'cartaio'; *claudar* 'chiodaio, chi fabbrica o vende chiodi'; *comatar* 'chi fa o vende i collari per il cavallo'; *coraçar* 'corazzaio, artigiano che costruisce le armature'; *fornadresa, fornedresa* 'fornaia'; *fornesar* 'fornaciaio, mattonaio, addetto alla fornace'; *fusar* 'fusaro, chi costruisce e vende fusi'; *lanar* 'lanaiolo'; *palotar* 'chi costruisce o vende le *palote*, mestolaio'; *stuvar* 'costruttore o venditore di stufe' o 'operaio addetto alla costruzione di opere idrauliche'; *taconedor* 'rappezzatore, rattoppatore'; *temesar* (e *temesarie*) 'stacciaio, chi fa o vende stacci e cri-

---

[16] Sui mestieri cf. Vicario (2009a).
[17] Cf. DESF: 107 (con altri rinvii) e Piccini (2006: 79).

velli'; *turner* 'tornitore, tornaio'. Per indicare il sarto non si usa più il germanismo *snaider* bensì *sartôr*.

La perdita di lemmi specifici investe anche settori dell'artigianato che non possono essere considerati estinti. Nell'ambito della confezione e della riparazione di calzature, per esempio, nelle nostre carte troviamo i seguenti termini, pressoché sinonimi: *chaliar, chialiar* 'calzolaio'; *chialçar* 'chi fa o vende calzari, calzolaio, scarpaio'; *scharpar* 'scarpaio, calzolaio'; *scarpator* 'calzolaio, colui che fa le scarpe'; *zerdon* 'cuoiaio, calzolaio, pellicciaio', anche 'ciabattino'. Attualmente è in uso soltanto *cjaliâr* 'calzolaio'.

Perdite cospicue si rilevano nei diversi settori del lessico relativo all'edilizia:

tipologie di edifici: *bratadarga forse 'bertesca, opera leggera di fortificazione antica'; *brotonesche* 'bertesche, opere fortificate';
elementi strutturali di edifici, manufatti e materiali: *chavridol* 'monaco, corto pezzo di trave verticale'; *mel* 'asse, incastro'; *petenegli* 'pettinelle, pettini fitti' o anche 'cantinelle'; *pidignul* 'puntello, piede o asta di sostegno'; *plumaç* 'traversino per opere di muratura'; *slosy* 'serrature, chiudente';
azioni e operazioni: *aplanchà* 'munire di pavimento di tavole'; *aplonbar* 'impiombare, rivestire o riempire di piombo'; *tulinar* 'sollevare (un carico) con il verricello', cioè con il *tulin* (in tutti i casi si tratta di verbi indicati come antichi già dal *Nuovo Pirona*).

Resistono in zone conservative (o sono comunque rare) voci come *iona* 'trave' e *ionela* 'piccola trave', *soie* 'fune, corda' e *siulin* 'cordicella', e infine *varis* 'cataletti, lettighe, barelle' (nell'espressione: *in varas*, riferita alle salme in attesa del funerale).

Un altro ambito che ha subito perdite considerevoli è quello del vestiario e dei tessuti:

indumenti: *berc(h)ant* 'capo di biancheria o di vestiario (di lino o di cotone)' ma anche 'barracano, tessuto forte'; *blancheta* 'casacca, camiciola bianca che portavano i contadini'; *çupa* 'farsetto' e *çupirel* 'giubbetto, piccolo farsetto'; *pelanda* 'giacchettone, casacca da contadino'; *sloyro* 'velo da testa'; *slucha* 'veste che soleva darsi alle spose novelle'; *uarnaçon* 'guarnacca, ampia e lunga sopravveste senza maniche';
tessuti, rifiniture e simili: *baratin* 'berrettino, tela grossa e cruda, di scarso valore'; *blaf* 'tessuto azzurro'; *bochasin* 'sorta di stoffa'; *cendal* 'cendado alla veneziana'; *frisidura* 'gallone, orlo appariscente del vestito'; *samit* 'sciamito, tessuto simile al velluto'; *scharlatin* 'scarlattino, drappo scarlatto'.

Uno dei settori più delicati è quello dei rapporti socioeconomici, che è stato interessato da cadute di numerosi termini e da adattamenti di altre voci sul modello del tosco-veneto, ma anche da fenomeni di conservazione che si sono verificati perfino a fronte dei molteplici cambiamenti di consuetudini che sono avvenuti nel corso del tempo. Come si è visto in precedenza, in ciascuno dei tre repertori considerati questo ambito è testimoniato da una percentuale piuttosto elevata di lemmi, e non è agevole scegliere quelli più adatti a rappresentare la perdita lessicale, l'adattamento ai modelli più prestigiosi o la conservazione fino ai nostri giorni. Tuttavia, se circoscriviamo l'analisi al piccolo campione di 32 lemmi settoriali ricavati dalle carte di Odorlico di Cividale, osserviamo che:

- 22 termini si sono conservati pressoché identici (69 %)[18],
- 4 hanno subito modifiche formali più sensibili, e in un caso anche con cambiamento semantico (12,5 %)[19],
- 2 sono stati mantenuti ma con altro significato (6 %)[20],
- 4 sono usciti dall'uso (12,5 %)[21].

Prima di segnalare alcune singole voci scomparse, mi soffermo su un'intera categoria – quella dei nomi astratti ricavati mediante la terminazione *-ura* (*-uria*) – che ha perduto un buon numero di voci: *charadura* 'carreggio, trasporto con carro'; *çirchiduris* forse 'ricerche'; *dispigniduris* 'riscatti'; *dutura* 'trasporto' e *aduturis* 'trasporti'; *lavoriduris* 'lavorazioni, fatture'; *minidura* e *meniduri* 'trasporti'; *misituria* 'spedizione'; *misuraduris* e *misuriduris* 'misure, misurazione, stima'; *vindeduris* 'vendite, ricavi'.

Analoga sorte è toccata a un altro gruppo di sostantivi, caratterizzati in questo caso dalla terminazione *-arìa*: *caniparia* 'caniparia, ufficio del cani-

---

[18] *achordà* 'accordare, dare', *chomandament* 'ordine, comando', *chomperà* 'comperare', *achomperà* 'comperò', *chostarin* 'costarono', *diferençiis* 'controversie, differenze, diatribe' (con minimo slittamento), *difiniçion* 'delibera, decisione', *difinit* 'definito, stabilito', *fit* 'affitto', *inprest* 'prestito', *inprestà* 'prestò' (e *inprestaç* 'prestati'), *invistì* 'investire, nominare', *letiro* 'lettera', *montin* 'ammontano', *nauly* 'nolo, noleggio', *om* 'uomo, persona, messo, incaricato', *pagà* 'pagare' (e *apagay* 'pagai', *inpagay* 'pagai'), *pagament* 'pagamento', *salary* 'salario, paga', *sentençio* 'sentenza', *spesis* 'spese', *statuç* 'statuti', *vendy* 'vendere'.

[19] *chustigon* 'questione, contenzioso' (oggi *cuistion*), *intradet* 'interdetto, interdizione' (oggi *interdet*), *roson* 'ragione, buona ragione' (oggi *reson*, con limitazioni semantiche), 'crediti, conti', *sentençeat* 'sentenziato' (oggi *sentenziât*).

[20] *chompedà* 'contare, numerare' (oggi 'raccontare, spiegare'), e *inchiantarin* 'diedero all'incanto, assegnarono' (oggi 'incantare, ammaliare' e simili, chiaramente su pressione semantica dell'italiano).

[21] *chunchordy* 'accordo', *dilivrat* 'deliberato, deciso' (oggi *deliberât*), *prestement* 'prestito' (oggi *prestit*), *protestaçion* 'protesta' (oggi *proteste*).

I linguaggi tecnici nelle carte friulane del tardo Medioevo

pario'; *chiamerarie* 'cameraria, compito, ufficio del cameraro'; *inbasaria* 'ambasceria, ambasciata'; *merchandaria* 'mercanzia, merce, prodotto'; *prochuraria* 'procura, delega, incarico'; *sindicharia* 'atto amministrativo dei sindaci'.

La desinenza *-son* (*-çon*) si riscontra in alcuni altri termini in gran parte astratti, e solitamente deverbali, afferenti al lessico giuridico e amministrativo (cf. Vicario 2009b: 145–147), spesso (ma non sempre) in corrispondenza del lat. -TIONE(M); già nelle carte sembra cedere il passo alla desinenza *-sion*, *-zion* (anche con la grafia *-çion*), che è oggi nettamente prevalente (salvo rari casi, come *reson*): *abitison* (ma anche *habitaçion*) 'abitazione'; *achordeson* o *chordeson* (e *cordesone*, ma anche *acordament*; da *achordà* 'accordare') 'accordo' (oggi sostituito dall'italianismo schietto *acordo*); *afitison* 'affittanza' e *fitison* 'affitto, canone, affittanza' («voce tecnica e storica» per il DESF: 25, s.v. *afitisón*); *condanason* o *condeneson* 'condanna', 'condanna' (DESF: 462, s.v. *condanesòn*); *consignaçon* 'consegna, deposito, custodia'; *desegnason* 'designazione'; *donason* (ma anche *donaçion* e *donation*) 'donazione, lascito' (DESF: 636, s.v. *donesòn*); *invistison* 'passaggio di proprietà, assegnazione, concessione'; *renunçiaçon* 'rinuncia'; *staçon* 'bottega, negozio' (e quindi *staçonar* 'bottegaio').

Concludo la sezione dei tecnicismi scomparsi suddividendo in due gruppi quelli riferibili al linguaggio amministrativo (alcuni dei quali sono già stati citati):

> ruoli pubblici o funzioni: *bric(h)* 'banditore, messo fiscale'; *cumsiorç* 'consorti, utenti per turno di un pascolo comunale'; *çurar* 'giurato, membro della rappresentanza e dell'amministrazione del comune' (sopravvive, però, *sindi(c)s* 'sindaci');
> contratti, accordi, atti, documenti, computi: *achordeson* 'accordo'; *briviler* 'privilegio, atto notarile'; *debençi* 'dovuto, conto, parcella'; *fitison* 'affitto, affittanza'; *pontasio* 'pontatico, pontaggio, pedaggio per il passaggio di un ponte'; *sc(h)osa* 'incasso, introito'; *soço* 'soccida, comproprietà'; *spensari* 'spesa, denaro speso'; *taulina* 'quota, contributo'.

4.2 Casi di influenza del tosco-veneto

Sono già stati ricordati in precedenza alcuni «doppietti» di voci ereditarie e voci influenzate dal tosco-veneto (cf. 3.2). Sono altresì numerosi gli esiti regolari dal latino che sono stati in seguito accantonati a causa della pressione di simili forme italiane o venete, o che sono stati interessati direttamente da tale influenza. Sintomatico è il caso di *devide* e *devida* (e *deveda*, *devita*, *devit*, ma anche *debita*) 'debito', dal lat. DĒBĬTA, neutro plurale reinterpretato come femminile singolare e colpito da spirantizzazione della labiale intervocalica e sonorizzazione dell'occlusiva alveolare sorda (cf. Vicario 2012c:

83

111). La variante *debita* è aderente al latino; in *devita* manca la sonorizzazione dell'occlusiva alveolare sorda; più che partire dal latino *debitum*, la forma *devit* potrebbe essere già influenzata dalla forma italiana *debito*, che poi ha effettivamente preso piede con *debit*. Curiosamente il DESF, in questo caso, pur indicando la forma *dèbit* come letteraria, non fa riferimento all'italiano, bensì soltanto al lat. DĒBĬTUM (cf. DESF: 577–578, s.v. *dèbit*). Invece *periul* 'pericolo' (< lat. PĔRĪCŬLUM) mostra regolarmente il dileguo della velare intervocalica che ha fatto seguito alla lenizione; tuttavia nel friulano attuale la forma comune, evidentemente influenzata dall'italiano, è *pericul*. Analoghi i casi di *iudià* e *çudià* 'giudicare' (< lat. JŪDĬCĀRE), sostituito oggi da un *judicâ* dove la velare appare reintegrata sul modello dell'italiano.

Per quanto riguarda l'occlusiva alveolare, sono degni di nota *vendide* 'vendita' (oggi *vendite*, con sorda reintegrata), e *tudor* 'tutore, responsabile', che ha poi lasciato il posto a *tutôr* (ma persistono molti altri: *chiarador* 'carrettiere', *vendidor* 'venditore' ecc.). Un fenomeno analogo riguarda le forme *provededor*, *provededors*, *pervededor*, *pervedadors* (o anche *pervededò*, *pervedò*, con la caduta della vibrante tipica del cividalese antico: cf. Vicario 1998: 168), tutte caratterizzate dalla sonorizzazione della alveodentale sorda intervocalica, a differenza dell'attuale *provediôr*.

Per quanto riguarda le forme deverbali ricavate mediante suffissazione, osserviamo la terminazione astrattiva *-ment* nel termine *prestement* 'prestito', costruito in modo analogo a *pagament*[22] ma poi sostituito da *prestit* (parola vicinissima all'italiano *prestito*).

4.3 Casi di conservazione

Non sono numerosi i casi di conservazione con slittamento semantico. Tra i più singolari ricordiamo *çesendeli* < lat. CĪCĬNDĒLA (DESF: 332, s.v. *cesendéli*), originariamente 'lampada, lanterna', ma attualmente usato per indicare una persona particolarmente alta e magra, uno 'spilungone'. Analogamente, *pesonal* significava 'pesinale, antica unità di misura', mentre oggi denota, con un traslato non opaco, chi si contraddistingue per forme fisiche abbondanti. Anche *muedul*, che per il *Nuovo Pirona* significava ancora 'cerro, quercia', oggi viene usato piuttosto per caratterizzare una persona impacciata o rigida.

Nel significato di 'contare, numerare' il verbo *chompedà*, regolarmente disceso dal latino, è stato sostituito dall'italianismo *compitâ*, mentre è usato ancora, seppure raramente, con il significato di 'raccontare, spiegare'. Il

---

[22] Si osservi che in *pagament* ⟨g⟩ vale [j]: cf. Vicario (1998: 61–63).

verbo *playdar*, invece, significava 'accordarsi, conciliare, trovare un accomodamento'; ora sopravvive, a un livello di linguaggio ricercato, con il significato di 'arringare, concionare, perorare, sostenere', mentre per 'conciliare' si usano *conciliâ*, *acuardâ*. Anche *fisich* ha perduto il significato di 'medico' (contrapposto a chirurgo) tipico dei documenti antichi, conservandosi soltanto come aggettivo (ma con il supporto dell'italiano)[23].

Infine, come si è già visto in precedenza, molte parole si sono conservate senza modifiche di forma o di significato. Al contrario di quanto si potrebbe ipotizzare, il lessico specifico relativo all'agricoltura appare generalmente conservato (almeno nei repertori), anche se sono venute meno alcune figure, funzioni o consuetudini, o se alcune coltivazioni sono scomparse[24]. Oggi sono rari, per esempio, gli allevatori di capre, ma il termine *chavrar* o *chiavrar* è ancora presente. È inconsueta, benché ancora vitale, la voce *çochul* 'capretto', mentre sono completamente scomparsi *multulina* 'pecorella' e *palombo* 'colombo'. Significativi i casi di conservazione anche nel settore dell'artigianato, in particolare nell'edilizia: *armadura* 'armatura, sostegno, impalcatura'; *chiarmat* 'ponte mobile'; *chiavilis* 'caviglie, cavicchie'; *chuvirtura* (e *covridura*) 'copertura'; *modoglons* 'modiglioni, bracci di legno infissi nei muri per sostenere le pergole'; *pidignul* 'puntello, piede o asta di sostegno'; *rudina* 'ghiaia minuta' ecc. Ma anche nell'ambito della lavorazione dei metalli: *açar* 'acciaio'; *aram* 'rame'; *aur* 'oro'; *arigint* 'argento'; *bront* 'bronzo'; *fiar*, *fier* 'ferro'; *plomp* 'piombo'; *stang* 'stagno'; e ancora: *faria* 'fucina, bottega del fabbro'; *fusina* 'fucina, focolare con mantice'; *magl(i)s* 'magli, delle ferriere o simili'; *saldador* 'saldatore, stagnatore'; *clostri* 'chiavistello, catenaccio'.

5. Conclusioni

Anche a fronte dell'importante lavoro di pubblicazione delle fonti realizzato negli ultimi due-tre decenni, l'impressione è che le conoscenze non siano ancora sufficienti a formulare ipotesi più articolate, né tantomeno a trarre conclusioni di ampio respiro. I notevoli scarti negli usi scritti tra autore e autore rendono molto difficile l'individuazione di linee di tendenza, per giunta in una situazione che non può che essere fluida (e non soltanto a causa dell'ampiezza dell'arco temporale esaminato). Risulterebbe peraltro di grande utilità anche un confronto con l'analoga documentazione dei territori non friulani, in particolare di quelli veneti limitrofi (cf. Vicario 2010).

---

[23] Cf. in merito le osservazioni di Vicario (1998: 126).
[24] Per esempio, già il *Nuovo Pirona* non registrava più termini come *managlons* 'manciate, fasci' o *cata* 'cumulo, catasta, pila'.

In linea di massima si può osservare che i documenti superstiti, pur numerosi, risalgono a un'epoca in cui, grazie al nuovo orientamento politico assunto dal patriarcato tra 1250 e 1420 e alla presenza di figure professionali provenienti da fuori regione (soprattutto banchieri), la pressione esercitata dai modelli tosco-veneti era ormai cospicua. Tale pressione – che consiste soprattutto in modifiche a livello fonologico, eliminazione di tratti ritenuti eccentrici, sostituzione di voci friulane patrimoniali o integrazione mediante prestiti – si esercita comunque su una base friulana tutt'altro che fragile, ma già molto ampia e dotata di un numero di tecnicismi (in alcuni casi di carattere colto) che copre diversi ambiti della vita sociale. In questo quadro non può essere trascurato il fatto che il friulano delle carte usuali del Tre e del Quattrocento si è ulteriormente arricchito di elementi lessicali desunti non soltanto dal latino, ma anche dai codici di più ampia diffusione nella Cisalpina, talvolta continuando ancora ad adattarli sottoponendoli a processi di cambiamento linguistico.

Ad ogni modo, se è vero che lo sviluppo di un sistema di scrittura e la messa in atto di una forma linguistica riservata alla distanza comunicativa costituiscono i due principali aspetti richiesti dal passaggio di una qualsiasi lingua alla forma grafica (cf. Koch/Oesterreicher 2001: 610–612), si è visto come il primo problema fosse già stato affrontato dal friulano sin dalla fine del XIII secolo, cioè dall'epoca in cui in diverse località del Friuli emersero in quantità significativa delle *scriptae* legate a precise tradizioni discorsive.

Per assistere nuovamente non soltanto allo sviluppo di un sistema di scrittura, ma anche alla diffusione massiccia di una forma della distanza comunicativa che non fosse di tipo strettamente letterario, si dovette attendere il Settecento, con l'affiorare dei documenti di scrittura omiletica in friulano; ma questa tradizione discorsiva poneva, in modo più marcato rispetto alle esperienze precedenti (di tipo sia amministrativo che letterario), anche l'esigenza di una maggiore compatibilità con i dialetti locali, in un primitivo spazio variazionale regionale.

L'ottenimento di alcuni gradi di elaborazione attraverso la tradizione discorsiva delle omelie ha in seguito permesso, soprattutto al friulano centrale, di raggiungere lo *status* di lingua *media* sia in rapporto con l'italiano, sia con le varietà friulane locali. La crescente fortuna che esso avrebbe avuto nell'Ottocento induce a riflettere anche sui due stadi del processo di standardizzazione. Il primo di essi, cioè la *selezione*, lo si vede in opera anche nella predicazione in friulano già nel momento in cui si osservano tentativi di demunicipalizzazione. La seconda fase, quella della *codificazione*, sarebbe giunta più tardi e in modo più graduale, ma un significativo segnale in questa direzione può essere riconosciuto nell'allestimento del *Vocabolario friulano* di Pirona, comparso nel 1871.

I linguaggi tecnici nelle carte friulane del tardo Medioevo

Bibliografia

Cadorini, G. 2015. Friulano, veneto e toscano nella storia del Friuli. In Heinemann, S. / Melchior, L. Eds. *Manuale di linguistica friulana*. Berlin / Boston: De Gruyter, 316–337.

Degrassi, D. 1988. L'economia del tardo medioevo. In Cammarosano, P. / De Vitt, F. / Degrassi, D. *Il Medioevo*. Tavagnacco (Udine): Casamassima, 269–435.

DEI = Battisti C. / Alessio G. 1950–1957. *Dizionario etimologico italiano*. Firenze: Barbera.

DESF = Zamboni, A. 1984/1987. *Dizionario etimologico storico friulano*, 2 voll. Udine: Casamassima.

Figliuolo, B. 2012. La vita economica e le presenze forestiere. In Figliuolo, B. Ed. *Storia di Cividale nel Medioevo. Economia, società, istituzioni*. Cividale del Friuli: Città di Cividale del Friuli, 111–170.

Francescato, G. / Salimbeni, F. 1977. *Storia, lingua e società in Friuli*. Tavagnacco (Udine): Casamassima.

Koch, P. / Oesterreicher, W. 2001. Gesprochene Sprache und Geschriebene Sprache. Langage parlé et langage écrit. In Holtus G. / Metzeltin, M. / Schmitt, Chr. Eds. *Lexikon der Romanistischen Linguistik*, vol. I,2, *Methodologie (Sprache in der Gesellschaft / Sprache und Klassifikation / Datensammlung und -verarbeitung), Part 1*. Tübingen: M. Niemeyer, 584–627.

Londero, A. / Begotti, P.C. / Mazzanti, G. / Vale, M. 2020. *Gli Statuti di Gemona. Per il governo della Magnifica Comunità*. Gemona del Friuli (Udine): Adriano Londero Editore.

Meyer-Lübke, W. 1894. *Grammatik der Romanischen Sprachen. 2. Formenlehre*. Leipzig: O. R. Reisland. [riproduzione facsimilare: Hildesheim / New York: Olms, 1972]

Nuovo Pirona = Pirona, G.A. / Carletti, E. / Corgnali, G.B. 2004. *Il Nuovo Pirona. Vocabolario friulano*. Udine: Società Filologica Friulana.

Piccini, D. 2006. *Lessico latino medievale in Friuli*. Udine: Società Filologica Friulana.

REW = Meyer-Lübke, W. 2009. *Romanisches etymologisches Wörterbuch*. Heidelberg: Carl Winter.

Vicario, F. Ed. 1998. *Il quaderno di Odorlico da Cividale. Contributo allo studio del friulano antico*. Udine: Forum.

Vicario, F. Ed. 1999. *Il quaderno dell'Ospedale di Santa Maria Maddalena*. Udine: Comune di Udine / Biblioteca Civica «V. Joppi».

Vicario, F. 2006. Cividale 1340. Note di cameraria tra friulano e tosco-veneto. *Revue de Linguistique Romane* 279–280, tomo 70, 471–518.

Vicario, F. 2009a. Appunti su nomi di mestiere in carte friulane tardomedievali. In Borghello, G. Ed. *Per Teresa. Dentro e oltre i confini. Studi e ricerche in ricordo di Teresa Ferro*, vol. 1. Udine: Forum, 357–371.

Vicario, F. 2009b. Cultismi nelle carte usuali friulane tra Tre e Quattrocento. In Marcato, C. Ed. *Lessico colto, lessico popolare*. Alessandria: Edizioni Dell'Orso, 139–154.

Vicario, F. 2010. *Il lessico friulano. Dai documenti antichi al dizionario storico*. Udine: Forum.

Vicario, F. 2012a. Appunti sul cividalese antico. In Figliuolo, B. Ed. *Storia di Cividale nel Medioevo. Economia, società, istituzioni*. Cividale del Friuli: Città di Cividale del Friuli, 27–36.

Vicario, F. 2012b. Note di lessico da un quaderno della Fabbrica del Duomo di Udine (anno 1440). In Borghello, G. Ed. *Per Roberto Gusmani. Linguaggi, culture, letterature. Studi in ricordo*, vol. 1. Udine: Forum, 481–491.

Vicario, F. 2012c. *Repertorio del friulano antico*. Udine: Comune di Udine / Biblioteca Civica «V. Joppi».

Vicario, F. 2013. *Quaderni gemonesi del Trecento. V. Repertori*. Udine: Forum.

Lorenzo Tomasin

Più *trasmigratori* che *poeti*. Percorsi non letterari nella storia e nella lessicografia dell'italiano

Abstract. Studies on History of Italian language are frequently biased by a traditional privileged focus on the literary language, and/or on the Tuscan tradition. It is a situation often complained also for the history of some other Romance languages, that can be explained in Italy by different and specific historical and cultural reasons. An example is chosen in this paper as a study case. The bilingual (or multi-lingual) Italian early modern lexicography produced outside Italy and largely independent both from literary tradition and from Tuscan primacy, opens some alternative paths to the research on the history of language, on its diffusion and on its learning in the European society. Three *lignées* are considered here in particular: the lexicographical descent of the German-Italian glossaries originally published in Venice in 1424, John Florio's dictionaries (started with *A Worlde of Wordes*, 1598), and the long series of bi- or multi-lingual dictionaries opened by Antoine Oudin and culminating in the *Dittionario imperiale* signed by Giovanni Veneroni (Jean Vigneron), first published in 1700.

Abstract. Gli studi sulla storia della lingua italiana sono spesso influenzati da un tradizionale primato concesso alla lingua letteraria, oppure alla tradizione toscana, o a entrambe simultaneamente. Il primo di questi aspetti è spesso lamentato anche da studiosi della storia di altre lingue romanze; per l'Italia questa circostanza può spiegarsi con specifiche ragioni storiche e culturali. In questo articolo, si discute un esempio particolare proponendolo come particolarmente significativo. La lessicografia bilingue (o multilingue) dell'italiano in età moderna prodotta fuori dall'Italia e largamente indipendente sia dalla tradizione letteraria, sia dalla centralità del toscano, apre vari percorsi alternativi alla ricerca sulla storia della lingua, sulla sua diffusione e sul suo apprendimento in Europa. Si considerano in particolare tre *lignées*: la discendenza lessicografica dei glossari veneto-tedeschi composti originariamente a Venezia nel 1424; i dizionari di John Florio (a partire dal *Worlde of Wordes*, 1598) e la lunga serie di dizionari bilingui o multilingui aperta dalle opere di Antoine Oudin e culminante nel *Dittionario imperiale* di Giovanni Veneroni (Jean Vigneron) pubblicato per la prima volta nel 1700.

1. Premessa

Come le omologhe discipline relative a varie altre lingue europee, la storia della lingua italiana nasce e prospera lungamente all'ombra della storia letteraria, cosicché ancora oggi la struttura e l'impostazione di molte ricerche in questo campo riflettono piuttosto fedelmente ambiti d'interesse, criteri di scelta, periodizzazione e articolazione complessiva provenienti dalle storie letterarie.

Le pagine che seguono si propongono di mettere a fuoco nel suo stato presente e nei suoi limiti il rapporto tra storie delle lingue romanze e storie degli usi colti e letterari, con particolare attenzione all'italiano. Come esempio rivelatore di tendenze più generali si eleggerà qui la lessicografia. In questo settore, cruciale per la standardizzazione e la codificazione, ben si osserva lo squilibrio tra studio della tradizione colta (e accademica, e puristica) da un lato, e da un altro quello di una plurima tradizione parallela, legata all'uso della lingua fuori d'Italia, in contesti tipicamente mercantili, tecnici e itinerari.

Le premesse storiche e culturali del problema che qui si affronta sono state nitidamente illuminate da Alberto Varvaro (1972–73: 33), per il quale la «riduzione della lingua alla lingua letteraria è [...] implicita, anche fuori d'Italia, in qualsiasi tentativo di legare lingua e cultura»; esse si riflettono puntualmente sullo studio dello svolgimento storico di lingue come il francese, in opere come quella pionieristica di Brunot (1896–99), o lo spagnolo, in testi ancor oggi di riferimento come quello di Lapesa (1942).

Mezzo secolo dopo l'acuto saggio di Varvaro, la situazione non sembra molto mutata, e il legame tra studi storico-linguistici e studi storico-letterari continua ad essere un punto critico della romanistica nel suo complesso, e di vari suoi singoli distretti nazionali. Così, anche nei manuali di storia della lingua italiana più recenti è normale che la scansione di capitoli e paragrafi assomigli in molti punti a quella che ci si attenderebbe da un manuale di storia della letteratura; ad esempio nell'attenzione prioritaria riservata ad autori del canone letterario fondamentali anche per il canone linguistico – a partire dalle *tre Corone*, vera *intersezione* tra storie della lingua e storie letterarie –, o nella costante tendenza a descrivere le vicende della lingua poetica come particolarmente rilevanti, anche per epoche come quella contemporanea, in cui di fatto la lingua letteraria – massime quella della poesia – influisce poco o per nulla sugli sviluppi dell'italiano comune, sulla sua diffusione sociale, sulla sua norma e sulle sue tradizioni discorsive.

2. Storia linguistica e storia letteraria

Il capostipite degli storici della lingua italiana, Bruno Migliorini (1960: 3), metteva in guardia saggiamente, nella premessa alla sua *Storia*, dalla sovrapposizione troppo rigida o automatica tra storia della lingua e storia della letteratura, che secondo lui era stata tipica degli studi ottocenteschi, e salutava come proficua novità uno spostamento del baricentro che nei fatti, dopo il suo capolavoro, non si è ancora confermato così nettamente:

> L'attenzione quasi esclusiva accordata alla lingua quale strumento letterario ha fatto sì che nel passato parlando di storia della lingua ci si riferisse principalmente allo stile degli scrittori e si tendesse piuttosto a tracciare delle storie dello stile, trascurando invece tanti altri aspetti, sia pur modesti, che appaiono nella complessa realtà dell'uso linguistico quotidiano. Così le pagine dedicate alla "storia della lingua" dal Parini, dal Baretti, dal Foscolo, dal Giordani, dal Capponi e gli spunti talora felici che esse contengono concernono piuttosto la storia della letteratura che quella della lingua.

Il rapporto squilibrato tra storia della letteratura e storia della lingua e la confusione della prima con la seconda sarebbero dunque, a parer di Migliorini, fatti ormai trascorsi che avrebbero dovuto lasciare spazio, nel territorio della nuova disciplina, a una più bilanciata considerazione.

È chiaro che un eventuale mantenimento dello scompenso di cui si dice anche *dopo* la nascita e la consacrazione della *Storia della lingua* come disciplina autonoma potrebbe dipendere dalla ben nota asimmetria tra vicende storiche della lingua letteraria italiana e usi linguistici extra-letterari almeno nell'Italia preunitaria, cioè in quella che è stata felicemente definita *Italia disunita* (con formula di Trifone 2010). Se si ammette, in altri termini, che la storia dell'italiano è per secoli quasi solo storia di una lingua letteraria, si spiega anche la ragione per cui la storia della lingua ha dato più peso alla lingua dei testi letterari che a quella dei documenti e in generale dei testi non letterari, che in quest'ottica sarebbero più legati alla dimensione locale.

Converrà intanto osservare che in tradizioni culturali distinte da quella italiana (e diversamente *strutturate* al loro interno), il problema del rapporto tra studio della lingua letteraria e studio della lingua non letteraria si pone in termini simili, ma comparativamente interessanti. Di recente, due avvertite storiche della lingua spagnola, Mónica Castillo Lluch ed Elena Diez del Corral Areta (2019: 9), hanno osservato che lo studio del castigliano documentario sembra aver avuto fino ad oggi una funzione di *supplenza* o di *complemento*, essendosi limitato a indagare le epoche nelle quali la documentazione *letteraria* (e s'intende proprio: poetica, di prosa d'arte, di teatro) fosse insufficiente:

> Tradicionalmente, el estudio histórico de la lengua española se ha fundado en una mayoría de textos literarios, pues, desde sus inicios, la Escuela de filología española siguió el criterio de su fundador, Ramón Menéndez Pidal, quien dio prioridad al análisis lingüístico de tales escritos y relegó el de los documentos de archivo únicamente a los periodos desiertos de producción literaria, en particular a los orígenes de la lengua.

Analogamente, sul versante galloromanzo Martin Glessgen ha lamentato la marginalità degli studi sulla lingua documentaria:

> L'écrit documentaire reste le grand absent des études de linguistique historique, alors qu'il représente quantitativement l'ensemble de loin le plus important. Les textes littéraires, religieux ou d'un savoir spécialisé ont été rédigés par les mêmes personnes que les textes documentaires et leurs auteurs ont connu la même formation dans les mêmes lieux. Sans la prise en considération des ensembles textuels de la pratique administrative et juridique, l'histoire des langues romanes reste donc partielle.[1]

Se la si compara a quella dell'ispanistica e della francesistica, la situazione della storia della lingua italiana pare da questo punto di vista anche migliore: nel senso che lo studio linguistico di testi documentari, piuttosto intenso in Italia sul versante medievale, si è spesso esteso qui anche ad altre epoche storiche, altrove oggetto di studi incentrati quasi solo sulla lingua letteraria. È il caso, ad esempio, del ricco filone delle ricerche sulla lingua dei semicolti (applicatosi perlopiù a documenti non letterari d'epoca moderna e contemporanea), o a quello poco meno ampio degli studi sulla lingua giuridica.[2]

Ma è un fatto che oggi tra gli storici della lingua italiana pochissimi sono quelli che hanno potuto costruire interi percorsi di ricerca indipendentemente dallo studio – in un modo o nell'altro *anche* letterario – di testi letterari. Tra i pochi campi extra-letterari a ricevere attenzione sono quelli schiacciati su un presentismo mediatico a bassissima tensione culturale e di scarso impegno storico, per cui si tratta più spesso di commentare l'attualità che di ricostruire e comprendere il passato.

Illuminante, per spiegare questo stato di cose, la posizione di Carlo Dionisotti, storico della letteratura e recensore tra i primi e più attenti della *Storia della lingua* di Migliorini, secondo il quale

> il nodo fra lingua e letteratura risulta in Italia più stretto che altrove, e scusabile è la riluttanza dimostrata dai linguisti a sciogliere quel nodo, l'inclinazione loro a lasciare la bisogna agli storici della letteratura (Dionisotti 1967: 80–81).

Il che può comprendesi, mentre meno condivisibili appaiono, col senno di poi (cioè dopo sessant'anni di studi), altre sue convinzioni, che pure sono rivelatrici:

---

[1] Cf. Descriptif du projet, in *Documents linguistiques galloromans. Edition éléctronique*, dirigée par Martin Glessgen, in rete: https://www.rose.uzh.ch/docling/descriptif.php?d=g.

[2] Sullo studio della lingua dei semicolti in Italia si vedano i recenti bilanci di Fresu (2014) e Di Caprio (2019); per la lingua giuridica, Fiorelli (2008), Bambi (2009) e la recente sintesi di Lubello (2021).

Più trasmigratori *che* poeti

Il discorso ci ha ormai portato a gonfie vele nel mare della storia letteraria. E certo lo storico della lingua italiana, come di ogni altra lingua, non può esimersi dal correre questo mare. Per i motivi già detti le scritture non letterarie in Italia sono scarse e infide; la preponderanza della letteratura è quantitativamente e qualitativamente assoluta. (Dionisotti 1967: 83)

Ovviamente così non è nella realtà, ma solo negli occhi di chi osserva (o osservava). Ma se ci si pone quest'ottica, si capisce come agli storici della lingua italiana lo studio della lingua letteraria sia parso una sorta di passaggio obbligato per il concorso di orientamenti critici tra loro antitetici. Da un lato, la storiografia letteraria che, con Dionisotti, trasfonde nel Novecento la tradizione della scuola storica italiana, d'orientamento positivista; da un altro, l'idealismo, che accorda un netto privilegio alla scrittura letteraria, poiché nell'approccio crociano la letteratura è di fatto il *primum* di qualsiasi storia linguistica, e la sua stessa ragion d'essere. L'intensa, e a tratti quasi ipertrofica fioritura italiana della *stilistica* intesa appunto come branca della storia della lingua italiana (anziché della critica letteraria) è evidentemente un riflesso dell'ipoteca posta dall'idealismo sugli studi linguistici. Non a caso, d'altra parte, la stilistica italiana – a differenza sia di quella che fa capo a Spitzer, sia di quella fondata da Bally – si è esercitata praticamente solo su testi letterari, dialogando in particolare con la metrica, con cui assai spesso si accompagna.

Ancora, la produzione poetica e generalmente colta si presenta in Italia per gli storici della lingua come un ampio *corpus* di testi ben editi (da *filologi... della letteratura italiana*, come oggi si titolano ufficialmente i curatori di quei testi: e ancora una volta l'etichetta tradisce forse la priorità degli interessi, più che l'abbondanza o il pregio delle testimonianze), omogeneamente distribuiti nel tempo e di solito ben studiabili dal punto di vista linguistico, a differenza delle fonti non letterarie (documenti, ma anche cronache, testi giuridici, materiale privato), spesso pubblicate da storici con criteri filologico-editoriali che le rendono purtroppo inservibili per il linguista.

Non basta. La stessa *questione della lingua*, cardine ineludibile di qualsiasi discorso sulla storia della lingua italiana, avrebbe teoricamente potuto svilupparsi in ambiti diversi da quello letterario, incentrandosi, ad esempio, sulla scelta dei modelli linguistici nel campo della produzione giuridica, della scrittura filosofica o di quella scientifica. Ma di fatto, essa si risolse quasi per intero in un dialogo tra poeti e – modernamente – prosatori, da Dante a Manzoni, e si tradusse in (o fu letta come) una disputa sulla lingua più conveniente alla produzione in versi e a quella narrativa in prosa.[3] Ne derivò,

---

[3] Interessanti i casi di Calvino e Pasolini, che pur essendo scrittori parteciparono alla questione della lingua guardando soprattutto alla lingua non letteraria (e

tra l'altro, quel complessivo ritardo della presa di coscienza circa le possibilità dell'italiano in campi diversi da quello letterario, che all'Italia appena unificata Graziadio Isaia Ascoli (1873) indicherà con chiarezza e severità.

È ben vero che uno degli snodi cruciali di quella *questione* consiste nell'allargamento del canone strettamente letterario delineato dal Bembo verso la produzione *anche* non letteraria dell'aureo Trecento fiorentino, allargamento promosso da Salviati e dalla prima Crusca.

Ma di fatto l'autocoscienza linguistica altrove secondata dall'opera delle corti e delle cancellerie (nella Toledo alfonsina o nella Parigi capetingia, alla metà del Duecento, e ancora durante l'età moderna) si descrive comunemente in Italia come un percorso quasi tutto interno alla letteratura e alla riflessione su poesia e prosa letteraria. Alla *questione della lingua* in Italia sembrano mancare per secoli – apparendo tardivamente, o non apparendo affatto – figure non isolate o eccezionali di legislatori, di filosofi, di scienziati o di tecnici, insomma di autori di testi *non letterari* capaci di spostare il baricentro del dibattito dal problema del *bello scrivere* a quello dello *scrivere bene* (o del *parlar chiaro* di galileiana memoria).

Non stupisce insomma che la storia di una lingua – l'italiano comune – che si presume *soprattutto letteraria* da parte di studiosi con una formazione prevalentemente letteraria abbia alimentato circolarmente il privilegio concesso allo studio della lingua poetica, qualificando la letteratura e in genere la tradizione colta come componente fondamentale, se non proprio unica forza motrice, negli sviluppi storici di una lingua che in realtà è stata silenziosamente alimentata da correnti ben più numerose e variegate. Insomma, la prevalente preoccupazione letteraria di chi scrisse d'italiano (non forse di chi scrisse in italiano) ha fatto a volte trascurare parti cospicue della storia linguistica.

Lo spostamento dell'attenzione dalla produzione colta verso tradizioni discorsive indipendenti dalla letteratura può dare conto di ambiti trascurati ma importanti per la diffusione e la circolazione dell'italiano in Europa. Nel seguito di questo lavoro prenderemo ad esempio, come si è detto, il campo della lessicografia. In quest'ambito – fondamentale per la concreta diffusione e per la standardizzazione delle grandi lingue europee durante la prima età moderna, e perciò cruciale per la storia della lingua – il privilegio concesso alla letteratura si combina in Italia con un altro carattere tipico, cioè il primato della tradizione toscana, la cui enfatizzazione porta spesso a ulteriori deformazioni prospettiche, che si ripercuotono non solo, come è noto, sulla

---

già Carducci nel 1896 scriveva che «la lingua comune tutti i giornali la scrivono; la lingua letteraria, lo dicemmo già, c'è sempre stata; e non occorre da vero incomodarsi a rifarne un'altra a posta de' nuovi bisognosi», cf. Tomasin 2007: 191).

produzione di vocabolari a lungo sbilanciati verso il lessico della letteratura toscana, ma anche sugli stessi studi di storia della lessicografia, che alle trafile colte e letterarie hanno concesso quasi tutto lo spazio.

Da un lato, ciò che non è letterario rischia di essere negletto, *di fatto*, da storici della lingua troppo influenzati dall'idea per cui le scritture non letterarie in Italia sarebbero, con le parole di Dionisotti, «scarse e infide» e la preponderanza della letteratura «quantitativamente e qualitativamente assoluta». Da un altro, ciò che non è toscano tende naturalmente ad essere considerato lontano da quel nucleo ristretto e individuato attorno al quale si sarebbe costruito e consolidato nel tempo lo *standard* dell'italiano comune: una sorta di appendice aneddotica, o al più di partecipante occasionale al percorso di diffusione, espansione e affermazione della lingua a base toscana. Risultato: come in quello dei testi, anche nello studio dei *luoghi della codificazione* dell'italiano comune, ciò che non è letterario tende ad essere oggetto d'interesse soprattutto *se almeno toscano*, e ciò che non è toscano *se almeno letterario*.

3. Tre filiere lessicografiche e la loro importanza per la diffusione dell'italiano

Nel campo degli studi sulla lessicografia dell'italiano, le opere e gli autori che non concorrano alternativamente alla registrazione monumentale della lingua letteraria o all'affermazione del modello toscano hanno dunque rischiato di restare in una zona d'ombra che occulta, di fatto, una porzione importante e assai ricca della storia culturale.

Un attento scrutinio della produzione lessicografica che riguarda l'italiano durante la prima età moderna mostra una realtà molto frastagliata: una grande varietà di prospettive e di assetti caratterizza la storia della lessicografia italiana *prima* e *durante* i secoli nei quali il vocabolario della Crusca istituisce e consolida un canone non solo toscanocentrico, ma di fatto anche dominato dalla produzione letteraria, a dispetto del dichiarato interesse per la documentazione non letteraria da parte di un purismo disposto ad accogliere *tutto* il lascito testuale dell'*aurea aetas* fiorentina (compresi «i libri delle ragioni dei mercanti, i maestri delle dogane, gli stratti delle gabelle e delle botteghe» evocati in un famoso passo del Cesari [2002]: 45).

In realtà, prima ancora della monolingue e fiorentinocentrica filiera cruscante, la lessicografia bilingue e plurilingue aveva già fondato la codificazione lessicale dell'italiano su un canone largamente *non letterario*.

Tra i dizionari che fecero conoscere e circolare il volgare d'Italia in Europa nella prima età della stampa ve ne sono certo di legati alla produzione letteraria più illustre, come quello *de las dos lenguas toscana y castellana* di Cristóbal de las Casas, sicuro debitore di Francesco Alunno e Niccolò Minerbi, che si basavano essenzialmente sullo spoglio di Boccaccio. Ma vi sono anche opere di tutt'altro orientamento, di cui vorremmo illuminare qui tre insiemi significativi, sorti rispettivamente in ambiente germanico, in Inghilterra e in Francia.

A ben vedere più antica e più ramificata della tradizione lessicografica monolingue capitanata dal vocabolario fiorentino è quella bi- e plurilingue di eredità medievale, cioè anteriore all'età della stampa. I glossari italo-tedeschi attribuiti a un non meglio identificato Giorgio da Norimberga, studiati già da Adolfo Mussafia (1873), e poi riscoperti e ben inquadrati storicamente da Alda Rossebastiano (1984), costituiscono – come quest'ultima ha minuziosamente ricostruito – il punto di partenza d'una ininterrotta serie di lessici plurilingui che ha origine attorno al 1424 a Venezia, nell'ambiente del Fondaco dei tedeschi, che approda alla stampa con l'*Introito e porta* (quasi 'avviamento' allo studio del «latino cioè italiano», cf. Tomasin 2011: 85) impresso per la prima volta da Adam von Rottwil nel 1477, e che attraverso plurime riprese e ampliamenti si estende su almeno tre secoli.

I vocabolari a stampa usciti tra i secoli XVI e XVII che discendono da quell'antico esperimento lessicografico manoscritto accostano parole di un numero crescente di lingue: agli originari italiano di base veneziana e tedesco di base bavarese, progressivamente appannati nella loro matrice regionale, si aggiungono un po' alla volta il latino, il francese, il fiammingo, lo spagnolo, l'inglese e il portoghese variamente rappresentati nelle diverse famiglie di questa affollata tradizione, di cui la stessa Rossebastiano (1984) rintraccia una novantina di titoli che giunge fino a un *Dictionnaire de six langages* stampato a Rouen nel 1636. Capisaldi di questa tradizione, oltre alla citata stampa di Rottwil, la *Introductio quaedam utilissima sive vocabularius quattuor linguarum latinæ, italicæ, gallicæ et alamannicæ* che Jacobus Mazochius stampa a Roma nel 1510, il *Quinque linguarum utilissimus vocabulista* edito a Venezia da Melchiorre Sessa nel 1513, una *Nomenclatura quattuor linguarum* di Cracovia, del 1532 (editore Florian Ungler), una *Nomenclatura sex linguarum* uscita a Vienna nel 1538 per i tipi di Johannes Singrenius, e il *Dilucidissimus Dictionarius* apparso ad Anversa nel 1534 presso Ioannis Steels: sono i capostipiti di altrettante famiglie individuate dalla Rossebastiano, per i quali date e luoghi bastino a documentare l'ampiezza di un successo editoriale internazionale e non effimero.

In queste opere, le liste lessicali (normalmente non alfabetiche) dei glossari veri e propri sono di norma introdotte da un repertorio di frasi, di scambi di battute e di situazioni che compongono un vero, seppur conciso, manuale di conversazione, ben più ampio del glossario stesso.

Al modello *istituzionale* di codificazione basato sull'accostamento di *grammatica* e *vocabolario monolingue*, quest'ampia e ramificata filiera culturale contrappone insomma un'alternativa basata sulla combinazione di *manuale di conversazione* e *vocabolario plurilingue*, che avviano all'apprendimento della lingua in modo completamente diverso – e su basi culturali del tutto distinte – rispetto a quelle proposte dai *luoghi della codificazione* più noti e studiati. D'altra parte, se la stagione delle grammatiche stampate delle lingue romanze si era aperta con la descrizione del castigliano di Antonio de Nebrija (1492), che comprendeva un intero libro dedicato all'apprendimento dello spagnolo come lingua straniera, nulla di simile offrirà la *linea maestra* delle grammatiche italiane a stampa, visto che né Fortunio, né Bembo, né i continuatori di questo paiono preoccuparsi della circolazione internazionale della «lingua senza impero» (secondo la famosa formula di Bruni 2001).

È rivelatrice la formula con cui già a partire dall'edizione di Domenico de Lapi (Bologna 1479) si individua chiaramente il pubblico dei glossari plurilingui di cui diciamo (Rossebastiano 1984: 45, corsivo nostro):

> Solenisimo vochabuolista e utilissimo a imparare legere per q(ue)li che desiderase senza a(n)dare a schola, como è *artesani e done*.

E la formula, con esplicita menzione di *artigiani* e *donne*, sarà ripetuta ancora nelle edizioni cinque- e seicentesche (di «profani e donne» parlerà l'edizione cracoviense del 1532). Si tratta in effetti di prontuari il cui pubblico tipico non era quello degli aspiranti poeti o dei letterati desiderosi di leggere comprendendole le opere di Petrarca o di Ariosto, bensì un'anonima e ben più vasta compagine di donne, commercianti, uomini d'armi, ecclesiastici e diplomatici che all'italiano si accostava per ragioni affatto pratiche e in circostanze del tutto indipendenti dal successo non solo dei capolavori letterari italiani, ma anche di quelli musicali, figurativi o architettonici che in altri ambiti determinavano il successo dell'italiano fuori d'Italia.

La seconda filiera che vorrei richiamare, come ho detto, porta in Inghilterra. Spesso ricordato, ma come se si trattasse di un anticipatore delle fortune del poco più recente *Vocabolario degli Accademici della Crusca*, è il capolavoro lessicografico di John Florio, cioè le due edizioni del suo dizionario (*A Worlde of Wordes*, 1598, poi *New World of Words*, 1611: ed. Haller 2013, basato sulla prima). Autore che in Italia probabilmente non visse mai nel corso della sua vita, John Florio si mostra fedele alle profonde convinzioni anti-puristiche che avevano mosso già il padre Michelangelo a schierarsi contro «quelle regole del parlare, e de lo scrivere, le quale essi o nel Bembo, o nel Fortunio si trovano haver studiate & apparate» (il passo è stato ben illustrato da Andrea Bocchi 2014: 54).

Il *thesaurus* del Florio conta 44mila lemmi nella prima edizione e addirittura 74mila nella seconda, laddove la prima Crusca si fermerà a 28mila, e si fonda su un canone di ben 252 *citati* che include non solo un'abbondante messe di autori letterari cinquecenteschi che saranno ovviamente evitati dal primo Frullone (dal Machiavelli al Bruno, dal Brucioli al Doni), ma anche vari titoli originali e numerose traduzioni italiane di opere riconducibili alla trattatistica scientifica e a quella tecnica (da Conrad Gessner all'Alessandro Capobianco di Vicenza autore di un trattato sull'artiglieria), alla storiografia e alla cronachistica (Olao Magno e un'anonima *Historia della China*), nonché ricettari (il Messi Sbugo del *Libro nuovo d'ordinar banchetti, et conciar vivande*) e, ovviamente, letteratura religiosa soprattutto eterodossa, dalle traduzioni bibliche alle riflessioni teologiche di protestanti e dissidenti religiosi (dal Brucioli al Diodati, a Juan de Valdes). Ben nota è poi la disponibilità floriana ad attingere ai dialetti, cooptando nell'edizione definitiva quasi trecento venezianismi, un centinaio di napoletanismi e varie decine d'altre voci regionali.[4]

Più che precorrere il successo della Crusca, dunque, Florio rappresenta uno degli episodi più illustri di una linea parallela e alternativa a quella consacrata dal purismo.

Parimenti affrancata dalla tradizione cruscante, e complessivamente indipendente dal modello basato sulla centralità della letteratura toscana o toscaneggiante nella descrizione e codificazione dell'italiano è una terza filiera della tradizione lessicografica. Si tratta della serie di opere che dalle *Recherches Italiennes et Françoises* di Antoine Oudin (1639–1640, poi *Dittionario italiano e francese* a partire dall'ediz. del 1693) porta ai vocabolari di Jean Vigneron (*alias* Giovanni Veneroni) e infine al *Dittionario imperiale* pubblicato per la prima volta a Francoforte nel 1700, e poi rivisto da Niccolò da Castelli nel 1714 e ristampato nel 1743, nonché ripreso da una nebula di analoghi dizionari settecenteschi per i quali sarebbe utile disporre di un censimento *ragionato* simile a quello procurato da Rossebastiano per la trafila che mette capo ai glossari veneto-tedeschi, anche per riscattare questa *lignée* dal silenzio riservatole da molti tra i principali studi recenti sulla storia della lessicografia italiana.[5] Per ora, si osserverà che la bibliografia analitica dei dizionari bilingui dedicati a italiano e francese di Lillo (2019: 12) assegna al Veneroni ben 41 edizioni tra il 1681 e il 1769 (e parla di «enorme successo»), in un intervallo temporale in cui la Crusca produce due (la terza e la quarta) delle sue impressioni.

---

[4] Sui venezianismi del Florio, cf. Ferguson (2012).

[5] Non fanno menzione né dell'Oudin, né del Veneroni le panoramiche storiche di Della Valle (2005) e di Marazzini (2009), mentre solo un cenno al primo si nota in Schweickard (2016: 505): e l'assenza non denota tanto una lacuna in questi lavori, quanto l'obiettiva marginalità di queste opere negli studi attuali (solo due corrive menzioni per l'uno, e una per l'altro vocabolario occorrono ad esempio negli atti del convegno ASLI dedicato una decina d'anni fa alla storia della lessicografia italiana, cf. Tomasin 2012).

Prendo ora a riferimento proprio il *Dittionario imperiale* nell'edizione del 1714 (recentemente ristampata in un'edizione anastatica dalla Città di Lugano: Veneroni 2011): in questo ideale punto d'arrivo di una tradizione che si svolge contemporaneamente al periodo di più intensa produzione del cantiere cruscante non è difficile individuare varie voci italiane che, oggi comunemente accolte anche dalla lessicografia *dell'uso*, sono lungamente ignorate dalla tradizione del purismo.

Emblematico il caso della parola *ditale*, oggetto di una famosa pagina ascoliana sugli eccessi del toscanismo. Nel senso di «dé à coudre», *ditale* è registrato sia dall'Oudin sia dal Veneroni, mentre solo la quarta impressione del Vocabolario della Crusca ammetterà, *obtorto collo*, l'accezione più comune in Italia («si dice anche l'anello da cucire»). Analogo è il caso di altre voci considerate regionali e perciò escluse dalla lessicografia cruscante, sebbene da tempo fossero penetrate nella lingua comune, come ad esempio:

- *inalborarsi* 'impennarsi', che entrerà solo nella quinta Crusca, ancorché sia voce già sacchettiana;
- *magari*, accolta nel *Dittionario imperiale* come «mot vénitien» (dei regionalismi dichiarati riparleremo sotto) ed esclusa dalla Crusca fino alla quinta impressione;
- *manizza*, 'manubrio', 'maniglia', assente in tutta la tradizione cruscante e accolto nella lessicografia monolingue all'altezza del Tommaseo-Bellini (*TB*);
- *ne(g)rofumo* 'polvere nera di fumo', accolto solo nella quinta Crusca (e cf. Alessio 1957–58, s.v.);
- *pupazza* «poupée», assente in tutta la tradizione cruscante, sia nella forma femminile sia in quella maschile in cui si è affermato nell'italiano comune, nel quale è spesso riguardato come un dialettalismo d'origine romana (cf. Avolio 1994: 571);
- *sommoz(z)are* «quand le cheval baisse la tête, ou l'appuye sur la bride, & tire la main de celuy qui est dessus», presente già nel Las Casas, e riportato dall'Oudin e dal Veneroni: è la base di un altro fortunato regionalismo (un napoletanismo), *sommozzatore*, per cui invano si cercherebbero riscontri nella Crusca;
- *zanzeriere* (s.m.) «un pavillon en Lombardie, parce qu'il empêche les moucherons», spiega il *Dittionario imperiale*: altra parola esclusa da tutte le impressioni della Crusca, per cui il GDLI riporta esempi già quattrocenteschi nel Belcari;[6]
- *zattera* «radeau», che entra nella Crusca all'altezza della IV edizione, ed è voce già registrata dal Florio nel *Worlde of Wordes*, riportata sia da

---

[6] Cf. anche il *DELIN* s.v. *zanzara*, che significativamente riporta *zanzeriere* anche dal *Vocabolario bresciano e toscano* del 1789.

Oudin sia da Veneroni senza le marche regionali che, come diremo ora, sono riservate a molti altri lemmi.

In molti casi, in effetti, quella che abbiamo indicato come la trafila dei vocabolari originariamente italiano-francesi di Oudin e Veneroni, poi quadrilingui (con tedesco e latino) nel *Dittionario imperiale*, dà ampio spazio ed esplicita trattazione ad ambiti lessicali vivissimi, ma esclusi dalla tradizione puristica, come le voci gergali e quelle dialettali o regionali.

Basandomi sulla prima parte (quella le cui entrate sono in italiano) del *Dittionario imperiale* nella già citata edizione del 1714, ho contato ben 38 voci chiosate come *jargon* nella sola lettera *A*. Si tratta in effetti di parole che in vari casi trovano riscontro nel Brocardo del *Modo nuovo* e in generale nella letteratura gergale cinque-seicentesca, come nel caso di *alberto* «oeuf», *albume* «de l'argent», *allumare* «voir», *alzare* «manger et boire», *amore* e *antona* «non», *ansare* «brûler», *antiporto* «une ceinture», la serie *aronte*, *artibio* e *artone* «du pain», *attencare* «voir», voci tutte rintracciabili nel repertorio del Prati (1978) sulle *Voci di gerganti, vagabondi e malviventi*.

L'Oudin, il Veneroni e i loro continuatori sono altrettanto generosi con le voci dialettali e regionali, che mostrano di riconoscere come tali e di cooptare accanto a quelle di uso comune. Come venezianismi sono dunque segnalati (mi fondo sempre sull'ediz. 1714 del *Dittionario imperiale*) *androna* «privè», *bigolo* «bâton à porter les seaux», *bisatti* «petites anguilles», *bòvoli* «escargots», *calicione* «sorte de pain d'épice», *cinquadea* «épée», *dao* «pour *dato*», *drio* «derrière», *fio* «fils», *fruare* «user des habits», *ingramire* / *ingramare* «doventar gramo», il già citato *magari*, *moja* «interjection venitienne quand on est en colère», *nezza* «nièce», *ninfa* «nom d'une fraise de toile», *parazonio* «sorte d'épée», *piègora* «brebis», *scoazze* «ballieures», *scobbia* «gauge de maréchal», *spuazzo* «un gros crachat», *zotto* «boiteux», *zane, zanni* «des quilles»[7].

Come «mots napolitains» poi figurano *bertola* 'borsa, tasca' nel proverbio «cuor contento, e la bertola al collo» (una voce di matrice comunque gergale), *chianare* «applanir, monter», *chisto/chisso* «pour *questo*», *chiù* «pour *più*, mots calabrois et napolitain», *diraggio* «pour *dirò*», *granne* «pour *grande*», *impiso* «pendu», *malaggia* «mal luy vienne», *puccia bianca* «sort de pain», *annare* «pour *andare*», *mandrollo* «un cachot».[8]

Ancora più numerosi, tanto che non si possono riportare qui se non in parte, sono i «mots lombards», cioè le voci genericamente settentrionali, che

---

[7] Per le voci *androna, bigolo, bisatti, bovoli, calison, cinquedea, fruar, neza, piègora, scoazze, zotto* cf. il *VEV*, on-line; *zanni* è errore per *zoni* 'rocchetti per giocare' (cf. Boerio 1856 s.v.).

[8] Cf. per *bertola, chisto, chiù, puccia* Galiani (1789), s.vv. Per *chianare* e *mandrollo, DEDI* s.v. *chiano* e *mandrùllë*.

ricorrono a decine, e comprendono intere serie lessicali, come quella composta dalla coppia *ameda/amida/amita* «tante» e *barba* «oncle», nonché voci del lessico più elementare come *ancò/ancuo* «aujourd'hui», *assentarsi* «s'asseoir», *cariega* «une chaire», *drean* «dernier», *giobba* «jeudy», *nigotta* «rien», *ponaro* «le nid où la poule pond», *preda* «proye, pour *pietra*», *prèvede* «prêtre», *a provo* «auprés», *smalza* «du beurre», *strangualzare* «engloutir», *toso* «un garçon», e così via.

Ma ciò che mostra nel modo più evidente la profonda diversità d'impostazione tra questa filiera lessicografica e quella dei puristi è la qualifica di alcuni termini come *fiorentinismi*, cioè come voci locali al pari degli altri regionalismi e dialettalismi segnalati per altre parti d'Italia: è il caso di *serqua*, voce di Crusca definita «quarteron, une douzaine, *mot florentin*» (corsivo mio), e di *canciola* «tumeur en l'aîne, &c.; il se prend aussi pour chancre, malediction dont se servent les florentins» (e in effetti si tratta di voce puntualmente registrata dalla Crusca) o di *chintana*, cioè quintana, di cui si dice che «les Florentins se servent de ce mot pour une bague que l'on court à cheval».

Nel caleidoscopio della lessicografia plurilingue europea, che per molte ragioni guarda all'italiano *dall'esterno*, il fiorentino è descritto in un certo senso come *dialetto tra i dialetti d'Italia*, con anticipazione mirabile – ma perlopiù inosservata dalla storiografia – dei futuri acquisti della scienza glottologica e della dialettologia moderna. Visioni come quelle di un Melchiorre Cesarotti, che di lì a qualche decennio descriverà la panoplia dialettale italiana come carattere precipuo di una lingua comune *in se* policentrica, trovano forse maggior senso e un più chiaro radicamento nella lessicografia plurilingue, che rappresenta l'italiano con maggiore ampiezza e obiettività di quella assicurata dalla coeva produzione monolingue.

4. Conclusioni

La *Tebe dalle sette porte* dell'italiano come lingua comune e come lingua d'Europa fu insomma costruita – per ricalcare una famosa metafora brechtiana – anche da una folta schiera di glossari, vocabolari, prontuari e libri didattici che prescindevano dalla produzione letteraria e non dipendevano da quella toscana, contraddicendo il *cliché* dell'italiano come lingua necessariamente legata alla sua tradizione colta e quasi vincolata, in ogni suo sviluppo, ai successi dei suoi autori di poesia e di prosa e alla loro progressiva adesione al modello toscano.

Lingua *ascoltata* e *parlata* oltre che (o più che) *letta* e *scritta*, l'italiano dei numerosi utenti di opere come quelle che abbiamo richiamato si diffonde attraverso canali distinti da quelli che consacrano Petrarca, Boccaccio, Ariosto o Della Casa.

Sono i percorsi di un italiano *itinerario* saturo d'elementi regionali assimilabili a quelli per cui Enrico Testa (2014) ha discorso d'*italiano nascosto*. E sono percorsi che anticipano quelli attraverso i quali l'italiano ha continuato a diffondersi anche in età contemporanea, dopo il drastico ridimensionamento della sua visibilità letteraria in un panorama ormai globale: è come lingua dell'emigrazione, più ancora che della poesia o dell'arte, che l'italiano si diffonde nel mondo nell'ultimo secolo e mezzo.

Piuttosto noto tra gli italiani, o almeno tra i romani dei nostri giorni, è il testo di una roboante iscrizione che campeggia sulla facciata di un palazzo costruito dal regime fascista nel cuore del quartiere dell'EUR: quello italiano vi è descritto come un «popolo di poeti, di artisti, di eroi, di santi, di pensatori, di scienziati, di navigatori, di trasmigratori», citazione di un discorso di Benito Mussolini del 2 ottobre 1935 in cui sequenza e gerarchia delle qualifiche riflettono perfettamente il pregiudizio concettuale da cui siamo partiti: una scala evidentemente in discesa che ha in cima i *poeti* e agli ultimi gradini i *navigatori* e i *trasmigratori* (o come forse si potrebbe dire oggi, i *migranti*).

Le reti lessicografiche attraverso le quali l'italiano si è diffuso capillarmente in Europa durante tutta l'età moderna mostrano che la tradizione della lingua letteraria e i successi di poesia e prosa d'arte rappresentano solo una porzione – e forse nemmeno la più rilevante, in vari periodi e in vari ambiti – di ciò che contribuì alla costruzione, alla circolazione e al progressivo rafforzamento dell'italiano comune. Una storia della lingua che dalla storia della letteratura è complessivamente piuttosto autonoma.

Bibliografia

Alessio, G. 1957–1958. Postille al dizionario etimologico italiano. *Quaderni linguistici, Università di Napoli* 3–4, 1–260.

Ascoli, G.I. 1873. Proemio. *Archivio glottologico italiano* 1, V–LIV.

Avolio, F. 1994. I dialettismi dell'italiano. In Serianni L. / Trifone, P. Eds. *Storia della lingua italiana*, vol. III *Le altre lingue*. Torino: Einaudi, 561–595.

Bambi, F. 2009. *Una nuova lingua per il diritto. Il lessico volgare di Andrea Lancia nelle* Provvisioni fiorentine *del 1355-57*. Milano: Giuffrè.

Bocchi, A. 2014. I Florio contro la Crusca. In Daniele, A. Ed. *La nascita del vocabolario. Convegno di studio per i quattrocento anni del Vocabolari della Crusca*. Padova: Esedra, 51–80.

Boerio, G. 1856. *Dizionario del dialetto veneziano*. Venezia: Cecchini.

Bruni, F. 2001. *Una lingua senza impero: l'italiano*. Venezia: Ca' Foscari.

Più trasmigratori *che* poeti

Brunot, F. 1896–1899. *Histoire de la langue française*. Paris: Colin.
Castillo Lluch M. / Diez del Corral Areta, E. 2019. *Reescribiendo la historia de la lengua española a partir de la edición de documentos*. Bern: Peter Lang.
Cesari, A. 2002. *Dissertazione sopra lo stato presente della lingua italiana*. Padova: Antenore.
Cortelazzo, M. 2007. *Dizionario veneziano della lingua e della cultura popolare nel XIV secolo*. Limena: La Linea.
DEDI = Cortelazzo, M. / Marcato, C. 1992. *Dizionario etimologico dei dialetti italiani*. Torino: UTET.
DELIN = Cortelazzo, M. / Zolli, P. 1999. *Dizionario Etimologico della Lingua Italiana*. Seconda edizione, a cura di M. Cortelazzo e M.A. Cortelazzo. Bologna: Zanichelli.
Della Valle, V. 2005. *Dizionari italiani: storia, tipi, struttura*. Roma: Carocci.
Di Caprio, C. 2019. Il tempo e la voce. La categoria di semicolto negli studi storico-linguistici e le scritture della storia (secc. XVI–XVIII). In Malato, E. / Mazzucchi, A. Eds. *La critica del testo. Problemi di metodo ed esperienze di lavoro*, atti del convegno di Roma, 2017. Roma: Salerno editrice, 613–664.
Dionisotti, C. 1967 [1962]. Per una storia della lingua italiana. In Dionisotti, C. Ed. *Geografia e storia della letteratura italiana*. Torino: Einaudi, 75–102.
Ferguson, R. 2012. Primi influssi culturali italo-veneti sull'inglese. Le testimonianza dei venezianismi in Florio, Coryate e Jonson. *Quaderni veneti* 1/1, 57–82.
Fiorelli, P. 2008. *Intorno alle parole del diritto*. Milano: Giuffrè.
Fresu, R. 2014. Scritture dei semicolti. In Antonelli, G. / Motolese, M. / Tomasin, L. Eds. *Storia dell'italiano scritto*. Vol. III. *Italiano dell'uso*. Roma: Carocci, 195–223.
GDLI = Battaglia, S. Ed. 1961–2002. *Grande dizionario della lingua italiana*. Torino: UTET.
Haller, H. Ed. 2013. John Florio, *A Worlde of Wordes*. Toronto: University of Toronto.
Lapesa, R. 1942. *Historia de la lengua española*. Madrid: Escelicer.
Lillo, J. 2019 (2020). *1583–2010. Quattro secoli e più di lessicografia italo-francese. Repertorio analitico dei dizionari bilingue* [sic]. Bologna: Clueb.
Lubello, S. 2021. *L'italiano del diritto*. Roma: Carocci.
Marazzini, C. 2014. *L'ordine delle parole. Storie di vocabolari italiani*. Bologna: il Mulino.
Migliorini, B. 1960. *Storia della lingua italiana*. Firenze: Sansoni (nuova ed. Milano: Bompiani, 2007, da cui si cita).
Mussafia, A. 1873. *Beitrag zur Kunde der Norditalienischen Mundarten*. Wien: Gerold.
Prati, A. 1978. *Voci di gerganti, vagabondi e malviventi studiate nell'origine e nella storia*. Nuova edizione. Pisa: Giardini.

Rossebastiano Bart, A. 1984. *Antichi vocabolari plurilingui d'uso popolare. La tradizione del "solenissimo vochabuolista"*. Alessandria: Edizioni dell'Orso.

Schweickard, W. 2016. La lessicografia. In Lubello, S. Ed. *Manuale di linguistica italiana*. Berlin: De Gruyter, 509–534.

Testa, E. 2014. *L'italiano nascosto. Una storia linguistica e culturale*. Torino: Einaudi.

Tomasin, L. 2007. *«Classica e odierna». Studi sulla lingua di Carducci*. Firenze: Olschki.

Tomasin, L. 2011. *Italiano. Storia di una parola*. Roma: Carocci.

Tomasin, L. Ed. 2012. *Il Vocabolario degli Accademici della Crusca (1612) e la storia della lessicografia italiana*. Firenze: Cesati.

Trifone, P. 2010. *Storia linguistica dell'Italia disunita*. Bologna: il Mulino.

Vàrvaro, A. 1972–1973. Storia della lingua: passato e prospettive di una categoria controversa. *Romance Philology* 26, 16–51, 509–531 (poi in Id., *La parola nel tempo. Lingua, società e storia*. Bologna: il Mulino, 1984, 9–77).

Veneroni, G. 2011. *Dizionario imperiale* (1714), ristampa anastatica, Bologna / Lugano: Forni / Archivio Storico della Città di Lugano.

VEV = Tomasin, L. / D'Onghia, L. Eds. *VEV – Vocabolario storico-etimologico del veneziano*, http://vev.ovi.cnr.it.

Tabea Salzmann*

Standardisierungsprozesse in der administrativen Schriftlichkeit des *Estado da Índia* im 16. Jahrhundert

Abstract. What effects can a multilingual space have on written communication? This article pursues the objective of considering contact effects on the standards of administrative documents in form, text and scripts. The documents under consideration pertain to the colonial administration of the *Estado da Índia* of the 16th century. While they represent a broad of contents in one text type and involve many different writers they were all written in the main ports of Portuguese India between 1512 and 1612. Their fairly homogeneous form suggests a well-developed professional system of writing, writers and postal exchange that implements and develops standardised forms of administrative communication in a written context in a give and take between mother country and colonies, between institutions and individual professionals, between rules and regulations and everyday practice.

Abstract. Welche Auswirkungen hat ein multilingualer Raum auf geschriebene Kommunikation? In diesem Artikel werden die Auswirkungen von Sprachkontakt auf den Standard portugiesischer administrativer Dokumente in Form, Text und Schrift untersucht. Die herangezogenen Dokumente stammen aus der Verwaltung des *Estado da Índia* im 16. Jahrhundert. Während diese Dokumente ein breites Inhaltsspektrum in einer Textart abdecken und von vielen verschiedenen mit dem Schreiben offiziell beauftragten sowie nicht-professionellen Schreibern stammen, wurden sie alle in den größeren Häfen des portugiesischen Indiens zwischen 1512 und 1612 verfasst. Die relativ homogene Form legt ein gut ausgebildetes professionelles System des Schreibens, der Schreiber und der Post nahe, welches in einem Geben und Nehmen zwischen Kolonien und Mutterland, zwischen Institutionen und individuellen Experten, zwischen Regeln und Vorschriften und alltäglicher Praxis standardisierte Formen von administrativer Kommunikation entwickelt und implementiert.

1. Einleitung

Kolonialisierung schafft einen ganz spezifischen, neuen Raum, der den Kontakt zwischen den Sprachen und Kulturen wesentlich prägt. Dieser Kontakt kann direkte Auswirkungen in der Sprache, wie den Einbezug neuen Voka-

---

* Universität Bremen, gefördert durch die Deutsche Forschungsgesellschaft (DFG) – GZ: SA 3224/2–1.

bulars oder auch die Entstehung neuer Sprachvarietäten haben. Er kann sich aber auch indirekt manifestieren. Ich möchte im Folgenden die indirekten soziokulturellen Auswirkungen eines solchen Raumes auf Sprache und Text untersuchen. Dies erfolgt, indem ich auf der einen Seite die soziale und sprachliche Geschichte des Kontaktes nachverfolge und dabei einen Fokus auf das Schreibertum lege (siehe Kap. 2) und auf der anderen Seite durch eine Korpusanalyse, in der ich Tendenzen der Vereinheitlichung über das 16. Jahrhundert in Dokumentenform, Textformat und Schriftarten von administrativen Dokumenten des portugiesischen *Estado da Índia*, speziell solchen Dokumenten, die in Indien verfasst wurden, aufzeige (siehe Kap. 3). Diese Mischung aus sprachgeschichtlicher und korpusbasierter textinterner Analyse ermöglicht es, zuverlässige Daten angemessen zu interpretieren (siehe Kap. 4). Ich behandle mit den ausgewählten Texten einen sehr kleinen Ausschnitt aus den sprachbezogenen Entwicklungen im *Estado da Índia* des 16. Jahrhunderts, der aber interessante Rückschlüsse auf das Gesamtszenario zulässt. Spezifischer untersuche ich formale und textuelle Merkmale von portugiesischen Dokumenten anhand eines Briefkorpus zwischen 1512 und 1612 aus dem geographischen Bereich Indien als Zentrum der kolonialen Administration im *Estado da Índia* und dem Hauptverknüpfungspunkt zu Portugal. Zur Einordnung gebe ich zuerst einen kurzen geschichtlichen Abriss und beschreibe die Verhältnisse in Administration und Handel des *Estado da Índia* (Kap. 2). Danach analysiere ich die Dokumentform und das Textformat und die in den Dokumenten verwendeten Schriftarten (Kap. 3), um dann zu einer standardisierungsgeschichtlichen Interpretation zu kommen (Kap. 4).

2. Zur Geschichte der portugiesischen Kolonien in Indien und der Handelsnetzwerke des *Estado da Índia*

Nach einem knappen Jahrhundert der kolonialen Expansion entlang der Küsten Afrikas gelangten die Portugiesen mit Vasco da Gama 1498 erstmals auf dem Seeweg nach Indien. Mit seiner Ankunft in der Nähe von Calicut begann die schrittweise Etablierung von Handels- und Militärstützpunkten entlang den indischen und ostasiatischen Küsten. Die Ostküste Indiens war zu diesem Zeitpunkt in kleine Reiche unterteilt, die durch eine hoch komplexe soziale, politisch-administrative und ökonomische Struktur gekennzeichnet waren. Diese Reiche wurden von Fürsten (*Rajas*) regiert, die mit den Portugiesen Handelsabkommen unterzeichneten.[1]

---

[1] Kenntnisse über die vorherrschenden soziopolitischen Strukturen und die Handelsnetzwerke und -güter hatten die Portugiesen bereits zuvor über Gesandtschaften erhalten, die Indien über den Landweg erreicht hatten. Nach der

Administrative *Schriftlichkeit des* Estado da Índia

Der Sitz des ersten Vizekönigtums, in Cochin 1506 etabliert, wurde 1510 nach Goa verlegt. Um 1535 hatten sich die Portugiesen an den Küsten Indiens von Daman im Nordwesten über die gesamte Küste bis nach Bangalore im Nordosten niedergelassen. Bereits 1511 eroberten die Portugiesen östlich von Indien Malakka im heutigen Indonesien. Im Jahr 1514 erreichten sie die Molukken. Die militärische Vormachtstellung im Indischen Ozean, deren Hauptstütz- und Ausgangspunkt Goa war, war die Voraussetzung für die vornehmlich handelsbezogene Präsenz der Portugiesen in diesem Raum. Damit handelte es sich hier, anders als in Amerika, nicht um Siedlungskolonialismus, sondern um Handelskolonialismus (Schneider 2012: 573, basierend auf Mufwene 2001). Trotzdem konnte sich das Portugiesische mit diversen Kontakteinflüssen als *lingua franca* des Handels und der Diplomatie mit europäischen Mächten schnell im *Estado da Índia* etablieren und wurde damit im gesamten östlichen Kolonialraum gesprochen (cf. Boxer 1984).

Die Schiffsroute der sogenannten *Carreira da Índia* blieb in den ersten 300 Jahren mehr oder weniger unverändert. Ein Weg dauerte bei besten Bedingungen zwischen sechs und acht Monaten, der Hin- und Rückweg insgesamt ca. 1,5 Jahre (cf. Diffie/Winius 1977: 199–201). Wegen der Monsunzeiten konnte nur eine Flotte pro Jahr entsandt werden (cf. Mathew 1988: 232–234), deren Größe also bestimmte, wie viele Personen und wie viele Waren hin und her verschifft wurden. Für die Verschiffung der Korrespondenz etablierte die Krone 1520 ein Postsystem, den *serviço de correio público*, damit Nachrichten und Dokumente besser und schneller zwischen den Kolonien und Portugal transportiert werden konnten.[2] Die Post wurde in den jährlichen Flotten mitgeführt (cf. Diffie/Winius 1997: 235).

Wir können für das 16. Jahrhundert von einer konstanten und progressiven Emigration von ca. 200.000 Portugiesen, hauptsächlich von Männern, in den *Estado da Índia* nach Indien und in der zweiten Hälfte des Jahrhunderts auch weiter nach Osten ausgehen. Davon verblieben nach Verlusten in der Passage von bis zu einem Drittel der Personen (cf. Diffie/Winius 1977: 199–

Entdeckung des Seewegs sammelten die ersten Expeditionen der sogenannten *Carreira da Índia* unter anderem mithilfe der dabei erstellten *Roteiros* (Logbüchern) weitere Informationen. Auf dieser Basis konnten die Portugiesen vor Ort schnell ein Netz von diplomatischen Beziehungen zu den lokalen Herrschern aufbauen (cf. Diffie/Winius 1977: 228).

[2] Die Post nahm ihren Dienst erst 1533 auf. Sie war über Jahrhunderte dem Verantwortungsbereich des Königs unterstellt. „Assim, a 6 de novembro de 1520, D. Manuel I publicou a Carta Régia que criava o ofício de Correio-mor [...]. O serviço de Correio-mor era público e qualquer cidadão podia utilizálo mediante o pagamento de uma quantia. O Correio-mor foi um cargo de nomeação régia até 1606, quando foi vendido pelo Rei Filipe II a Luís Gomes da Mata [...]" (https://www.bancoctt.pt/home/marcos-historicos, 10.03.2022).

201) und nach der Rückkehr eines weiteren Drittels wohl etwa 60 000 Portugiesen im Indischen Ozean (cf. Russell-Wood 2007: 176; Duncan 1986: 22, nach Schiffspassagierlisten errechnet).

Die Haupteinnahmequelle für den *Estado da Índia* und damit gewissermaßen seine Raison d'Être war der interkontinentale Handel zwischen Asien, Südostasien, Südasien, Afrika und Europa. Über das sich schnell ausbreitende portugiesische Handelsnetzwerk von Siedlungen mit Häfen, Festungen und Handelshäusern zwischen Ostafrika und Ostasien wurden viele verschiedene Waren, vor allem Gewürze und Luxusgüter, verschifft und gehandelt.

Zum Erhalt des Systems von Stützpunkten und Handelshäusern entstand über die erste Hälfte des 16. Jahrhunderts schnell ein komplexer administrativer Apparat.[3] Siedlungen, wie z.B. Goa[4], die um Handelsstützpunkte und gegebenenfalls Festungen herum entstanden, konnten portugiesisches Stadtrecht erwerben. Diese Siedlungen als administrative Einheit waren die zentrale Komponente der portugiesischen Kolonialstrukturen (cf. Russell-Wood 2007: 182) und basierten auf administrativen und physischen Strukturen, die die Portugiesen aus dem Mutterland mitgebracht und für den kolonialen Kontext angepasst hatten.

Die größte portugiesische Besitzung Goa kann als Beispiel für die Etablierung von urbanen portugiesischen Kolonialsiedlungen in Indien und Asien dienen. Die Bevölkerung Goas macht im 16. Jahrhundert wohl zwischen 50.000 und 70.000 Einwohner aus. Davon sind die zwei kleinsten Gruppen diejenigen mit der meisten Entscheidungsgewalt. Das sind zum einen die kleine Gruppe der portugiesischen Funktionäre und zum anderen die lokale Oligarchie der (einfluss)reichen Händler und Bürger. Außerdem gibt es zwischen 1.000 und 2.000 Soldaten und ca. 2.000 sogenannte *casados* – also Soldaten, die aus dem Militär ausscheiden, sich mit einheimischen Frauen verheiraten und in Indien, zumeist als Händler, ansässig werden (cf. Feldbauer 2003: 92–93). Dazu kann man wohl noch relativ viele europäische Geistliche als Repräsentanten der Kirche und kirchlichen Orden rechnen. Der Rest der Einwohner sind in Asien geborene Nachkommen von Portugiesen und solche aus Mischehen, die für rechtliche und administrative Zwecke beide gleichermaßen nicht als Portugiesen zählen, sowie autochthone Bevöl-

---

[3] Erfahrung mit der Etablierung einer solchen Administration hatten die Portugiesen (ja) bereits in den vorangegangenen 100 Jahren an den Küsten Afrikas gemacht.

[4] Das Stadtrecht Goas hatte das Stadtrecht Lissabons zum Vorbild (cf. Boxer 1969: 277–278).

Administrative Schriftlichkeit des Estado da Índia

kerung und Sklaven, die eine ethnische Mischung aus Asiaten und Afrikanern bildeten.[5] Der Alltag der Bevölkerung wurde in Goa durch den *senado da Camara*, die Stadtverwaltung, organisiert. Deren Aufgaben waren die Steuerverwaltung, die Organisation der öffentlichen Infrastruktur sowie die Preisfixierung für Grundnahrungsmittel. Goa hatte ein Eichamt und ab 1545 eine eigene Rechtsverwaltung mit Gericht, (Staats-)Anwaltschaft und Schatzmeister (cf. Boxer 1969: 273). Die untersten Ränge des öffentlichen Dienstes bestanden aus Marktaufsehern, Pförtnern, Standartenträgern, Vorarbeitern, dem Kerkermeister und dem Waisenrichter, sowie Repräsentanten der Gilden (cf. Boxer 1969: 277–279). Dem Ganzen stand der *Governador* bzw. Vizekönig mit seinem administrativen Korps vor. Die höheren sozialen Schichten, wie der Adel, das höhere administrative Personal, wichtige Händler und Unternehmer und das gebildete Bürgertum, zeichneten sich unter anderem dadurch aus, dass sie das Schreiben als Teil ihrer Kultur und Arbeit ausübten, aber nicht speziell nur dafür ausgebildet wurden. Von diesen zu unterscheiden sind Sekretäre, Schreiber, Archivare, Buchhalter und Kontoristen, für die das Schreiben zentraler Teil ihrer Ausbildung und späteren Arbeit ist. Administrative Aufgaben, wie die Ämter von Schreibern, Notaren oder Funktionären, durften nur in Portugal geborene Portugiesen übernehmen. Eine Ausnahme galt für Übersetzer und Dolmetscher. Die oberen Ränge wurden alle drei Jahre aus Portugal neu besetzt und die entsprechenden Dreijahresschaften (*triénio*) schon bald gewinnbringend verkauft oder sogar vererbt (cf. Diffie/Winius 1977: 324), während die unteren Ränge meist lebenslange Posten von Personen waren, die in Indien ansässig blieben.

Außerdem waren die autochthonen Ortschaften des Umlands, die tributpflichtig waren, über die Dorfvorsteher – *tanadares* oder *gancares* – in die administrative Struktur einbezogen (cf. Diffie/Winius 1977: 333). Die Stadtverwaltung in Goa und anderen portugiesischen Kolonialorten wurde auch mit der Instand- und Aufrechterhaltung der Festungen, Garnisonen und der Küstenwache beauftragt (cf. Boxer 1969: 284). Die Armen-, Kranken- und Gefängnispflege, sowie Bestattungsdienste übernahmen in Goa die *miseri-*

---

[5] Feldbauer (2003: 95) rechnet pro Haushalt eines *casado* mit ca. zehn Sklaven. Je nach Rang und Funktion des portugiesischen Personals nimmt die Anzahl an Sklaven eines Haushaltes stark zu. Boxer (1969: 306) geht für normale europäisch geführte Haushalte von 15 bis 20 Sklaven aus, für wichtige oder ökonomisch gut gestellte Funktionäre von zwischen 50 und 100 Sklaven pro Haushalt und für reiche Händler und ranghohe Funktionäre von über 300 Sklaven.

cordias, Laienbruderschaften, die zur Hälfte aus adeligen und zur Hälfte aus nichtadeligen Portugiesen[6] bestanden (cf. Boxer 1969: 294–295).

Der Verwaltungsapparat, der alle sozialen, ökonomischen und weiteren Aspekte des Alltags organisierte, war, um es mit Diffie und Winius (1977: 325) zu sagen, auf eine „enorme Armee von Schreibern, Inspektoren, Richtern und Funktionären" (eigene Übersetzung) angewiesen. Die hier erwähnten Posten, die mit dem Schreiben befasst sind, finden sich auf allen Ebenen der Administration. Bei den Schreibern lässt sich zwischen Sekretären und Schreibern unterscheiden. Sekretäre waren im Allgemeinen aus den höheren sozialen Klassen und einem bestimmten Amt oder einer bestimmten Institution oder Person zugeteilt. Sie hatten dort vertrauliche Angelegenheiten zu betreuen und waren besser bezahlt. In vielen Fällen hatten sie gleichzeitig mehrere Ämter inne – so zum Beispiel das des Sekretärs, wie auch des Verwalters eines Handelshauses. So war es denn auch wahrscheinlicher, dass sie selbst als Akteure in Erscheinung traten und in ihrem eigenen Namen schrieben. Schreiber und Büroangestellte dagegen waren den Sekretären untergestellt und kamen als *homes letrados* eher aus dem aufkommenden mittleren Bildungsbürgertum. Sie erhielten ihre Ausbildung oftmals in Handelshäusern und Niederlassungen.

Die Arbeit der Schreibkräfte war stark reguliert durch die Manuelinischen Verordnungen von 1512/13 und 1521[7] mit Paragraphen zu Dokumentenform, Aufbewahrung und Postgang, die zum Beispiel besagen, dass offizielle Dokumente in den Schreibstellen unter Verschluss und in Kopie aufzubewahren sind, und durch die Philippinischen Verordnungen von 1597, die für die koloniale Administration und die Rolle der Sekretäre und Schreiber wenige Änderungen enthielten. Die niedergeschriebenen Regelungen sind Zeugnis einer langen mediterranen Kanzleitradition (cf. Wansborough 1996) und wurden hier auch für die Kolonien festgeschrieben. In Kombination mit der traditionellen Schreiberausbildung boten diese Regelungen klare Strukturen für eine Arbeit, die inhaltlich sehr variabel sein konnte und in einem hochkomplexen multilingualen und multikulturellen sozioökonomischen Umfeld stattfand.

Ab Anfang des 17. Jahrhunderts bekamen die Portugiesen im asiatischen Raum mehr und mehr Konkurrenz von anderen europäischen Mächten. Gleichzeitig befand sich Portugal, und damit auch seine Kolonien, ab 1580

---

[6] Bis weit in das 19. Jahrhundert hinein waren auch hier keine Nichtportugiesen zugelassen (cf. Boxer 1984).

[7] Zum Beispiel im Livro 1, título 13, 18, 35–37 und 59 (de Almeida Costa, M. J. Ed.: Ordenaçoens do Senhor Rey D. Manuel, da Real Imprensa da Universidade, levada a efeito em Coimbra, no ano de 1797, facsimile. Lisboa: Fundação Calouste Gulbenkian, 106–111, 142–144, 225–232, 400–419).

Administrative Schriftlichkeit des Estado da Índia

unter Phillip II. in Personalunion mit Spanien, bekam jedoch vom spanischen König das Recht, seine Kolonien nach wie vor autonom zu verwalten (cf. Newitt 2005: 175–176). Die europäischen Kriege und ab Mitte des 17. Jahrhunderts die koloniale Expansion der Niederländer, Franzosen und schließlich Briten in Indien führten zum Verlust zahlreicher Besitzungen. Spätestens 1844 befanden sich nur noch Goa und die Malabarküste sowie Daman und Diu in Gujarat im Besitz Portugals. 1961 wurde schließlich der Sitz des Vizekönigtums Goa als letzte Besitzung Portugals von Indien eingenommen. Der Verlust wurde allerdings erst 1975 von Portugal anerkannt.

3. Dokumente des 16. Jahrhunderts aus dem *Estado da Índia*

3.1 Die Quellenlage

Die Dokumentenlage für den *Estado da Índia* des 16. Jahrhunderts ist, was ihre Menge angeht, relativ übersichtlich. Das Erdbeben in Lissabon im Jahr 1755 hat viele Dokumente aus dieser Zeit zerstört. Die heute noch erhaltenen Dokumente finden sich vor allem im *Arquivo Histórico Ultramarino* (AHU) in Lissabon, in welchem Dokumente von verschiedenen Orten zusammengeführt wurden, in den *National Archives of Goa* (NAG) in Panjim, Goa, im Nationalarchiv *Torre do Tombo* (TT), Lissabon, und in der Staatsbibliothek Portugals (*Biblioteca Nacional de Portugal*, BNP).

Die Dokumente liegen in den Archiven in unterschiedlicher Form vor.[8] Im TT, aus dem die hier ausgewählten Dokumente stammen, sind die Dokumente in der digitalen Sammlung chronologisch und nach ihrem ursprünglichen Standort in digitale „Kisten" (*maços*) innerhalb der Sammlung *Corpo Cronológico* (CC) aufgeteilt.[9] Im CC sind normalerweise Dokumente, die in

---

[8] Das bezieht sich nicht nur auf ihre archivarische Aufbereitung als Originaldokumente oder Kopien und Mikrofilme (aus den 1950er Jahren wegen schlechten Zustands der Originale) oder digitalisierte Versionen, sondern auch auf die Tatsache, dass bereits die Originaldokumente unterschiedliche Formen haben. In Goa zum Beispiel finden sich aktuell nur noch Sammelbände von Dokumenten, wie Original-Abschriften für die Buchführung von unterschiedlichen Institutionen des *Estado da Índia* und Kopien von Dokumenten.

[9] Die Sammlung *Corpo Cronológico* ist in drei Teile aufgeteilt, welche grob verschiedenen Textsorten entsprechen. Teil 1 besteht vornehmlich aus Briefen, Teil 2 überwiegend aus Befehlen und Teil 3 aus Miscellanea. Es fällt auf, dass in der Sammlung *Corpo Cronológico* (CC) Teil 1 des TT ca. ab den 70er Jahren des 16. Jahrhunderts weniger Dokumente aus Indien zu finden sind. Einige Dokumente sind im CC Teil 2 und 3 zu finden. Dies kann aber unter anderem auch damit zusammenhängen, dass im AHU ungefähr ab demselben

einem inhaltlichen Zusammenhang stehen, in einer Mappe zusammengefasst. Diese Ordnung der Dokumente ist bei der Digitalisierung verloren gegangen. Von jedem Dokument gab es theoretisch mindestens zwei Exemplare: Das Originaldokument, das an den Adressaten ging, wurde als Einzeldokument auf dem Seeweg zwischen Indien und Portugal verschifft. Bereits in Indien wurde eine Abschrift erstellt, die in der schreibenden Stelle oder im zugeordneten Archiv als Kopie in Büchern oder Bänden[10] verblieb. Auch in Portugal wurden Abschriften erstellt und archiviert. Kopien können damit entweder aus derselben Schreiberhand wie das Original stammen – ersichtlich sowohl an der Handschrift, als auch an Formatmerkmalen wie Originalunterschriften –, es kann sich um zeitgenössische Abschriften handeln oder aber um archivarische Kopien aus dem 18. und 19. Jahrhundert.[11]

Insgesamt handelt es sich um formelle administrative Dokumente. Dies zeigt sich in der Dokumentenform, zum Beispiel in den Absendern und Adressaten, der Form und Sprache der Dokumente, den administrativen Dienstgängen, die die Dokumente durchlaufen, und inhaltlich.

Die Archive unterscheiden dabei verschiedene DOKUMENTENTYPEN, deren Benennung zum Teil aus den Dokumenten selbst stammt. Ich habe diese hier nach Formalitätsgrad geordnet:

Bula (Bulle), *Mandado* (Befehl), *Provisão* (Maßnahme, Vorschrift, Verfügung zu allen Lebenslagen), *Conhecimento* (Bekanntmachung), *Procuração* (Vollmacht), *Ordem* (Anordnung), *Carta patente* (Patente), *Certidão* (Urkunde, Bescheinigung), *Carta de confirmação* (Bestätigungsschreiben), *Informação* (Auskunft, Nachricht), *Justificação* (Rechtfertigung), *Parecer* (Gutachten, Meinung), *Alvará* (Lizenz, Genehmigung, Bescheinigungen jeglicher Art, von Soldanweisungen und Schuldscheinen bis zu Bestätigung der Identität einer Person oder Heiratserlaubnissen), *Recibo* (Quittung), *Rol da entrega* (Übergabeprotokoll, aus der Briefpost) und *Carta* (Briefe allgemein).

Für die vorliegende Analyse der Dokumentenform, des Textformats und der Schriftarten habe ich aus einem Gesamtkorpus von ca. 880 Dokumenten

---

Zeitpunkt das Volumen an Dokumenten aus Indien deutlich zunimmt, während hier für die vorhergehenden Jahrzehnte des 16. Jahrhunderts sehr wenige Dokumente zur Verfügung stehen (insgesamt nur 1 Kiste).

[10] Z.B. Kontorbücher aus der Verwaltung des *Estado da Índia*, in denen Kopien aller versandten oder ausgehändigten Dokumente gesammelt wurden. Andere Bände sind nachträgliche archivarische Zusammenfassungen von Originaldokumenten oder von ihren Kopien.

[11] Archivarische Kopien – vor allem von solchen Dokumenten gemacht, die als besonders wichtig oder erhaltenswert erachtet wurden – wie auch erhaltene Originale sind größtenteils an den König gerichtete Dokumente.

Administrative Schriftlichkeit des Estado da Índia

aus drei Archiven (AHU, NAG, TT), deren Emissionsort überwiegend Goa, für einige Dokumente auch Diu, Cochin, Chaul, Chale, Cranganor und Cananor ist, 70 Originaldokumente mit insgesamt 85 Texten aus dem Nationalarchiv TT in Lissabon ausgewählt. Diese sind Teil des CC, Teil 1, und reichen in ihrer Datierung relativ gleichmäßig verteilt von 1512 bis 1612.

Der hier untersuchte Korpus aus dem TT, CC, 1. Teil, besteht vornehmlich aus Briefen, *cartas*. Dieser Dokumententyp ist der am ehesten erzählende und damit am wenigsten formelle Typ der beschriebenen Bandbreite. Zum Vergleich, vor allem für die Auswertung der Analyseergebnisse, wurden aus den folgenden Dokumentensorten jeweils einige Einzeltexte mit einbezogen: *provisão, ordem, certidão, carta de confirmação, recibo, rol da entrega, parecer, justificação*.

Inhaltlich decken die hier zusammengestellten Dokumente eine breite Spanne von Themen ab. Dies ist unter anderem der Tatsache zuzuschreiben, dass alle Aspekte des alltäglichen Lebens, von der Struktur der Kolonien, über den Handel und Ausbau von Netzwerken bis hin zu Fragen des Zusammenlebens mit der autochthonen Bevölkerung im Austausch mit der Krone in Portugal geregelt werden mussten. Es gibt Dokumente über Diplomatisches, über Eroberungen und Schlachten, Jahresberichte, Administratives, Postversand und -empfang, Informationen zu und Bitte um Schiedssprüche in Konflikten zwischen verschiedenen Personen der Administration, Bittschreiben um Sold und Posten oder um Rückkehr nach Portugal nach vollendetem *triénio*, Anforderung von Personal, Listen besoldeter Soldaten, Bitten um Instandhaltung der Festungen und der öffentlichen Infrastruktur, Kirchenangelegenheiten, Beschwerde- und Bittbriefe der Einwohner von Goa und Cochim, Steuerangelegenheiten, Gutachten zum Markt bestimmter Güter, über die *Carreira* des Jahres, über Vergabe von (Jahres)Verträgen (der *carreira* z.B. Pfeffer und Gewürze, Bau, Holz oder Grundnahrungsmittel), Geschäftsschreiben, Warenanforderung, Warenerhalt und Quittungen, Warenausgabe für Schiffsladungen und Zahlungsanweisungen.

Form und Inhalt der Dokumente sind eng miteinander verknüpft und bestimmen zusammen den Formalitätsgrad. Die Textsorten, die sich dabei ergeben, sind offensichtlich auch den Schreibenden als solche bewusst, was sich darin zeigt, dass die Formalia in Form und Sprache jeweils recht homogen eingehalten werden. So haben Schiffsladelisten eine andere Form als Regelungen zum sozialen Zusammenleben in den kolonialen Besitzungen der Portugiesen. Trotz breiter inhaltlicher Variation handelt es sich aber immer um Dokumente der Distanzsprache, die in ihrer Form einer Tradition der administrativen und juristischen Dokumente sowie dem traditionellen Briefwechsel in der Administration folgen.

Bezeichnend ist, dass mit dem Formalitätsgrad auch eine Richtung in der Adressierung einhergeht: formellere Dokumententypen, also etwa die *pro-*

visão, gehen immer von höheren administrativen Stellen an niedrigere Stellen.[12] Weniger formelle Dokumente sind häufig umgekehrt an höhere Stellen der Administration gerichtet, wie zum Beispiel Bittschreiben oder Informationsschreiben. Auch deswegen werden Dokumente vom Vizekönig an den König, meist schlicht als *cartas* – Briefe – bezeichnet. Die Verbindung zwischen Adressaten und Textsorte könnte damit zusammenhängen, dass rechtlich bindende Texte, in Form und Funktion hoch formell, nur von offiziellen administrativen Stellen ausgestellt werden können und der Inhalt in den meisten Fällen weisende Funktion hat.

3.2 Analysen von Dokumentenform, Textformat und Schriftarten

Die DOKUMENTENFORM innerhalb der *Cartas* ist, auch über den Verlauf von 100 Jahren, recht homogen. Da es sich in diesem Korpus durchweg um Dokumente handelt, die versandt wurden, liegen sie physisch alle gleich vor: Es sind Einzelseiten, die zum Teil zusammengenäht, geheftet oder geknickt wurden. Das MATERIAL der Dokumente ist, soweit sich das erkennen lässt, durchweg Papier. Dazu finden sich aber in dem Onlinearchiv keine Angaben. Einige Dokumente sind in nicht besonders gutem Zustand. Die Ränder sind ausgefranst, Insekten haben mit der Zeit Löcher hineingefressen oder die Seiten haben Wasserschäden. Bei manchen ist nach Angaben des Onlinearchivs die Tinte ätzend oder wurde digital nachgearbeitet, weil sie verblasst ist. Bei anderen ist das Papier so dünn, dass die Tinte auf die Rückseite durchgedrückt hat und inzwischen beide Seiten kaum mehr lesbar sind. Wenige Dokumente befinden sich in gutem Zustand. In zahlreichen Fällen finden sich noch Markierungen des originalen Versands wie Löcher und Faden der Bindung oder des Verschlusses, Siegel(abdrücke) oder Knicke im Papier, aus denen sich klar erkennen lässt, wie das Dokument für den Versand gefaltet war.

---

[12] Bei den Vergleichsdokumenten handelt es sich fast ausschließlich um Schreiben von höheren administrativen Stellen an gleichrangige oder niedrigere Stellen oder an Einzelpersonen mit Anweisungen zu einem Sachverhalt. Einzig die *justificação* als Verteidigung bei einer Anschuldigung und das *parecer* als von Einzelpersonen eingefordertes Gutachten zu einem Sachverhalt richten sich an die Administration. Aber auch sie sind eben Reaktionen auf eine Anforderung von Informationen von höheren Stellen. So gibt es zum Beispiel 1545 ein Schreiben des *Governador* an die wichtigsten Mitglieder der Gesellschaft in Goa mit der Anweisung, ihre Meinung zum Pfeffermarkt in Form eines Gutachtens darzulegen (PT/TT/CC/1/77; Originalzitierweise des Archivs hier übernommen. Besagt in diesem Fall, dass die Dokumente sich in der Kiste 77 des ersten Teils des CC finden).

Administrative Schriftlichkeit des Estado da Índia

Die SEITEN stehen im Hochformat.[13] Die letzte Seite wird meist nur zur Hälfte beschrieben, sei es hochkant oder quer. Wenn diese Seite gleichzeitig die beim Versand außenliegende Seite ist, nach zweimaligem Falten gewissermaßen der Umschlag, wird die freie Hälfte mit Empfänger und Absender versehen. In der ANSCHRIFT steht im Empfänger der Titel und Name der Person, manchmal auch mit vorangestellter Präposition und Artikel, z.B. „a El Rey" – „an den König". In seltenen Fällen findet sich darunter eine Art Kurzzusammenfassung oder Betitelung des Inhalts des Schreibens. Eine Adresse im heutigen Sinne gibt es nicht. Gegen Ende des Jahrhunderts ist offensichtlich das Postsystem weiterentwickelt worden. Ab dieser Zeit finden sich manchmal Angaben zum Postweg wie „primeira via" oder „segunda via", ähnlich dem englischen „priority". Sichtbar abgesetzt vom Empfänger steht im Normalfall der Absender, entweder nur mit seinem Namen, oder mit seinem Titel und nicht immer dem Namen. Manchmal findet sich auch die Präposition „do" – „vom". ABSENDER der untersuchten Dokumente sind die Vizekönige oder Stadtverwalter, die Verwalter der Handelshäuser, die Kapitäne, die Finanzverwalter, Vertreter von Kirche und Orden, Sekretäre und Schreiber, die Rentmeister, Händler und Diplomaten, Ombudsmänner, Einwohner von Goa und Cochim und Personen mit geringeren administrativen oder militärischen Posten. ADRESSATEN sind der König, der Vizekönig, der Kardinal, die Allgemeinheit, Vorgesetzte/Inhaber höherer administrativer Posten im Estado da Índia (z.B. der *secretario de estado*) oder im Finanzministerium (*vedor da Fazenda*) und Geschäftspartner. Ebenso finden sich (An)Weisungen an Untergebene/Mitarbeiter/Verwaltung und Schreiben an Familienangehörige wie Geschwister oder die Ehefrau.

Als ABSENDEORTE, sofern sie angegeben werden oder sich aus dem Inhalt erschließen lassen, finden sich in den hier behandelten Dokumenten Goa, Cochim, Cannanor, Chaul und Chale in Indien. Um einen Eindruck von der gesamten Ausdehnung des portugiesischen Kolonialreichs im indischen Ozean zu bekommen, habe ich außerdem je zwei Dokumente aus Malakka und Ormuz und eines aus Ceilao eingeschlossen.

Die ERSTE SEITE wird mit „snor" (senhor) und einem Serif sowie einem Kreuz in der Mitte der Seite überschrieben (siehe Fig. 1). Darunter wird Platz frei gelassen, bis der Text beginnt. Um den Text herum befindet sich normalerweise ein bis zur Papierkante frei gelassener Rand. Dieser kann variieren, beträgt aber meist ähnlich wie bei heutigen Dokumenten 2–3 cm. Der rechte Rand ist derjenige, der am stärksten variiert. Hier ist manchmal kaum noch Rand vorhanden. Dies ist zum einen der Fall, wenn das Blatt bis an den Rand beschrieben wird, entsteht zum anderen aber auch dadurch, dass vor allem

---

[13] Ausnahme sind Urkunden, die insgesamt einer anderen Form folgen.

in der ersten Jahrhunderthälfte platzraubende Serife als Zeilenauslauf vorhanden sein können. Dabei läuft der letzte Buchstabe einer Zeile, entweder in allen Zeilen oder nur ab und zu, waagerecht bzw. in einer leicht schräg abwärts gerichteten Linie aus.

Fig. 1. PT/TT/CC/1/12/44, Brief von António Real an den König, 15.12.1512, Cochim.

Die BLATTEINTEILUNG beim Schreiben ist bis 1604 über das Jahrhundert relativ unverändert. Ab 1607 zeigt sich erstmals, dass nicht mehr über die ganze Breite des Papiers geschrieben wird, sondern ein breiter Rand an der linken Seite auf jeder beschriebenen Seite freigelassen wird. Das Verhältnis beträgt dabei fast 2/3 beschriebener Text zu 1/3 freigelassenem Platz. Ab 1610 ist diese Aufteilung in allen Dokumenten, auch in privaten Briefen, zu finden. Das linke Drittel wird freigelassen und für Antwortschreiben oder Notizen aus weiteren Geschäfts- oder Verwaltungsgängen genutzt. Zuvor standen Antwortschreiben[14] oder Notizen von Verwaltungsgängen unterhalb des Originaltextes oder umseitig. In manchen Fällen führte diese Technik dazu, dass es so viele solcher Zusätze gab, dass ein oder mehrere weitere Blätter Papier beigelegt wurden.[15]

Der TEXT hat keine Anrede oder Einleitung, sondern beginnt immer direkt mit seinem Anliegen. Als formale Auszeichnung des Textbeginns wird

---

[14] Solche Schreiben machen ein Dokument besonders interessant für den Vergleich von Handschriften und gebräuchlichen Schriftarten.

[15] Es gibt eine ganze Bandbreite an Umsetzungsmöglichkeiten für Absätze. Absätze kommen in manchen Dokumenten häufig, also alle paar Zeilen vor. In anderen Dokumenten finden sich keine Absätze, sondern das Dokument besteht aus einem einzigen Fließtext. Dies scheint auch nicht von der Textlänge abzuhängen, da es beide Varianten für sehr unterschiedliche Gesamttextlängen gibt. Vielmehr scheint es sich hierbei um ein Merkmal zu handeln, das vom Schreibenden abhängig ist und manchmal mit der Textstruktur zusammenhängt.

Administrative Schriftlichkeit des Estado da Índia

in offizielleren Dokumenten manchmal der erste Buchstabe als Initiale umgesetzt. Das Textende zeichnet sich meist durch eine *lauda*[16], eine Abschiedsformel, aus. Danach folgen standardmäßig der Absendeort, das Datum und die Unterschrift des Absenders. Diese wird über das hier untersuchte Jahrhundert traditionell in der rechten unteren Ecke des Blattes platziert. Erst gegen Ende des 16. Jahrhunderts gibt es Abweichungen, bei denen sich die Unterschrift entweder in der Mitte am unteren Rand oder direkt am Ende des Textes findet (z.B. in PT/TT/CC/1/82/33 oder PT/TT/CC/1/91/59). Wenn viele Personen den Text unterschreiben (müssen), wird der gesamte Platz unterhalb des Textes verwendet und manchmal noch eine weitere Seite oder ein weiteres Blatt hinzugenommen. Bei offizielleren Dokumenten steht nach dem Ort, aber vor dem Datum, der Name des Schreibers und des Auftraggebers. Manchmal, sofern zutreffend, wird hinzugefügt, für wen dieser Auftrag übernommen wurde (z.B. PT/TT/CC/1/55/25).

Die DATIERUNG ist von Beginn des 16. Jahrhunderts an standardisiert und steht am Textende.[17] Eine Veränderung stellt man nur in der Schreibweise fest: Zu Beginn des Jahrhunderts werden Tag und Jahr noch in römischen Ziffern geschrieben und der Monat abgekürzt. Aber schon ab 1513 wird für die Datierung der Tag regulär in römischen Ziffern, der Monat als Abkürzung und das Jahr in arabischen Ziffern geschrieben, manchmal, vor allem mit Fortschreiten des Jahrhunderts, ohne das Jahrtausend (z.B. 533). In manchen Dokumenten wird das Datum durch die Einleitung „ano de" oder die Zwischenschübe „no mes de", „dias do mes de", oder „annos" (sic) am Ende erweitert. Dies ist offensichtlich ein administrativer Standard, der für eine große Bandbreite an Texttypen eingesetzt wird.[18]

Damit zeigt sich, dass trotz kontinuierlicher Entwicklungen über das Jahrhundert kaum von den vorgegebenen Textformaten und etablierten Dokumentenformen abgewichen wird. Es ist nicht erkennbar, dass die Administration sehr streng bei der Durchsetzung der Textformate vorging. Den-

---

[16] Je nach Adressat, z.B. „noso snor prospere a vida e istado de V.A." (PT/TT/CC/1/103/130), „noso sor acresemte o Real estado he vyda de V.A." (PT/TT/CC/1/106/152) oder „beiso as maos de V.m." (PT/TT/CC/1/83/53). Die *lauda* variiert stark.

[17] Ausnahmen z.B. 1527 (PT/TT/CC/1/35/69): Datum in erster Linie; 1538 (PT/TT/CC/1/63/68): Ort und Datum am Textanfang, am Textende wiederholt.

[18] Im Gegensatz dazu findet sich das Datum in Urkunden, zum Beispiel in *certidões* und *alvarás* des Königs und weiteren Dokumenten solchen Formalitätsgrades, am Anfang des Textes und wird sowohl orthographisch ohne Abkürzungen und in Lettern, als auch textuell mit der Einleitung „do ano do Nacimento de Noso snor JH" angegeben – hier im Korpus z.B. in einer *carta de mercê* von 1535.

Tabea Salzmann

noch kam es zu einer weitgehenden Angleichung der Formen, weil die Schreiber es offensichtlich sinnvoller fanden, die von der Administration entwickelten Lösungen zu übernehmen, statt eigene Lösungen entwickeln zu müssen und weil sie die Grundzüge dieser Formen bereits vom Erlernen ihres Handwerks her kannten. Die Textformate entstehen und etablieren sich hier also in einem neuen Raum im Zuge der Kolonialisierung für und in der Administration. Gleichzeitig werden in ihnen Vorgaben aus dem Mutterland umgesetzt, die schon zu Beginn des 16. Jahrhunderts in den Manuelinischen Verordnungen festgehalten werden, welche wiederum auf einer langen mediterranen Schreibtradition beruhen.

Diese relative Einheitlichkeit im Format steht im Gegensatz zu der Vielfältigkeit und individuellen Ausprägung der Handschriften, die sich in den Dokumenten des 16. Jahrhunderts finden. Offensichtlich sind Schriftarten im 16. Jahrhundert, gerade auch durch die Entstehung des Buchdruckes, starken Veränderungen unterworfen. Die Handschriften lassen sich insgesamt in vier verschiedene SCHRIFTARTEN einordnen. Im vorliegenden Korpus wird als schreibschriftliche Abwandlung und Weiterentwicklung der *cortesana*[19] vor allem die *escritura procesal* genutzt, welche sich von Italien ab Mitte des 15. Jahrhunderts in die übrigen romanischsprachigen Länder verbreitet. Die *cortesana* selbst findet sich nur noch in wenigen sehr formellen Dokumententypen wie etwa der *provisão, ordem, certidão* oder *carta de confirmação* zu Beginn des 16. Jahrhunderts. Sie wird jedoch durch die *procesal* abgelöst, so zum Beispiel 1522 in einer *justificação* über die Fähigkeiten eines Schreibers in recht unleserlicher *procesal* (PT/TT/CC/1/28/5). Der Name *procesal* rührt daher, dass sie ursprünglich für Schnellschrift entwickelt und zur platzsparenden Mitschrift in Gerichtsprozessen genutzt wurde. Damit ist sie für administrative Zwecke besonders geeignet. Die *procesal* zeichnet sich durch relativ runde Formen und viele horizontale Ligaturen über den Wörtern aus (siehe Fig. 1). Aus ihr geht die *escritura procesal encadenada* hervor, deren Verwendung zeitgleich mit dem Auftauchen der *escritura procesal* erscheint – hier im Korpus erstmals 1513 (siehe Fig. 2). Hierbei handelt es sich um eine sehr runde Schreibschrift, deren Duktus keine Unterbrechungen des Textflusses und keine Lücken zwischen Wörtern in einer Zeile zeigt. Aus demselben Grund finden sich bei dieser Schriftart fast keine Ober- oder Unterlängen, keine Majuskeln und keine Serife.

Die *procesal* wird, nachdem sie die *cortesana* in sehr formellen Textsorten ablöst, in eigentlich allen Textsorten verwendet. Ab den 20er Jahren des Jahrhunderts über eine Zeitspanne von rund 20 Jahren sind die meisten Dokumente, die in *procesal* geschrieben sind, wegen der Menge an Abkür-

---

[19] Die *escritura cortesana* war vor allem im 15. Jahrhundert in den romanischsprachigen Ländern am Hof als formelle Schriftart in Gebrauch.

zungen und Ligaturen sowie einer Tendenz zur *procesal encadenada* kaum lesbar.

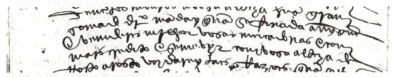

Fig. 2. PT/TT/CC/1/13/80, Ausschnitt aus Brief von Francisco Corvinel, feitor de Goa, an den König, Goa, 22.10.1513.

Ca. ab der Mitte des Jahrhunderts sind die Handschriften allerdings auch in der *procesal* leserlicher. Vor allem bei Schreibern[20] ist das Schriftbild der Handschriften in den vorliegenden Dokumenten ab 1538/39 wieder klarer und Wörter werden sichtbarer abgegrenzt. Ab der zweiten Hälfte des 16. Jahrhunderts beginnt der Duktus der *procesal* in vielen Handschriften weniger rund und zunehmend vertikaler mit leichter Schräglage nach rechts zu werden, so zum Beispiel in Dokumenten von 1539, 1544, 1545 und 1555. Auch in einem der Dokumente aus Ormuz (PT/TT/CC/1/83/53) verwendet der Schreiber 1549 einen vertikaleren Duktus mit weniger Ligaturen und einem klaren Einsatz von Ober- und Unterlängen, sowie Majuskeln. Dadurch ist die Handschrift, trotz vieler Abkürzungen, lesbar.[21]

Etwa ab Mitte des Jahrhunderts, ungefähr zu demselben Zeitpunkt, als Handschriften in der *procesal* lesbarer werden, beginnt eine dritte Schriftart, die *escritura itálica, humanística cursiva* oder *cancilleresca*, in sehr formellen Dokumenten Verwendung zu finden. Sie entsteht zu Beginn des 15. Jahrhunderts aus der *gótica cursiva libraria* (cf. Galende Diaz 1998: 212) und verdankt ihren Namen *itálica* ihrer Entstehung in Italien[22], den Namen *cancilleresca* ihrem Einsatz in den Kanzleien. Die Bezeichnung *cursiva* oder *humanística cursiva* gibt die Form der Schriftart mit langem vertikalem,

---

[20] Dies ist möglicherweise der Effekt einer Veränderung in der Ausbildung zum Schreiber. Bei anderen Schreibenden, wie gebildeten Händlern oder Mitgliedern des Adels, lässt sich in diesem Korpus keine solche Veränderung zum selben Zeitpunkt feststellen.

[21] Gleichzeitig gibt es nach wie vor viele Handschriften, wie zum Beispiel in einem Dokument von 1542, die sich durch einen runderen und kleineren Duktus auszeichnen. Allerdings unterscheiden sie sich von der vorhergehenden Phase, indem sie trotzdem Ober- und Unterlängen einsetzen und Wortgrenzen ganz gut zu erkennen sind.

[22] Die Schriftart unterliegt einigen Veränderungen. Im 16. Jahrhundert ist sie als *humanística redonda* wegen fehlender Ligaturen noch eine Druckschrift und entwickelt sich bis Anfang des 17. Jahrhunderts zu einer Schreibschrift.

leicht schräg nach rechts liegendem Duktus an. Sie wird in der Staatskanzlei Spaniens unter Karl V. ab Mitte des 16. Jahrhunderts[23] verwendet, von wo aus sich ihr Gebrauch bis Mitte des 17. Jahrhunderts in alle anderen Bereiche der schriftlichen Kommunikation Spaniens verbreitet. Auch in Portugal und den Kolonien wird sie ab der Mitte des 16. Jahrhunderts verwendet. Die Verwendung der *itálica* in Dokumenten der Kirche und der Orden zeigt zudem, dass unter dem Einfluss des Vatikans und der Orden diese Schriftart im kirchlichen Bereich schon früh für vielfältige Texttypen verwendet wird.[24] Unter diesen Vorzeichen der administrativen und kirchlichen Verwendung breitet sich dann über die 2. Hälfte des Jahrhunderts der Gebrauch der *itálica* auch in andere Textsorten aus. Spätestens 1596 wird die Schriftart auch in Briefen, *cartas*, aus dem gesamten *Estado da Índia* benutzt (siehe Fig. 3). Während in den ersten Jahrzehnten ihrer Nutzung zeitgleich auch noch die *procesal* und die *procesal encadenada* weiter genutzt werden, nimmt die *itálica* spätestens ab 1610 bis hin in das private Briefeschreiben z.B. 1611 (PT/TT/CC/1/115/121) die Domänen der anderen Schriftarten ein. Trotz der Domänenübernahme durch die *itálica* am Ende des Jahrhunderts ist allerdings auch die *procesal encadenada* weiterhin im Einsatz und wird bis in das 17. Jahrhundert hinein immer wieder verwendet, zum Beispiel in den untersuchten Dokumenten aus den Jahren 1540, 1549, 1588, 1604 und 1607.

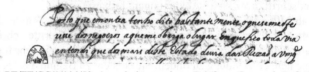

Fig. 3. PT/TT/CC/1/114/53, Ausschnitt aus einem Brief von Cosme de Lafetá an den König, Cochim, 15.01.1602.

Es zeichnet sich damit eine chronologische Entwicklung von der Verwendung der Schriftart *cortesana* zur *itálica* ab, wobei die *procesal* dem größten Wandel unterworfen ist. Diese Veränderungen gehen jedoch nicht linear vonstatten. Veränderungen in den Vorschriften und wohl in der Lehre des Schreibertums in den königlichen Kanzleien sickern über die nächsten Jahrzehnte durch die unterschiedlichen Schreibbüros der administrativen Institutionen, von wo aus sie sich auch auf das Schreiben von nicht administrativen

---

[23] Cf. Galende Díaz, J. C. 1998. La escritura humanística en la Europa del Renacimiento. *Espacio, Tiempo y Forma*. Serie III, Historia Medieval, Núm. 11, 187–230, hier 205.

[24] Hier im Korpus finden sich zum Beispiel Briefe von Mönchen wie der von de Frei Antonio do Rosario 1556 in einer sehr klaren, vertikalen und leicht nach rechts geneigten *itálica*.

Schreibenden auszuwirken scheinen. Diese Entwicklungen breiten sich zeitversetzt vom Mutterland in die Kolonien aus.

4. Standardisierung von administrativen Schreibtraditionen und Texten im multilingualen Raum

Die Unterschiede in der Umsetzung der neuen Schriftarten und in ihrer textsortenbezogenen Verbreitung zeigen sich vor allem im Vergleich zwischen Handschriften von Schreibern und Handschriften von anderen Schreibenden und gerade im Vergleich der verschiedenen im Korpus vorliegenden Textsorten. Hinweise sowohl auf die textsortenspezifische Umsetzung der Schriftarten als auch auf die Unterschiede zwischen Autor und Schreiber finden sich in zweierlei Hinsicht. Erstens etabliert sich in den späteren Jahrzehnten des 16. Jahrhunderts das namentliche Festhalten des Schreibers und Autors, in dieser Reihenfolge, am Textende. Dies dürfte aus den juristischen oder gesetzgebenden Texten der Kanzleien resultieren, wo es vorgeschriebene Form war. Zweitens gibt es einige Dokumentensorten, in denen ein erster offizieller Text vom Schreiber begleitet wird durch einen zweiten Text des Autors selbst, so zum Beispiel in den Wirtschaftsgutachten. Dieses zweite Schreiben des Autors unterscheidet sich im Allgemeinen sehr deutlich in der Handschrift und verwendeten Schriftart. Auch in Dokumentensorten wie den Bittschreiben zeigt sich, dass ein erster, von einem Schreiber aufgesetzter Text, in Form und Schriftart bestimmten Regeln folgt und dann ergänzt wird durch weitere Schreiben, die zum Beispiel die Legitimität des Anspruchs oder Erklärungen zu den Bearbeitungsvorgängen abgeben, aus anderen Händen und unter Verwendung anderer Schriftarten. So wird zum Beispiel das Originalschreiben von Schreiberhand in einer klaren *procesal* geschrieben, die möglicherweise schon Züge der *itálica* zeigt. In den Folgetexten eines Dokuments wird dann aber von anderen Schreibenden eine schnell geschriebene runde *procesal* verwendet, teilweise auch die *procesal encadenada*. Dies zeigt zum einen, wer die folgenden Schreibenden sind, nämlich zum Beispiel höheres Administrationspersonal, aber eben nicht Schreiber, oder juristisches Personal, das die rechtlichen Ansprüche des Originalschreibens prüft. Zum anderen zeigt es aber auch die Textabhängigkeiten im Dokument selbst. Weitere Texte werden offensichtlich als vom Originaltext abhängige Reaktionen und damit abhängig von diesem Schreiben betrachtet und unterliegen damit anderen textinternen Regeln in Bezug auf Sprache, Form und Schrift. Dies zeigt sich bei Bearbeitungsvermerken zum Beispiel in vermehrten Abkürzungen, Telegrammstil, aber eben auch in der gewählten Schriftart. Aus diesen Hinweisen lässt sich dann auch in den *cartas* darauf rückschließen, ob der Text von einem Schreiber oder dem Autor selbst aufgesetzt wird, auch wenn sich kein Vermerk hierzu findet. Und wir können die Entwicklungen in der Nutzung von Schriftarten und ihre Verbreitung in andere Textsorten im Zusammenspiel zwischen (neuen) Schreibtraditionen und der sozialen oder administrativen Stellung des Schreibenden ablesen. Damit zeigen Handschriften in Kombination mit der Eruierung der soziokulturellen Schreibgeschichte der Schreibenden und mit der Analyse der Umsetzung von Schreibtraditionen und Regeln in Bezug auf Schriftart und Text- und Dokumentensorte eine Möglichkeit, Schreiber und Autor eines Dokuments textintern zu unterscheiden. Autoren sind meist sozial höher gestellte Personen mit Entscheidungsgewalt und daher Agenten, während Schreiber das Handwerk besitzen, um einen Text unter Anwendung ihres administrativen und Textsortenwissens in eine für die weitere Verwendung des Schreibens angemessene Form zu bringen. Die Analyse von Handschriften in Kombination mit soziolinguistischer Information wie der sozialen Stellung und dem Posten des Schreibenden kann also Auskunft darüber geben, wie Bildung, soziale Klasse und Position in der Administration im *Estado da Índia* ineinandergreifen.

Die relative Homogenität der Dokumentenform im Verlauf des Jahrhunderts legt nahe, dass bereits zu dessen Beginn Standards für die Erstellung von Dokumenten administrativer Art vorhanden sind, die in den Kolonien angewandt werden, und zwar für viele Textsorten und Inhalte. In der konkreten Form, in der die hier untersuchten Dokumente vorliegen, zeigen sich also indirekt auch die Auswirkungen der geographischen Ausbreitung des portugiesischen Kolonialreiches und die soziokulturelle „Neuerfassung" eines Raumes inklusive seiner administrativen Aspekte. Die Veränderungen, die sich dann im Schreibwesen der kolonialen Administration ergeben, sind in vielen Fällen praktischen Problemen geschuldet. Dazu gehören nicht zuletzt logistische Details der Globalisierung wie die platz- und geldsparende Form der Dokumente, die Lesbarkeit sowie die Nachverfolgung und Überprüfung der Zuverlässigkeit eines Dokuments.

Neue Entwicklungen kommen dann entweder aus der hierarchisch höheren Administration, werden meist erst für formellere Texte verwendet und breiten sich dann nach und nach in andere Textsorten aus. Ein Beispiel dafür, dass es trotz der Manuelinischen und Phillipinischen Verordnungen von Seiten der Herrschenden einen Bedarf für klare Regeln gab, ist das Gesetz zu Stilen und Arten des Schreibens und Redens – „Provisão dos estilos e modos de escrever e falar" von 1597. Die Einleitung liest sich wie eine Protestreaktion auf vermeintliche Abweichungen von den Regeln in Bezug auf blumigen Stil und unangemessene Betitelung von Personen:

sendo eu informado das grandes desordens e abusos que se têm introduzido no modo de falar e escrever, e que vão continuamente em crescimento e têm chegado a muyto excesso, de que têm resultado muytos inconvenientes.[25]

Der König Don Philippe gibt in besagter *Provisão* an, dass er, unter Heranziehen von Experten, beschließt, die Dokumentenform unabhängig vom Texttyp vorzugeben. Unter anderem bestätigt er hier Regeln, die über das Jahrhundert bereits in Gebrauch sind, wie die Überschreibung des Dokuments mit „Senhor", das Weglassen einer Einleitung und die *lauda* und Form des Textschlusses. Der König unternimmt hier also Maßnahmen gegen Veränderungen vor allem in der Titulierung, die sich möglicherweise auch in den Kolonien ergeben haben[26], zumindest werden die Kolonien als Wirkfeld des Gesetzes explizit mit einbezogen.

Auch entstehen neue Entwicklungen, weil vor allem Schreiber in ihrem hoch komplexen kolonialen Umfeld, das sich auf allen Ebenen geographisch, klimatisch, soziokulturell hochgradig vom Mutterland unterscheidet, vor neue Herausforderungen gestellt werden und diese in Text und Form umsetzen müssen. Es zeigt sich die Spannung zwischen der aus portugiesischer Sicht peripheren fernen Situation der Kolonien und der Notwendigkeit sie trotzdem eng an das Mutterland zu binden. Hierbei wird dann vor allem deutlich, dass sie auf bereits vorhandenes Wissen, Traditionen und Regeln zurückgreifen. Dadurch werden Standards ausgebreitet, ausdifferenziert, aber eben auch gefestigt. Die kolonialen Verwaltungen entwickelten über die Zeit eigene Strukturen und Dokumentengänge. In diesen peripheren Regionen waren die Portugiesen mit einer vielschichtigen sprachlich-kulturellen Situation konfrontiert. In Indien wurden neben den regionalen indoarischen Sprachen Gujarati in Gujarat (Nordwestindien), Marathi in Maharashtra, Konkani um Goa herum (zentrale Westküste) und dem dravidischen Malayalam an der Malabarküste, dank der bestehenden Handelskontakte zu Afrika und dem mittleren Orient Arabisch und durch die Etablierung des Mogulreiches Persisch gesprochen. Diese komplexen Sprachtraditionen brachten ein ebenso komplexes Schreibwesen mit sich, das sich in vielerlei Hinsicht von dem Portugiesischen unterschied – andere Sprachen, andere Schriftsysteme, andere Texttraditionen und ein anderes Bildungssystem. Der Kontakt mit den

---

[25] „informiert über das große Durcheinander und den Missbrauch, der sich in die Sprech- und Schreibart eingeschlichen hat und der kontinuierlich wächst und einen großen Exzess erreicht hat, woraus sich viele Unannehmlichkeiten ergeben" (eigene Übersetzung, Don Phillipe, *Provisão del Rey Nosso Senhor, de como se ha de falar, & escrever* 1596, nach Caruso 1993).

[26] Da im vorliegenden Korpus die meisten Dokumente an den König gerichtet sind, findet sich wenig Variabilität in der Anrede und Titulierung. Der Grund für diese *Provisão* ist damit hier nicht nachzuvollziehen.

regionalen Kulturen und ihren Bildungs-, Schreib- und Administrationstraditionen dürfte die Etablierung eines Standards in verschiedenen Domänen des portugiesischen Kolonialsystems beeinflusst haben, wie z.B. in der Verwaltung und im Bereich des Handels mit Einflüssen darauf, wie man schriftliche Vertragsabschlüsse, diplomatische Verhandlungen, Währungsfragen etc. handhabt. Dieser interpersonelle Kontakt fand nach Disney (2007: 304–305) durch den Handel mit asiatischen Kaufleuten „right across the social spectrum, from viceroy to apprentice seaman" statt. Umso bedeutender ist die relative Homogenität der vorliegenden Dokumente in Form und Format, die auf eine starke Ausrichtung der Kolonien auf Lissabon und eine relativ große soziokulturelle Abgrenzung zu den regionalen Kontaktsprachen und -kulturen deuten. Der multikulturelle, multilinguale Raum führt dann dazu, dass sich Kontakteinflüsse in Dokumenten- und Textform, vor allem im Austausch mit dem Mutterland, in einer stärkeren Standardisierung der portugiesischen administrativen Textsorten niederschlagen.

Bibliographie

Arévalo Jordán, V. H. 2003. *Introducción a la Paleografía Hispanoamericana.* Cordoba: Ediciones del Sur.

Biedermann, Z. 2014. *The Portuguese in Sri Lanka and South India. Studies in the history of diplomacy, empire and trade, 1500–1650.* Wiesbaden: Harrasowitz.

Boxer, C. R. 1984. *From Lisbon to Goa 1500–1750, Studies in Portuguese Maritime Empire Enterprise.* Alderhorst: Variorum.

Boxer, C. R. 1969. *The Portuguese seaborne Empire 1415–1825.* New York: Alfred A. Knopf.

Caruso, P. 1993. Sobre o estilo e modo de falar e escrever. *Alfa* 37, 205–208.

Clements, C. J. 2009. *The linguistic legacy of Spanish and Portuguese. Colonial expansion and language change.* Cambridge: Cambridge University Press.

Diffie, B. / Winius, G. 1977. *Foundations of the Portuguese Empire, 1415–1580.* Minneapolis: University of Minnesota Press.

Disney, A. 2007. Portuguese Expansion, 1400–1800: Encounters, negotiations, and interactions. In Bethencourt, F. / Ramada Curto, D. Eds. *Portuguese Oceanic Expansion 1400–1800.* Cambridge et al.: Cambridge University Press, 283–313.

Feldbauer, P. 2005. *Estado da Índia. Die Portugiesen in Asien 1498–1620.* Essen: Magnus.

Galende Díaz, J. C. 1998. La escritura humanística en la Europa del Renacimiento. *Espacio, Tiempo y Forma.* Serie III, Historia Medieval, Núm. 11, 187–230.

Gómez Gómez, M. 2017. *Secretarios del rey y escribanos de cámara en el Consejo de Indias: oficiales de la pluma para el gobierno de la monarquía.* Nuevo Mundo Mundos Nuevos, Open Ed. https://doi.org/10.4000/nuevomundo.71367

Loureiro, S. 2007. Reconstituição e análise da documentação produzida por Afonso Mexia, escrivão da Câmara e da Fazenda de D. Manuel I e de D. João III. *Cadernos do Arquivo Municipal* 9, 12–49.

Matthew, K. M. 1988. *History of the Portuguese navigation in India, 1497–1600.* Delhi: Mittal Publications.

Mufwene, S. 2001. *Ecology of language evolution.* Cambridge: Cambridge University Press.

Newitt, M. D. D. 2005. *A history of Portuguese overseas expansion, 1400–1668.* London: Routledge.

Pelúcia, A. 2007. Os Funcionários Administrativos do Estado da Índia na Epoca de D. Manuel – Notas sobre os Escrivães. In Freitas de Meneses, A. / Oliveira e Costa, J. P. Eds. *O Reino, as Ilhas e o Mar Oceano.* Lisbon-Ponta Delgada: Universidade dos Açores & CHAM, 657–667.

Russell-Wood, A. J. R. 2007. Patterns of settlement in the Portuguese Empire 1400–1800. In Bethencourt, F. / Ramada Curto, D. Eds. *Portuguese Oceanic Expansion 1400–1800.* Cambridge et al.: Cambridge University Press, 161–196.

Salzmann, T. 2021. Portugiesisch und die indischen Sprachen – Verschlungene Entlehnungswege und ihre Bedeutung für den multilingualen Raum. In Haßler, G. / Schäfer-Prieß, B. Eds. *Sprachkontakte im Rahmen der portugiesischen Expansion / Contatos linguísticos na sequência da expansão (marítima) portuguesa.* Frankfurt a. M.: Peter Lang, 81–108.

Schneider, E. 2012. Contact-induced change in English worldwide. In Nevalainen, T. Ed. *The Oxford Handbook of the History of English.* Oxford: Oxford University Press, 572–581.

Wansborough, J.E. 1996. *Lingua Franca in the Mediterranean.* Richmond, Surrey: Curzon Press.

Marina Albers

Knowledge and Writing in the Spanish Colony. The Promotion of Education and Literacy by the Jesuits and internal epistolary communication in the eighteenth-century Province of Paraguay

Abstract. The aim of this contribution is to investigate the role of the Jesuit Order in disseminating education, knowledge and literacy in the historical religious Province of Paraguay, and to explore the extent to which their own writing activity represents the characteristics of the European epistolary discourse tradition. From a socio-cultural point of view, the Jesuits were committed to providing outstanding education in the colonial society through the *Colegios* which they founded and directed, and they disseminated knowledge and culture through libraries and printing presses. Against this background of increasing literacy in the colonies, a corpus of letters written in the 18th century in historical Paraguay by Jesuits, as writing experts, will be classified and analyzed from a discourse-traditional and pragmatic perspective. The focus will be on the questions of which textual elements of communicative distance of the European epistolary tradition are followed in the corpus texts and in which areas innovations or even linguistic novelties are implemented in the discourse tradition of the letter during the so-called *primer español moderno* (1675–1825).

1. Education and Writing in the Spanish Colonies

In the colonial empires of the Spanish Crown, the dissemination of the Spanish language and promotion of literacy went hand in hand with the expansion of knowledge, education and European culture. Although reading and writing had little significance for everyday life in the colonies, for the educated minority, these competences were nevertheless "el acceso al mundo de los privilegios europeos" (Bertolotti/Coll 2013: 24), which was initially reserved for the male members of the so-called *élite hispanocriolla* (cf. Chocano Mena 2000: 186). As a result, education initially functioned as a social and ethnic distinctive feature that separated the indigenous population from the Spaniards and their descendants, the *criollos*.

Education and literacy played a role not only in colonial administration and in the juridical context, but was also connected to religion from the beginning (cf. Elizaincín et al. 1997: 15–16). This was due to the fact that the Spanish Crown and the Catholic Church were closely linked and both pursued the same objective of disseminating of the Christian faith throughout the world:

> La educación estaba íntimamente unida a la religión, característica común a toda la colonización española que refleja la fuerte relación entre la Corona Española y la Iglesia Católica. Los objetivos de la educación básica eran tanto la enseñanza de la lectura, la escritura y las funciones matemáticas como la transmisión de los valores religiosos. (Elizaincín et al. 1997: 14)

In addition, education also played a key role in the evangelization of the indigenous population groups in the colonies, the responsibility for which fell under the purview of the various Christian orders. Within this framework, the *Compañía de Jesús*, "una Orden eminentemente intelectual y universitaria" (Gracia 2007: 143), was particularly distinguished by its commitment to education and its highly respected Jesuit educational institutions.

The main objective of this contribution is to focus on the interplay between socio-cultural and linguistic aspects of written language. In a first step (2.), I will analyze the role of the Jesuit Order in promoting education and literacy in the Jesuit Province of Paraguay, which was founded in 1607 and comprised the present-day republics of Argentina, Paraguay and Uruguay. For this purpose, I will briefly discuss the Jesuit *Colegios*, libraries and printing presses, which were considered important educational institutions and sources of knowledge and culture in the Spanish colony. In a next step (3.), the focus will be on the question of the extent to which the highly educated members of the order, as writing experts, themselves contributed to the development of the Spanish language in the epistolary discourse tradition. To this end, I will draw on a corpus[1] of one hundred manuscripts written between 1728 and 1765 by members of the *Compañía de Jesús*, who were born and worked in the order's Province of Paraguay, intended for internal epistolary communication within the order. In doing so, I will examine and show, on the basis of concrete passages from my corpus, to what extent the textual European epistolary tradition was carried on by the Jesuits who were expe-

---

[1] This corpus is the basis of my ongoing dissertation project on 18th century Spanish in the religious Province of Paraguay. The corpus was created through a digitization project in a cooperation between the *Universidad Católica Argentina* and the *Centro Universitario de Digitalización de Documentos e Investigación*, which initially made more than 5,000 manuscripts available as scans in the *Archivo General de la Nación* in Buenos Aires (cf. Archivo General de la Nación 2011). From this extensive corpus, I selected those texts for my working corpus that were written by Jesuits born in the Province of Paraguay (cf. Storni 1980) and then transcribed them manually. In the selected passages, "//" stands for a new paragraph and "/" for a new line. The resolution of abbreviations such as "V.Ra." is done by italics: "V*uestra* R*everencia*".

rienced writers and in which areas discourse-traditional innovations or even linguistic novelties of the so-called *primer español moderno* (1675–1825) appeared in the Jesuit letters. A brief conclusion (4.) will bring together the results from the socio-cultural and the linguistic points of view.

2. The Jesuit commitment to education

In addition to the evangelization of the indigenous peoples (which culminated in the famous *Reducciones Jesuíticas del Paraguay*[2]), the provision of education was one of the main objectives of the Jesuit Order throughout the Spanish empire. Due to the fact that, contrary to Spain, there were no municipal educational institutions in the colonies, the Jesuit-run institutions quickly established themselves and were sometimes among the most important in the colonial cities (cf. Chocano Mena 2000: 186–194; O'Malley 2014: 45).

2.1 Jesuit Colegios and the University of Córdoba

Providing a solid educational foundation and thus increasing literacy amongst the *criollos* was, among others, the focus of the Jesuits and other Christian orders, who established so-called *Escuelas de Primeras Letras* for this purpose. In Montevideo, for example, the Jesuits established the first *Escuela de Primeras Letras* in 1745, just twenty years after the city was founded in 1724, and it remained in existence until the order was expelled in 1767. In addition to basic skills such as reading, writing and mathematics, the Jesuits primarily taught Christian doctrine (cf. Ferres 1975: 50; Elizaincín et al. 1997: 13–14).

The *Colegios* were, after all, the institutions that provided the Spanish elite and their descendants in the colonies with higher education and, along with it, access to European culture and knowledge. In the Jesuit Province of Paraguay, the religious founded a total of twelve *Colegios* in the largest cities of the province: Asunción, Tarija, Mendoza, Santa Fe, San Miguel de Tucumán, Santiago del Estero, Salta, La Rioja, as well as the *Colegio Máximo* in Córdoba and in Buenos Aires the *Colegio Chico de Nuestra Señora de Belén* and the *Colegio Grande de San Ignacio de Buenos Aires* (cf. Page 2011: 114–121). As in the European *Colegios* of the order, great importance was placed on traditional humanistic education, which included grammar and

---

[2] On reductions in Paraguay cf. Armani (1988), González Rodríguez (1992), Hartmann (1994), Luna (2009), O'Malley (2014), Santos (1992), among others.

Latin lessons as well as rhetoric and, in larger *Colegios*, theology, philosophy, scholasticism and morals (cf. Page 2011: 439). The educational plan of the order, *Ratio Studiorum*, served as a guideline, setting the educational direction from 1599 to 1773 and thus guaranteeing the homogeneity and excellence of all Jesuit *Colegios* and universities throughout the world (cf. Gracia 2007: 148; O'Malley 2014: 50).

The most prestigious of the Jesuit educational institutions in the religious Province of Paraguay was undisputedly the University of Córdoba: "La Universidad de Córdoba, ha sido la expresión más elocuente de la cultura jesuítica colonial, y que todavía ejerce su influjo en nuestros días" (Gracia 2007: 137). After its initial foundation by the Jesuits in 1613, Pope Gregory XV and King Philip IV designated the *Colegio Máximo* a university in 1621 and 1622 respectively (cf. Rodríguez Cruz 1977: 341). Up until that point, higher education in the Viceroyalty of Peru (to which the Jesuit Province of Paraguay belonged) could only be obtained at the University of San Marcos in Lima, an institute established by the Dominicans in 1551. Now however, *criollos* from the entire province could also receive a highly regarded humanistic education in Córdoba (cf. Gracia 2007: 123; Rojas 1985: 68; Chocano Mena 2000: 201).

No less an example than the University of Salamanca served as a model, and just as in the latter, the philosophy of Aristotle and the theology of St. Thomas Aquinas were the main influences on the university education in Córdoba. Morals, canon law, sacred scripture and, later, mathematics and indigenous languages were also taught (cf. Albers 2022: 22–24; Gracia 2007: 130–142; Rodríguez Cruz 1977: 342). The close networking of the academic education, administration and bureaucracy ultimately led to the students enjoying a high position in later fields of activity such as the priesthood or the civil service (cf. Rojas 1985: 68; Chocano Mena 2000: 211). Thanks to the great prestige of the Jesuit-run university, Córdoba developed into an important center for education, knowledge and culture in the Spanish colonies (cf. Gracia 2007: 138).

2.2 Jesuit libraries and printing works

A further important source for the promotion of knowledge and education in the colonies were libraries and printing presses, with Jesuit institutions again taking a leading role:

> Los colegios más importantes contaban, además, con imprentas y grandes bibliotecas en las que había libros publicados en la zona, pero también importados de Europa, sobre casi todas las materias. (O'Malley 2014: 78)

Among books on theology and religion, which made up about 75 % of the colonial libraries' holdings, there were also classics of literature such as *Don Quijote* or other chivalric novels, as well as works such as Nebrija's *Gramática de la lengua castellana*, which found an interested readership among the literate elite (cf. Chocano Mena 2000: 224–225). As the example of the library in Montevideo, which contained over 2,000 books, shows, the libraries of the order were often the most important in the city (cf. O'Malley 2014: 78; Elizaincín et al. 1997: 14). This illustrates the extent to which the Jesuits were concerned with disseminating culture and knowledge in the colonies, as well as making it accessible to the elite.

In contrast to the libraries, which largely contained European culture and knowledge tradition, the aim of the American printing presses[3] – the first one being established in 1539 in *Nueva España* – was above all the generation of innovative types of knowledge (cf. Chocano Mena 2000: 225–226), such as works on autochthonous languages and peoples or translations of the catechism into indigenous languages "dado que solo a través del conocimiento del idioma autóctono —o más bien de las lenguas generales de cada región— […] se garantizaba una evangelización verdadera y profunda" (Albers 2022: 25). It was in this context that the Jesuits built the first printing press of the La Plata region in 1705, in the reductions in Paraguay. In that same year, they published the first printed work of the region, a Guaraní translation of *De la diferencia entre lo temporal y lo eterno* by the Jesuit Juan Eusebio Nieremberg. This *imprenta ambulante*, which travelled between the various reductions, was also intended to educate and promote the Guaraní population, as many of the books were produced in their autochthonous language. Works written by Nicolás Yapuguay, an educated indigenous man, were also printed there between 1724 and 1727 (cf. Gracia 2007: 164; Cerno/Obermeier 2013: 47–48; Chocano Mena 2000: 227).

This commitment to the promotion of indigenous culture by the Jesuits makes it clear that it was not only the education of the Hispanic elite that was in their interest, but also that of the indigenous population. While the printing press of the *Reducciones* began its work at the beginning of the 18th century, the towns in the order's Province of Paraguay had to wait until the second half of the century. It was not until 1761 that a printing press was bought in Spain for the University of Córdoba, as the increasing intellectual life made a dedicated printing press indispensable (cf. Gracia 2007: 165).

---

[3] The most important printing centers in the Spanish colonies were initially the capitals of the viceroyalties, Mexico (1539) and Lima (1584), but later also Puebla (1640) and Guatemala (1660). In other cities, printing presses such as those of the Jesuit Order only emerged in the course of the 18th century (cf. Chocano Mena 2000: 228).

Thanks to the commitment of the *Compañía de Jesús* to the dissemination and promotion of education and knowledge, the *Colegios* and the university were able to train not only civil servants and administrators, but also religious clerics and priests, who had always belonged to the *criollo* elite, and who worked as experts in the service of the Spanish Crown, the Catholic Church or even the Jesuit Order in the colony. Against this background, it is therefore of particular interest not only to look at the Jesuit institutions in a socio-cultural way, but also to ask how the written language of this highly educated generation of Jesuits developed within the framework of epistolary correspondence within the order and how this can be evaluated.

3. The literacy in the Jesuit Order

The corpus, which represents the literacy of the Jesuits in a medial as well as conceptual sense according to Koch/Oesterreicher (1985), is comprised of one hundred texts written by members of the order born in the Province of Paraguay (cf. 1. fn. 1), which served the communication of the religious among themselves.[4] The Jesuit texts in my corpus thus correspond exactly to the guidelines of the *Compañía de Jesús*, which has always attributed an important role to the epistolary correspondence within the order (cf. Morales 2005: 22):

> Las cartas [según las Constituciones] son lazos de unión, motivo de emulación, fuente de consejos, son el modo para tener una idea universal del gobierno, ocasión de acción de gracias, alimento para la oración común, aumento de la gloria de Dios. (Morales 2005: 22)

3.1 Discourse-traditional and pragmatic classification of the corpus texts

With a share of 88 %, letters take up the majority of the Jesuit corpus, but other smaller text types are also represented, as Table 1 (cf. Appendix) shows. Although the texts contained in the corpus belong to different text types, they can all be assigned to the same discourse tradition of 'letter' according to Koch's (2008: 62) definition: "No se trata de una tradición discursiva única, sino más bien de un conjunto de tradiciones discursivas que estaban organizadas en torno a la idea de carta". Finally, this discourse tra-

---

[4] Nevertheless, three of the letters of my corpus are not addressed to religious. These include two letters (JIU99, JIU102) from Joseph Ignacio Umeres to the governor of Buenos Aires, Don Pedro de Cevallos, and one letter (JDe503) from Juan Delgado to Doña María Teresa Rondón.

dition also includes diplomas, deeds and official documents of an ecclesiastical and secular nature (cf. Koch 2008: 62).

A general definition of 'letter' goes beyond the pure form of written communication and social interaction and also includes aspects such as the emerging communicative distance as well the possibility of planning the discourse to a certain extent, among others (cf. Álvarez 2002: 11; Bouvet 2006: 23–24; Koch 2008: 64).

Not only in linguistics is the letter considered an interesting object of study, but also in other disciplines such as history, textual criticism, sociology, anthropology of writing or history of editing (cf. Mosqueda 2021: 40–58). In linguistics, letters not only provide information about pronunciation, language change, linguistic history or sociolinguistic aspects such as the writers' degree of literacy, but can also "escibir la historia del lenguaje desde abajo" (Mosqueda 2021: 49), especially when the writers are so-called *peu-lettrés* or *semianalfabetos* (cf. Cano Aguilar 1996: 379). Even though the aspects mentioned can hardly be analyzed separately, the possibility of tracing the epistolary tradition in different historical and social contexts through the study of letters is considered the most important function in the context of this contribution (cf. Mosqueda 2021: 49).

Under the term *ars dictaminis*, the art of writing letters, the origin of the epistolary discourse tradition goes back to the Middle Ages and has its roots in ancient rhetoric. In 12th century Bologna, letter writing was analyzed according to the model of Roman rhetoric and reduced to a system, whereby a five-part paradigmatic scheme, modelled on Cicero's speech, was adopted (cf. Ueding 1992: 1040–1041; Pontón 2002: 40–41):

Part	Function
salutatio	Greeting (reference to the relationship between writer and addressee)
captatio benevolentiae	Winning the reader's favor, creating a respectful atmosphere
narratio	Statement of the facts
petitio	Request for action
conclusio	Conclusion (forms of politeness, well wishes, farewell)

Tab. 2. Scheme of the *ars dictaminis* according to the model of ancient rhetoric.

The art of the *ars dictaminis* was disseminated throughout Europe during the Middle Ages through practice-orientated manuals which were initially written in Latin, but from the 13th century onwards, they began appearing in the vernacular.[5] The five-part structure was adopted beyond the Middle Ages, especially for public and official letters, as these were often read aloud to the addressee and were thus similar in function to rhetorical speeches (cf. Ueding 1992: 1041–1044).

Accordingly, the letters of the Jesuits can be classified overall as a reproduction and continuation of the *ars dictaminis*, as within a traditional order structure in the context of the colonial period, they are considered as official rather than private letters.

In the conceptual continuum of immediacy and distance according to Koch/Oesterreicher (1985), private letters are classified in the range of immediacy due to the familiarity of the communication partners, spontaneity or affective and expressive participation, etc. In contrast, letters such as those in the corpus, which correspond to the epistolary tradition, are more likely to be classified as communicative distance due to the paradigmatic conditions of communication such as publicity, physical distance, reflection or absence of emotional involvement (cf. Koch/Oesterreicher 1985: 19–23; Koch 2008: 64; 1988: 26).

3.2 Continuation of traditional epistolary patterns

Letters that are part of the *ars dictaminis* tradition not only follow the traditional five-part structure – the order of the segments was, however, variable – but also strive to continue the formulas and rhetorical procedures rooted in the epistolary formulations of Latin (cf. García-Godoy 2012b: 360; Pontón 2002: 50). As was also prescribed in the numerous letter-writing manuals, formulaic constructions, especially in the parts of *salutatio* and *conclusio*, were intended to follow the applicable forms of politeness and address[6] that traditionally depended on the addressee of the letter and the relationship between the latter and the writer (cf. Ueding 1992: 1041; Cano Aguilar 1996: 380; Álvarez 2002: 13–15; Koch 2008: 62; Pontón 2002: 41). In the following steps, I will therefore limit the scope of this contribution to the *salutatio* and *conclusio* of a few prototypical letters from my corpus.

---

[5] On the history of the *ars dictaminis* cf. Ueding (1992: 1042–1044), for the *ars dictaminis* in Spain cf. Pontón (2002: 39–79).

[6] After the downgrading of the medieval reverential form of address *vos*, abstract nominal forms of honorific address of the 3rd ps. sg. according to the scheme [possessive 2nd ps. pl.] + [abstract noun], which were adopted from Latin, filled this gap, especially from the 15th century onwards: *Vuestra Excelencia* for viceroys and dukes, *Vuestra Majestad* for kings, *Vuestra Reverencia* for clerics, *Vuestra Santidad* for the pope, *Vuestra Merced* etc. (cf. Bertolotti 2015: 92–93; Koch 2008: 59–76; García-Godoy 2012a: 126–127).

Knowledge and Writing in the eighteenth-century Province of Paraguay

In the letters of the Jesuits, which were usually addressed to higher-ranking, venerable members of the order, the *salutatio* contained an individual salutation which at the same time expressed the rank or function of the addressee within the Jesuit Order, as excerpts (1), (2) and (3) from the corpus texts illustrate:

(1) Mi P*adr*e R*ec*tor Ygn*ac*io Xavi*er* de Leyva.// Aunq*ue* en estos meses imediatos e escritos varias/ a V*uestra* R*everencia*, q*ue* no se si an lleg*a*do, repito esta, saluda/ ndole afectuosame*n*te, y dandole la noticia [...] (FR450, 1760)

(2) Mi P*adr*e Visitad*o*r Nicolas Contucci.// Recibo la de V*uestra* R*everencia*, y digo q*ue* me alegro mucho de/ la determinacion de V*uestra* R*everencia* [...] (RdR449, 1760)

(3) Mi P*adr*e Proc*urad*or Juan Franc*is*co Carrio.// Aviendo llegado a este Pueblo con los/ 1530 y tantos Indios el dia 12 del Corri/ ente, no puedo menor de saludar a V*uestra*/ R*everencia*, y darle por esta, siquiera de a/ longe, un abrazo estrecho [...] (IR817, 1765)

In the examples, the *salutatio* shows the individual form of vocative address according to the scheme [possessive 1st ps. sg.] + [title/rank/function] + [first name and surname], while in the main body of the letter the reverential abstract nominal form of allocutive address *Vuestra Reverencia* for members of the clergy is used.[7] At the same time, these salutations create a respectful and honorific atmosphere within the framework of the *captatio benevolentiae* with greetings and well wishes (cf. Koch 2008: 65).

The letters that were not addressed to members of the Compañía de Jesús nevertheless followed a similar pattern:

(4) Mi Señora D*oñ*a M*ar*ia Teresa Rondon.// Muy Señ*o*ra mia, despues de saludar a V*uestra* m*erce*d, passo a dezirle [...] (JDe503, 1754)

(5) Ex*elen*tisimo Señor// He recivido anoche con la estimacion q*ue* debo la/ de V*uestra* Ex*elenci*a [...] (JIU102, 1759)

On the one hand, in the *salutatio* (4) to Doña Maria Teresa Rondón, the same scheme [possessive 1st ps. sg.] + [title/rank/function] + [first name and surname] is used, and the *captatio benevolentiae* also corresponds to the procedure in the other letter excerpts (1) – (3). In contrast however, the traditional scheme is dispensed with in (5) and the addressee Don Pedro de Cevallos, governor of Buenos Aires, is addressed by the honorific *Excelentísimo Señor*, followed by the abstract nominal form of honorific address *Vuestra Ex-*

---

[7] In the letters of the corpus, *Vuestra Reverencia, Vuestra Merced* etc. are used in the function of personal pronouns of politeness, with which the congruence takes place accordingly in the 3rd ps. sg., as shown in examples (14) and (16) (cf. Koch 2008: 77).

celencia, which was diversified for political figures (cf. Bertolotti 2015: 92–93; Koch 2008: 76).

On the other hand, the formulaic nature of the traditional letters was even more pronounced in the *conclusio*, where, in addition to politeness, well wishes and respect, a certain servility and humility were expressed. This is shown by the Spanish formulations fossilized in the epistolary tradition, such as *muy humilde servidor que su mano besa* or corresponding variants (cf. García-Godoy 2012b: 371; Pontón 2002: 54), which also appear in a similar variant in the letters to Doña Maria Teresa Rondón (6) and Don Pedro de Cevallos (7):

(6) [...] D*ios* me g*uar*de a V*uestra* merced m*uchos* años. Colegio, y Julio 12 de/ 1754.// B*eso* L*a* M*ano* de V*uestra* merced.// Su Serv*ido*r y Capellan// Juan Delgado (JDe503, 1754)

(7) [...] a cuyos ordenes estare siempre pronto sin cesar/ de rogar al S*eñ*or g*uar*de a V*uestra* Exelenci*a* m*uchos* años como deseo./ S*an*to Thome, y Junio 13 de 1759.// Ex*el*entisi*mo* Señor// B*eso* L*a* M*ano* de V*uestra* Ex*el*enci*a*// su humilde Serv*ido*r y Capellan// J*oseph* Yngacio Vmeres (JIU102, 1759)

It was precisely this traditional "besalamanos de las despedidas epistolares" (García-Godoy 2012b: 369) that was criticized in the eighteenth-century letter-writing manuals[8] for its formality and formulaic nature; it was no longer considered appropriate, and new formulations such as *Dios guarde a V.md. muchos años* were proposed instead (cf. García-Godoy 2012b: 371). In (6) and (7), the traditional and the innovative formulas coexist in the *conclusio*, while in the letters to members of the Jesuit Order (8) – (10), God's protection for the addressee is requested and submissiveness and devoutness are expressed:

(8) [...] encomendandome en sus s*an*tos sacrificios, y ruego a N*uestro*/ Señ*or* le gu[a]rde m*uchos* años. Cordova, y Dic*iembr*e 6 de 1760// M*uy* afecto siervo de V*uestra* Reverencia// Franci*sco* Ruiz (FR450, 1760)

(9) [...] No se ofrece otra cosa al presente, sino enco/ mendarme en los s*antos* sacr*ifi*cios y oraci*ones* de V*uestra* Reverencia,/ rogando a N*uestro* Señor g*uar*de a V*uestra* R*everencia* m*uchos* años con perfecta/ salud. Cordoba, y Dic*iembr*e 9 de 1760.// Mui rend*ido* s*iervo* de V*uestra* Reverencia// Roque de Ribas (RdR449, 1760)

(10) [...] Todos los PP*adres* saludan a V*uestra* Reverenci*a*, a qui*e*n N*uestro* Señor/ g*uar*de m*uchos* años no olvidandome en sus santos sacr*ific*ios. Santo/

---

[8] On the letter-writing manuals (sp. *manuales de correspondencia, tratados epistolares* or rather *tratados de cartas misivas*) in the *primer español moderno* (1675–1825) cf. García-Godoy (2012b) and Medina Morales (2012).

Domingo, y septiembre 22 de 1765.// M*uy* S*iervo* de V*uestra* R*everencia*.//
Isidro Rojas (IR817, 1765)

Despite the omission of the "besalamanos", these farewell phrases still seem very formulaic, rigid, planned and syntactically complex. They thus testify to little spontaneity and once again confirm the communicative distance of these letters, which are part of the tradition of the *ars dictaminis*.

3.3 Innovations and novelties in the discourse tradition

The epistolary discourse tradition reached a high point in the 18th century, especially within the framework of the Enlightenment; with the increasing publication of manuals, letters gained in popularity and took on an important role within the social culture of politeness. Therefore, the epistolary tradition had to adapt to the opening of the letter to new social, more private contexts and a larger field of writing experts created by the increasing access to written forms of communication and the growth of literacy (cf. García-Godoy 2012b: 368; Medina Morales 2012: 195). The most important innovations in the epistolary tradition involved the inclusion of everyday and private topics, the opening up to private individuals as addressees, and the expansion of the discourse tradition to new subgenres such as short messages (cf. García-Godoy 2012b: 364–367).

The discussion of everyday and private matters in letters is not a real innovation, since these have always been addressed by private writers, especially by *semianalfabetos* or *peu-lettrés*, in their letters. However, due to their expressivity, familiarity and spontaneity, these types of letters have hitherto belonged to the range of communicative immediacy and have hardly laid claim to a sophisticated style or adherence to rhetorical formulas and procedures (cf. Cano Aguilar 1996: 379–380). Thus, the inclusion of these new everyday topics in the epistolary tradition and at the same time in the letter-writing manuals represents a novelty in the *primer español moderno*.[9]

With the emergence of new subgenres such as short messages, etc. in the epistolary tradition, the discourse tradition expanded. In contrast to the traditional letter, the new text types are characterized by their simplified structure, their brevity and their simpler, syntactically less complex and reverential style (cf. García-Godoy 2012b: 367–368). The corpus texts of the Jesuits

---

[9] The letters of the Jesuit corpus also address personal issues such as health, material necessities, one's own experiences and desires, but also other novel topics such as the indigenous world etc. Due to the associated conditions of communication, such as greater familiarity, more affective participation, etc., the letters move more into the direction of communicative immediacy.

also include representatives of such text types with the designation "Papel de libranza":

(11) He recivido del Señor Alferez/ Don Fernando Arenas cinquen/ ta pesos de plata secilla p*ara* mis/ menesteres. Rio Negro, y Septiem/ bre 20 de 1765.// Isidro Rojas. (IR865, 1765)

(12) S*eñor* D*on* Gregorio Bachiller estimare, que por este entriegue/ por mi quenta al S*eñor* D*on* Thomas Lopez novecientos y 13 p*esos*/ y 4 r*eales* que seran bien dados. y quedo a los ordenes de V*uestra* merce*d*./ en B*uenos* Ayres y Oct*ubre* 11 de 1730.// Son 913 *pesos*. 4 r*eales*.// Raphael Cavallero (RC350, 1730)

In addition to the clear brevity, these two confirmations of payment are distinguished by the fact that they each dispense with the formal, schematic forms of address of the epistolary tradition and instead address the person in question according to the scheme [Señor] + [title] + [first name and surname]. Furthermore, the *conclusio* in (11), which has traditionally been characterized by formulaicness and respect, is omitted entirely, while the idea of servility for the addressee in (12) is expressed only by "quedo a los ordenes de Vuestra merced". On the other hand, individual parts of the epistolary tradition such as date, place and signature are retained (cf. Koch 1988: 28).

With the opening of the discourse tradition to new, shorter text types, a change in linguistic style also took place. Instead of the syntactically complex, reverential and formulaic style, shorter, more concise formulations were more appropriate for the new purposes, as the example excerpts (13) – (15) from corpus letters of the Jesuit Antonio Gutiérrez show:

(13) […] porque aun/ que siento que la Estancia quede sin Sacerdote/ pero sera esso menor inconveniente que el que/ se dexe tambien la Mission, como el año pass/ ado. Nada de nuevo por aca. N*uestro* S*eño*r g*uar*de a V*uestra* R*e*verenci*a* […] (AG166, 1761)

(14) […] y creo no sera la ultima, y no me fal/ tan bastantes ocupaciones que me llaman a di/ versas partes. Ba la cera, que es una arroba. Del trigo de alla no se cosa de cierto… El/ H*erman*o me dize io no no se si cojeremos trigo con/ dos negaciones. V*uestra* R*everenci*a nada me dize […] (AG494, 1758)

(15) […] y segun el numero, que avisan; para que/ aca no andemos como locos buscando, y/ haziendo diligencias para hallar lo que no/ ai. No mas. N*uestro* Señ*o*r g*uar*de a V*uestra* R*everenci*a m*uchos* años […] (AG174, 1759)

These examples illustrate how these clearly less syntactically complex, partly even incomplete, elliptical sentences were incorporated into the *narratio* of the letters, which otherwise correspond to the *ars dictaminis*. The change from syntactically complex, partly formulaic, traditional structures to the telegram style, which serves the pure transmission of information ("nada nuevo por aca" (13), "ba la cera" (14), "no mas" (15)), occurs abruptly and only selectively. Such extreme syntactic shortenings and simplifications break with the style of the inherited epistolary tradition and open up the discourse tradition to a new style.

The abstract nominal addresses according to the scheme [possessive 2nd ps. pl.] + [abstract noun] were highly diversified in the epistolary tradition, especially after the 15th century, depending on the social position and status of the addressee, and possessed a ceremonial, reverential character (cf. Bertolotti 2015: 92–93; Koch 2008: 72–76; Pontón 2002: 40–41). The 18th century saw a slow simplification of forms of honorific addresses within the epistolary tradition, adapted for the newly emerging audiences and addressees which no longer included only persons of higher rank and dignity, but also equals (cf. García-Godoy 2012b: 365; Medina Morales 2012: 196):

> Las transformaciones en las formas de trato se reflejaron de forma gradual y lenta en la tradición epistolar por dos motivos: de un lado, por la *(sic)* propias características del tipo textual, la fijación implícita que conlleva, y, de otro lado, porque la gran mayoría de los tratamientos usados en estos textos fueron realmente productivos en este género discursivo […]. (Medina Morales 2012: 195)

The form of allocutive address *Vuestra Merced*[10], which had been vital in the language since the 15th century and was already largely grammaticalized by the 18th century, finally replaced the traditional, deferential and highly diversified forms such as *Vuestra Reverencia, Vuestra Excelencia, Vuestra Nobleza* etc. in the epistolary tradition (cf. Medina Morales 2012: 202–203; García-Godoy 2012a: 112; 2012b: 368). From a pragmatic point of view, *Vuestra Merced*, which was neither limited to a certain social position nor to a certain relationship between writer and addressee, was also suitable for letters to equals and persons of any social position (cf. Medina Morales 2012: 202–204).

In the letters of the Jesuit corpus, *Vuestra Merced* in the abbreviation *V.md.*, which had been established since the 15th century, is not used for intra-order correspondence, but in the short message to Don Gregorio Bachiller (12) as well as in the letter to Doña María Teresa Rondon:

---

[10] The form *Vuestra Merced* was to evolve from the abstract nominal form of address to the polite personal pronoun *usted* through the new form of abbreviation *V.(d.)* (previously *V.md.*), which was also innovatively established in the epistolary tradition in the 18th century (cf. García-Godoy 2012b: 368; 2012a: 112–113). On the diachronic development of *Vuestra Merced* in general, cf. García-Godoy (2012a: 125–130).

(16) Mi Señora Doña Maria Teresa Rondon.// Muy Señora mia, despues de saludar a Vuestra merced, passo a dezirle, como/ el Maestro Don Roque Martinez, me dize, que Vuestra merced le ha facilitado/ el subministrarle luego veinte y cinco pesos delos reditos, que Vuestra merced/ me ha de entregar; por mi parte no ay dificultad, y assi sien/do del gusto de Vuestra merced, y dando dicho Don Roque recibo, seran/ bien dados. Dios me guarde a Vuestra merced muchos años. Colegio, y Julio 12 de/ 1754.// Beso La Mano de Vuestra merced.// Su Servidor y Capellan// Juan Delgado (JDe503, 1754)

The expression of politeness is clearly given by *Vuestra Merced* in (16), without losing communicative distance, respect or the complex elaborated style. This form of address is not limited to the social position of the lady in this example, but could also be used for any person, making *Vuestra Merced* polyvalent. Due to this unmarkedness and profitability, this form of address became generalized in the epistolary tradition of the 18th century as a general polite form of address (cf. Koch 2008: 76; Medina Morales 2012: 202–205).

4. Conclusions

This contribution was able to illustrate the interplay of socio-cultural factors, such as the promotion of education in institutions, and linguistic aspects of written language, which relates to the analysis and contextualization of the European epistolary discourse tradition represented in the corpus, thus demonstrating the significant role of the Jesuit Order in promoting literacy.

In summary, it can be said that in terms of socio-cultural aspects, the *Colegios* founded by the Jesuits and the University of Córdoba enjoyed a high prestige due to the excellent traditional humanistic education and they introduced important generations of the *élite hispanocriolla* to knowledge, eventually educating them to become experts themselves. While the Jesuit libraries disseminated traditional European thought and knowledge, the printing presses in the *Reducciones del Paraguay* served above all to generate new and innovative kinds of knowledge, which also included the indigenous world and its languages for the purpose of evangelization.

In this context, the members of the order who were active in the Jesuit Province of Paraguay were also writing experts themselves, demonstrating their written language skills through lively epistolary communication within the order and, in some cases, to the outside colonial world. The letters from the corpus of the 18th century, written by members of the *Compañía de Jesús*, fit into the tradition of the *ars dictaminis*, as they continue the traditional structure, rhetorical procedures and reverential style of letters belonging to the communicative distance. The use of the abstract nominal forms of address and the strict formulaic expressions in the *salutatio* and *conclusio* which characterize the European epistolary tradition, could be shown on the basis of example passages from the corpus. However, the developments in the discourse tradition that began in the 18th century also shaped the Jesuits' letters. In the *primer español moderno,* the epistolary tradition experienced an opening towards more private topics as well as new groups of people and formed novel text types. The Jesuit corpus illustrates these discourse-traditional innovations in that it also includes texts similar to letters, such as payment confirmations, and shows isolated changes in linguistic complexity through a shorter, telegram-like style. Furthermore, the letters that are not addressed to members of the order demonstrate the change in the polite form of address to *Vuestra Merced* that took place in the epistolary tradition in the 18th century.

All in all, these three aspects of opening changed the European epistolary discourse tradition in the *primer español moderno,* so that it moved with the demands and the changed social conditions of the 18th century, without completely abandoning the epistolary tradition and its patterns. In this way, the European epistolary tradition adapted to the increasing literacy in the colonies and the ever-growing circle of writing experts that emerged in the religious Province of Paraguay through the institutions and commitment of the Jesuit Order.

References

Albers, M. 2022. La proyección de la Universidad de Salamanca en las Universidades de la Compañía de Jesús en Hispanoamérica. In Torrijos-Castrillejo, D. / Gutiérrez, J. L. Eds. *La Escuela de Salamanca: La primera versión de la modernidad.* Madrid: Sindéresis, 17–27.

Álvarez, M. 2002. *Tipos de escrito III: Epistolar, administrativo y jurídico.* Madrid: Arco Libros.

Archivo General de la Nación 2011. *Fondos Documentales del Departamento. Documentos Escritos. Período Colonial.* Buenos Aires.

Armani, A. 1988. *Ciudad de Dios y ciudad del sol. El "Estado" jesuita de los guaraníes (1609-1768).* México D.F.: Fondo de Cultura Económica.

Bertolotti, V. 2015. *A mí de vos no me trata ni usted ni nadie. Sistemas e historia de las formas de tratamiento en la lengua española en América.* México D.F.: Universidad Nacional Autónoma de México.

Bertolotti, V. / Coll, M. 2013. *Contacto y pérdida: el español y las lenguas indígenas en el Río de la Plata entre los siglos XVI y XIX.* Boletín de Filología XLVIII/2, 11–30.

Bouvet, N. 2006. *La escritura epistolar.* Buenos Aires: Eudeba.

Cano Aguilar, R. 1996. Lenguaje 'espontáneo' y retórica epistolar en cartas de emigrantes españoles a Indias. In Kotschi, T. / Oesterreicher, W. / Zimmermann, K. Eds. *El español hablado y la cultura oral en España e Hispanoamérica.* Frankfurt a. M.: Vervuert, 375–404.

Cerno, L. / Obermeier, F. 2013. Nuevos aportes de la lingüística para la investigación de documentos en guaraní de la época colonial (siglo XVIII). *Folia Histórica del Nordeste* 21, 33–56.

Chocano Mena, M. 2000. *La América colonia (1492-1763). Cultura y vida cotidiana.* Madrid: Síntesis.

Elizaincín, A. / Malcuori, M. / Bertolotti, V. 1997. *El español en la Banda Oriental del siglo XVIII.* Montevideo: Universidad de la República.

Ferres, C. 1975. *Época colonial. La Compañía de Jesús en Montevideo.* Montevideo: Biblioteca Artigas.

García-Godoy, M. T. 2012a. El *tratamiento de merced* en el español del siglo XVIII. In García-Godoy, M. T. Ed. *El español del siglo XVIII. Cambios diacrónicos en el primer español moderno.* Bern: Peter Lang, 111–152.

García-Godoy, M. T. 2012b. Una tradición textual en el primer español moderno: Los tratados de misivas. *Études romanes de Brno* 33, 357–376.

González Rodríguez, J. 1992. El sistema de reducciones. In Borges, P. Ed. *Historia de la Iglesia en Hispanoamérica y Filipinas: siglos XV–XIX/ 1: Aspectos generales.* Madrid: B.A.C., 535–548.

Gracia, J. 2007. *Los jesuitas en Córdoba. Desde la Colonia hasta la Segunda Guerra Mundial. Tomo III: 1700–1767.* Córdoba: Universidad Católica de Córdoba.

Hartmann, P. C. 1994. *Der Jesuitenstaat in Südamerika 1609–1768.* Weißenhorn: Anton H. Konrad Verlag.

Koch, P. 1988. Fachsprache, Liste und Schriftlichkeit in einem Kaufmannsbrief aus dem Duecento. In Kalverkämper, H. Ed. *Fachsprachen in der Romania.* Tübingen: Narr, 15–60.

Koch, P. 2008. Tradiciones discursivas y cambio lingüístico: el ejemplo del tratamiento *vuestra merced* en español. In Kabatek, J. Ed. *Sintaxis histórica del español y cambio lingüístico: nuevas perspectivas desde las tradiciones discursivas.* Madrid: Iberoamericana, 53–88.

Koch, P. / Oesterreicher, W. 1985. Sprache der Nähe – Sprache der Distanz. Mündlichkeit und Schriftlichkeit im Spannungsfeld von Sprachtheorie und Sprachgeschichte. *Romanistisches Jahrbuch* 36, 15–43.

Luna, F. 2009. *Historia integral de la Argentina. Tomo II. El sistema colonial.* Buenos Aires: Booket.

Medina Morales, F. 2012. Los títulos de tratamiento en la España del siglo XVIII: la perspectiva de los tratados de cartas ilustrados. In García-Godoy, M. T. Ed. *El español del siglo XVIII. Cambios diacrónicos en el primer español moderno.* Bern: Peter Lang, 195–218.

Morales, M. M. 2005. *A mis manos han llegado. Cartas de los PP. Generales a la Antigua Provincia del Paraguay (1608-1639)*. Madrid: Universidad Pontificia Comillas.

Mosqueda, A. 2021. *Cartas sobre la mesa. Correspondencias editoriales en la Argentina moderna, 1900–1935*. Buenos Aires: Eudeba.

O'Malley, J. W. 2014. *Historia de los jesuitas. Desde Ignacio hasta el presente*. Bilbao: Mensajero.

Page, C. A. 2011. *Relatos desde el exilio. Memorias de los jesuitas expulsos de la antigua provincia del Paraguay*. Asunción: Servilibro.

Pontón, G. 2002. *Correspondencias. Los orígenes del arte epistolar en España*. Madrid: Biblioteca Nueva.

Rodríguez Cruz, Á. M. 1977. *Salmantica docet. La proyección de la Universidad de Salamanca en Hispanoamérica*. Tomo I. Salamanca: Universidad de Salamanca.

Rojas, E. M. 1985. *Evolución histórica del español en Tucumán entre los Siglos XVI y XIX*. San Miguel de Tucumán: Universidad Nacional de Tucumán.

Santos, Á. 1992. El Plata: La evangelización del antiguo Paraguay. In Borges, P. Ed. *Historia de la Iglesia en Hispanoamérica y Filipinas: siglos XV–XIX/ 2: Aspectos regionales*. Madrid: B.A.C., 673–690.

Storni, H. 1980. *Catálogo de los jesuitas de la provincia del Paraguay (Cuenca del Plata) 1585–1768*. Roma: Institutum Historicum.

Ueding, G. Ed. 1992. *Historisches Wörterbuch der Rhetorik. Band 1: A-Bib*. Tübingen: Niemeyer.

Appendix

Text type	Number	Characteristics
Carta	88	Letter to addressees Epistolary elements
Papel de libranza	2	Short legal acknowledgement of receipt Epistolary elements
Relación (de costos)	2	Statement of costs in bill No epistolary elements
Testimonio/Papel sobre testimonio de elección	2	Report on results of election/ election protocol No epistolary elements

Ajuste de cuentas/ Cuenta corriente	2	Statement of trade relations and costs in bill No epistolary elements
Estado del Colegio	1	Balance sheet of credit, purchase and sale No epistolary elements
Acta de venta	1	Sales contract with legal language No epistolary elements
Respuesta a reparos	1	Enumeration of invoice elements No epistolary elements
Contrato	1	Continuous text with details of deadlines, prices No epistolary elements

Tab. 1. Text types of the corpus texts and characteristics.

Katharina Fezer

„Le parfait négociant" als vollendeter Sprecher?
Wirtschaftsfachsprache und Sprachnormierungsdebatte im
Frankreich des 17. Jahrhunderts

Abstract. This paper aims to shed light on the language of trade used by merchants in seventeenth-century France, specifically on the relationship between this linguistic variety and the standardization debate fostered by the courtly and literary institutions of the time. The theoretical and practical sides of this relationship will be taken into consideration: First, it will be shown that an examination of the metalinguistic treatises of this century reveal both prescriptive, and therefore derogatory, attitudes towards this variety, as well as more descriptive and tolerant stances. Second, some select examples of syntactical and lexical features in model commercial letters, found in both handbooks for merchants and other letter-writing manuals of this era, will be compared to the corresponding norms advocated by the treatises. This analysis leads to the conclusion that the model letters, rather than complying with codified and prescriptive norms, demonstrate an adherence to their own standards which are guided by the practical requirements of commercial processes.

Abstract. Der Beitrag untersucht die Handelssprache im Frankreich des 17. Jahrhunderts, insbesondere die Wechselwirkungen, die zwischen dieser Varietät und der zeitgleich von den höfisch-literarischen Institutionen vorangetriebenen Sprachnormierungsdebatte bestehen. Hierbei werden sowohl die sprachtheoretische als auch die sprachpraktische Ebene berücksichtigt: Indem in einem ersten Schritt die metalinguistischen Traktate jener Epoche auf ihre Behandlung dieser Varietät hin untersucht werden, kann dieser Beitrag zeigen, dass sowohl präskriptive (und infolgedessen ablehnende) als auch deskriptive, tolerierende Haltungen gegenüber der Handelssprache in diesen Texten kookurrieren. In einem zweiten Schritt werden ausgewählte syntaktische und lexikalische Charakteristika der geschäftlichen Musterbriefe, die in den Handbüchern für Kaufleute sowie in weiteren Briefstellern jener Epoche enthalten sind, mit den in den Traktaten postulierten entsprechenden Normen verglichen. Diese Analyse erlaubt es, zu belegen, dass diese Briefe eigene Standards aufweisen, die sich nach den funktionellen Erfordernissen von Handelsroutinen richten, anstatt die kodifizierte Norm zu erfüllen.

1. Handelsmilieu und Sprachnormierung im *siècle classique*: drei Schlaglichter

Im Frankreich des 17. Jahrhunderts ist das Verhältnis der Sprache der Kaufleute zur gleichzeitig stattfindenden Sprachnormierungsdebatte von starken Widersprüchlichkeiten geprägt. Eine anfängliche Impression hiervon geben die drei folgenden Schlaglichter:

Erstens macht ein kleines Ereignis des Jahres 1698 deutlich, wie wenig vereinbar die Welt der Kaufleute und die höfisch-akademischen Kreise der Sprachnormierungsdiskussion scheinen. Damals widmet der Literat und Sprachtheoretiker Pierre Richelet die Neuauflage seiner Musterbriefsammlung *Les plus belles lettres françoises sur toutes sortes de sujets* nicht, wie sonst meist üblich, einer einflussreichen Persönlichkeit der höfischen Welt, sondern einem „Monsieur Burgeat, Marchand de Paris" (Richelet 1698: ii) – und sorgt damit für großes Aufsehen, wie aus den zahlreichen Kritiken, die diese Zueignung thematisieren, abzulesen ist: So kommentiert der anonyme Autor des *Théophraste moderne* spöttisch, dass ein Autor, der sein Werk einem Händler widme, sicherlich dringend neue Kleidung benötige.[1] Dem widerspricht ein weiterer Rezensent – schließlich handle jener Burgeat nicht mit Stoffen, sondern nur mit Spitzen – und hält diese Widmung für reine Satire, ähnlich einer Dedikation Scarrons an seinen Hund (cf. [Anonymus] 1701: 76). Eine derart offen gezeigte Beziehung zum Handelsstand wird demnach als schlicht nicht mit dem Anspruch der metasprachlichen Diskussion kompatibel gewertet.

Zweitens demonstriert eine nur wenige Jahre zuvor erschienene Publikation unstrittig, dass die umfassenden Normierungsbestrebungen des *siècle classique*, die neben der Sprache auch viele weitere Bereiche des gesellschaftlichen Lebens betreffen, den Handelsstand keineswegs ausschließen: Im Jahr 1675 erscheint Jacques Savarys *Le parfait Negociant*, dessen Titel bereits an weitere (auch) sprachnormierende Schriften derselben Epoche wie den Briefsteller *Le parfait secrétaire* (1646) oder die Übersetzung des *Cortegiano* von Baldassarre Castiglione, *Le parfait courtisan* (1580) erinnert und in dessen Vorwort auch auf einige sprachliche Charakteristika dieses Werks eingegangen wird. Savary schreibt:

> Il ne me reste plus pour finir cette Preface, que de prier ceux qui liront ce Livre d'excuser les fautes que je pourrois avoir faites dans la diction; ils doivent d'autant plus les excuser, que je n'ay jamais appris la Grammaire, ni les autres choses que sçavent ordinairement ceux qui ont appris la langue Latine. J'avoüe ingenuement ma foiblesse, mais heureusement pour moy il n'estoit

---

[1] „Un Auteur qui dédie à un Marchand, avoit certainement besoin d'un habit" (Anonymus 1700: 20).

„Le parfait négociant" als vollendeter Sprecher?

> pas necessaire d'un stile si relevé, pour écrire les matieres que j'ay traitées, & il suffisoit que je m'attachasse seulement, ainsi que j'ay fait, à si bien m'expliquer, que le moindre apprenty pust entendre, & concevoir toutes les choses que je luy propose, pour bien apprendre sa profession. (Savary 1675: [xii])

Einerseits wird eine grammatisch korrekte Sprache hier als nicht notwendig eingeordnet: Nur die inhaltliche Verständlichkeit, nicht aber die Form des Geschriebenen klassifiziert Savary als relevant. Trotz dieser vermeintlichen Irrelevanz findet die sprachliche Korrektheit jedoch Erwähnung – und allein diese Tatsache lässt darauf schließen, dass diesem Aspekt durchaus Wichtigkeit beigemessen wird. Andernfalls wäre eine derartige *captatio benevolentiae* kaum für notwendig erachtet worden. Auch bei einem ausschließlich auf den Handelsstand zugeschnittenen Werk scheint demnach keineswegs ausgeschlossen, dass die Rezipierenden an einer nicht formvollendeten Sprache Anstoß nehmen könnten.

Drittens und letztens können von Kaufleuten verfasste Texte gar von solch hoher sprachlicher Qualität sein, dass sie in Musterbriefsammlungen aufgenommen werden – wenn man der folgenden Erläuterung zu einem Brief in Barthélémy Piélats *Secrétaire inconnu* Glauben schenkt. Wie der Konzessivsatz darin gleichwohl deutlich macht, entspricht dies keinesfalls der Regel:

> C'est une lettre étrangere que l'Autheur insere dans les siennes, & certes soit que l'on remarque la grande cordialité de celuy qui l'écrit soit que l'on s'areste à la maniere judicieuse dont elle est composée, l'on trouvera qu'encore que ce soit un Marchand qui l'a faite, elle n'est pas moins bonne qu'elle est obligeante. (Piélat 1677: 89)

Der vorliegende Beitrag möchte dieses komplexe und widersprüchliche Verhältnis des Handelsstandes und seiner Sprache sowie der Sprachnormierungsdebatte in Teilen systematisieren.[2]

Vor allem zwei Bereiche werden näher betrachtet: Der erste betrifft die rein theoretische Ebene der Sprachnormierungsdiskussion im *siècle classique* und fokussiert den Status der Handelssprache in den französischen metasprachlichen Werken des 17. Jahrhunderts. Zu klären ist hier, ob und, wenn ja, auf welche Weise diese Sprache dort Erwähnung findet: Wird sie als eigenständig betrachtet? Wird sie bewertet und, wenn ja, wie? Und: Erstrecken sich die Normierungsbestrebungen explizit auch auf sie?

---

[2] Die bislang existierenden Forschungsbeiträge, die die Handelssprache näher betrachten, sind nur wenige an der Zahl und widmen sich vorwiegend oder ausschließlich den lexikalischen Charakteristika dieser Varietät, cf. Kelz (1994), Kuhn (1931), Wilhelm (2013).

Der zweite Bereich betrifft die sprachliche Praxis: Es werden Muster-Geschäftsbriefe, wie sie in Handbüchern für Kaufleute, aber auch in allgemeinen Briefsammlungen zu finden sind, auf die Übereinstimmung mit einigen der zur selben Zeit postulierten sprachlichen Normen hin überprüft und auf Basis dieser Kriterien mit Musterbriefen anderer Art, die oft Teil derselben Briefsammlungen sind, kontrastiert. So soll herausgefunden werden, ob die in diesen typischen Handelsdokumenten gebrauchte Sprache insofern eigenen Standards folgt, als dass die präskriptiven Sprachnormen in diesen Texten in anderem Maße realisiert werden.

Es werden also nicht authentische Briefe, sondern gedruckte Vorlagen untersucht, bei denen aufgrund ihrer Vorbildfunktion ein erhöhter Grad der Einhaltung dieser präskriptiven Normen und eventuell nur geringe Unterschiede zu den sonstigen Briefmustern erwartet werden könnten.[3] Da diese Werke jedoch auf die Bedürfnisse der Kaufleute zugeschnitten sind und ihre Verfasser:innen meist auch dem Handelsstand angehören, befinden sich die vorliegenden Quellen an der Schnittstelle zweier unterschiedlicher – und möglicherweise in Teilen entgegengesetzter – Bestrebungen: dem Streben nach (auch sprachlicher) Vorbildhaftigkeit entsprechend der höfisch-literarischen Vorgaben einerseits und dem Streben nach größtmöglicher Funktionalität andererseits.

2. Der Status der Wirtschaftsfachsprache in den *grammaires* und *remarques*

Für die Beantwortung der theoriebezogenen Fragen habe ich auf das von *Classiques Garnier Numérique* bereitgestellte *Grand Corpus des grammaires et des remarques sur la langue française* (Colombat/Fournier/Ayres-Bennett 2011) zurückgegriffen, welches die gleichzeitige automatische Durchsuchung aller enthaltenen Werke gestattet. Für das 17. Jahrhundert sind dies 26 verschiedene Schriften, die, um möglichst sämtliche Passus aufzufinden, in denen das Handelsmilieu Erwähnung findet, auf die fünf Begriffe *affaire**, *march**, *négoc**, *commerc** und *trafi** hin durchsucht wurden. Einige der Treffer wurden (vor allem aufgrund der Polysemie der Lexeme *affaires* und *commerce*) wieder aussortiert. Übrig blieben rund zwanzig für die Analyse geeignete Textstellen. Angesichts des großen Umfangs der durchsuchten Werke ist dies keine sonderlich hohe Zahl. Dennoch lässt sich auch in diesen Abschnitten eine Tendenz erkennen, die Wendy Ayres-Bennett bereits für die *remarques* von Vaugelas bezogen auf diastra-

---

[3] Für einen allgemeinen Überblick über die französischen Briefsteller und ihr Verhältnis zur Norm cf. Große (2017).

„Le parfait négociant" als vollendeter Sprecher?

tische und diaphasische Varietäten im Allgemeinen herausgearbeitet hat: die Kopräsenz zweier unterschiedlicher Einstellungen gegenüber Varietäten. Wie Ayres-Bennett (2018: 67–92) aufzeigt, vertritt Vaugelas einerseits ein präskriptives Modell, das von einer strikten Dichotomie zwischen richtig und falsch – dem *bon usage*, gleichgesetzt mit dem *bel usage*, und dem *mauvais usage* – ausgeht. Dem *bon usage* entspricht in diesem Modell nur eine Varietät: die Sprechweise der „plus saine partie de la Cour, conformément à la façon d'escrire des meilleurs Autheurs" (Vaugelas 1647, Préface II.3). Andererseits lassen Vaugelas' Ausführungen an anderen Stellen einen deskriptiven Ansatz erkennen. Dieser geht von relativen Werten aus, billigt unterschiedliche Varietäten und sieht je nach Kontext, Register, Stil etc. mehr oder weniger angemessene Varianten als gegeben an. Dieser Ansatz toleriert also auch fachsprachliche Charakteristika.

Eben diese beiden Ansätze lassen sich auch in einigen weiteren metasprachlichen Werken bezogen auf die Varietät des Handelsstandes erkennen, wie die folgenden Beispiele illustrieren.

Das präskriptive Modell tritt beispielsweise in Louis Alemands Bemerkung bezüglich des Verbs *défalquer* hervor:

> Bien des gens s'en servent en France; mais […] ce ne sont gueres que les Marchands ou gens d'affaires ou de Palais. Avec tout cela ce mot n'est gueres bon, il est fort bas, & je ne voudrois pas l'écrire. (Alemand 1690: 83)

Das Lexem wird klar den Berufsbereichen des Handels und der Justiz zugewiesen, damit gleichzeitig als diastratisch niedrig bewertet und abgelehnt.

Auch Marguerite Buffet stellt Kaufleute in ihrer Bemerkung zu den Zahlwörtern als unverbesserlich dar:

> On ne dit plus parlant des nombres, septante, octante, nonante, il faut dire soixante & dix, quatre-vingt, quatre vingt dix: il y a des marchands qui ne peuvent s'en corriger. (Buffet 1668: 87)

Der Ausschnitt aus dem Werk Pierre de La Touches schließlich ist im vorliegenden Kontext besonders relevant, weil er sich speziell auf Handelskorrespondenzen bezieht:

> Il n'y a que les Marchans qui commencent leurs lettres par, *J'ai reçu la vôtre*; il faut dire, *J'ai reçu votre lettre*. Les Pronoms possessifs absolus sont rélatifs; ils se raportent toujours à quelque nom qui précéde. (La Touche 1730 [1696]: 262)

Der Hauptsatz vor dem ersten Semikolon scheint zwar noch keine Ablehnung auszudrücken, sogleich folgen jedoch die für die präskriptive Haltung charakteristische Phrase *il faut dire* sowie die zugehörige allgemeinere

149

Grammatikregel, gegen die in handelstypischen Briefanfängen verstoßen werde. Andere Textauszüge dagegen demonstrieren eine deskriptivere Haltung: So finden sich bei Denis Vairasse d'Allais sowie bei La Touche unter anderem Definitionen und Präzisierungen zu Lexemen aus dem Wirtschaftskontext. Beispielsweise wird die Erweiterung der Semantik von *faillir* und *faire faillite* im Handelswesen oder der Unterschied zwischen *crédit* und *débit* präzise erläutert, ohne dass hierbei eine Wertung zu erkennen wäre:

> Les marchands disent *Faillir*, & *faire faillire* pour faire banqueroute. (Vairasse d'Allais 1681: 365)

> *Achalander, acréditer. Ce Marchand est bien achalandé. Ce Marchand est bien acrédité*, sont des expressions qui signifient deux choses diférentes. La prémiére veut dire *un Marchand qui a un bon débit*, & la séconde signifie *un Marchand qui a un bon crédit*. (La Touche 1730 [1696]: 10)

Eine Bemerkung Dominique Bouhours' schließlich zeugt von einem Bewusstsein für die Durchlässigkeit der einzelnen Varietäten. Ein möglicher Einfluss der Wirtschaftsfachsprache auf die Varietät des höfisch-galanten Kontextes wird hier – zumindest bezüglich der lexikalisch-semantischen Ebene – nicht als negativ bewertet:

> [On] a dérobé aux Marchands celle (l'expression, Anm. KF) d'un bon *commerce*, pour exprimer que ceux à qui on l'applique sont gens avec qui on peut vivre commodement. (Bouhours 1693: 113)

Allen bislang gezeigten Erwähnungen ist jedoch gemeinsam, dass diese zwar auf einige sprachliche Details hinweisen, jedoch nicht von der Sprache der Kaufleute (oder auch der jeweiligen Sprache anderer Berufsgruppen) als eigenständiger Sprache mit eigenen Bedürfnissen sprechen. Ansätze eines solchen Bewusstseins finden sich lediglich bei Jean Macé, der zwischen den Erfordernissen der *langues d'érudition et de doctrine* und der *langues du pays et de commerce* unterscheidet:

> Surquoy il est encore besoin de remarquer vne *distinction* importante. C'est que dans les Langues du bas degré, ou de commerce: il faut plustost aprandre tout le menu détail, & les mots particuliers qui viennent en vzage: que non pas la phraze, & les delicatesses. Au contraire, dans les Langues d'erudition, au degré mediocre & exquis, c'est superfluité d'aprandre mille vetilles; estant assez de sçauoir la phraze, les ornemans, & ce qui entre dans l'emploi des Sçiences. Car je demande au mieux disant Latin, qui soit en France; que sert de sçauoir en cete Langue Romaine, tout le menu équipage d'vn Nauire? tous les vtansiles d'vne cuisine? tous les outils d'vn Cordonnier? […] A parler sinceremant, tout ce ménage n'est bon que dans les Langues du pays & de commerce. […] Il faut sçauoir precisémant ce qu'on appelle le couuert sur vne

"Le parfait négociant" als vollendeter Sprecher?

table, le cabinet dans vne chambre, le degré ou l'escalier dans vne maison, le pont-leuis dans vn château: non pas en ces occasions s'amuzer à faire des periphrazes, & des circonlocutions. (Macé 1651: 13–14)

Macé nennt hier zwar einige Berufsbereiche, differenziert aber nicht genauer zwischen einzelnen Fachsprachen und meint mit *langue de commerce* zudem vermutlich ohnehin weniger die Sprache des Handels als – allgemeiner – das, was man die Sprache des täglichen Umgangs nennen könnte. Auch widerspricht sich Macé teils, wenn er die *langues de commerce* als die in allen Bereichen am wenigsten ausgebauten Sprachen ansieht, ihnen aber gleichzeitig den differenziertesten Wortschatz zuweist. Dennoch zeigen auch seine Ausführungen, dass es zu kurz greifen würde, die metasprachlichen Werke des *siècle classique* als Schriften darzustellen, die nur eine einzige Varietät vorschreiben, zeugen sie doch von einem Bewusstsein für unterschiedliche sprachliche Bedürfnisse und betonen die Wichtigkeit der Funktionalität von Sprachen in verschiedenen Bereichen.

3. Musterkorrespondenzen als Ort der Realisierung präskriptiver Sprachnormen?

3.1 Das Untersuchungskorpus

Ob sich diese Funktionalität auch in der Praxis an den Musterkorrespondenzen aus dem Handelskontext zeigt, soll nun in einem zweiten Schritt diskutiert werden. Das Korpus dieser Pilotstudie besteht aus allen Briefvorlagen, die in den folgenden sieben Werken enthalten sind:

- Anonymus: *Der neue Wegweiser der Französischen Sprach* (1686)
- Irson, Claude: *Pratique generale et methodique des changes etrangers* (1687)
- La Grue, Thomas: *La grammaire françoise* (1678)
- La Porte, Mathieu: *La science des Negocians et Teneurs de Livres, ou Instruction generale Pour tout ce qui se pratique dans les comptoirs des Negocians* (1704)
- Marin, Pieter: *Nouvelle metode pour apprendre les Principes & l'Usage des langues françoise et hollandoise* (1712)
- Piélat, Barthélémy: *L'anti-grammaire* (1673)
- Savary, Jacques: *Le parfait Negociant* (1675)

Insgesamt handelt es sich um 180 Briefe, die zusammen rund 21.000 *tokens* umfassen. 113 Briefe hiervon sind als Handelsbriefe einzuordnen. Sie enthalten vor allem Musterlösungen für folgende Themenstellungen: Zahlungs-

oder Kreditaufforderungen und -bestätigungen, Empfehlungsschreiben, Begleitschreiben für Warensendungen, Informationsschreiben über getätigte Geschäfte sowie über neu eingetroffene oder gewünschte Waren samt Kaufempfehlungen oder auch Planungen für den Aufbau eines gemeinsamen Geschäfts. Die Themen der übrigen 67 Briefe sind sehr unterschiedlich: Galante Korrespondenzen samt Liebeserklärungen finden sich darunter, aber auch Schreiben an Familienmitglieder, Einladungen zu Hochzeiten und Taufen, Beileidsschreiben und Ratschläge für eine angemessene Lebensführung. Da Handelsbriefe tendenziell kürzer und oft sehr formelhaft sind – insbesondere, wenn es sich um sogenannte Wechselbriefe handelt – ist das Verhältnis zwischen beiden Textgruppen bezüglich der Wortanzahl wieder ausgewogen: Auf beide Bereiche entfallen gut 10.000 Wörter.

	Handelsbriefe	sonstige Briefe
Anzahl Briefe	GESAMT: 113 Anonymus: 7 Irson: 14 La Grue: 32 La Porte: 10 Marin: 13 Piélat: 19 Savary: 18	GESAMT: 67 Anonymus: 4 La Grue: 12 Marin: 20 Piélat: 31
Anzahl Wörter	10.747	10.565

Tab. 1. Das Untersuchungskorpus in Zahlen.

Die ersten vier der aufgeführten Werke sind für Sprachlernende aus dem deutschen oder flämischen Sprachraum bestimmt, die übrigen drei für französische Kaufleute. Wie sehr sich die Sphären des Handelswesens und der Sprachdebatte überschneiden können, wird an der Person von Claude Irson deutlich: Dieser ist sowohl Philologe als auch Mathematiker, verfasst dementsprechend sowohl die *Nouvelle méthode pour apprendre facilement les principes et la pureté de la langue françoise*, die Teil des *Grand Corpus* ist, als auch verschiedene, für unterschiedliche Berufszweige konzipierte Lehrwerke der Arithmetik, darunter den hier berücksichtigten Ratgeber für Kaufleute. Von den übrigen Autoren sind La Grue, Marin und Piélat aus Frankreich stammende, in die Niederlande emigrierte Hugenotten. La Porte und Savary gehören dagegen dem Wirtschaftsmilieu Frankreichs an: La Porte ist als Rechnungsbuchhalter tätig, Savary zunächst als Kaufmann und anschließend in der königlichen Staatskanzlei.

Auch bei den zu untersuchenden sprachlichen Merkmalen musste für die Pilotstudie eine Auswahl getroffen werden. Ausgewählt wurden Normen, die besonders relevant für Briefe erscheinen oder, wie bereits in den Zitaten von Alemand und Buffet gesehen, typische Fehler des Handelsstandes postulieren. Weitere Auswahlkriterien waren die Häufigkeit des normierten Sprachphänomens in den Texten sowie die leichte, möglichst (teil)automatisierte – d.h. mittels einer Volltextsuche erfolgende – Überprüfbarkeit der Regeln und schließlich die Relevanz dieser Regeln innerhalb der Sprachnormierungsdebatte, die sich daran messen lässt, wie häufig und intensiv die entsprechenden Phänomene in den metasprachlichen Werken diskutiert werden.[4]

Auf Basis dieser Kriterien wurden drei Gruppen von präskriptiven Normen selektiert: erstens die Regeln bezüglich einiger Ellipsen, die typischerweise in den formelhaften Wendungen zu Beginn eines Briefs auftauchen, zweitens die Vorgaben zu Zahlwörtern und drittens die Vorschriften zu weiteren elliptischen Satzkonstruktionen, so zur Auslassung des Subjektpronomens oder der Weglassung weiterer Satzelemente in Koordinationskonstruktionen.

3.2 Elliptische Formeln am Briefbeginn

Die erste der untersuchten Normvorgaben wird von den weiteren elliptischen Konstruktionen gesondert behandelt, weil es sich um eine briefspezifische Regel handelt, gegen die – laut dem bereits zitierten Pierre de La Touche – gerade Kaufleute besonders oft verstoßen. Kaufleute, so La Touche, bestätigen den Empfang einer Korrespondenz zu Beginn des eigenen Briefs schriftlich, indem sie das Wort *lettre* auslassen und lediglich Pronomen verwenden, die sich darauf beziehen (cf. La Touche 1730 [1696]: 262). Die Forderung La Touches, das Bezugswort immer auszudrücken, findet sich auch in vielen weiteren *grammaires* und *remarques*, unter anderem in Gilles Ménages *Observations sur la langue françoise*. Ménage erwähnt zusätzlich weitere Beispiele für Ellipsen dieser Art, wie die Weglassung des Monats in „le premier du courant, du passé":

> *I'ay reçû la vostre. I'ay reçû l'honneur de la vostre. Le premier du courant, du passé.* [...] Toutes ces façons de parler ne sont pas du bel usage. Dites, *I'ay reçû vostre lettre*: [...] Le premier de ce mois: Le premier de l'autre mois: Le premier du mois passé [...]. Il faut dire aussi, *Ie vous écris cette lettre*: ou simplement, *Ie vous écris*. (Ménage 1675: 506)

Die Ergebnisse der Durchsuchung des Korpus auf diese beiden Phänomene hin zeigen deutliche Unterschiede zwischen den Handels- und den sonstigen Briefen: 70 Auslassungen von *lettre* in den Handelsbriefen stehen lediglich

---

[4] Auch hierfür ist die Möglichkeit der Volltextsuche im *Grand Corpus* sehr nützlich.

9 in den weiteren Korrespondenzen gegenüber. Die Auslassungen des Monats belaufen sich auf 24 versus 2 Okkurrenzen.

	Handelsbriefe	sonstige Briefe
Auslassung *lettre*	GESAMT: 72 Anonymus: 3 Irson: 20 La Grue: 20 La Porte: 10 Marin: 14 Piélat: 3 Savary: 2	GESAMT: 9 Anonymus: 2 La Grue: 1 Piélat: 6
Auslassung Monat	24	2

Tab. 2. Anzahl der Auslassungen des Lexems *lettre* sowie des Monats.

Dieses grammatisch-diskursive Merkmal scheint demnach in der Tat typisch für Briefe aus dem Handelskontext zu sein, was vermutlich durch deren stärkere Formalisierung bedingt ist: Typischerweise beginnen sie mit der Empfangsbestätigung des letzten erhaltenen Schreibens samt Datumsangabe, wie an den im Folgenden aufgeführten zwei Beispielen ersichtlich ist – ein Usus, der von großem praktischem Nutzen im geschäftlichen Kontext ist, da er die chronologische Einordnung der Korrespondenzen erleichtert und diesbezüglichen Verbindlichkeiten wie beispielsweise die Setzung und Einhaltung von Bestell- und Zahlungsfristen entgegenkommt:

(1) Monsieur. La chere vostre du 9. Courant m'a esté doublement agreable [...]. (La Grue 1678: III, 84)

(2) Le 7. du courant fut le jour de ma derniere, à laquelle je me refere. (La Porte 1704: 333)

Offenbar bestand also nicht die Absicht, diese Praxis in den Mustervorlagen an die Vorgaben der Sprachtheoretiker:innen anzupassen. Vor allem im Falle Claude Irsons verwundert dieser Widerspruch zwischen Sprachtheorie und Sprachpraxis zunächst, da Irson beide Bereiche repräsentiert. Ein Blick in Irsons *Nouvelle methode pour apprendre facilement les principes et la pureté de la langue françoise,* zeigt jedoch, dass Irsons der einzige Sprachtheoretiker ist, der Auslassungen dieser Art gutheißt und ihnen gar „plus de grace & de netteté" (Irson 1662: 85) zuschreibt. Ob er zu diesem Urteil aufgrund seiner Eingebundenheit in den Wirtschaftskontext gelangt ist, ob hier also die ihm vertraute Praxis seine Sprachtheorie beeinflusst haben könnte, ist eine Frage, die mangels weiterer Daten zum gegenwärtigen Zeitpunkt offenbleiben muss.

3.3 Zahlwörter

Ein eindeutigerer Widerspruch zwischen Theorie und Praxis findet sich bei Irson, was die Zahlwörter betrifft. Auch diesbezügliche „Fehler" werden teils explizit dem Handelsstand zugeschrieben – siehe die in Abschnitt 2 bereits erwähnte Bemerkung Marguerite de Buffets – und hier herrscht absolute Einigkeit unter den *grammairiens* und *remarqueurs*. Dementsprechend urteilt auch Irson klar: „SEPTANTE ne se dit point pour *soixante-dix*, non plus qu'*octante*, ny que *nonante* pour signifier *quatre-vingt* ou *quatre-vingt-dix*" (Irson 1662: 117). Bereits Claude Favre de Vaugelas kommt zum selben Schluss:

> *Septante, octante, nonante. Septante*, n'est François, qu'en vn certain lieu où il est consacré, qui est quand on dit *la traduction des septante*, ou *les septante Interpretes*, ou *simplement les septante*, qui n'est qu'vne mesme chose. Hors de là il faut tousjours dire *soixante-dix*, tout de mesme que l'on dit *quatre-vingts*, & non pas *octante*, et *quatre vingt-dix*, & non pas *nonante*. (Vaugelas 1647: 420 [380])

Bedauerlicherweise werden Zahlwörter im hier vorliegenden Korpus jedoch höchst selten verwendet – auch, weil die Musterbriefe teilweise Formularen ähneln, in die Zahlen dann bei Bedarf eingefügt werden können. So finden sich nur sieben Okkurrenzen der entsprechenden Zahlwörter. Sechsmal davon handelt es sich um die als falsch klassifizierten Formen. Aus dieser geringen Vorkommenszahl lassen sich selbstverständlich keine verlässlichen Aussagen ableiten.

„korrektes" Zahlwort	„falsches" Zahlwort
GESAMT: 1	GESAMT: 6
soixante-dix: 0	septante: 2 (Irson)
quatre-vingts: 1 (Marin)	huitante: 0
quatre-vingts-dix: 0	nonante: 4 (Savary: 1, Irson: 3)

Tab. 3. Verteilung der Zahlwörter in den Musterkorrespondenzen.

3.4 Weitere elliptische Konstruktionen

Ergiebiger sind die Ergebnisse beim dritten Merkmal, das überprüft wurde. Die Ablehnung von Ellipsen ist ein wiederkehrender Bestandteil der Mehrzahl der *grammaires* und *remarques* des *siècle classique*, werden Satzkonstruktionen, bei denen nicht alle Konstituenten an der Satzoberfläche erscheinen, doch als gegenläufig zur erwünschten *clarté* der Sprache erachtet (cf. Siouffi 2003: 38–47). In der sprachlichen Praxis des 16. Jahrhunderts und zu Beginn des 17. Jahrhunderts waren elliptische Konstruktionen noch weit verbreitet und akzeptiert, ihre Häufigkeit nahm jedoch zumindest in einigen Textsorten bereits massiv ab.[5] Bei der Lektüre der metasprachlichen Werke des *siècle classique* fällt auf, dass die ablehnende Haltung gegenüber Ellipsen im Laufe des Jahrhunderts immer rigider wird, so etwa bezüglich der Auslassung der Subjektpronomina.[6] Die folgenden Ausschnitte aus den *remarques* von Vaugelas und aus dem mehr als fünfzig Jahre später erschienenen Kommentar der *Académie Française* zeigen, dass es hier große Veränderungen gab:

> Suppression des pronoms personnels devant les verbes.
> Cette suppression a tres-bonne grace, quand elle se fait à propos, comme *nous auons passé les riuieres les plus rapides, et pris des places que l'on croyoit imprenables, & n'aurions pas fait tant de belles actions, si nous estions demeurez oisifs, etc.* Il est bien plus elegant de dire, *& n'aurions pas fait tant de belles actions,* que si l'on disoit *& nous n'aurions pas fait.* […] Mais plusieurs abusent de cette suppression […]. L'vn de nos plus celebres par exemple a escrit, *car une chose mal donnée ne sçauroit estre bien deüe, & ne venons plus à temps de nous plaindre, quand nous voyons qu'on ne nous la rend point.* Il falloit dire, *& nous ne venons plus à temps,* parce que la construction change. De mesme en vn autre endroit, *nous ne sommes pas contens de nous informer du fonds de celuy qui emprunte, mais foüillons jusques dans sa cuisine.* Il faut dire *mais nous foüillons,* parce que cette particule *mais,* fait vne separation qui rompt le lien de la construction precedente, et demande une nouuelle. (Vaugelas 1647: 420–421 [380–381])

Laut Vaugelas darf das Subjektpronomen demnach nur im zweiten von zwei koordinierten Sätzen weggelassen werden, wenn dasselbe Subjekt im ersten Satz ausgedrückt wurde und die Sätze zudem mit *et*, nicht aber mit *mais* oder *ou* verbunden wurden. Die *Académie* jedoch lehnt auch diese Ausnahme ab und erachtet den Ausdruck des Subjektpronomens immer für zwingend notwendig:

> Non seulement on n'a point trouvé que dans la phrase de M. de Vaugelas, il soit plus élegant de dire, *& n'aurions pas fait tant de belles actions,* que si l'on disoit, *& nous n'aurions pas fait.* Mais on a regardé la suppression du pronom *nous* comme une faute. Il n'est presque jamais permis de supprimer les pronoms personnels devant les verbes, quoy qu'ils ayent esté exprimez dans le premier membre de la periode. (Académie Française 1704: 416)

---

[5] Cf. beispielsweise die Studie von Baudry (2003) zu Koordinationskonstruktionen in Reiseberichten des 16. und 17. Jahrhunderts.

[6] Die allgemeine Entwicklung dieses grammatischen Merkmals während des *siècle classique* wurde bereits wiederholt in der Forschung behandelt, cf. u.a. Fournier (1998: 21–23), Marchello-Nizia (1995: 82).

"Le parfait négociant" als vollendeter Sprecher?

Ein ähnliches Bild ergibt sich bei der Auslassung anderer Elemente in Koordinationskonstruktionen, seien es direkte Objektpronomina, Adjektive, Präpositionen, Artikel, die Partikel *plus* und *si* oder Possessivpronomina. Während Vaugelas hier aber noch Ausnahmen zulässt, sofern die koordinierten Nomina oder Verben Synonyme oder Quasi-Synonyme sind, lehnt die *Académie* Ellipsen auch bei Quasi-Synonymen ab.

Ellipse betrifft:	abgelehnt wird:	befürwortet wird:
direktes Objektpronomen	Pron. + V + *et* + V	Pron. + V + *et* + Pron. + V
Adjektiv	Art.+ Adj. + N + *et* + N (sofern die Nomina nicht Synonyme bzw. Quasi-Synonyme sind)	Art. + Adj. + N + *et* + Art. + Adj. + N
Präposition	PP + NP/VP + *et* + NP/VP (sofern die Nomina nicht Synonyme bzw. Quasi-Synonyme sind)	PP + NP/VP + *et* + PP + NP/VP
Artikel	Art. + N + *et* + N	Art. + N + *et* + Art. + N
plus / si	plus/si + Adj. + *et* + Adj.	plus/si + Adj. + *et* + plus/si + Adj.
Possessivpronomen	Poss.pron.(Pl) + N + *et* + N (sofern die Nomina nicht Synonyme bzw. Quasi-Synonyme sind)	Poss.Pron(Sg.) + N + *et* + Poss.Pron(Sg.) + N

Tab. 4. Synopse der *remarques* in Vaugelas (1647) bezüglich Koordinationskonstruktionen.

Im untersuchten Korpus wurden sämtliche Subjekt-Verb-Konstruktionen auf den Ausdruck des Subjekts hin überprüft. Ebenso wurden alle Koordinationskonstruktionen auf Ellipsen hin untersucht. Wieder zeigen die Ergebnisse deutliche Unterschiede zwischen den Handelskorrespondenzen und den sonstigen Briefen, insbesondere, was die Auslassung der Subjektpronomina betrifft: In 94 Fällen fehlen letztere in den Handelsbriefen an Stellen, wo dies von keinem metasprachlichen Werk, auch nicht von Vaugelas, toleriert wird. In den sonstigen Briefen tritt dieses Phänomen nur viermal auf. Die Konstruktion, die die *remarques* von 1647 noch akzeptieren, tritt mit 21 versus 10 Fällen nicht ganz so häufig auf. Die weiteren Ellipsen sind ebenfalls nur wenige an der Zahl, wenngleich auch hier die Okkurrenzen in den Handelsbriefen mit 19 zu 8 deutlich häufiger sind.

	Handelsbriefe	sonstige Briefe
Auslassung des Subjektpronomens - verschiedene Subjekte - selbes Subjekt in Koordinationskonstruktion (ohne *mais/ou*)	94 21	4 10
weitere Ellipsen in Koordinationskonstruktionen	19	8

Tab. 5. Anzahl der elliptischen Konstruktionen.

Am markantesten sind die fehlenden Subjektpronomina. Die Ausmaße, die dieses Phänomen teils annimmt, lassen sich an den Musterbriefen La Grues am besten demonstrieren, bei denen in insgesamt annähernd vierzig Prozent der Fälle, in denen die erste oder zweite Person Singular oder Plural das Subjekt ist, letzteres nicht ausgedrückt wird. Zur Veranschaulichung sei hier noch einer der Musterbriefe, in dem dieses Phänomen besonders häufig auftritt, vollständig wiedergegeben: Ein einziges Mal, ganz am Schluss, erscheint das Subjekt an der Textoberfläche, in den übrigen Fällen fehlt es:

> Monsieur.
> Par la mienne du 20. passé **aurez pû** apprendre l'expedition qu'**ay fait** selon vos ordres de vos six tonneaux d'huile: en responce à la chere vostre du 12. Courant, **vous diray**, m'estre desia prevalu sur Mr. le Blanc d'icy, de tout le monter de mes provisions; si bien que **vous remercie** de l'offre. **Verray** aujourdhuy par les lettres de Venise ce qu'il y aura à faire pour les soyes greges, & **vous en aviseray** sans dilay; l'on doute cependant de leur bonne debite, à cause de la grande quantité qu'on en attend de Smirne, par avis; **Pourrez** en pressentir quelqu; chose de nos amis d'Amsterdam, ils ne m'en marquent rien pour asteure, peut estre par oubly; Cy joinct **trouverez** sur Eux une lettre de change de mille Ducats en espece à huict jour de veue; de laquelle vous plaira procurer acceptation & payement en son temps pour du reçeu m'en crediter avec avis, ce qu'attendant **ie** demeure, &c. (La Grue 1678: III, 84–86, Hervorhebungen KF)

Zudem lassen sich die zuvor erläuterten Auslassungen des Wortes *lettre* sowie des Monats im ersten Satz dieses Musterbriefs feststellen.

Insgesamt sind deutliche Unterschiede zwischen den Handelsbriefen und den Briefen anderer Art feststellbar, was den Grad der Realisierung der präskriptiven Sprachnormen betrifft. Dieser ist in den Briefen aus dem Handelskontext deutlich geringer. Insbesondere bei der Nutzung von Ellipsen zeigt sich, dass die im 16. Jahrhundert verbreiteten Strukturen hier extensiv weiter genutzt werden – wohl gerade aufgrund der Funktionalität dieser traditionellen Muster: Durch sie werden Texte um einiges kürzer und damit im Kontext des Handelsalltags effizienter. Zumindest in diesem Bereich entsprechen die fachsprachlichen Texte des Handels anderen Standards als jenen, die die höfisch-literarischen Kreise vorschreiben möchten.

4. Ausblick

Um umfassendere und wirklich verlässliche allgemeinere Aussagen machen zu können, müsste das Korpus selbstverständlich erweitert werden: erstens um weitere Musterbriefe aus früheren oder späteren Werken, um mögliche diachrone Entwicklungen präziser darstellen zu können (also vom Ende des 16. Jahrhunderts bis ins 18. Jahrhundert), und zweitens vor allem um authentische Briefe von Kaufleuten der betreffenden Epoche. Diese sind in den Archiven in großer Zahl vorhanden. Ihre Transkription stellt jedoch ein sehr zeitaufwändiges Projekt dar. Eine erste von mir vorgenommene Sichtung einiger Handelskorrespondenzen, die in den *Archives départementales d'Ille-et-Vilaine* in Rennes und den *Archives du Calvados* in Caen lagern,[7] wies auf ein hohes Vorkommen elliptischer Konstruktionen – insbesondere bei den typischen Empfangsbestätigungen – hin. Genaue Zahlen hierzu müssen aber noch erhoben werden.

Außerdem sollten die bisher überprüften sprachlichen Normen erweitert werden, so beispielsweise um die Vorgaben, die weitere umstrittene syntaktische Konstruktionen (unter anderem die Nutzung bestimmter Relativpronomina, unterschiedliche Verbvalenzen oder die Angleichung des *participe passé*) betreffen. Auch die lexikalische Ebene kann stärker eingebunden werden: So könnte überprüft werden, in welchem Maße sich der in den Briefen verwendete Fachwortschatz erweitert und inwieweit diese Änderungen sich in den während dieser Epoche erscheinenden Wörterbüchern Antoine Furetières, Pierre Richelets, der *Académie française* etc. widerspiegeln. Die vorliegende Pilotstudie zeigt bereits, dass weitere wichtige Erkenntnisse zum spannungsgeladenen Verhältnis zwischen dem präskriptiven Diskurs und der kaufmännischen Schriftpraxis zu erwarten sind.

---

[7] Gesichtet und digitalisiert wurden Teile des *Fonds Lion* (Signatur H/SUPP/ 1719–1721, *Archives du Calvados*) sowie die Korrespondenzen mit den Signaturen 2ED/6, 2ED/45, 2EH/6, 2EL/281 und 2ER/138 der *Archives d'Ille-et-Vilaine*.

Bibliographie

Académie française = Corneille, T. 1704. *Observations de l'Académie Françoise sur les Remarques de M. de Vaugelas*. Paris: Barbin.

Alemand, L.-A. 1690. *Nouvelles Remarques de M. de Vaugelas sur la langue françoise. Ouvrage posthume. Avec des observations de M.******. Paris: Desprez.

Anonymus. 1686. *Der neue Wegweiser der Französischen Sprach in Französisch und Teutsch*. Schaffhausen: Meisters.

Anonymus. 1700. *Le Théophraste moderne ou nouveaux caractères sur les moeurs*. Paris: Brunet.

Anonymus. 1701. *Sentimens critiques sur les caractères de Monsieur de la Bruyère*. Paris: Brunet.

Ayres-Bennett, W. 2018. Bon usage et variation sociolinguistique. In Vaugelas, C. F. de. *Remarques sur la langue françoise*. Édition de Wendy Ayres-Bennett. Paris: Classiques Garnier, 67–92.

Baudry, J. 2003. Les syntagmes nominaux coordonnés par "et". In Combettes, B. Ed. *Évolution et variation en français préclassique. Études de syntaxe*. Paris: Champion, 139–169.

Bouhours, D. 1693. *Suite des Remarques nouvelles sur la langue françoise*. Paris: Josse.

Buffet, M. 1668. *Nouvelles Observations sur la langue françoise, où il est traitté des termes anciens & inusitez, & du bel usage des mots nouveaux. Avec les éloges des illustres sçavantes, tant anciennes que modernes*. Paris: Cusson.

Colombat, B. / Fournier, J.-M. / Ayres-Bennett, W. Eds. 2011. *Grand Corpus des grammaires françaises, des remarques et des traités sur la langue (XVIe–XVIIe siècles)*. Paris: Classiques Garnier Numérique. https://classiques-garnier.com/grand-corpus-des-grammaires-francaises-des-remarques-et-des-traites-sur-la-langue-xive-xviie-s.html (30.09.2022).

Fournier, M. 1998. *Grammaire du français classique*. Paris: Bélin.

Große, S. 2017. *Les manuels épistolographiques français entre traditions et normes*. Paris: Champion.

Irson, C. 1662. *Nouvelle methode pour apprendre facilement les principes et la pureté de la langue françoise contenant plusieurs traitez*. Paris: Baudouin.

Irson, C. 1687. *Pratique generale et methodique des changes etrangers*. Paris: Jombert.

Kelz, I. 1994. *Das Französische als Handels- und Geschäftssprache vom Ausgang des Mittelalters bis zum 19. Jahrhundert. Eine Untersuchung an Lehrwerken für den berufsbezogenen Französischunterricht*. Augsburg: Universität Augsburg.

Kuhn, A. 1931: *Die französische Handelssprache im 17. Jahrhundert*. Leipzig / Paris: Selbstverlag des Romanischen Seminars / Droz.

„Le parfait négociant" als vollendeter Sprecher?

La Grue, T. 1678. *La grammaire françoise, nouvellement traduite en allemand du Latin.* Heidelberg: Zubrodt.

La Porte, M. 1704. *La science des Négocians et Teneurs de Livres, ou Instruction générale Pour tout ce qui se pratique dans les comptoirs des Négocians.* Paris: Cavelier / Osmont.

La Touche, P. 1730 [1696]. *L'art de bien parler françois, qui comprend tout ce qui regarde la grammaire, & les façons de parler douteuses.* Quatrième édition. Amsterdam: Wetsteins & Smith.

Macé, J. 1651. *Methode universelle pour apprandre facilemant les langues, pour parler puremant et escrire nettemant en françois. Recueillie par le sieur du Tertre.* Paris: Iost.

Marchello-Nizia, C. 1995. *L'évolution du français. Ordre des mots, démonstratifs, accent tonique.* Paris: Colin.

Marin, P. 1712. *Nouvelle méthode pour apprendre les Principes et l'usage des langues françoise et hollandoise.* Amsterdam: Van Eyl.

Ménage, G. 1675. *Observations de Monsieur Ménage sur la langue françoise.* Paris: Barbin.

Piélat, B. 1673. *L'anti-grammaire.* Amsterdam: Van Waesberge.

Piélat, B. 1677. *Le secrétaire inconnu. Contenant des Lettes sur diverses sortes de matieres. Seconde Edition, Reveüe & Corrigée.* Lyon: Larchier.

Richelet, P. 1698. *Les plus belles lettres françoises sur toutes sortes de sujets, tirées des meilleurs Auteurs, avec des Notes.* Paris: Brunet.

Savary, J. 1675. *Le parfait Negociant ou instruction generale pour ce qui regarde le commerce de toute sorte de Marchandises, tant de France, que des Pays Estrangers.* Paris: Billaine.

Siouffi, G. 2003. Le regard des grammairiens. In Combettes, B. Ed. *Évolution et variation en français préclassique. Études de syntaxe.* Paris: Champion, 19–67.

Vairasse d'Allais, D. 1681. *Grammaire Méthodique contenant en abrégé les Principes de cet art et les règles les plus nécessaires à la langue française.* Paris: Vairasse d'Allais.

Vaugelas, C. F. de. 1647. *Remarques sur la langue françoise utiles à ceux qui veulent bien parler et bien escrire.* Paris: Camusat.

Wilhelm, E. 2013. *Italianismen des Handels im Deutschen und Französischen. Wege des frühneuzeitlichen Sprachkontakts.* Berlin / Boston: De Gruyter.

Laura Linzmeier

"Navigating" the visual surface – the writing strategies of French navigational experts in the seventeenth and eighteenth centuries

Abstract. The seventeenth and eighteenth centuries in Europe were a time of knowledge accumulation and documentation. Navigation was a sector affected to the same degree by the authorities' attempts to accurately sort and store information too. This article considers French navigational journals, which were increasingly strictly controlled and regulated by the authorities in the seventeenth and eighteenth centuries. The focus is on the journals' visual aspects, namely, the layout constraints present in tables, which significantly influenced the navigators' writing behavior. By analyzing a journal from the mid-eighteenth century, this article shows that the advantages associated with the table format – that is, the collection of a large amount of information and the ability to retrieve it quickly thanks to its conciseness – conflicted with the writing needs of navigators who thus used narrative strategies to balance out this conflict.

1. Introduction

This article deals with writing strategies in maritime texts, with a focus on French navigational journals in the seventeenth and eighteenth centuries. After a brief introduction in which the historical context and the diffusion and use of *navigational journals* in France are presented (section 2), section 3 provides a theoretical framework that emphasizes the role of the visual surface in the structuring and perception of textual content. A particular role became assigned to the use of standardized tables in maritime documents, which were intended to guarantee quick documentation as well as fast comprehension of structures and contents. Section 4 provides a detailed overview of the development of navigational journals during the seventeenth and eighteenth centuries and of the underlying official regulations that guided the changes in layout. By analyzing a typical example of a table-like navigational journal from the mid-eighteenth century (sections 5 & 6), this article will discuss whether and if so, how layout-specific standards influenced navigational experts' writing process.[1]

---

[1] This study was carried out as part of my wider present research project that deals with the writing strategies of French maritime expert writers in the seventeenth

2. Maritime writing in its historical context

Especially from the seventeenth century onward, a transition from coastal navigation to the "new seafaring" ("Neue Schifffahrt", Novi 1999: 113), that is, transoceanic navigation, can be observed in Europe.[2]

The discovery of distant lands, the pursuit of raw materials and space for overseas settlements, and the administrative tasks and demands of the major European powers resulted in an increased desire to document, that is, "to map, measure, collect, describe and classify all manner of things and beings" (Sankey 2010a: 107). In seventeenth-century France, this culminated with Jean-Baptiste Colbert (1619–1683) as Secrétariat d'Estat à la Marine, with whom "as pluripotent minister, France's colonial and scientific endeavors became transformed" (McClellan/Regourd 2011: 43). Indeed, (international) trade and manufacturing were reformed, and the maritime sector was reorganized and ruled directly by the king (cf. Leroy-Turcan 1999: 71; McClellan/Regourd 2011: 35, 43, 52):

> On the eve of the French Revolution, then, the French state possessed a huge bureaucracy devoted to overseas expansion and colonial development. A noteworthy set of scientific and technical institutions functioned within a larger administrative structure, and these specialized institutions collectively constituted the largest and most complex "scientifico-medico-technical" bureaucracy in the history of the world to that point. (McClellan/Regourd 2011: 47)

Navigation was historically assigned to the less prestigious *artes mechanicae*. But from the second half of the seventeenth century, with the founding of the Académie Royale des Sciences in 1666, "the mechanical arts became objects of political interest and learned scrutiny" (Bertucci 2017: 23). The handling of maritime activities and findings was now strictly regulated, documented, evaluated, and made available to later navigators. This is why "the Marine Royale needs to be considered a specialist and expert institution underwritten

---

    and the eighteenth centuries. The project combines a linguistic-historical approach (it has a sociocultural background) with an analysis of linguistic, textual, and discourse-traditional features of French administrative-maritime writing. The project is based on a rich corpus of French *journaux de bord* and *journaux de navigation*, mainly taken from the microfilmed Fonds de la Marine of the National Archives in Paris (the navy and the Compagnie des Indes; Series 4JJ, MAR/4JJ/1–431) and the Archives départementales de Loire-Atlantique (merchant marine).

[2]   For historical contextualization, the training of navigators, and the creation, dissemination, and design of journals and handbooks (sections 2 & 4), I refer in particular to the works by Berthiaume (1990), Sankey (2010a/b), Schotte (2013a/b), and Linzmeier (2022a).

"Navigating" the visual surface

by the state" (McClellan/Regourd 2011: 58). The Dépôt des Cartes et Plans was established in 1720 to examine, collect, and inventory material such as ship logs, maps, reports etc., and it thus "served as the central clearinghouse for cartographical, navigational and hydrographic information" (McClellan/Regourd 2011: 60; cf. Trevisan 2021: 74).

Besides putting stricter legal principles into practice, the French navy's professionalization was advanced by the expansion of training centers, the provision of teaching materials, the establishment of an Académie de Marine in Brest in 1752, and the collection and provision of maritime expertise and vocabulary through lexicons, (also multilingual) dictionaries, and navigation manuals. Several hydrography schools had been established by 1785 for the training of merchant marine seafarers. Three training schools for young officers – the Écoles des Gardes du Pavillon et de la Marine – were opened in 1689 in Brest, Rochefort, and Toulon (cf. Boistel 2010, Vol.1: 25; Trevisan 2021: 71). Teachers and examiners working at these schools were often famous hydrographers (Esprit Pézenas) or astronomers (Pierre Bouguer) who published navigational and hydrographic instructions and were closely tied to the Académie Royale des Sciences in Paris (cf. McClellan/Regourd 2011: 59–60). While in the late seventeenth century the intendant complained about the cadets' lack of reading and writing skills, the situation improved with Colbert's efforts and the Ordonnance from 1689 (cf. Artz 1937: 514–516). Not only were navigation-specific subjects taught, such as shipboard training, mathematics, astronomy, mechanics, hydrography etc., but the English language was occasionally taught too (cf. McClellan/Regourd 2011: 58–59; Artz 1937: 516), alongside calligraphy and letter writing among other skills (cf. Lutun 1995: 16).

Navigational journals were an essential part of the documentation policy used by Colbert and his successors. These journals normally served for "the day-to-day recording of information, mostly written up at the end of each day" (Sankey 2010a: 113). Legal regulations – the Ordonnances for the merchant marine (1681) and for the navy (1689) – stipulated the obligation of keeping and later submitting onboard documents or copies to an official after the voyage. The regulations from 1765 and 1786 underlined and reinforced this necessity once again (cf. Schotte 2013a: 294–295; Trevisan 2021: 71–72; Berthiaume 1990: 53).[3] The documentation policy and the reinforcement of the training structure were also manifest in the manuals that emerged at this time as guidance on keeping onboard documents. Manuals, courses, and examinations in navigation schools were used as pedagogical measures intended to teach young seafarers how to deal with the form and content of these documents; they illustrated the authorities' attempt to guide and codify

---

[3] Cf. Ordonnance (1786: 473–474).

the writing process (cf. Schotte 2013b: 99, 106, 112). These materials contained not only preformulated phrases, short forms to be used, and (rather indirect) indications of the morphosyntactic arrangement of the journal entries, but also specific recommendations about layout (cf. Linzmeier 2022a: 266–267, 287, 289). Nevertheless, navigational journals varied in response to official orders, individual observations, and the navigator's writing attitude. They are therefore hybrid texts that may combine sections of text from different discourse traditions (cf. Linzmeier 2022b, 2023).[4] Because of the multifunctionality and individuality of the journals, Sankey (2010a: 115) speaks of "a hybrid genre, bringing together different levels and categories of information".[5]

3. Navigational journals as technical texts during the seventeenth and eighteenth centuries

Maritime texts like logbooks and journals written on official orders are first and foremost technical texts: "en premier lieu des documents techniques" (Llinares 2019: 259).[6] These texts are functional with a clear purpose. They fulfill mainly an informative function and aim for precision and efficiency by using standardized forms.[7]

Technical texts, thus, follow their own conventions, and they differ from the standards and ideals of institutions promoting language norms (such as the Académie Française), which were directed at the courtly elites. Nevertheless, the Enlightenment was a time when the study of technical subjects became increasingly popular. Consequently, the discourse-traditional features of specialized genres were accepted and valorized by language standardizing institutions as part of copresent diaphasic varieties.[8]

---

[4] *Discourse traditions* are historically conventionalized patterns of linguistic utterances (oral or written) that are susceptible to change over time (cf. Wilhelm 2001: 470; Aschenbrenner 2003: 5).

[5] See also footnote 18 of the present article.

[6] Cf. the German term "Gebrauchstexte" (Rolf 1993: 125–128).

[7] In addition to hydrographic and nautical details, the documents also contain information on all sorts of observations related to the journey, the crew, the situation on board, conflicts and diseases, religious practices, etc. (cf. Bonnichon 1997: 25–26, 43).

[8] Vaugelas' *Remarques* were known to take a normative approach; nevertheless, they were not necessarily prescriptive but, in some cases, to be understood as descriptive observations: Vaugelas was well aware of the coexistence of linguistic varieties, such as technical language, which he tolerated and considered justified in certain contexts (cf. Große 2020: 424). I refer here to the

Technical language is not only marked by the use of technical terms but also by the use of brevity and condensation strategies to ensure precision and the removal of ambiguity. The correct use and interpretation of these structures, which are standardized within a specific technical language, must be learned by expert users (cf. Göpferich 2007: 419). Common strategies include a recourse on "terms as text condensates" (ibid.: 414), "short forms and abbreviations" (ibid.: 415), "syntactic condensation" (such as nominalization, ellipses, prepositional phrases instead of conjunctions; ibid.: 415), "formulaic writing" (ibid.: 419), and "non-verbal information carriers" (ibid.: 418), such as illustrative figures. In addition, content structuring strategies related to layout, such as the use of tables, increased in prestige and extended their range of application from the seventeenth century onward, when tables were no longer just used in mathematics, but entered written language texts too, including grammars like the one by Port-Royal (1660), where they were used to illustrate grammatical and syntactical rules (cf. Raible 1991: 16–17).[9]

The verbalized sections of navigational journals in the seventeenth and eighteenth centuries made the information adhere to norms and become more repetitive (cf. Llinares 2019: 259). Condensation strategies were common (for instance, the frequent use of abbreviations, ellipsis of subject pronouns, the use of participial constructions and formulaic units – cf. Linzmeier 2022a: 282, 287–291) and heavy recourse to numbers. The study of navigational journals also reveals that while these journals are fundamentally characterized by condensation, such strategies are employed to varying degrees in the individual subtexts that make up the document. As mentioned earlier, journals are often hybrid documents in which subtexts of different discourse traditions alternate: this is reflected in the use of different surface patterns and layouts in which cargo lists and nautical tables can be found alongside linear and narrative written comments and report sections.

The focus of this analysis is on the interaction of verbal forms and non-verbal features structuring the visual surface during a time when the authorities' standardization of layout became crucial: special attention is paid to layout-specific factors such as the use of tables and lists and writers' ways of dealing with these formats in their writing process.

---

article by Katharina Fezer (in the present volume), who draws a comparable conclusion on commercial letters.

[9] The first models moving toward the development of diagrams and tables are schematic arrangements, for example, in the form of tree diagrams for illustrating kinship relations, which could themselves bring together several two-dimensional tables (cf. Raible 1991: 25).

3.1 The interaction of verbal and nonverbal elements on the visual surface – theoretical underpinning

Traditionally, text-linguistic analyses use well-known textuality features (for example, those defined by Beaugrande/Dressler 1981) to examine texts of various kinds. These analyses focus on mainly verbal phenomena, taking apparently less interest in other elements operating on the visual surface[10] and guiding text structuring and comprehension, such as (typo)graphic features and layout (cf. Stöckl 2005: 205; Spitzmüller 2016: 226–228).

More recent models of text analysis argue for a holistic concept of text that allows not only linguistic elements but also nonverbal elements to be included in text perception and to reveal texts' "semiotic potential" (Spitzmüller 2016: 233). Fix (2008a: 32), for example, proposes a multicodal concept of text, as she emphasizes that typographic, pictorial, and material elements (such as writing support and paper texture) also "participate in the text's offer of meaning",[11] as do other nonverbal elements such as mediality and locality (cf. Fix 2008b: 343–345). This also includes typographic elements in a broad sense, such as features that transmit connotative meaning (e.g., paper size and format) and means of structuring like charts and tables (cf. Spitzmüller 2016: 229, 233).[12]

It must also be noted here that in the research on the visual surface there are different terminologies for typographic elements and levels. Since this paper focused on navigational journals, which often used tables to document nautical observations, I refer here to Stöckl's (2005: 210) idea of macrotypography,[13] which entails a means of structuring the visual surface, such as paragraphing, emphasis, orientation aids (e.g., lists and tables) and the

---

[10] Cf. Schmitz's paper on "Sehflächenforschung" (Schmitz 2011).

[11] Transl. from German: "am Sinnangebot des Textes teilhaben" (Fix 2008a: 32). One may think here, for example, of gestures of respect in the eighteenth and nineteenth century in letters to socially superior persons, such as the practice of keeping a margin (cf. Spitzmüller 2016: 233) or a devotional gap on the page.

[12] It has to be noted, however, that typographic structuring (e.g., by tables, spatia) and highlighting (e.g., by italics, boldface, spacing) refer to the *typo-script*, strictly speaking. Nevertheless, the notion of *typography* is often also used to refer to the structuring and emphasizing means used in handwriting (*manu-script*) – from where it also historically stems (cf. Dürscheid 2016: 55, 303–304).

[13] Stöckl's (2005: 210) four-part model distinguishes between *micro-*, *macro-*, *meso-* and *paratypography*. Macrotypography involves a) paragraphing, indentations, caps, ornamented content; b) emphatic means (e.g., italics); c) orientation aids (heading hierarchies, lists, tables, charts, indexes, footnotes, marginalia, etc.); and d) montage text and graphics (images).

"Navigating" the visual surface

montage of text and graphics (images). Stöckl (2005: 213) points out that this subtype of typography "creates optical balance, shapes textual order and guides readers' attention by providing a page-map to navigate".

However, this article does not understand macrotypographic elements (such as tables) exclusively as structure-giving and attention-directing devices, since a major advantage of the "table" lies in its ability to express semantic and cognitive added value: the categorization and combination of details gives rise to new semantic information (cf. section 3.2).

3.2 Tables as a means of information condensing, storing, and retrieving

The table format is a commonly used macrotypographic feature in navigational journals. Tables are based on lists. When used in technical texts, lists are purpose-oriented (cf. Koch 1990: 131). Since a list does not have to be read entirely and linearly, "[o]ne does not *read* but only *uses* a list" (Doležalová 2009: 1; italics in the original). Lists are an advancement not only for information retention but also for information processing; an essential premise is that the correct way of decoding a list has been learned beforehand (cf. Koch 1990: 141, 144).

While a list is a "one-dimensional matrix", a table is "two-dimensional" (Raible 1991: 9, 15). Consequently, a table is "a complex list with paradigmatic, vertical and syntagmatic, horizontal relations" (Waldispühl 2019: 202, fn. 12).[14] As with lists, tables are texts that "do not want to be read at all (from front to back), but only want to be searched specifically and are designed for this reading-as-searching-and-finding" (Hausendorf 2009).[15] Tables allow for information to be conveyed more quickly and precisely (cf. Raible 1991: 38) since they can "arrange linguistic elements into an overall meaning" through brevity, without requiring complex grammatical structures (Schmitz 2011: 29).[16] This also means, as is generally the case with technical language structures (e.g., condensation strategies, formulas), that the correct use and decoding of tables must be learned as well (cf. Raible 1991: 38). When there are many columns, tables often rely on abbreviations to include all the details.

---

[14] Transl. from German: "eine komplexe Liste mit paradigmatischen, vertikalen und syntagmatischen, horizontalen Beziehungen" (Waldispühl 2019: 202, fn. 12).

[15] Transl. from German: "gar nicht gelesen werden wollen (von vorne bis hinten), sondern nur gezielt durchsucht werden wollen und auf dieses Lesen-als-Suchen-und-Finden hin angelegt sind" (Hausendorf 2009).

[16] Transl. from German: "arrangieren zwar sprachliche Elemente zu einer Gesamtbedeutung" (Schmitz 2011: 29).

4. The development of navigational journals' design in the seventeenth and eighteenth centuries

The layout of navigational journals likely developed between the seventeenth and eighteenth centuries.[17]

Thus, from the seventeenth century and certainly in the early eighteenth century, numerous suggestions for the design of navigation journals emerged (cf. Schotte 2013a/b; Linzmeier 2022a: 266–267). The authorities' desire for uniformity in layout was directly reflected in the Ordonnance issued in 1689 demanding navigators to respect a "prescribed form" ("forme préscrite"), but this form basically remained an "abstract model" ("modèle abstrait", Berthiaume 1990: 38–39, 410).

The idea of implementing a fixed model was advanced by Minister Maurepas from 1735 onward. The journals had to match the spirit of the Enlightenment, which was devoted to science, with a focus on emphasizing the scientific character of the maritime journals ("accentuer le caractère scientifique des journaux de mer", Berthiaume 1990: 41). The journals were to have around twelve columns, as it was hoped that in this way, information about the day, wind, distance, longitude, latitude, compass variation, flow, etc. could be made available immediately not only to the navigator, but also to scientists and geographers (cf. Berthiaume 1990: 38, 41–44). However, the reality was somewhat different: the writers dealt with these specifications with varying degrees of strictness and initially still enjoyed freedom and flexibility in how they kept their journals without fear of serious consequences (cf. Schotte 2013a: 295–297; Berthiaume 1990: 48): Instead of numerous narrow columns, the writers used the margins to document latitude, longitude, and compass directions (as in the manual that Dechales proposed in 1677). Consequently, they also structured the visual surface into spaces. Yet when using the margins, there were often only three parts and not the twelve columns desired by the authorities and theorists in their "imposed model" ("modèle impose", Berthiaume 1990: 46).[18]

---

[17] Cf. Schotte (2013a), who examined the development in detail. Cf. also Linzmeier (2022a: 259–267).

[18] However, "disregarding" the guidelines may also be related to the documentation and archiving culture itself: the term *navigation journal* (*journal de bord/journal de navigation*) is not a technical term and was often used (by the writers themselves and later by the archives) to designate different types of documents. The documents stored in the depots and archives, which we use for scientific analysis today, are often copies made after or during the journey by the navigator himself or even by employees because of legal requirements (cf. Berthiaume 1990: 37–38, fn. 19). They are not necessarily one-to-one copies but also include summaries and syntheses of the *journaux* (the "extraits").

Since the navigators rejected the authorities' demands for a standardized journal layout, even stricter regulations were devised from the second half of the eighteenth century onward. This "surveillance from the shore" (Schotte 2013a: 300) took on new dimensions: with the Ordonnance issued in 1765 and the Règlement sur la forme & la tenue des Tables de Loch & Journaux à bord des Vaisseaux (this was part of the Ordonnances et règlements concernant la Marine, Paris, 1786) for the navy, the authorities were trying to impose "la plus grande uniformité" (Ordonnances 1786: 448). According to the theorists and the authorities, navigation-specific observations should now be documented in even more detail – in ever more and narrower columns of tables – with a clear focus on technical information. The Ordonnance of 1786 (454–459) and the *Encyclopédie Méthodique – Marine* (Vial Du Clairbois/Blondeau 1787: 860–861) provided a log table model (to be completed by the *maître pilote* of the quarter) and a journal template (to be completed by the captain) (cf. Llinares 2019: 262), which had to be respected (cf. Ordonnances 1786: 448).

The aim was not only to create a uniform structure and to guarantee precision and completeness, but also to enable the rapid comprehension and translation of information into nautical charts by experts (cf. Berthiaume 1990: 45). The advantage of the table format – its propensity for quick information retrieval and the extraction of individual pieces of information – should prove its worth here. For this purpose, journals with table preprints were distributed to navigators (these were known as "formulaire pré-imprimé", Berthiaume 1990: 415), especially from the second half of the eighteenth century onward, to exercise even more control (cf. Berthiaume 1990: 45, 49–50). This related to a "normalization of instruction" that had begun at that time (McClellan/Regourd 2011: 58). For instance, Étienne Bézout's (1739–1783) textbook *Cours de mathématiques à l'usage des Gardes du Pavillon et de la Marine* became the official, mandatory manual for naval cadets in 1764 (cf. McClellan/Regourd 2011: 58–59). Many hydrography schools were established from the mid-eighteenth century onward, and so the 1786 regulations, Concernant les Écoles d'Hydrographie, et la réception des Capitaines, Maîtres et Patrons, consisted of an attempt to achieve a certain uniformity in teaching ("une certaine uniformité dans l'en-

---

Sometimes extracted results were interwoven into letters to the authorities (the Council): nautical details were here summarized in lists and alternated with narrative passages that served to reproduce individual observations during the voyage (cf. Linzmeier 2023). Thus, there may be "some slippage between the categories" (Sankey 2010a: 124). Compare with a discussion on the terms used in the works by Schotte (2013a/b), Berthiaume (1990), Sankey (2010a/b), and Linzmeier (2022a: 260–261, 274, 276).

seignement", Trevisan 2021: 71), which had not been successfully implemented up to that point.

Whereas writers had previously drawn tables by hand,[19] the preprinted forms now led to a restructuring of media and a necessary interaction between print and handwriting (cf. Hausendorf 2009). The following case study considers how the writers approached these layout-specific constraints.

5. "Navigating" the visual surface – a case study

In this article, I will limit myself to a qualitative analysis of a navigational journal whose macrotypography is dominated by the table format. The journal was written by the French East India Company (Paris, MAR 4JJ/77/48),[20] and it summarizes a journey completed from 1750–1752 on the ship *La Fière* from Penmance[21] to the *îles de France et Bourbon* (= today's islands of Mauritius and Réunion), and back to Lorient. The captain, Louis Caro, did not write the journal, but the *pilote écrivain*, Claude Georges Renier, did. According to the Archives Nationales, it is an "original" and not a copy.

The journal consists of twenty-four folios; it contains preprinted pages coded from fol. 3r to 14r – in total, there are sixteen columns to be completed daily! From fol. 14v there are ruled pages for the writer to synthesize observations made of individual days in paragraphs and lists. The description of the journey undertaken in 1752 starts at fol. 18r.

In the following analysis, I will only take a more detailed look at the table format, which is structured and preprinted in the document as follows (cf. Fig.1/2):

---

[19] A good example can be found in the *Médiathèques de Quimper Bretagne Occidentale*: https://mediatheques.quimper-bretagne-occidentale.bzh/iguana/www.main.cls?surl=search&p=af3e6a0a-94ab-11e8-a80b-0050568050bf#recordId=1.407281 (2022-12-10).

[20] The journal is part of the 4JJ-subseries *Journaux de bord* MAR/4JJ/15-MAR/4JJ/144/G – *Campagnes de traite négrière au XVIIIe siècle*, which is available on the National Archives homepage: https://www.siv.archives-nationales.culture.gouv.fr/siv/rechercheconsultation/consultation/multimedia/Galerie.action?irId=FRAN_IR_050747&udId=A1_117 (2022-12-15).

[21] In the *Petit Atlas Maritime* by Jacques Nicolas Bellin (cf. 1764: 70), Penmance is indicated as a small spot situated on the Blavet river in the northern part of Locmiquélic (located in today's arrondissement of Lorient).

"Navigating" the visual surface

MOIS D								
JOURS.			Vents.	Force du Vent.	Temps & état de la Mer.	Air de vent qu'a valu la Route eſtimée.	Chemin eſtimé.	Air de vent de la Route corrigée.	Chemin corrigé.
De la ſemaine.	du mois.	de la Lune.							

Fig. 1. Left-hand page of the pre-ruled navigational journal (my own copy).

ANNÉE						
Latitude eſtimée.	Latitude obſervée.	Longitude Meridien de	Variations obſervées, ocçaſes, ortives ou azimuts	Variations eſ- timées.	Vûës des Terres & les Relevemens ; Sondes, Mouillages, Courans & Marées, & diverſes Remarques.	

Fig. 2. Right-hand page of the pre-ruled navigational journal (my own copy).

A first glance at the document indicates that the writer has consistently completed the columns accurately, precisely, and fully. His neat handwriting suggests that he has fulfilled his obligation to complete the journal in an attentive and highly organized manner. There are hardly any corrections or sloppiness in the handwriting. One can see that the writer copes very well with the table format. This is clear despite the fact that the sixteen narrow columns force him to use very small and closely spaced characters, which certainly required careful concentration.

The first fifteen columns have been completed in a nominal style and use conventionalized abbreviations or formulas. Consider these examples from fol. 8v/9r and 11v/12r:[22]

- **Force du Vent** column: *Grand vent; Petit frais Et calme; Joly frais; Petit frais Calme; Bon frais; Grand frais*, etc.
- **Temps & état de la Mer** column: *Beau tems Belle mer; tems sombre Belle mer; tems à grains Belle mer, Beau tems Groſse mer; Brume Groſse mer*, etc.

The noun phrases (mostly adjective + noun) are fixed standardized forms that are even taught in manuals. Therefore, they are easily recognized as semantic units and do not necessarily have to be separated from each other with punctuation (e.g., *Beau tems Belle mer*) (cf. Linzmeier 2022a: 285–287).

The remaining columns are strongly marked by the use of abbreviations (see the three columns *Air* and *Air de vent*: *SE, SSO; SE¼E; NO¼N*) or numbers (e.g., the columns on latitude and longitude in Fig. 3).

---

[22] The transcription is as close to the original as possible, i.e., punctuation and orthography are reproduced as in the manuscript.

The sixteenth column (the *Remarques* section "Vûës des Terres & les Relevemens; Sondes, Mouillages, Courans & Marées, & diverses Remarques") is for the writer to note individually observed details of the journey and other details:

- **sightings of other ships**: *à 6 h^e: ½ du matin Nous avons vû un v^{au} que Nous avons Cru Estre le 13 Cantons* ... (fol. 5r)
- **interactions with other navigators**: *les 13 Cantons Comandé Par Mr Bouvet au quel Nous avons parlé à 8 h: ½* (fol. 7r)
- **the spotting of territories, animals, plants, etc.**:
  o *Dimanche 9e: hier à 3 h^e: ½ apres midy Nous avons vû l'isle de France dans Le OSO Distante de 18 Lieux Nous avons Continué La Route du O¼NO* ... (fol. 9r)
  o *Nous avons vû D'Eux Loups Marins* ... (fol. 8r)
  o *au jour nous avons vû Cantité Doiseaux* ... (fol. 9r)
  o *Nous avons Sondé Et trouvé 100 B^e: fond de Gravier taché de Diverses Couleurs Et quantité de Coquillages fins Et pouris.* (fol. 8r)
- **the documentation and justification of navigational details and processes (wind, weather, direction, distances, etc.)**:
  o *Mais ayant Reconnu que Ce v^{au} Etoit Portugais Nous avons fait Servir Et Continué Notre Route alors il Nous à tiré d'Eux Coups de Canons à Boulets* ... (fol. 5r)
  o *Levent augmentant toujours Nous avons Serré peu à peu nos voilles*... (fol. 8r)
  o *à 9 h^e: Nous avons fait le ONO* ... (fol. 9r)
  o *Vendredy 7e à midy Rodrigue Suivant La Carte françoise me Reste au ONO Distante de 15 Lieux
  Et Suivant pietergos*[23] *L'isle de France au Ouest Distante de 34 Lieux* (fol. 9r)

The contents of this column are also characterized by conventionalized abbreviations (e.g., *v^{au}* = *vaisseau*); however, these are integrated into mainly complete sentence structures formulated in the first person (singular or plural), which may consist of main and subordinate clauses (with a participle or conjugated verb + conjunction).

A closer look at the document reveals, however, that the writer skips numerous days (e.g., in June; see Fig. 4). Fol. 8v and fol. 9r show that the writer does not respect the table format throughout (see Fig. 3): he lacks room for maneuver because of the table format's rigid structure. The writer

---

[23] The writer refers here to the maps made by the Dutch cartographer Pieter Goos (1616–1675).

"Navigating" the visual surface

uses the sixteenth column so extensively that the line available per day is not sufficient to communicate all of his observations. Hence, there is an asymmetry on the visual surface and the problem remains of assigning observations to the days mentioned on the left in the first column. Thus, the writer lacks space on the page to write down observations for all the days.

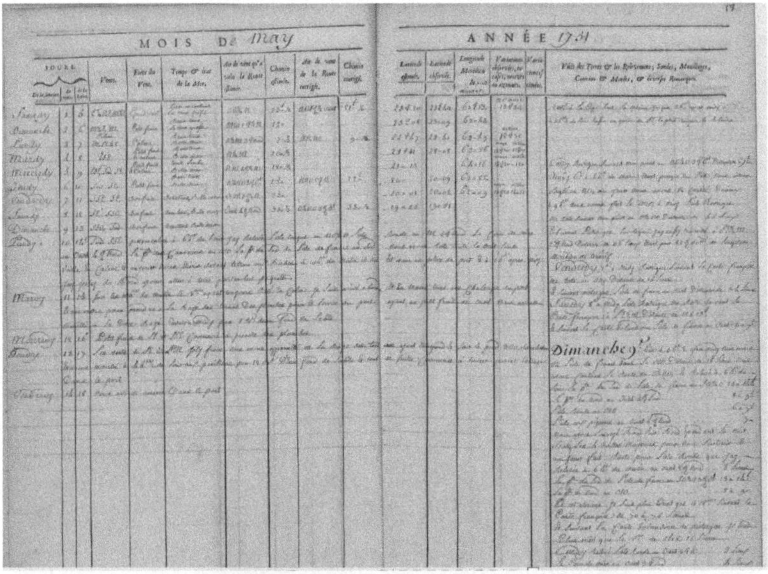

Fig. 3. Journal de bord de Claude Georges Renier, pilote et écrivain (original), MAR 4JJ/77/48, Archives Nationales Paris, fol. 8v/9r.

He compensates for this by filling the columns *JOURS*, *Vents*, and *Force du Vent* from May 10/Monday, but from the sixth column onward (*Temps & état de la Mer.*), he no longer respects the table format and writes across the columns. He therefore slips directly into the narrative style of the sixteenth column: *à 6 h^e: du Soir Jay Relevé L'isle longue au NO½O [...] à 10h^e: du Matin il Nous est venu un pilote du port Et à 1 h^e : apres midy Jay [traty?]*[24] *du Bord pour aller à terre porter les paquets.* The measured values to be documented in detail (wind direction, route, latitude, longitude) are consequently not recorded at all or are woven directly into the narrative text passages (see also fol. 10v/11r).

---

[24] Unclear word.

On fol. 9v and 10r (the month of June), only the *Remarques* field has been filled, while the other columns remained completely empty (see Fig. 4). His disrespect for the table format becomes even more obvious at the back of document: fol. 14v shows that the writer is moving to the ruled pages in the back of the document, which he uses to describe, in a narrative style, observations about individual days in the month of June.

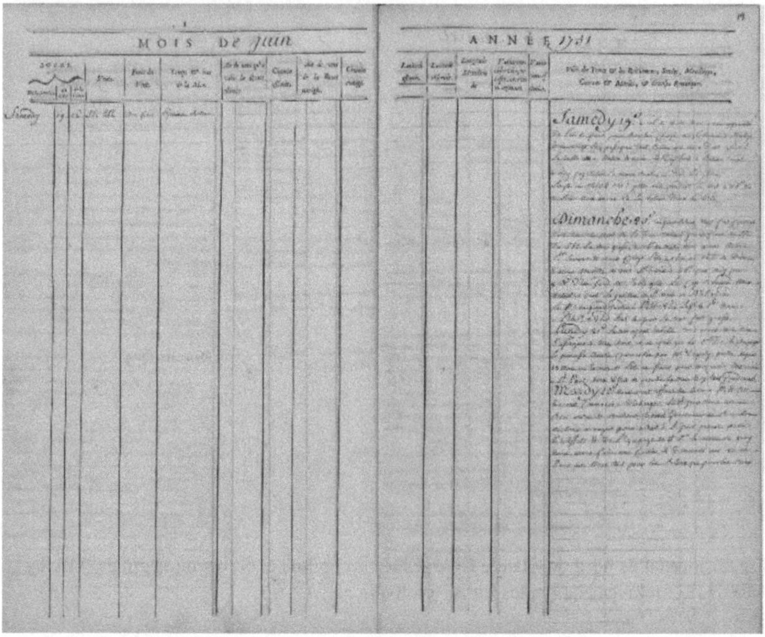

Fig. 4. Journal de bord de Claude Georges Renier, pilote et écrivain (original), MAR 4JJ/77/48, Archives Nationales Paris, fol. 9v/10r.

Dimanche 20e: au jour le tems Etant fort Couvert
Nous Navons point vû La terre ventant grand frais du SSE
Du SSE La mer grofse, à 10h^e: du Matin Nous avons Reconu
Ste Susanne Et avons Cotoyé L'isle à 1 Lieu ou 1L ½ de Distance
Et avons Mouillé devant St Denis à 3h^e : apres midy par
9 B^e: D'Eau fond de Sable gris Le Cap Bernard Nous
Restant au Ouest Le pavillon de S.^{t} denis au SE¼S 3 d[égres] Sud
La p^{te}. du grand Jardin à L'ESE 3 d[égres] Sud La p^{te}. de S^{te}. Marie
à L'E¼SE 3 d[égres] Sud tous le jour la mer fort grofse (fol. 10r)

This passage very clearly demonstrates the advantages of narrative style over condensed table contents: the table format allows for storage and information processing, but – as Freyberg (2021: 109) pointed out – "[o]verall, however, the visual presentation is static and aspects such as synchronicity and dynamics are lacking."[25] The table format does not permit individual observations and decisions (the course taken, etc.) to be related to one another, whereas the *Remarques* field does. Here, the advantage of narrative structures with complete sentences becomes apparent.

Navigational journals are not just a means of knowledge storage – they are also legal documents with which navigators can justify their actions and prove their skills (cf. Llinares 2019: 262): The narrative style permitted in the sixteenth column allows the table content to be placed in context and the causal, temporal, and concessive relations to be established through the use of, for example, adverbs (e.g., *au jour, tout le jour, à 10h^e*, fol. 10r), prepositions (e.g., *malgré*, fol. 11r; *pour nous approcher*, fol. 14v) or subordinate clause constructions with conjunctions or participles (e.g., *le tems Etant fort Couvert Nous Navons point vû La terre*, fol. 10r). This allows the writer to specify how, for example, wind, weather, and swell affected the journey and why, as a result, the navigator reached certain decisions (e.g., to change course, to take in the sails, to set anchor, to extend the journey). Even if ellipsis is used without a conjugated verb (e.g., *tous le jour La mer fort groſse*, fol. 10r), the advantage over a table is that the information on the condition of the sea can be related to time (*tous le jour*). This relationship cannot be established by the table alone, which is oriented to the day in general and not to individual phases of the day.

6. Synthesis and conclusion

What becomes very clear is that the visual surface, here in the form of a table, was not accepted by the writers because the rationalization of the text structure and mathematization of the content prevented individual and creative writing (cf. Berthiaume 1990: 96). The numerous columns to be filled with measured values (e.g., longitude, latitude, wind strength, etc.) already demand high precision and attention from the writers and at the same time the use of conventionalized forms and abbreviations does not stimulate their creativity. The *Remarques* column could sometimes compensate for this, as it allowed the writers to individually and creatively record their own observations in narrative form. However, the balance between rigid standardized structures and

---

[25] Transl. from German: "Insgesamt ist die visuelle Darstellung jedoch statisch und Aspekte wie Synchronizität und Dynamik fehlen" (Freyberg 2021: 109).

free passages was disturbed by the increasingly narrow table format: as the number of columns increased, the *Remarques* section, which the writers basically used to narratively document and communicate their personal and individual observations, then shrank to a small table column (cf. Berthiaume 1990: 51), and so the writers' only option was to reject the table format.

This case study clearly shows that the strict standards set by the authorities did not necessarily lead to greater accuracy, but rather to pressure and ultimately rejection by the writers. This was manifest in their not respecting the journals' pre-set layout: "In an age when mariners frequently expressed their distaste for mathematical calculation, it is unsurprising to find a preference for prose records over numerals" (Schotte 2013a: 306).

Schotte (2013a: 306) pointed out that while some mariners may have seen an advantage in replacing long words with short numbers, layout factors associated with lists and tables such as "panoptic information retrieval" – for later expert readers – were probably of less interest to the writers. Therefore, we see here a conflict triggered by the macrotypography, that is, by the layout. The table format was primarily intended to serve the later evaluation of the nautical details by the authorities and scientists – but the writers saw less benefit in the format. They likely felt patronized and unappreciated by the authorities, as the given structure could not be adjusted flexibly to their needs and interests. Because of the strict supervision and the obligation to keep the journal accurately, it was simply impossible for these writers to achieve such perfection. For this reason, the documents "were losing the aura of certainty and skill" (Schotte 2013a: 300) that they were originally famous for. This "idiolect made of signs and numbers",[26] which the authorities desired in order to control the navigators' writing, seemed extremely unsuitable to the writers (Berthiaume 1990: 95). Thus, they tried to regain control by writing across the columns, as they felt that important details could not be squeezed into narrow columns using numbers and symbols (cf. Schotte 2013a: 300).

References

Artz, F. B. 1937. Les débuts de l'éducation technique en France (1500–1700). *Revue d'histoire moderne*, tome 12 N°29/30, 469–519. https://doi.org/10.3406/rhmc.1937.3890 (2022-12-10).

Aschenbrenner, H. 2003. Diskurstraditionen – Orientierungen und Fragestellungen. In Aschenbrenner, H. / Wilhelm, R. Eds. *Romanische Sprachgeschichte und Diskurstraditionen*. Tübingen: Narr, 1–18.

---

[26] Transl. from French: "idiolecte fait de signes et de chiffres" (Berthiaume 1990: 95).

Beaugrande, R. A. de / Dressler, W. U. 1981. *Einführung in die Textlinguistik*. Tübingen: Niemeyer.

Bellin, J. N. 1764. *Petit Atlas Maritime, Recueil De Cartes Et Plans Des Quatre Parties Du Monde: Contenant Les Cotes de France et Les Places Maritimes Sur l'Ocean et sur la Mediterranée*. Vol. 5. Paris. https://gallica.bnf.fr/ark:/12148/bpt6k1073258x.r=Petit%20Atlas%20Maritime?rk=64378;0 (2022-12-10).

Berthiaume, P. 1990. *L'aventure américaine au XVIIIe siècle. Du voyage à l'écriture*. Ottawa: Les Presses de l'Université d'Ottawa.

Bertucci, P. 2017. *Artisanal Enlightenment: Science and the Mechanical Arts in Old Regime France*. New Haven: Yale University Press.

Boistel, G. 2010. *Diffusion et mutation des méthodes de l'astronomie nautique, 1749–1905: Accompagné du mémoire d'habilitation, « Une école pratique d'astronomie au service des marins et des explorateurs : l'observatoire de la Marine et du Bureau des longitudes au parc Montsouris, 1875–1914 ». Histoire, Philosophie et Sociologie des sciences*. Nantes: Université de Nantes.

Bonnichon, P. 1997. Pratiques maritimes, d'après les journaux de bord: la croisière de la frégate l'Adelayde pour les Mascareignes et retour, à la fin de la guerre de succession d'Espagne. In Association des Historiens Modernistes des Universités Ed. *Les européens et les espaces océaniques au XVIIIe siècle. Actes du colloque de 1997*. Paris: Presses de l'Univ. de Paris-Sorbonne, 25–54.

Dechales, C. F. M. 1677: *L'art de naviger demontre' par principes & confirmé par plusieurs observations tirées de l'experience*. Paris: Etienne Michallet. https://archive.org/details/bub_gb_wBl2i8gxXjcC (2022-12-10).

Doležalová, L. 2009. The Potential and Limitations of Studying Lists (Introduction). In Doležalová, L. Ed. *The Charm of a List: From the Sumerians to Computerised Data Processing*. Cambridge scholars publishing, 1–8.

Dürscheid, C. [5]2016. *Einführung in die Schriftlinguistik. Mit einem Kapitel zur Typographie von Jürgen Spitzmüller*. Göttingen / Stuttgart: Vandenhoeck & Ruprecht.

Fix, U. 2008a. Text und Textlinguistik. In Janich, N. Ed. *Textlinguistik: 15 Einführungen*. Tübingen: Narr Francke Attempto, 15–34.

Fix, U. 2008b. Nichtsprachliches als Textfaktor: Medialität, Materialität, Lokalität. *Zeitschrift für Germanistische Linguistik* 36/3, 343–354.

Freyberg, L. 2021. *Ikonizität der Information: Die Erkenntnisfunktion struktureller und gestalteter Bildlichkeit in der digitalen Wissensorganisation*. Berlin: Institut für Bibliotheks- und Informationswissenschaft der Humboldt-Universität zu Berlin.

Göpferich, S. 2007. Kürze als Prinzip fachsprachlicher Kommunikation. In Bär, J. A. / Roelcke, T. / Steinhauer, A. Eds. *Sprachliche Kürze. Konzeptuelle, strukturelle und pragmatische Aspekte*. Berlin / New York: De Gruyter, 412–433.

Große, S. 2020. Normative Grammars. In Lebsanft, E. / Tacke, F. Eds. *Manual of Standardization in the Romance Languages*. Berlin / Boston: De Gruyter, 417–440.

Hausendorf, H. 2009. Kleine Texte – über Randerscheinungen von Textualität. Germanistik in der Schweiz. *Online-Zeitschrift der Schweizer Akademischen Gesellschaft für Germanistik* 6. http://www.sagg-zeitschrift.unibe.ch/6_09/hausendorf.html (2022-12-10).

Koch, P. 1990. Vom Frater Semeno zum Bojaren Neascu. Listen als Domäne früh verschrifteter Volkssprache in der Romania. In Raible, W. Ed. *Erscheinungsformen kultureller Prozesse. Jahrbuch 1988 des Sonderforschungsbereichs 'Übergänge und Spannungsfelder zwischen Mündlichkeit und Schriftlichkeit'*. Tübingen: Narr, 121–165.

Leroy-Turcan, I. 1999. Modalités de création d'une base informatisée « Vocabulaire de la marine au 17e siècle »: problèmes relatifs aux corpus de référence et aux documents permettant de vérifier la vitalité des termes. In Newman, D. L. / van Campenhoudt, M. Eds. *Maritime Terminology: Issues in Communication and Translation. Proceedings of the First International Conference on Maritime Terminology*. Bruxelles: Editions du Hazard, 70–92.

Linzmeier, L. 2022a. Die Schriftlichkeit französischer Seefahrtsexperten im 17. und 18. Jahrhundert: "ungeübte" Schreiber oder Experten der pragmatischen Schriftlichkeit? In Schöntag, R. / Schäfer-Prieß, B. Eds. *Romanische Sprachgeschichte und Sprachkontakt – Münchner Beiträge zur Sprachwissenschaft*. Frankfurt a. M.: Peter Lang, 245–303.

Linzmeier, L. 2022b. La houle et la plume: la scripturalité des groupes d'experts maritimes en France aux XVIIe et XVIIIe siècles entre document institutionnel et ego-document. *Linx* [En ligne], 85. Revue des linguistes de l'Université Paris Ouest Nanterre La Défense. Special Issue: Bergeron-Maguire, M. Ed. *Pour une histoire de la langue «par en bas»: Textes documentaires (privés) et variation des langues dans le passé*. https://journals.openedition.org/linx/9430 (2023-02-22).

Linzmeier, L. 2023. What shall we do with the "writing" sailor? – Style-shifting and individual language use in a French navigation journal from the eighteenth century. In Schiegg, M. / Huber, J. Eds. *Intra-Writer Variation in Historical Sociolinguistics*. Oxford: Peter Lang, 407–429.

Llinares, S. 2019. La République en mer, le journal de navigation de la frégate l'*Insurgente* de Lorient à Cayenn, 1798. In Acerra, M. / Michon, B. Eds. *Horizons atlantiques. Villes, négoces, pouvoirs*. Rennes Cedex: Presse Universitaires de Rennes, 259–268.

Lutun, B. 1995. Des Ecoles de marine et principalement des écoles d'hydrographie (1629–1789). *Sciences et techniques en perspective* 34, 3–30.

McClellan, J. E., III / Regourd, F. 2011. *The Colonial Machine: French Science and Overseas Expansion in the Old Regime*. Turnhout: Brepols.

Novi, C. 1999. Multilingual Harmonization and Standardization of Technical Terminology at the International Maritime Organization. In Newman, D. L. / van Campenhoudt, M. Eds. *Maritime Terminology: Issues in Communication and Translation. Proceedings of the First International Conference on Maritime Terminology*. Bruxelles: Editions du Hazard, 110–125.

Ordonnance 1681 = Louis XIV (1638–1715; roi de France). 1714. *Ordonnance de la marine. Du mois d'aoust 1681. Commentée & conferée avec les anciennes ordonnances, & le droit écrit : avec les nouveaux règlemens concernans la marine*. Paris: Guillaume Cavelier. https://gallica.bnf.fr/ark:/12148/bpt6k960 6758r.texteImage (2022-12-10).

Ordonnance 1689 = Louis XIV (1638–1715; roi de France). 1764. *Ordonnance de Louis XIV pour les armées navales & arsenaux de marine. Du 15 avril 1689. Nouvelle édition augmentée des deux reglemens par colonnes. Le premier, pour les appointemens des officiers à la mer, & solde des équipages. Le second, pour la quantité des munitions, agrez, aparaux & ustensiles dont les vaisseaux de chaque rang doivent être munis*. Paris: Père Prault. https://gallica.bnf.fr/ark:/12148/bpt6k9661196g.texteImage (2022-12-10).

Ordonnance 1765 = Louis XV (1710–1774; roi de France). 1765. *Ordonnance du Roi, concernant la Marine. Du 25 mars 1765*. Paris: Imprimerie Royale. https://gallica.bnf.fr/ark:/12148/btv1b8625496x.image (2022-12-10).

Ordonnance 1786 = Louis XVI (1754–1793; roi de France). 1786. *Ordonnances et règlements concernant la Marine*. Paris: Imprimerie Royale. https://gallica.bnf.fr/ark:/12148/bpt6k3044098n.r=Ordonnances%20et%20r%C3%A8 glements%20concernant%20la%20Marine%2C%201786?rk=21459;2 (2022-12-10).

Raible, W. 1991. *Die Semiotik der Textgestalt. Erscheinungsformen und Folgen eines kulturellen Evolutionsprozesses*. Heidelberg: Winter, 5–44. https://www.leibniz-publik.de/de/fs1/object/display/bsb00054798_00006.html (2022-12-10).

Rolf, E. 1993. *Die Funktionen der Gebrauchstextsorten*. Berlin / New York: De Gruyter.

Sankey, M. 2010a. Writing and Rewriting the Baudin Scientific Expedition to the Southern Hemisphere, 1800–1804. In Fornasiero, J. / Mrowa-Hopkins, C. Eds. *Explorations and Encounters in French*. Adelaide: University of Adelaide Press, 103–134.

Sankey, M. 2010b. Writing the Voyage of Scientific Exploration: The Logbooks, Journals and Notes of the Baudin Expedition (1800–1804). *Intellectual History Review* 20/3, 401–413.

Schmitz, U. 2011. Sehflächenforschung. Eine Einführung. In Diekmannshenke, H.-J. / Klemm, M. / Stöckl, H. Eds. *Bildlinguistik. Theorien, Methoden, Fallbeispiele*. Berlin: Erich Schmidt, 23–42.

Schotte, M. E. 2013a. Expert Records: Nautical Logbooks from Columbus to Cook. *Information & Culture* 48/3, 281–322.

Schotte, M. E. 2013b. Leçons enrégimentés : l'évolution du journal maritime en France. *Annuaire de Droit Maritime et Océanique* 31, 91–115.

Spitzmüller, J. 2016. Typographie. In Dürscheid, C. *Einführung in die Schriftlinguistik*, 5th ed. Göttingen: Vandenhoeck and Ruprecht, 209–241.

Stöckl, H. 2005. Typography: Body and dress of a text – a signing mode between language and image. *Visual Communication* 4/2, 204–214.

Trevisan, N. 2021. *Une histoire de l'hydrographie française*. Brest Cedex: Amhydro.

Vial Du Clairbois, H. / Blondeau, E. 1787. *Encyclopédie Méthodique – Marine*. Vol. 3. Paris: Panckoucke. https://gallica.bnf.fr/ark:/12148/bpt6k62944172/ (2022-12-10).

Waldispühl, M. 2019. Die Liste als Ordnungsmedium in mittelalterlichen Libri vitae. *Zeitschrift für Literaturwissenschaft und Linguistik* 49, 197–218.

Wilhelm, R. 2001. Diskurstraditionen. In Haspelmath, M. / König, E. / Oesterreicher, W. / Raible, W. Eds. *Language Typology and Language Universals. An International Handbook*. Vol. 1.1. Berlin: De Gruyter, 467–477.

Anne Weber, Daniele Moretti and Vahram Atayan

Ways of wisdom: the transfer of knowledge into German-speaking countries discussed on the basis of the *Heidelberg Bibliography of Translations of Nonfictional Texts*

Abstract. In the early modern period nonfictional texts in the broadest sense were dominant in both text production and translation. After the invention of the printing press, more and more translations were published in the vernacular, predominantly requested by noblemen and produced by scholars. Traditionally however, linguistics and translation studies have focused on literary texts. As a result, we lack well-founded historically oriented research focusing on the translation of specialized texts, while at the same time, bibliographies that would enable or support comprehensive analyses do not exist. Within the context of the *Digital Humanities*, the *Heidelberg Bibliography of Translations of Nonfictional Texts* pursues two objectives. First of all, we compile a comprehensive bibliography of early modern translations from seven (mostly Romance) source languages, integrating two earlier projects (focusing on the Romance languages and Latin as source languages) with a new collection of English-German and Dutch-German translations published between 1450 and 1850. Second, our technical infrastructure will be made accessible for interested researchers to create their own similar databases in the future. After a brief introduction (Section 1), the present contribution will provide an overview of the bibliography as a whole and discuss the current status, as well as the thematic distribution, of the data sets registered so far (Section 2). To illustrate how the collection can be used within Romance Studies, we will then proceed to a statistical analysis of the metadata of the collected works (Section 3). Finally, we will discuss the evolution of the titles of nonfictional texts on the basis of the use of chosen keywords (Section 4) before finishing with some concluding remarks (Section 5).

1. Introduction: specialized texts, cultural contact and translation in the early modern period

Research on translation in the Modern Era has traditionally considered literature in the narrowest sense. However, as Spieckermann (1992: 193) points out, around 75 % of all new publications on the German book market were 'scholarly' in the broadest sense until 1740. To focus on literary texts therefore

> is to ignore the large amounts of translation which went on in the fields of medicine, mathematics and astronomy, law and government, art and architec-

ture [...], agriculture, military science, and technology in its various branches. (Gillespie 2007: 1441)

For instance, physicians and surgeons did not usually speak foreign languages or even Latin and were consequently dependent on German translations of relevant texts to broaden their knowledge (cf. Haage/Wegner 2007: 52). Despite this, German became the main language of publication only in the 17th century: the proportion of publications in the vernacular increased from a mere 5 % in around 1520 to approx. 30 % by 1570, and only from 1681 onwards did German texts prevail (cf. Hartweg 2000: 1686). There was also a significant proportion of translations on the German book market; estimations for the late 18th century range from a humble 15 % to a staggering 75 % (cf. Willenberg 2008: 175) with the real figure presumably falling somewhere in-between.

In the beginning, translations were predominantly produced by scholars and clerics by order of aristocrats with an interest in the respective works (cf. Albrecht 1998: 273). From the middle of the 18th century, it became common for translators to receive remuneration for their work, which led to a considerable increase in the number of translations published, but also to significant reductions in quality (cf. in detail Fränzel 1914: 74–100); according to Seibicke (2003: 2382), who analyses specialized translations from French and English into German published in the second half of the 18th century, translators' lack of expertise results in numerous untranslated terms, unnecessary doublets and mistranslations. Translation was not established as a profession until the 19th century (cf. Albrecht 1998: 273).

It is generally accepted that throughout history different nations and hence different languages have been considered role models: French in the 12th–14th century and then again in the 17th/18th century; Italian from the 13th/14th century; English from the 18th century (cf. Albrecht 2007: 1094–1095; Koller 2007: 1704). Latin, in contrast, is obviously not linked to a specific country but served as an international lingua franca throughout the Middle Ages and beyond (cf. IJsewijn 2007: 1429) and maintained its status in the sciences in particular until the 20th century (cf. Müller 2003: 3). However, the mere non-availability of an original would sometimes force a translator to opt for a text in an intermediary language (cf. Spieckermann 1992: 195; Willenberg 2008: 166). In other cases, translations were simply preferred as source texts for translations into German due to the exemplarity of a particularly prestigious (intermediary) language, most commonly French for its supposed "clarté" (cf. Willenberg 2008: 173). Since the Netherlands were an important center for literature and printing, Dutch became another popular intermediary language, particularly for translations from English into German (cf. Willenberg 2008: 158; Price 1941: 118).

Ways of wisdom: the Heidelberg Bibliography of Translations

As to German as a target language, two different 'varieties' must be mentioned, "gemaines Teutsch" and "aigen Teutsch": the former refers to what might be considered a common vernacular focused on content, while the latter was a variety of German used and understood only by scholarly people (cf. Hohmann 1977: 258–259). Although many German Humanists considered their native tongue to be inadequate for cultural and intellectual life, even 'barbarous' (IJsewijn 1990: 48), translators typically preferred to take an integrative approach to appeal to their readers (cf. Koller 2007: 1702–1703; Koller 2008: 220).

Though not concerned with the contents of the collected works itself, the *Heidelberg Bibliography of Translations of Nonfictional Texts*[1] aims to provide a comprehensive database for researchers interested in the questions addressed in the present Section 1. We will now discuss the bibliography in the context of the Digital Humanities (cf. 2). Following this, it will be shown that specific analyses can be conducted using only the metadata (Section 3) or the titles of the works included in the database (Section 4).

2. The *Heidelberg Bibliography of Translations* (HÜB) in the context of the Digital Humanities

The expression *Digital Humanities* (DH) has become widely accepted since 2004, although other terms (such as *eHumanities* – the *e* meaning *enhanced* here – or *Humanistic Computer Science*) emerged as early as the 1980s, and the phenomenon itself has existed since the 1950s (cf. Vogeler 2018: 15–16). For the purpose of the present publication, a slightly outdated understanding can shed some light on the concept:

> Die Digitalen Geisteswissenschaften, die Digital Humanities (DH), kann man in diesem Sinne auch als eine Hilfs- und Grundwissenschaft bezeichnen, d.h., dass man mit digitalen Methoden etwas 'macht', damit man richtige Wissenschaft machen kann [...]. (Vogeler 2018: 12)

Although Vogeler (2018: 12) states that the above definition of *Digital Humanities* is no longer valid in today's scholarly reality, we consider it pertinent with regard to our database. While the compilation (as a result) can be of great use to scholars aiming to analyze phenomena of cultural transfer, the history of translation and/or of a specific field (this would be the 'genuinely scholarly' part), the process of compilation is generally considered mere

---

[1] Officially named the *Heidelberger Übersetzungsbibliographie nichtfiktionaler Texte (HÜB)* and funded by the Deutsche Forschungsgemeinschaft (DFG, German Research Foundation) – project no. 429695918.

"Fleißarbeit" (Koller 2008: 210–211), a laborious and perhaps even tedious, but intellectually rather undemanding task (and here is the 'making of a helpful something'), which must nonetheless be carried out for the sake of research (cf. ibidem; Nies 1986: 152; Fabian/Spieckermann 1980: 154). Moreover, when talking about bibliographies, we seem to be faced with a dilemma as to the prominence of technologies: while the use of digital tools and methods has been self-evident in the Humanities for quite some time now (cf. Kurz 2016: IX), bibliographies are often still published as printed monographies, even though online databases are only the next logical step.

2.1 Project aims and technical characteristics

The *Heidelberg Bibliography of Translations* aims to compile information on English-German and Dutch-German translations of nonfictional texts in the early modern period (1450–1850) and to provide this information to interested scholars online and free of charge, thus combining the use of digital tools and methods with what we might call a 'digital outcome'. It is the third project in a series, following the Romance-German *Saarbrücker Übersetzungsbibliographie* (project term 2005–2008) and the Latin-German *Saarbrücker Übersetzungsbibliographie – Latein* (project term 2011–2014), both also funded by the DFG. Across all three projects, information on translations from a total of seven different (source or intermediary) languages will be systematically collected. These include French, Italian, Spanish and Portuguese (though the two latter to a lesser extent) in the Romance-German database, Latin in the Latin-German database, and finally English and Dutch in the current bibliography. In addition to compiling the bibliography itself, we will make our technical infrastructure accessible for interested researchers to create similar collections, which may consider other languages and/or periods.

While previous data sets were stored in a MySQL database programmed in PHP, we are now using PostgreSQL and Python for the current bibliography, thus developing a new 'lean' structure.[2]

---

[2] Although the continuous development and releases of the last few years have led to a narrowing of the differences between MySQL and PostgreSQL, the former is a purely relational database, whereas the latter is an object-relational database (ORDB). This means that while MySQL was originally conceived (and tends to be used) for reading large amounts of data faster, PostgreSQL is more flexible, extendable and can handle concurrency better, i.e. it can perform multiple tasks at the same time (cf. among others https://www.integrate.io/blog/postgresql-vs-mysql-which-one-is-better-for-your-use-case/; https://www.geeksforgeeks.org/difference-between-mysql-and-postgresql/; 2022-02-11).

Ways of wisdom: the Heidelberg Bibliography of Translations

Fig. 1. Django administration website.

The previous data sets have been migrated to the new infrastructure so that all three collections can be used and searched together. The administration site with the entry interface uses Django CMS and is, of course, password protected.

Fig. 2. Publicly accessible search interface.

The public website offers a basic search function where users may enter specific title keywords, author/translator names, DDC categories (to search for specific subject matters, cf. below), years or languages. Search results can be sorted by year, title, author/translator or DDC class. Results can be exported using the export function.

2.2 Data compilation and current status

For all works identified through secondary literature or in library catalogues,[3] we collect basic bibliographic data – author/translator, title, publisher, place and year of publication, as well as up to four libraries where the work can be found (preferably in Germany). Wherever possible, we also add a link to a digitized version. In addition, we provide a thematic classification based on the two first levels of the *Deweys Decimal Classification* (DDC)[4] and assign a 'cultural area' to each work. This indicates the country – based on contemporary national borders – where the author was born and/or spent most of their working life, rather than the place of publication. This enables us not only to differentiate between two countries/cultures with the same national language (English for Great Britain vs. America), but also to conduct analyses of cultural transfer phenomena, e.g., translations of texts from France published either in French or in Latin.

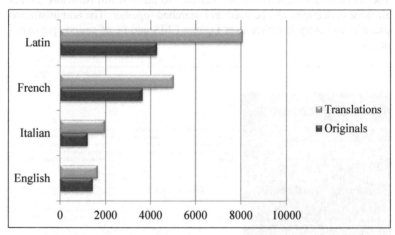

Fig. 3. Current project status (overall).

---

[3] NB: We create individual entries only for different translations and not for different editions of the same translation. Information on further editions may, however, be added in the edition and/or comments field.

[4] While we are conscious that the use of the DDC classes is not indisputable, we are keen to point out that we merely aim to hint at the subject matter covered in the respective work, even though the thematic classification is not our main concern. For this purpose, the DDC is considered sufficiently appropriate, seeing that it would be impossible to find the ideal thematic classification to cover a period of 400 years and more.

Ways of wisdom: the Heidelberg Bibliography of Translations

While the Romance-German and Latin-German databases can be regarded as complete (links to digitized versions that did not yet exist during the project terms will be added to account for the huge efforts that have been made in the last decade), the work on the English-German and Dutch-German collection is still in progress and all results and data must be considered preliminary (all numbers last updated in late 2021).

The Latin-German database contains information on a total of 8.066 translations and 4.276 original texts. There are two reasons why so many originals seem to be missing. First of all, it is not possible to identify all originals as the collected texts are up to 600 years old. Second, Latin was exceptionally prestigious and some scholars assume that authors may have claimed to be publishing a translation from Latin when a text was in fact a German original (cf. Weber 2015: 608). Despite this, and given that we had no means via which to verify each text's 'translation status', we collected all works that were *marked* as translations.

As for the thematic distribution of the works contained in our database, we consolidated some of the DDC main classes for Fig. 4.[5]

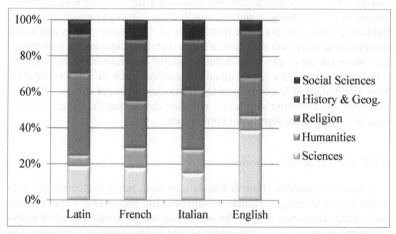

Fig. 4. Current project status (thematic distribution).

---

[5] *Social Sciences* = DDC 300 (same); *History & Geography* = 900 (same); *Religion* = 200 (same); *Humanities* = 100 (Philosophy & Psychology), 400 (Language), 700 (Arts & Recreation), 800 (Literature); *Sciences* = 000 (Computer Science, Information & General Works), 500 (Science), 600 (Technology).

It is obvious that the importance of the different subject matters of the collected works is not quite the same across all languages considered. In the case of Latin and Italian, there is a significant focus on *Religion* (46 % and 33 % of texts respectively). In contrast, the largest proportion of translations from French consider *History & Geography* (34 %), while the *Sciences* are a dominant subject matter for translations from English into German (39 %). The latter finding, however, is still preliminary.

Naturally, in a comprehensive study of the metadata, we would also have to take into consideration changes in thematic distribution over time. It is clear for example, that the importance of *Religion* decreased over time, while the *Sciences* gained increasing scholarly interest (cf. 3.2 below).

3. Statistical analysis of metadata

In our bibliography of translations, we primarily collect metadata regarding individual works. Although an examination of the texts' contents is not therefore possible, we are able to conduct statistical analyses of the data regarding subject matters, languages and/or cultural areas. This can be particularly enlightening since changes in the distribution of the subject matters and in the translation activity both over time and between languages and/or cultural areas can reveal the dynamics of cultural transfer; generally-speaking, cultural transfer is reflected by (interlingual) translation, such as it is investigated here with regard to German-speaking territories as 'target culture'. In order to render this evolution visible, we will first define specific parameters and then test our data for significant correlations.

3.1 Definition of the parameters

The database contains German translations from seven systematically collected source languages: French, Italian, Spanish, Portuguese, Latin, English and Dutch. However, it must be noted that we have also included works where the aforementioned languages served as intermediary languages. The database therefore includes additional original languages that appear less frequently, e.g., Armenian, Greek and Swedish.[6]

As shown above (cf. 2.2), we consolidated some of the DDC main classes to account for the different topics of the works contained in our database. This results in six more comprehensive thematic categories: *Humanities*

---

[6] For the purpose of the present contribution, we do not differentiate between the various 'functions', i.e., an example with Swedish in the Romance database might be either *Romance–Swedish–German* or *Swedish–Romance–German*.

(e.g., Philosophy, Ethics and Rhetoric), *History* (from a modern perspective, i.e., political events of the day) & *Geography* (including travel reports), *Sciences*, *Religion* (including theology), *Social Sciences*, *Other*.

The question of how to define specific periods, in contrast, is rather challenging as this involves dividing a continuum – which is already rather heterogeneous as different languages and cultural areas are concerned – into clearly defined segments. Nevertheless, in order to give a general overview of the translation activity in the German-speaking territories, we have established four different periods of approx. 100 years each which can be defined with reference to historical events and the history of ideas. For the purposes of the present contribution, we will use the following informal labels:

(1) *Printing Press + Protestantism* (up to approx. 1550): the invention of the printing press led to an immense acceleration in the circulation of knowledge. It was also the first phase of a time of upheaval in Europe initiated by the emergence of Protestantism and the beginning of the Counter-Reformation (the Council of Trent 1545–1563, the Peace of Augsburg 1555).

(2) *Religious Wars + Discoveries and Conquests* (1551–1650): this period is marked by religious wars (the Massacre of Vassy 1562, the St Bartholomew's Day massacre 1572, the Edict of Nantes 1598 in France, the Thirty Years' War ending in the Peace of Westphalia in 1648, the Wars of the Three Kingdoms in England, Scotland and Ireland, ending in 1651 with the Battle of Worcester) as well as by great geographical discoveries and the conquest of major parts of the new-found world.

(3) *(Early) Enlightenment* (1651–1750): this era is characterized by the accelerated development and institutionalization of the sciences (from Descartes and the formation of the Academies/Royal Society up to the *Encyclopédie*, the first volume of which appeared in 1751).

(4) *Revolutions to Modernity* (from 1751): the beginning of this period is marked by the (late) Enlightenment which led to political upheaval throughout Europe – from the French Revolution to the revolutions of 1848; thanks to scientific and technical progress, it also led to the emergence of Modernity.

3.2 Correlations original language – subject matter – period

The following four figures show the correlations between two different parameters each.

As shown by Fig. 5, there are clear differences between the individual (Romance) source languages over time. Italian is overrepresented as a source language in the first three periods. The same is true of Spanish in the second period, whereas French becomes clearly overrepresented during the transition from the Enlightenment to Modernity. From a purely quantitative perspective, French would already have been dominant in the '(Early) Enlightenment' period; due to the extremely high numbers in the fourth period, however, it is still underrepresented in the third.

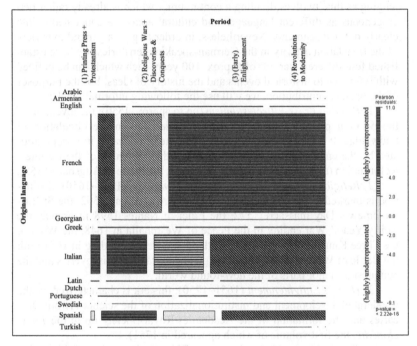

Fig. 5. Correlations original language – period (Romance database).[7]

With regard to the correlations between subject matter and period, we find that for Latin as a source language (cf. Fig. 6), *Religion* is extremely dominant in the first two periods with a massive decrease towards the end of the periods taken into consideration. In contrast, political events of the day as well as expedition reports play a major role in the second and third periods, whereas the *Sciences* become dominant in the fourth period. *Social Sciences* and the *Humanities* are mainly overrepresented in the '(Early) Enlightenment'.

---

[7] The height of each field represents the number of works in the respective category in relation to the number of works in the other categories in the left column; the width, similarly, refers to the number of works in the different categories in the same line.

Ways of wisdom: the Heidelberg Bibliography of Translations

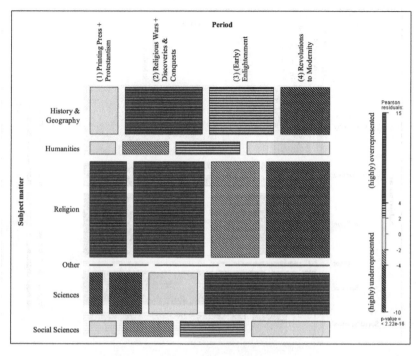

Fig. 6. Correlations subject matter – period (Latin database).

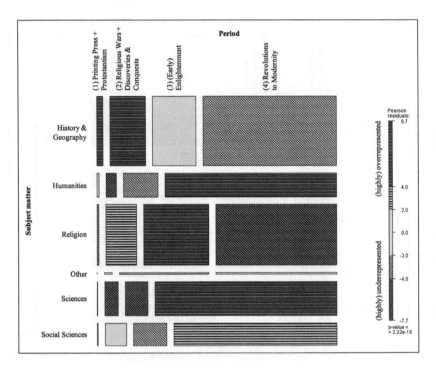

Fig. 7. Correlations subject matter – period (Romance database).

Considering the Romance-German database as a whole (cf. Fig. 7), we have similar findings, although the transition from Latin to the Romance vernacular languages for the religious discourse becomes visible in the second and third period. The *Sciences* and *Humanities* are overrepresented at the height of the Enlightenment as well as during the 'Revolutions to Modernity' period. However, it is necessary here to have a closer look at the role of the individual Romance languages.

As is clearly visible in Fig. 8, scholarly interest in Spanish original texts was particularly focused on *Religion*. In contrast, *Religion* and the *Humanities* are both overrepresented for translations from Italian. Meanwhile, *Religion* is rarely the subject of translations from French, with the *Sciences* being a dominant topic of focus here.

Ways of wisdom: the Heidelberg Bibliography of Translations

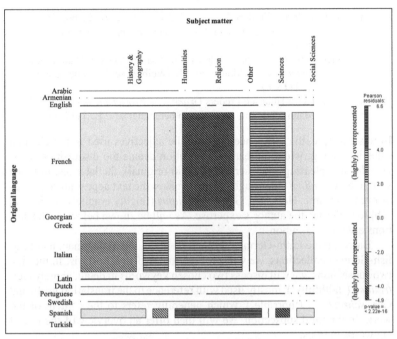

Fig. 8. Correlations source language – subject matter (Romance database).

All in all, our analysis of the metadata shows how the role of different source languages changed over time and with regard to different subjects, which illustrates the evolution of the international transfer of knowledge into German-speaking territories – or, as we like to call it, the ways of wisdom.

4. The evolution of the titles of nonfictional texts

When working with texts from the early modern period, it can be enlightening to focus on the titles in particular. Titles are often considered to be a text type of their own (cf. Nord 1993: 43–44) as they have specific characteristics. What seems most relevant in the present context is that they tend to emotionalize and feature elements of appraisal in order to appeal to the reader and incite them to read the related work (cf. Nord 1993: 168–171).

Earlier analyses were able to show that some keywords are particularly frequent in the titles of texts from those days (cf. Weber 2013: 410–415; Weber/Moretti/Atayan 2015: 683–685). Sometimes, two translations of the same original title contain different keywords, which shows how the interpretation of the same content can be steered by the translator and/or editor:

(1) a. Lat. Heinrici Frederi Dantiscani *Lusus juvenilis* de poenis uxoris, sive disquisitio, num fas sit vapulare uxores a maritis? (1627; Religion)
b. Ger. Des *Hochgelahrten* Herrn Heinrich Freders von Dantzig *Lustige Frage*: Ob ein Mann sein Ehe-Weib zu schlagen berechtiget sey […] (1656)
c. Ger. Herrn Heinrich Freders *Gründliche Erörterung der Frage*: ob ein Mann seine Frau zu schlagen berechtigt sey? […] (1738)

In this example, the difference between the adjectives used in the German titles is striking: while the earlier translation deems the disquisition to be Ger. *lustig* ('pleasing' – closer to the Latin original), the later one uses the word Ger. *gründlich* ('thorough'), which makes the text appear more serious or even academic. However, Ger. *hochgelahrt* ('highly erudite') is added in (1b) to underline the author's expertise. As will be shown below, such additions are not uncommon.

Based on the Latin-German, French-German, Italian-German, and English-German collections, we will proceed to a two-step analysis. In the first two subsections, we will discuss two chosen keywords in detail, namely Ger. *treulich* ('faithfully'), mostly used with reference to the translation itself, and Ger. *schrecklich* ('horrible'), which generally refers to the content of the work. In the third subsection, we will then offer an overview of the use of keywords in titles.

4.1 Discussion of chosen keywords: treulich

When working on the Latin-German database in particular, we had the impression that many translations were marked as *treulich* (including the typographic variations *tre(u)wlich*), so we wanted to verify this impression against actual data from our database.[8] It transpires that there are 105 occurrences in the translations from Latin for the period between 1551 and 1600 alone, as compared with only 24 in the translations from French (numbers are almost negligible for translations from Italian and English). Nevertheless, the number of occurrences is not as significant as the proportion of translations that are marked as particularly faithful, i.e., the number of occurrences in relation to the total number of translations we have collected for the different language pairs.

---

[8] Last updated for the present publication in early October 2021, the database contained the following number of translations from the respective source languages: 8.066 for Latin, 5.017 for French, 1.963 for Italian and 1.296 for English (the numbers for English are, however, still preliminary).

Ways of wisdom: the Heidelberg Bibliography of Translations

	Latin	French	Italian	English
1501–1550	0.9 %	0.0 %	0.0 %	0.0 %
1551–1600	8.3 %	13.5 %	1.4 %	0.0 %
1601–1650	7.2 %	6.1 %	2.2 %	15.4 %
1651–1700	3.5 %	2.3 %	2.4 %	2.6 %
1701–1750	2.8 %	0.9 %	1.0 %	2.2 %
1751–1800	0.4 %	0.0 %	0.0 %	0.8 %

Tab. 1. Proportions of *treulich* in the titles (chronology).

A closer look at these numbers shows that a marking as 'faithful' is actually not more frequent for translations from Latin than for other source languages. On the contrary, the most significant proportion (13.5 %) is reached for translations from French, a highly prestigious language as mentioned above (cf. 1), published between 1551 and 1600. Nevertheless, the faithfulness of the translation was commonly highlighted with regard to Latin original texts for a longer period of time. This might be due to the extraordinary status of this language, which translators regarded as a role model for their own mother tongues (cf. Limbeck 2005: 3). For translations from Italian, such markings are almost nonexistent, and with regard to the English-German database, we must emphasize that we are still working on this collection. The current figure of 15.4 % for the period 1601–1650 is likely misleading as it is based on only two actual occurrences of *treulich* in the titles. All in all, it seems that it is actually the prestige of the source language that motivates translators to mark a translation as faithful.

Furthermore, it becomes obvious that from 1751, such notes regarding the quality of the translation are far less common for all source languages. Given that the database contains only nonfictional texts, this may be due to changing 'scholarly' conventions (cf. 4.3).

With regard to the subject matters of the texts in which *treulich* is used in the title, we find that on the whole it is most frequent for texts relating to *History & Geography* and *Religion*, while it almost never appears in the titles of texts relating to the *Sciences*. In contrast to the other language pairs involved, it is comparatively common throughout all subject matters for translations from Latin.

	Latin	French	Italian	English
Humanities	1.7 %	0.2 %	0.0 %	0.0 %
History & Geog.	3.6 %	1.9 %	1.1 %	1.9 %
Sciences	1.0 %	0.5 %	0.3 %	0.0 %
Religion	4.3 %	0.7 %	0.9 %	1.4 %
Social Sciences	1.8 %	0.6 %	1.0 %	0.0 %

Tab. 2. Proportions of *treulich* in the titles (subject matters).

Although most occurrences of *treulich* refer to the translation itself and must consequently be deemed to be additions, we also find instances in which *treulich* refers to the faithfulness of the original account and was already contained in the title of the source text.

(2) a. En. [...] also from the more cruelly devouring jawes of the inhumane canibals of Florida. *Faithfully related* by one of the persons concerned therein. (1752; History & Geog.)
 b. Ger. [...] aus den noch grausamern Rachen der unmenschlichen Canibalen oder Menschenfressern in florida sind befreyet worden. *Getreulich aufgezeichnet* von einem welcher selbst persöhnlich dabey gewesen [...]. (1756)

In this example, it seems that the sensational contents of his account led the author to point out his own credibility.

4.2 Discussion of chosen keywords: schrecklich

Compared with *treulich*, we find a different situation for our second chosen keyword, *schrecklich* (including variations such as *erschröcklich*). First of all, this term is far less frequent than the one discussed before. However, while we find most occurrences between 1551 and 1600 for translations from Latin (16), their number is constantly elevated for translations from Italian in the three half-centuries from 1501 to 1650 (5/8/9 occurrences). This is particularly clear when we look at the percentages:

	Latin	French	Italian	English
1501–1550	0.3 %	0.0 %	6.2 %	0.0 %
1551–1600	1.3 %	1.7 %	5.6 %	0.0 %
1601–1650	1.3 %	1.0 %	4.0 %	0.0 %
1651–1700	0.2 %	0.5 %	0.8 %	0.0 %
1701–1750	0.0 %	0.2 %	0.0 %	0.7 %
1751–1800	0.1 %	0.0 %	0.0 %	0.0 %

Tab. 3. Proportions of *schrecklich* in the titles (chronology).

One presumable cause of this uneven distribution becomes apparent where specific examples are considered:

(3) a. It. Nuova, e *vera* relazione dello *spauentoso, & orribile terremoto* che fu l'ora 21. de' 14 aprile 1672. (1672; History & Geog.)
 b. Ger. Neue und *warhafftige* Relation Von dem grossen und *erschröcklichen Erdbeben* So sich den 14. Aprill Anno 1672. in der Statt Rimini [...] (1672)

Ways of wisdom: the Heidelberg Bibliography of Translations

(4) a. It. [Original unknown]
 b. Ger. *Warhafftiger* bericht, von dem *erschröcklichen Mordt*, an acht vnd achtzig Christlichen [..] personen, [...] begangen den 11. Junii 1561 (1561; History & Geog.)

It seems that this term is used mostly to refer to natural catastrophes (earthquakes, major floods), to designate impressive natural phenomena (the Niagara Falls in one example) or describe despicable human behavior (such as murder). Usually, a similar element of appraisal can also be found in the original title (or, as seen in example 3 above, even two such adjectives). Moreover, several of the Italian examples refer to the same earthquake as example 3 above. This peculiarity also explains why the term is by far most frequent in texts relating to *History & Geography* (1 % for translations from Latin, 3.6 % for translations from Italian; the numbers for the other categories are below 1 % and thus almost negligible).

As seen in examples 3 and 4 above, the use of *schrecklich* is often combined with an emphasis on the truthfulness of the account, probably in order to render such sensational reports more credible.

4.3 Overview of the use of keywords in titles

Naturally, there are many more emotive keywords and elements of appraisal that frequently appear in the titles of nonfictional texts from the early modern period. Tab. 4 gives an overview of some of them, starting with the two terms discussed in the Sections above (highlighted in italics), followed by a further eight terms (for some of them, variations are also indicated), which are sorted by frequency in Latin and French.

	Latin	French	Italian	English
treulich	3.2 %	1.0 %	0.8 %	0.9 %
schrecklich	0.4 %	0.2 %	1.2 %	0.1 %
berühmt	3.7 %	1.3 %	2.8 %	1.8 %
gelehrt	3.7 %	1.1 %	1.0 %	2.0 %
für-/vornehm	3.6 %	1.8 %	2.5 %	1.9 %
wahrhaft	3.6 %	1.6 %	4.1 %	0.6 %
für-/vortrefflich	1.5 %	0.9 %	1.2 %	0.4 %
grausam/gräulich	0.6 %	0.2 %	0.9 %	0.2 %
hochwürdigst	0.3 %	0.3 %	0.3 %	0.0 %
anmütig/-mutig	0.2 %	0.2 %	0.3 %	0.1 %
∅	2.1 %	0.8 %	1.5 %	0.8 %

Tab. 4. Proportions of chosen keywords in the titles (overview).

First of all, it becomes apparent that some keywords are more frequent than others, and that some of the most frequent words typically refer to the author of the original work (*berühmt*, 'famous'; *gelehrt*, 'erudite'). Second, frequency also seems to depend on the source language of the translation, which in turn might also correlate with the different thematic distribution for each source language. For example, we can assume that adjectives such as those listed above are more frequent in religious texts (the most important thematic field for translations from Latin) than in scientific ones (most frequent in our English-German collection so far). Moreover, some terms are very specific in their use as, for instance, *hochwürdigst* ('most reverend') usually refers to a bishop and thus can probably not be considered as an appraisal but simply corresponds to the then customary address. Of course, in order to identify the actual reasons for the differences in the use of these adjectives, a more comprehensive analysis would be required.

An earlier study has already shown that older texts usually have longer titles than more recent texts: the titles of translations from Latin into German that appeared between 1450 and 1550 ('period 1') comprise an average of 33.8 words, while those published between 1812 and 1912 ('period 2') contain only 22.5 words (cf. Weber/Lehmann/Moretti 2015: 310). Although in both periods, titles consisting of anything between 11 to 29 words are most frequent (47 % and 66 % respectively), 35 % of the titles dating from period 1 comprise 40 or more words, compared to only 8 % for period 2 (cf. ibidem). This tendency can be easily illustrated by an example where the Latin original was translated twice in different centuries:

(5) a. Lat. Raimundi Lullii Majoricani De alchimia opuscula quae sequuntur. Apertorium, item magica naturalis (1546; Sciences)
 b. Ger. Des Hochgelahrten und weitberühmten Philosophi Raymundi Lullii Apertorium, Von der wahren Composition des Steines der Weisen: In Deutsch übergesetzet von J. T. (1675)
 c. Ger. Raimundi Lullii Tractat vom philosophischen Stein (1770)

As can be seen, the 18th century title more closely resembles the titles of contemporary nonfictional texts, being written in nominal style and containing hardly any adjectives, let alone emotive or evaluative ones.

5. Concluding remarks

When considering our bibliography, we must bear some potential limitations in mind. First of all, we can obviously not be sure that our collection is anywhere near complete. Despite the general availability of modern tools, the ease with which information on texts from different periods can be found is highly variable. Second, for all our analyses, we have a limited statistic basis, and consequently the (relatively) high number of texts written by particularly industrious authors such as Erasmus of Rotterdam might distort our figures. Nevertheless, we are able to draw some general conclusions.

As far as our statistical analysis is concerned, and with regard to the importance of different source languages, it seems clear that the focus changes from Italian, Latin and Spanish to French, while the most common thematic focus progresses from *History & Geography* and *Religion* towards the *Sciences*. The strongest correlation can be seen between French (as a source language) and the *Sciences*.

The tentative analysis of the titles has shown that some conventions can be identified and that the use of specific keywords seems to depend mainly on the period in which the work is published and also on the contents. The translations are sometimes marked as particularly faithful, while some titles contain a negative evaluation of the content, often combined with another (positive) adjective to highlight the truthfulness of the account. The authors are recognized as *berühmt* ('famous') or *(hoch)gelehrt* ('(highly) erudite'), the works as *vortrefflich* ('excellent'). The more recent the translation, the shorter and more factual the title is likely to be.

The present contribution offers only a brief insight into the characteristics and the current status of the *Heidelberg Bibliography of Translations of Nonfictional Texts*, and exemplifies the opportunities for further research that it offers. More comprehensive and in-depth analyses will follow to illustrate the scholarly merits of our database.

References

Albrecht, J. 1998. *Literarische Übersetzung: Geschichte, Theorie, kulturelle Wirkung*. Darmstadt: Wissenschaftliche Buchgesellschaft.

Albrecht, J. 2007. Bedeutung der Übersetzung für die Entwicklung der Kultursprachen. In: Kittel, H. / Frank, A. P. / Greiner, N. / Hermans, T. / Koller, W. / Lambert, J. / Paul, F. Eds. *Übersetzung – Translation – Traduction*, 2nd vol. Berlin / New York: De Gruyter, 1088–1108.

Fabian, B. / Spieckermann, M.-L. 1980. Deutsche Übersetzungen englischer humanmedizinischer Werke 1680–1810. *Medizinhistorisches Journal* 15, 154–171.

Fränzel, W. 1914. *Geschichte des Übersetzens im 18. Jahrhundert*. Leipzig: Voigtländer.

Friendly, M. 1994. Mosaic Displays for Multi-Way Contingency Tables. *Journal of the American Statistical Association* 89, 190–200.

Gillespie, S. 2007. Vernacular translations of classical and neo-latin writings in the European Renaissance: the Germanic languages. In Kittel, H. / Frank, A. P. /

Greiner, N. / Hermans, T. / Koller, W. / Lambert, J. / Paul, F. Eds. *Übersetzung – Translation – Traduction*, 2nd vol. Berlin / New York: De Gruyter, 1441–1447.

Haage, B. D. / Wegner, W. 2007. *Deutsche Fachliteratur der Artes in Mittelalter und Früher Neuzeit.* Berlin: Erich Schmidt.

Hartweg, F. 2000. Die Rolle des Buchdrucks für die frühneuhochdeutsche Sprachgeschichte. In Besch, W. / Reichmann, O. / Sonderegger, S. Eds. *Sprachgeschichte*, 2nd vol. 2nd ed. Berlin / New York: De Gruyter, 1682–1705.

Hohmann, T. 1977. *Heinrichs von Langenstein 'Unterscheidung der Geister' Lateinisch und Deutsch. Texte und Untersuchungen zu Übersetzungsliteratur aus der Wiener Schule.* München: Artemis.

IJsewijn, J. 1990. *Companion to Neo-Latin Studies. Part I: History and Diffusion of Neo-Latin Literature*, 2nd ed. Leuven: Leuven University Press.

Koller, W. 2007. Übersetzung und deutsche Sprachgeschichte. In Kittel, H. / Frank, A. P. / Greiner, N. / Hermans, T. / Koller, W. / Lambert, J. / Paul, F. Eds. *Übersetzung – Translation – Traduction*, 2nd vol. Berlin / New York: De Gruyter, 1701–1712.

Koller, W. 2008. Übersetzungen ins Deutsche und ihre Bedeutung für die deutsche Sprachgeschichte. In Besch, W. / Reichmann, O. / Sonderegger, S. Eds. *Sprachgeschichte*, 1st vol. 2nd ed. Berlin / New York: De Gruyter, 210–229.

Kurz, S. 2016. *Digital Humanities. Grundlagen und Technologien für die Praxis*, 2nd ed. Wiesbaden: Springer Vieweg.

Limbeck, S. 2005. *Theorie und Praxis des Übersetzens im deutschen Humanismus. Albrecht von Eybs Übersetzung der 'Philogenia' des Ugolino Pisani*, Online Publication, https://freidok.uni-freiburg.de/data/2147.

Müller, J.-D. 2003. Latein als lingua franca in Mittelalter und Früher Neuzeit? In Ehlich, K. Ed. *Mehrsprachige Wissenschaft – Europäische Perspektiven. Eine Konferenz im Europäischen Jahr der Sprachen.* München: Institut für Deutsch als Fremdsprache / Transnationale Germanistik. http://www.eurosprachenjahr.de/Mueller.pdf (2012-08-06).

Nies, F. 1986. Vom Elend der Übersetzungs-Bibliographie. In Kortländer, B. / Nies, F. Eds. *Französische Literatur in deutscher Sprache. Eine kritische Bilanz.* Düsseldorf: Droste, 152–153.

Nord, C. 1993. *Einführung in das funktionale Übersetzen. Am Beispiel von Titeln und Überschriften.* Tübingen: Francke.

Price, L. M. 1941. Holland as a Mediator of English-German Literary Influences in the 17th and 18th Centuries. *Modern Language Quarterly* 2/1, 115–122.

Seibicke, W. 2003. Fachsprachen in historischer Entwicklung. In Besch, W. / Reichmann, O. / Sonderegger, S. Eds. *Sprachgeschichte*, 3rd vol. 2nd ed. Berlin / New York: De Gruyter, 2377–2391.

Spieckermann, M.-L. 1992. Übersetzer und Übersetzertätigkeit im Bereich des Englischen in Deutschland im 18. Jahrhundert. In Schröder, K. Ed. *Fremdsprachenunterricht 1500–1800. Vorträge gehalten anläßlich eines Arbeitsge-*

sprächs vom 16. bis 19. Oktober 1988 in der Herzog-August-Bibliothek Wolfenbüttel. Wiesbaden: Harrassowitz, 191–203.

Vogeler, G. 2018. Was ist „DH"? Probleme und Perspektiven der Digitalen Geisteswissenschaften. In Börner, I. / Straub, W. / Zolles, C. Eds. *Germanistik digital. Digital Humanities in der Sprach- und Literaturwissenschaft.* Wien: Facultas, 12–28.

Weber, A. 2013. Ceterum censeo versiones esse quaerendas: DFG-Projekt Saarbrücker Übersetzungsbibliographie – Latein. In Sergo, L. / Wienen, U. / Atayan, V. Eds. *Fachsprache(n) in der Romania. Entwicklung, Verwendung, Übersetzung.* Berlin: Frank & Timme, 403–419.

Weber, A. 2015. Tempus fugit – versiones manent: DFG Project *Saarbrücker Übersetzungsbibliographie – Latein.* In Steiner-Weber, A. / Enenkel, K. A. E. Eds. *Acta Conventus Neo-Latini Monasteriensis: Proceedings of the 15th International Congress of Neo-Latin Studies (Münster 2012).* Leiden: Brill, 604–613.

Weber, A. / Lehmann, A.-K. / Moretti, D. 2015. Saarbrücker Übersetzungsbibliographie – Latein. Eine ‚Fleißarbeit' des 21. Jahrhunderts!? In Gil, A. / Polzin-Haumann, C. Eds. *Angewandte Romanistische Linguistik. Kommunikations- und Diskursformen im 21. Jahrhundert.* St. Ingbert: Röhrig, 303–317.

Weber, A. / Moretti, D. / Atayan, V. 2015. Zwischen Deutschland und Romania: die Saarbrücker Übersetzungsbibliographien als Werkzeug der Sprach-, Kultur- und Translationswissenschaften. In Lavric, E. / Pöckl, W. Eds. *Comparatio delectat II. Akten der VII. Internationalen Arbeitstagung zum romanisch-deutschen und innerromanischen Sprachvergleich, Innsbruck, 6.–8. September 2012.* Frankfurt a. M.: Peter Lang, 679–692.

Willenberg, J. 2008. *Distribution und Übersetzung englischen Schrifttums im Deutschland des 18. Jahrhunderts.* München: Saur.

Martin Sinn

Sprachliche Vielfalt und disziplinäre Ausdifferenzierung: Dante in den Akademievorträgen Benedetto Varchis (1543–1547)

Abstract. Among the myths about the origin of language diversity, the biblical story of Babel is probably the most popular in Western culture. In its reception, the origin of language diversity is often linked to the different crafts involved in the construction of the tower. Against the background of this nexus linking disciplinary differentiation and language diversity, this article undertakes a contrastive analysis of the efforts for language elaboration as they can be found in Dante's *Convivio* and *Commedia* just as in the *lezioni* on Dante, which Benedetto Varchi delivered to the *Accademia Fiorentina* between 1543 and 1547. While the texts of the two authors are similar in their efforts to extend the vernacular into the domain of the scientific disciplines, they are fundamentally different in terms of the arrangement of the treated disciplines: Compared to Dante's *Commedia*, the reconstruction of his horizon of knowledge that Varchi undertakes in his academy lectures is accompanied by an increased awareness concerning the diversities and incompatibilities of the individual scientific disciplines. However, this brings into focus not only the individual scientific disciplines, but also the medium in which this content is conveyed: language itself. Language diversity, I propose in this article, is then no longer to be understood as the result of a divine vengeance, but as the result of an epistemological shift between the Middle Ages and the Renaissance, in which theology seems to forfeit its position as the ultimate purpose of all disciplines.

Abstract. Der in der westlichen Kultur wohl am meisten verbreitete Mythos zum Ursprung der Sprachenvielfalt ist die biblische Anekdote vom Turmbau zu Babel, in dessen Rezeption – etwa bei Dante – die Entstehung sprachlicher Vielfalt an die unterschiedlichen am Bau beteiligten Berufsgruppen geknüpft wird. Vor dem Hintergrund dieses Nexus von sprachlicher Vielfalt und disziplinärer Ausdifferenzierung unternimmt der folgende Beitrag eine kontrastive Analyse der Bemühungen um sprachlichen Ausbau, wie er sich einerseits im *Convivio* und in der *Commedia* Dantes, andererseits aber auch in den von Benedetto Varchi zwischen 1543 und 1547 vor der *Accademia Fiorentina* gehaltenen *lezioni* über Dante manifestiert. Während sich die Texte der beiden Autoren in ihrem Streben nach einem Ausbau der Volkssprache bis hinein in die wissenschaftlichen Disziplinen gleichen, erweisen sie sich im Hinblick auf die Ordnung dieser Disziplinen als grundsätzlich verschieden: Die Rekonstruktion des Wissenshorizontes Dantes, die Varchi in seinen Akademievorträgen unternimmt, geht mit einem gesteigerten Bewusstsein für die Verschiedenheiten und Inkompatibilitäten der einzelnen – in der *Commedia* weitaus weniger ausdifferenzierten – Disziplinen einher. Dies wiederum führt auch dazu, dass die Trennlinie zwischen literarischem und wissenschaftlichem Diskurs zunehmend an Schärfe gewinnt. Der Grund für die sprachliche und disziplinäre Ausdifferenzierung sowie die damit einhergehende sprachliche Vielfalt ist folglich nicht im – etwa von Dante postulierten – göttlichen Racheakt zu suchen, sondern im epistemologischen Wandel zwischen Mittelalter und Renaissance, in dem die Theologie ihre Position als Endzweck aller Disziplinen einzubüßen scheint.

1. Einleitung

Mythen über den Ursprung der Sprachenvielfalt gibt es viele: Die Hindu-Religionen etwa führen die sprachliche Vielfalt auf den Gott Brahma zurück, der die Äste des Lebensbaumes zurückschnitt und auf der ganzen Welt verteilte. Während sich zuvor noch alle Menschen unter dem bis zum Himmel reichenden Peepal-Baum versammeln konnten, wuchsen nun überall auf der Erde verteilt kleinere Banyan-Bäume, die allerdings weniger Menschen Schutz bieten konnten und so für die Entstehung unterschiedlicher Sprachen verantwortlich waren (cf. Żywiczyński 2019: 25–26). Die heilige Schrift des Islams hingegen, der *Qur'ān*, gibt diesbezüglich Anlass zu einer bis heute anhaltenden Diskussion, die sich insbesondere an der Auslegung von أَلْسِنَتِكُمْ (Transliteration: *alsinatikum*, dt. *eurer Zungen/eurer Sprachen*) entzündet – und damit an der Frage, ob die sprachliche Vielfalt menschlich und daher zu tadeln oder doch gottgegeben und daher auch gottgewollt ist (cf. Shah 2019: 182). Die Tukuna aus dem oberen Amazonasgebiet wiederum führen die Vielzahl der Sprachen auf einen Diebstahl zurück: Während des Versuchs, einen Erdhügel zu errichten, der bis zum Himmel reichen sollte, wurden zwei Kolibri-Eier, die als Nahrungsmittel für alle an der Erdarbeit Beteiligten vorgesehen waren, von einer einzigen Person verspeist. Schon bei dem Versuch, den Täter ausfindig zu machen, verstanden sie einander plötzlich nicht mehr – und der große Erdhügel zerfiel in die einzelnen Berge, die bis heute existieren (cf. Nimuendajú 1952: 130).

Vom Versuch, den Himmel zu erreichen, erzählt auch der biblische Mythos vom Turmbau zu Babel, der sich spätestens seit Augustinus nicht nur bei christlichen Theolog:innen großer Beliebtheit erfreut, sondern auch bei all jenen Gelehrten, die sich mit Fragen bezüglich der Sprachenvielfalt beschäftigen – schließlich sucht auch dieser Mythos nach einer Antwort auf die Frage des Ursprungs dieser Pluralität. So greift etwa auch Dante Alighieri in seiner ab 1304 verfassten Schrift *De vulgari eloquentia* (*DVE*) die biblische Anekdote auf, wenn er davon berichtet, dass sich in Babel das ganze Menschengeschlecht zusammengefunden habe, um – mit dem Ziel, den Schöpfer zu übertreffen – einen Turm zu errichten, der bis in den Himmel reichen sollte. Gott aber bestrafte den menschlichen Hochmut, indem er die Sprache der Menschen verwirrte, sodass diese vom Bau ablassen mussten, da ihnen die Möglichkeit der Verständigung genommen war. Eine Sprachen*vielfalt*

Dante in den Akademievorträgen Benedetto Varchis (1543–1547)

tritt an die Stelle der Sprache Adams, des bis dahin einheitlichen Hebräischen (cf. Coluccia 2021: 85). Doch während die mittelalterliche *vulgata* anschließend von der Zerstreuung der am Bau Beteiligten in die verschiedensten Länder berichtet (*BSV*, Gen. 11: 9), motiviert Dante die sprachliche Ausdifferenzierung auch semantisch-funktional:

> [6] Siquidem pene totum humanum genus ad opus iniquitatis coierat: pars imperabant, pars architectabantur, pars muros moliebantur, pars amussibus regulabant, pars trullis linebant, pars scindere rupes, pars mari, pars terra vehere intendebant, partesque diverse diversis aliis operibus indulgebant; cum celitus tanta confusione percussi sunt ut, qui omnes una eademque loquela deserviebant ad opus, ab opere, multis diversificati loquelis, desinerent et nunquam ad idem commertium convenirent.
>
> [7] Solis etenim in uno convenientibus actu eadem loquela remansit: puta cunctis architectoribus una, cunctis saxa volventibus una, cunctis ea parantibus una; et sic de singulis operantibus accidit. Quot quot autem exercitii varietates tendebant ad opus, tot tot ydiomatibus tunc genus humanum disiungitur; et quanto excellentius exercebant, tanto rudius nunc barbariusque locuntur. (*DVE* lat. 1188–1192)
>
> 6. Beinahe das ganze Menschengeschlecht war zu diesem Werk der Ungerechtigkeit zusammengeströmt: einige hatten die Leitung inne, einige die Bauplanung, einige errichteten die Mauern, einige begradigten sie mit Messleisten, einige verfugten sie mit Kellen, einige hauten Steine zu, einige wollten sie zu Wasser oder zu Lande befördern, einige widmeten sich diesen oder jenen Arbeiten, als sie auf einmal vom Himmel her mit einer derartigen Verwirrung geschlagen wurden, dass sie, die alle in einer und derselben Sprache das Werk angegangen waren, in verschiedene Sprachen zersplittert vom Werk ablassen mussten und nie wieder zu einer gemeinsamen Verständigung kommen konnten.
>
> 7. Nur die, die in derselben Tätigkeit vereinigt waren, behielten nämlich dieselbe Sprache. Also hatten alle Bauplaner eine gemeinsame Sprache, alle Steintransporteure eine, und so bei allen Tätigkeitsgruppen. Derart wurde damals das Menschengeschlecht in so viele Sprachen unterteilt, wie Berufssparten beim Werk beschäftigt waren, und je höher ihre Tätigkeit war, desto roher und barbarischer sprechen sie jetzt. (*DVE* dt. 47)

Im Unterschied zur *vulgata* schildert Dante, dass nach der Bestrafung Gottes jede Berufssparte ihre eigene Sprache erhalten habe. Die sprachliche Vielfalt resultiert bei Dante also auch aus der Vielfalt der am Bau beteiligten Tätigkeiten und kann daher mit Florian Mehltretter als eine Art „fachsprachliche Differenzierung" verstanden werden (Mehltretter 2010: 35).

Diesem Nexus von disziplinärer und sprachlicher Ausdifferenzierung widmet sich auch der vorliegende Beitrag, in dessen Zentrum ausgewählte, von Benedetto Varchi zwischen 1543 und 1547 vor der *Accademia Fiorentina* gehaltene *lezioni* über Dante stehen. Im ersten Abschnitt werden dazu zunächst zwei Werke desjenigen Autors näher betrachtet, der den zentralen Gegenstand der meisten Akademievorträge bildet: Anhand des *Convivio* und der *Commedia* soll zum einen aufgezeigt werden, dass sich Dantes Bemühen um einen sprachlichen Ausbau der Volkssprache (*volgare*) bis in den Bereich der Wissenschaft erstreckt. Zum anderen sollen die Disziplinen, die Eingang in die literarischen Texte Dantes finden, in die Wissensordnung der Zeit überführt werden und Überlegungen dazu angestellt werden, inwiefern in diesen Texten von einer strikten Trennung zwischen literarischem und wissenschaftlichem Diskurs ausgegangen werden kann.

Im zweiten Abschnitt stehen die oben bereits genannten Akademiereden Benedetto Varchis zu Textstellen der *Commedia* und insbesondere die darin enthaltenen metasprachlichen Kommentare im Mittelpunkt der Analyse. Ziel dieser Betrachtungen ist es einerseits, auch hier Aufschlüsse über das Vorgehen beim Sprachausbau im Bereich der Wissenschaften zu gewinnen, andererseits, durch die Analyse der in den *lezioni* vorgenommenen Rekonstruktion des Wissenshorizontes Dantes Erkenntnisse über das rinascimentale Verhältnis der einzelnen Disziplinen zueinander zu gewinnen. Die Akademien, hier insbesondere die *Accademia Fiorentina*, sowie die vor diesem Hintergrund entstehende Gattung des Akademievortrags, die in diesem Beitrag durch Benedetto Varchi vertreten wird, sollen dabei als Orte[1] verstanden werden, die sich dem sprachlichen Ausbau des *volgare* widmen, zugleich aber ein Bewusstsein für die disziplinäre Vielfalt schaffen und somit als Voraussetzung für die Entstehung ausdifferenzierter Fachsprachen betrachtet werden können. In einem abschließenden Abschnitt sollen die Ergebnisse der einzelnen Analysen zusammengetragen und in allgemeinere Überlegungen zum Verhältnis von Wissenschaft, Theologie und Literatur im Zeitalter der Renaissance überführt werden.

---

[1] An dieser Stelle sei auf das Forschungsprogramm des SFB 1391 *Andere Ästhetik* verwiesen, der sich bei der Untersuchung ästhetischer Akte und Artefakte in dreierlei Hinsicht von herkömmlichen Ästhetiktheorien unterscheidet: Er ist anders in der Zeit, insofern er sich vormodernen Gegenständen und Praktiken widmet und sich an einer Ästhetik vor der Ästhetik versucht, anders im Ort (sic!), insofern er nicht (nur) in normativen Werken wie Poetiken oder Rhetoriken nach Spuren des Ästhetischen sucht, und anders im Anspruch gesellschaftlicher Relevanz, insofern er stets in den Blick nimmt, wie die Akte und Artefakte in die Gesellschaft eingebunden sind, cf. Gerok-Reiter/Robert (2022).

Dante in den Akademievorträgen Benedetto Varchis (1543–1547)

2. Dante: Volkssprachlicher Universalitätsanspruch und mittelalterliche Epistemologie

2.1 Die Himmelssphären des Convivio und ein Titelblatt der Commedia

Kehren wir aber zunächst noch einmal zurück zu Dante. Dieser beginnt in den ersten Jahren des 14. Jahrhunderts, also ungefähr in jenem zeitlichen Rahmen, in dem er auch das *De vulgari eloquentia* niederschreibt, die Arbeit an einem weiteren Werk: dem *Convivio*. Im Unterschied zur Abhandlung über die Vulgärsprache verfasst er seinen philosophischen Kommentar eigener Kanzonen aber nicht auf Lateinisch, sondern im *volgare*. Dafür nennt er zugleich „tre ragioni, che mossero me ad eleggere innanzi questo che l'altro: l'una si muove da cautela di disconvenevole ordinazione; l'altra da prontezza di liberalitate; la terza da lo naturale amore e propria loquela" (*Convivio* 126). Zum einen seien auch seine Kanzonen in der Volkssprache verfasst worden (cf. *Convivio* 128), zum anderen schreibe er nicht für die Minderheit der Universitätsgelehrten, sondern für die weitaus größere Masse der „principi, baroni, cavalieri, e molt'altra nobile gente, non solamente maschi ma femmine" (*Convivio* 156). Als drittes Argument führt er an, dass er damit zudem die Leistungsfähigkeit des *volgare* unter Beweis stellen wolle:

> Chè per questo comento la gran bontade del volgare di sì [si vedrà]; però che si vedrà la sua vertù, sì com'è per esso altissimi e novissimi concetti convenevolemente, sufficientemente e acconciamente, quasi come per esso latino, manifestare [...]. (*Convivio* 164–166)

Die Versprachlichung von „altissimi" und „novissimi concetti" unternimmt er etwa bereits, wenn er im zweiten Buch die Himmelssphären mit den zeitgenössischen Disziplinen engführt: „[È] mestiere", so heißt es dort, „fare considerazione sovra una comparazione, che è ne l'ordine de li cieli a quello de le scienze" (*Convivio* 308). Leitend ist dabei das aristotelische Prinzip, man könne die Hierarchie der *scienze* anhand der Vornehmheit des jeweiligen Untersuchungsgegenstands bestimmen (cf. Maierù 1993: 158–159). Daraus ergibt sich eine Ordnung, in der die ersten sieben Himmelsbereiche den sieben *artes liberales* entsprechen: Die Disziplinen des Triviums – Grammatik, Dialektik und Rhetorik – bilden dabei die ersten drei Kreise ab, das Quadrivium – Arithmetik, Musik, Geometrie und Astronomie – die darauffolgenden vier. Der achten Sphäre, dem Fixsternhimmel, komme die Metaphysik gleich, der neunten die „scienza morale", dem letzten Kreis, dem sogenannten „cielo quieto" entspreche wiederum die „scienza divina, che è Teologia appellata" (*Convivio* 308–310). Somit steht letztere an oberster Stelle der Wissenschaften, was Dante einmal mehr auf die Vornehmheit und Gewissheit des untersuchten Gegenstandes zurückführt: „[N]on soffera lite alcuna d'oppinioni o di sofistici argomenti, per la eccellentissima certezza del suo subietto, lo quale è Dio" (*Convivio* 336). Der Philosophie kommt indessen eine besondere Rolle zu, die sich nur schwer in die Parallelisierung von Himmelssphären und *artes liberales* integrieren lässt: Sie ist nicht nur zentraler Bestandteil der philosophischen Disziplinen im engeren Sinne (gemeint sind „la Scienza Naturale, la Morale e la Metafisica"), sondern findet sich grundsätzlich in allen Disziplinen wieder – sie ist die „donna di questi autori, di queste scienze e di questi libri", bei der auch Dante selbst nach dem Tod Beatrices Trost findet (Maierù 1993: 162).

Damit finden wir im *Convivio* eine Wissensordnung vor, die in weiten Teilen der des Mittelalters entspricht: Während die Philosophie darin als Grundlage für die aus der Spätantike übernommenen *artes liberales* verstanden wird, dienen die sieben freien Künste der Vorbereitung auf die höchste Disziplin: die Theologie.[2]

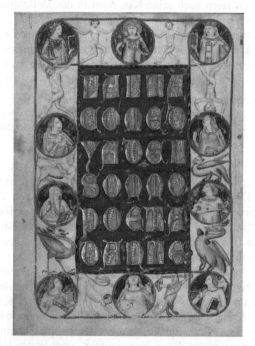

Fig. 1. Dante Alighieri: La divina commedia. [um 1360]. Codex Altonensis, Bibliotheca Christianei, Signatur: R 7/2.

---

[2] So stellt die Propädeutik der *artes liberales* auch im Universitätssystem die Voraussetzung für das Theologiestudium dar, cf. Lindgren (2012: Sp. 1101).

Dante in den Akademievorträgen Benedetto Varchis (1543–1547)

Ihr illustratives Pendant – insbesondere im Hinblick auf das Verhältnis zwischen den *artes* und der *teologia* – findet eine solche Epistemologie im Titelblatt einer auf die zweite Hälfte des 14. Jahrhunderts datierten Handschrift der *Commedia*, des sogenannten Codex Altonensis (cf. Fig. 1): „LALTA / COMED / YADEL / SOMMO / POETA / DANTE" benennt die Handschrift ihren Inhalt in der Mitte der Miniatur. Umgeben sind die auf blauen, rechteckigen Grund gesetzten goldenen Lettern von zehn Frauen-Medaillons, die sich um den Textkörper gruppieren: Ein Medaillon befindet sich jeweils an den vier Ecken des Quaders, an der längeren vertikalen Seite nehmen die Eckmedaillons zwei weitere Medaillons in ihre Mitte, an der kürzeren horizontalen Seite jeweils eines.

Auf der linken Seite identifiziert Klaus Arnold von unten beginnend die personifizierten Künste des Triviums: Die Dialektik mit Schere und Codex befindet sich am linken unteren Bildrand, darüber die gestikulierende Rhetorik und schließlich die Grammatik, die ihr Wissen durch Bücher, vor allem aber auch durch die Muttermilch weitergibt. Auch die *artes* des Quadriviums lassen sich unter den Medaillons ausmachen: Die zählende Arithmetik befindet sich in der unteren Bildmitte, die mit einem Messstab ausgestattete Geometrie in der rechten unteren Bildecke. Über ihr spielt die Personifikation der Musik auf einer Mandorla, die Astronomie, die über ihr steht, ist hingegen nur noch schwerlich zu identifizieren. In den restlichen drei Medaillons erkennt Arnold am linken oberen Bildrand die mit dem Reichsschwert und Reichsadler ausgestattete Personifikation des *imperium*, am rechten oberen Bildrand die Philosophie mit Buch, Szepter und Leiter, wie sie etwa bei Boethius imaginiert wird, und in der oberen Bildmitte die Gestalt der Theologie, symbolisiert durch den Seraph sowie die in der anderen Hand gehaltene Bibel (cf. Arnold 1999: 365–367). Nicht nur in der Analogisierung der Himmelssphären mit den wissenschaftlichen Disziplinen, wie wir sie im *Convivio* beobachten konnten, spiegelt sich also die mittelalterliche Epistemologie wider. Auch das Titelblatt der Handschrift aus dem 14. Jahrhundert bebildert eine Wissensordnung, in der sich die Theologie als höchste Disziplin präsentiert und die sieben *artes liberales* in ihren Dienst stellt. Dies zeigt sich einerseits räumlich, insofern die Theologie über den *artes* thront, andererseits aber auch durch die Blickführung der einzelnen personifizierten *artes*, die ihren Blick allesamt ehrfürchtig auf die Theologie richten.

2.2 Die Commedia *als Sammelbecken wissenschaftlicher und literarischer Diskurse*

Nicht nur im *Convivio*, auch und insbesondere in der *Commedia* stellt Dante die Leistungsfähigkeit des *volgare* unter Beweis. Im Rahmen seiner Jenseitsreise durchschreitet die *Figur* Dante die Abgründe der Höllenkreise bis hin zu den höchsten Sphären des Himmels, der *Autor* Dante erschließt diese sprachlich und kleidet von den niedrigsten bis zu den höchsten Gegenständen alles ihm Widerfahrene in ein volkssprachliches Gewand – und damit nicht zuletzt auch die unterschiedlichen Wissensgebiete der *scienze*: Von den Stadien der Verdauung und der Entstehung des Spermas bis hin zur Deutung von Mondkratern und dem Erscheinen von Regenbögen werden die unterschiedlichsten Themenbereiche und verschiedensten sprachlichen Register bedient. Überträgt man die Parallelisierung von Himmelssphären und Disziplinen aus dem *Convivio* zudem auf die Jenseitsreise der *Commedia*, entsteht das Bild, dass Dante – während er in Richtung Paradies schreitet – auch die unterschiedlichen wissenschaftlichen Disziplinen durchquert. So behandelt die *Commedia* „astronomia, astrologia, ottica, alchimia, matematica, geometria, logica, medicina nelle sue specializzazioni di fisiologia, anatomia ed embriologia" und kann deshalb mit Andrea Battistini verstanden werden als eine „sede in cui Dante dispiega tutte le sue molte conoscenze scientifiche" (Battistini 2013).

Die *Commedia* nimmt unterschiedliche Diskurse in sich auf, verwebt diese miteinander und wird zu einem literarischen Sammelbecken verschiedenster wissenschaftlicher Disziplinen. Möglicherweise manifestiert sich darin eine allgemeinere Tendenz früher volkssprachlicher Texte: nämlich die, dass darin in vielen Fällen keine klare Trennung von Wissenschaft und Literatur vorgenommen wird. „Ai tempi di Dante Alighieri, una vera distinzione tra le «due culture» non si poneva", postuliert Battistini und begründet dies einerseits etymologisch durch die Mehrdeutigkeit des Begriffs der *scienza*, andererseits durch die Stellung der Theologie innerhalb der Wissensordnung des Mittelalters: „A integrare tutto il sapere, e quindi anche la scienza e la letteratura, è la consapevolezza che tutto si riconduce a Dio [...]" (Battistini 2013). Und auch Claudio Giovanardi zieht einen vergleichbaren Schluss, wenn er sagt:

> [...] la linea di demarcazione tra testo scientifico e testo letterario non pare chiaramente evidente. Il Convivio dantesco è per larga parte interpretabile come un'opera scientifica; il Decameron boccacciano, a sua volta, non è privo di termini scientifici. È del resto noto che numerosi termini tecnico-scientifici sono penetrati nella nostra lingua per il tramite delle opere letterarie [...]. (Giovanardi 2006: 2197)

Das Streben nach der volkssprachlichen Erschließung sämtlicher Wissensgebiete wird Dante im ersten Drittel des 16. Jahrhunderts jedoch zum Verhängnis: In seinen *Prose della volgar lingua* entthront Pietro Bembo den Dichterkönig des 14. Jahrhunderts und schließt ihn – zumindest vordergründig – aus dem Kreis literarischer Autoritäten aus, denn „mentre che egli di ciascuna delle sette arti e della filosofia e, oltre acciò, di tutte le cristiane cose maestro ha voluto mostrar d'essere nel suo poema, egli men sommo e meno perfetto è stato nella poesia" (Bembo 1989: 178). Zu sehr habe sich Dante auf die Inhalte seiner Dichtung konzentriert, zu wenig auf die sprachliche Form, denn um alles ausdrücken zu können habe er „ora le latine voci, ora le straniere, che non sono state dalla Toscana ricevute, ora le vecchie del tutto e tralasciate, ora le non usate e rozze, ora le immonde e brutte, ora le durissime" verwendet – und damit nicht genug: selbst die „[voci] pure e gentili" habe er verdorben, sodass die *Commedia* nun eher einem „bello e spazioso campo di grano, che sia tutto d'avene e di logli e d'erbe sterili e dannose mescolato" (Bembo 1989: 178) gleiche. Umso überraschender scheint es, dass sich gerade ein Schüler Bembos des großen Vorhabens Dantes erneut annimmt – Benedetto Varchi.

3. Varchis Akademievorträge zwischen Sprachausbau und Wissensrekonstruktion

Das 16. Jahrhundert kann in Italien mit gutem Recht als das Jahrhundert der Akademien angesehen werden. In beinahe allen Regionen des polyzentrisch organisierten Italiens entstehen ab der Mitte des Jahrhunderts Sozietäten, die sich größtenteils in der Volkssprache – und damit unterscheiden sie sich von den lateinischsprachigen Universitäten (cf. Bätschmann/Weddigen 2013: 25) – den unterschiedlichsten Disziplinen widmen: die *Accademia delle Arti del Disegno* der bildenden Kunst, die *Accademia degli Intronati* dem Theater, die *Accademia degli Umoristi* der Politik und die *Accademia dei Lincei* den Naturwissenschaften. Mit der *Accademia della Crusca* und der *Accademia Fiorentina* sind darunter auch zwei Institutionen, die sich explizit der Sprachpflege – und insbesondere dem *volgare* – verschreiben. Selten sind diese Akademien in ihrem Handeln aber gänzlich ungebunden, ganz im Gegenteil: „Nicht wenige dieser Sozietäten in Italien", betonen Sarah Dessì Schmid und Jochen Hafner, „sind dabei in ihrer Existenz unmittelbar vom höfischen Leben abhängig, sei es ideell oder finanziell, oder gar in dieses integriert" (Dessì Schmid/Hafner 2016: 390). Auch in der 1540 unter der Schirmherrschaft von Cosimo de' Medici gegründeten *Accademia Fiorentina* gehen politische und sprachliche Fragen Hand in Hand – und das mit weitreichenden Folgen. So hebt etwa Eric Cochrane im Hinblick auf den Einflussbereich der florentinischen Akademie hervor:

> Life in Florence was also one in which class differences had not yet hardened into caste barriers, however much some philosophers might rant scornfully about the vulgar populace. Indeed, the elevation of the vernacular to the level of a literary and scientific language, which the new Accademia Fiorentina had

systematically promoted ever since its foundation in 1540, had obviated the once menacing split between a Latin-speaking elite and the rest of the citizenry. (Cochrane 1970: 47)

Ein einflussreiches Instrument, um eine solche Erhebung des *volgare* auf die Ebene der Literatur und der Wissenschaft durchzusetzen, kann in der neu entstehenden Gattung des Akademievortrags (cf. Kristeller 1960: 225) ausgemacht werden: Durch ihren besonderen medialen Status (schriftliche Konzeption, mündliche Realisierung (cf. Koch/Oesterreicher 2011)) bietet sie sich auch für die volkssprachliche Kommunikation wissenschaftlicher Inhalte für ein nicht latinophones Publikum an. Benedetto Varchi kann dabei als emblematischer Vertreter dieser neuen Gattung angesehen werden. Nach seiner Rückkehr aus dem Exil 1543 wurde er beauftragt, vor der versammelten Akademie *lezioni* über Dante zu halten und wurde, so Umberto Pirotti, recht bald zum

> most assiduous lecturer in the Florentine Academy; and there he used every subject as a pretext for nourishing the unlettered with the bread of science, cutting off the hard crust of scholastic Latin and then serving it with the elegance required by those used to magnificent banquets. (Pirotti 1970: 189)

Varchis metasprachliche Kommentare zum Ausbau des „unverkrusteten" *volgare* sowie seine Äußerungen zu den in der *Commedia* eng verwobenen Diziplinen sollen vor dem Hintergrund dieser neu entstandenen Gattung in den folgenden beiden Abschnitten genauer betrachtet werden.

3.1 Die Sprache der lezioni: ein volgare für die Wissenschaft

Wenngleich die Bewunderung Varchis für seinen Lehrer Bembo zeitweise ins Unermessliche zu steigen scheint – man denke etwa an Sonette wie „Non hanno il BEMBO le tue rive [...]" (Varchi 1555: 110) oder an die im Jahr 1546 gehaltene Grabrede zum Tode Bembos –, wäre es falsch, im Falle Varchis eine über alle Lebensphasen hinweg orthodox bembistische Prägung anzunehmen. Vielmehr oszilliert sein Werk in einem Spannungsfeld zwischen Bembismus einerseits und Florentinismus andererseits und unterscheidet sich somit in einigen Positionen beträchtlich von demjenigen seines Lehrers.[3]

---

[3] Dies zeigt sich auch schon in der Entstehungsgeschichte des *Ercolano*: Varchi soll in der Polemik zwischen Annibale Caro und Ludovico Castelvetro einschreiten – und zwar für seinen Freund Caro. Dieser aber vertritt in der Polemik den Standpunkt der Florentinisten, der konträr zu seiner bembistischen Prägung steht. Cf. hierzu etwa Pirotti (1971: 124).

Dante in den Akademievorträgen Benedetto Varchis (1543–1547)

Dies scheint etwa im Hinblick auf den Ausbau der Volkssprache der Fall zu sein: Während Bembo eine reine Sprache für die Literatur anstrebt und Dante aufgrund des Gebrauchs von Fremdwörtern und von Begriffen niederer sprachlicher Register aus dem Kreis der nachahmungswürdigen Autoren des Trecento ausschließt, verfolgt Varchi gemeinsam mit der *Accademia Fiorentina* das Ziel, das bereits Dante im *Convivio* und der *Commedia* anstrebte, nämlich das *volgare* auch in anderen Bereichen mit den antiken Sprachen konkurrenzfähig zu machen.

In seiner Rede zum Antritt seines Konsulats im Jahr 1545 konstatiert Varchi, dass sich seit der Gründung der Akademie dort derart beflissene Geister zusammenfanden,

> affinchè tutti gli uomini, e specialmente la gioventù fiorentina, potessero insieme con la bontà de' costumi e cognizione delle scienze, non solo apprendere, ma esercitare ancora la facultà del bene ed ornatamente parlare [...]. (*Lezioni* 175)

Im Vergleich zum Lateinischen fehle es der Vulgärsprache noch an Schmuck und Reichtum, gar vieles fehle ihr noch bis zu ihrem Höhepunkt, und dennoch sei die Sprache bereits jetzt in einem Zustand, der erlaube, „che ciascuno può non solo acconciamente e agiatamente, ma copiosamente ancora e leggiadramente sprimere con ella i concetti suoi tutti quanti" (*Lezioni* 178–179). Zwar führt er an dieser Stelle als Beispiel für beinahe göttliche Prosa und Dichtung noch seinen Lehrer Bembo an, doch wird schnell deutlich, dass es Varchi um weit mehr geht als um den Bereich der Literatur. Die „oratoria" (gemeint ist damit natürlich auch die volkssprachliche Redekunst) sei die Grundlage für sämtliche Disziplinen, denn „senza lei tutte l'arti e tutte le scienze di tutte le sorti sarebbono, si può dir, mutole, e tutte le cose o magnificamente fatte, o fortemente, o sapientemente, starebbono in oscuro ed al tutto nascose" (*Lezioni* 174). Ein schönes, wenn auch schwieriges Unternehmen sei es deshalb, den Menschen in diesem Bereich voranzubringen, der ihn vom Tier unterscheidet: der Sprache (cf. *Lezioni* 175).

In der *lezione* vom 25. Juni 1543, in der es – ausgehend vom 25. Gesang des *Purgatorio* – um die Entstehung des menschlichen Körpers geht, lässt sich anhand der metasprachlichen Kommentare Varchis erkennen, wie dabei vorgegangen werden soll: Man solle ihn entschuldigen, bittet er das Publikum zu Beginn seiner Rede,

> se in trattando di cose sì nuove e quasi del tutto inusitate nella lingua nostra, usarò necessariamente, seguitando in questo e i Greci ancora e i Latini, alcune parole e vocaboli i quali paressero alle vostre purgatissime orecchie, o più vili e plebei, o meno puri e onesti, che in questo castissimo e santissimo luogo tra persone tanto modeste e tanto disciplinate non si conviene [...]. (*Lezioni* 8–9)

215

Erneut wird deutlich, dass das *volgare* in manchen Bereichen, hier insbesondere in den wissenschaftlichen Disziplinen, noch hinter den antiken Sprachen zurückbleibt. Um aber zu diesen aufschließen zu können, bedient Varchi sich zur Versprachlichung neuer Inhalte im *volgare* genau dieser Vorbilder, was zur Verwendung von Wörtern führen kann, die dem Publikum unrein und niederträchtig erscheinen mögen. Einem hätte dies wohl besonders missfallen: seinem Lehrer Pietro Bembo.

3.2 Der Inhalt der lezioni: *Rekonstruktion und Ausdifferenzierung der Disziplinen*

Am Beispiel der *lezioni* zu Dante lässt sich aber nicht nur zeigen, in welcher sprachlichen Form die Inhalte vermittelt beziehungsweise welche sprachlichen Mittel für die Behandlung dieser Inhalte herangezogen werden sollen. Mit Blick auf den Inhalt der Vorträge vor der Akademie wird auch deutlich, dass Varchi sich in seinen Akademievorträgen zum Ziel setzt, dem Publikum die ausgewählten Textstellen der *Commedia* verständlich zu machen. Er ist sich dessen bewusst, dass Dante „seppe perfettamente tutte l'arti e scienze liberali" (*Lezioni* 8), und weiß darum, dass diese Eingang in den literarischen Text gefunden haben – also geht er den umgekehrten Weg und betreibt eine Rekonstruktion von Dantes Wissenshorizont.

So beginnt etwa seine Rede zum 25. Gesang des *Purgatorio*, die er im Dezember 1543 vor der versammelten Akademie hält, mit einigen philosophischen „primii principii e [...] prime cagioni", auf welche die Darlegung des wissenschaftlichen Hintergrunds folgt: „L'intendimento nostro nella presente lezione è dichiarare primieramente con più agevolezza che sapremo, e maggior brevità che potremo, la generazione e formazione dell'uomo [...]" (*Lezioni* 10). So behandelt er mit Autoritäten wie Aristoteles, Galenos und Averroes etwa die Themen Blut, Verdauung oder Menstruation, bevor dieses Wissen erneut an die Verse der *Commedia* rückgebunden wird. Ziel Varchis ist es, zu zeigen, dass Dante gleichermaßen als „ottimo medico e ottimo filosofo e ottimo teologo" (*Lezioni* 8) betrachtet werden kann. Dass es sich dabei um keinen Einzelfall handelt, wird etwa in der vierten *lezione* zum ersten Gesang des *Paradiso* deutlich, wo es im Hinblick auf die verschiedenen Arten des Sonnenaufgangs heißt:

> Ma perchè Dante favella in questo luogo non solamente come poeta ed astrologo, ma ancora come filosofo e teologo, per meglio intendere queste differenze è necessario che sappiamo prima alcune cose belle sì ed utilissime, ma fastidiose in vero e male agevoli a dichiarare così a mente senza strumenti, e massimamente in questa lingua ed a chi non n'avesse alcuna notizia da se. (*Lezioni* 256)

Dante in den Akademievorträgen Benedetto Varchis (1543–1547)

An gleich mehreren Stellen wird somit erkenntlich, dass sich die in der *Commedia* miteinander verwobenen Ansichten Dantes unterschiedlichsten Disziplinen zuordnen lassen und sich in manchen Fällen gar gegenüberstehen. Dies zeigt sich etwa in der dritten und vierten *lezione* zum zweiten Gesang des *Paradiso*, die um die Thematik der Mondflecken kreisen: Die großen Philosophen aller Nationen hätten sich bereits gefragt, „che cosa siano e donde procedano quelle varietà e diversità di parti che nella luna si vedono" (*Lezioni* 471). Selbsterklärend ist es an dieser Stelle, dass sich auch Dante in der *Commedia* mit dieser Problematik auseinandergesetzt hat – doch lässt sich seine Argumentation nicht auf eine einzige, sondern auf gleich mehrere Disziplinen zurückführen:

> E perchè l'oppenione di Dante non è tutta teologica, come si credono tutti, ma parte filosofica e parte astrologica, però è necessario dichiarare prima tutte e tre queste oppenioni, senza le quali è del tutto impossibile intendere pur una parola sola di quanto si deve dichiarare oggi [...]. (*Lezioni* 491)

In den darauffolgenden Abschnitten unternimmt Varchi den Versuch, diese drei Disziplinen voneinander zu trennen und die unterschiedlichen Meinungen vergleichend gegenüberzustellen: Anhand der philosophischen Lehre legt er die Anordnung der sieben Planeten mit dem Fixsternhimmel dar und erklärt, weshalb Saturn der „più perfetto tra i sette pianeti", der Mond hingegen der „più imperfetto" sei (*Lezioni* 494). Zu den acht Sphären der Philosophen treten in der Theologie zwei weitere Sphären hinzu, wobei der philosophische „motore primo" durch „Dio" ersetzt wird (*Lezioni* 497). Die Astrologen hingegen nehmen neben den acht Himmeln der Philosophen grundsätzlich nur einen weiteren an, den „primo mobile", und stellen für die unterschiedlichen Planeten unterschiedliche Temperaturen, Geschlechter und Effekte fest (*Lezioni* 499). „Ma tornando di nuovo a Dante", resümiert er sodann,

> dico che l'oppenione sua pare a me che sia mescolata di tutte e quattro l'oppenioni predette; perciocchè [...] egli piglia da Aristotile che le Intelligenze siano forme dei corpi celesti, come l'intelletto umano è forma degli uomini [...]; dai teologi piglia che l'ultimo cielo o piuttosto il primo sia immobile, la qual cosa è impossibile appresso Aristotile [...]; dagli astrologi piglia l'influenza [...]; e finalmente soggiugne l'oppenione sua [...] che le macchia che si veggono nella luna vi siano dentro sostanzialmente. (*Lezioni* 502–503)

Aus den Versen Dantes extrapoliert Varchi die einzelnen Disziplinen, auf die sich die Argumentation des *sommo poeta* zurückführen lässt. Doch belässt er es nicht dabei: Er hebt zudem hervor, an welchen Stellen sich die Disziplinen unterscheiden oder gar inkompatibel miteinander sind.

Dies betrifft nicht nur die einzelnen *artes*: Vor dem Hintergrund eines gesteigerten Bewusstseins für die Verschiedenheit der Disziplinen, das mit der Rekonstruktion des Wissenshorizonts Dantes einhergeht, wird auch die Unterscheidung von literarischem und wissenschaftlichem Diskurs zum Gegenstand. So stellt Varchi in der zweiten *lezione* zur *maggioranza dell'arti*, die er am 13. März 1547 vor der *Accademia Fiorentina* hält, vor dem Hintergrund einer Textstelle der *Commedia* einmal mehr verschiedene Disziplinen nebeneinander, hebt dabei aber nun auch die Besonderheit des literarischen Diskurses hervor:

> Ma queste [le scienze, Anm. M.S.] non sono quelle, che facciano il poeta, perché ne potrebbe scrivere e come Filosofo e come Medico e come Astrologo, e così di tutte l'altre; ma quello, che fa il poeta è il modo dello scriverle poeticamente [...]. (*Lezione seconda* 132)

Auch über Lukrez, so heißt es weiter, könnte man behaupten, dass er kein Dichter, sondern ein Philosoph sei, doch sei der philosophische Gegenstand an manchen Stellen auf solch poetische Art und Weise dargestellt, dass man ihn dort als Dichter betrachten könne – was sich auch an Dante zeige,

> che in molti luoghi tratta le quistioni e di teologia e di filosofia e di tutte l'altre scienze, la qual cosa non è da poeta; ma le tratta, oltre il numero, con parole e figure e modi di dire poetici. (*Lezione seconda* 132)

Was den Dichter auszeichnet, ist eine bestimmte Art, die Dinge zu betrachten und diese vor allem auch sprachlich – durch eigene „parole e figure e modi di dire" – darzustellen. Nur ist diese eben weder astrologisch noch medizinisch oder philosophisch, sondern schlicht und einfach poetisch. Während die *Commedia* sich als ein Sammelbecken unterschiedlichster Disziplinen präsentiert und keine Unterscheidung zwischen literarischem und wissenschaftlichem Diskurs vorzunehmen scheint, resultiert die disziplinäre Ausdifferenzierung, die Varchi in den *lezioni* vornimmt, nun auch in einer stärkeren Abgrenzung des wissenschaftlichen vom literarischen Diskurs, insofern nicht nur die Charakteristika der einzelnen *artes liberales* herausgearbeitet und gegenübergestellt, sondern auch die (sprachlichen) Besonderheiten des dichterischen Schaffens hervorgehoben werden. Florian Mehltretters These, man könne im 16. Jahrhundert, etwa bei Fortunio und Bembo, sehen, dass „[d]ie literarische Sprache [...] noch kein eigenes Subsystem [ist], das von anderen Arten der Schriftsprache getrennt wäre", scheint wenige Jahre später – zumindest in den *lezioni* Varchis – nicht mehr uneingeschränkt gültig zu sein (Mehltretter 2009: 36).

Darüber hinaus scheint es bei all dem beinahe so, als wäre die Theologie nur eine Disziplin unter anderen – und auch in der sechsten *lezione* zum ersten Canto des *Paradiso*, in der Varchi versucht, die Wissensordnung der

Dante in den Akademievorträgen Benedetto Varchis (1543–1547)

Commedia zu rekonstruieren, wird die Position der Theologie nicht expliziert. Varchi geht dort von der Unterscheidung zwischen den *parole* einerseits und den *cose* andererseits aus. Den *parole* ordnet er die Künste des Triviums (Poetik, Grammatik, Rhetorik) zu, den *cose* die des Quadriviums und die alles umfassende Philosophie ebenso wie Medizin, Politik und Jurisprudenz (cf. *Lezioni* 194–195). „Alle quali cose si deve aggiugnere la Teologia cristiana", fügt er dann hinzu, ohne aber zu spezifizieren, wie sich die Theologie in der Wissensordnung Dantes zu den anderen Disziplinen verhält (*Lezioni* 195). Zu untersuchen bleibt, inwiefern sich die (rekonstruierte) Epistemologie Varchis von der Dantes tatsächlich unterscheidet – die Theologie in der rinascimentalen Wissensordnung Varchis tatsächlich ihre Stellung als Endzweck aller Disziplinen verliert, die in der mittelalterlichen Epistemologie, etwa im *Convivio* oder der *Commedia*, noch unumstritten scheint.

4. Fazit

Anhand der Analyse ausgewählter *lezioni* zu Dante Benedetto Varchis konnte zum einen gezeigt werden, dass der Akademievortrag ein wichtiges Instrument für den Sprachausbau im *volgare* darstellt, insofern er sich zu einer bedeutenden, wenn nicht gar zur zentralsten Gattung des im 16. Jahrhundert aufblühenden Akademiewesens entwickelt, das sich wiederum der zumeist volkssprachlichen Behandlung wissenschaftlicher Gegenstände verschreibt. Zum anderen wurde deutlich, dass in den Akademievorträgen Varchis zur *Commedia* eine Rekonstruktion von Wissensbeständen zur Texterläuterung vorgenommen wird und diese Rekonstruktion mit einem Bewusstsein einerseits für disziplinäre Verschiedenheiten und Inkompatibilitäten und andererseits für die Besonderheiten der Dichtkunst, in der die wissenschaftlichen Gegenstände in der *Commedia* behandelt werden, einhergeht. Zur Folge hat dies, dass auch die Trennlinie zwischen literarischem und wissenschaftlichem Diskurs an Schärfe gewinnt, insofern durch die Rekonstruktion – so zumindest im Fall von Dantes *Commedia* und Varchis *lezioni* – ein „Herausschälen" der wissenschaftlichen Disziplinen aus dem literarischen Diskurs stattfindet.

Würde sich zudem der Verdacht bestätigen, dass die Theologie im Übergang von einer mittelalterlichen zu einer rinascimentalen Wissensordnung ihre Position als höchste Disziplin verliert, wäre die fachsprachliche Auffächerung also weniger ein göttlicher Racheakt im Sinne der babylonischen Sprachverwirrung als das Resultat einer disziplinären Ausdifferenzierung und einer epistemologischen Neuordnung: Wenn die Theologie nicht mehr den Endzweck aller wissenschaftlichen Bemühungen darstellt, ließe sich damit das gesteigerte Bewusstsein für die Verschiedenheit der Disziplinen und deren zunehmende Autonomie begründen, die sich – dies sei hier abschließend angemerkt – nicht zuletzt auch in der frühneuzeitlichen Behauptung der Philologie als Textauslegungswissenschaft jenseits der Bibelexegese manifestiert.

Diese Pluralisierung derjenigen Instanzen, die eine Deutungshoheit über Texte für sich beanspruchen, spiegelt sich in der Tatsache wider, dass offenbar ein und derselbe Gegenstand, so etwa die Mondflecken oder die Anordnung der Planeten, in ein und demselben Text, dem Akademievortrag (hier: Varchis), aus unterschiedlichen Perspektiven betrachtet werden kann. Die disziplinären Entfaltungen und die hermeneutischen Auslegungskonkurrenzen wären dann ein weiteres Indiz einer „generellen Pluralisierungstendenz der Diskurse" im Zeitalter der Renaissance, denn auch hier gilt die Regelmäßigkeitsannahme, die Klaus W. Hempfer voraussetzt: „[E]pistemologischer Wandel bedingt (in der Regel) Diskurswandel" (Hempfer 1991: 39).

Bibliographie

Arnold, K. 1999. Bildung im Bild: Darstellungen der *septem artes liberales* in der Kunst des Mittelalters und der Renaissance. In Schaefer, U. Ed. *Artes im Mittelalter*. Berlin: Akademie Verlag, 361–375.

Bätschmann, O. / Weddigen, T. 2013. Einleitung. In Bätschmann, O. / Weddigen, T. Eds. *Benedetto Varchi. Paragone – Rangstreit der Künste.* Darmstadt: WBG, 7–64.

Battistini, A. 2013. Lingua, letteratura e scienza da Dante a Calvino. *Il Contributo italiano alla storia del Pensiero – Scienze.* Rom: Istituto dell'Enciclopedia italiana. https://www.treccani.it/enciclopedia/letteratura-e-scienza-da-dante-a-calvino-lingua_(Il-Contributo-italiano-alla-storia-del-Pensiero:-Scienze)/ (04.10.2021).

Bembo, P. 1989. Prose della volgar lingua. In Dionisotti, C. Ed. *Pietro Bembo. Prose della volgar lingua. Gli Asolani. Rime.* Mailand: TEA, S. 71–309.

BSV = Biblia sacra vulgata. Genesis – Exodus – Leviticus – Numeri – Deuteronomium. Ed. von Beriger, A. / Ehlers, W.-W. / Fieger, M. 2018. Bd. I. Berlin / Boston: De Gruyter.

Cochrane, E. 1970. A Case in Point: The End of the Renaissance in Florence. In Cochrane, E. *The Late Italian Renaissance* 1525–1630. London: Macmillan, 43–73.

Coluccia, R. 2021. Il mito di Babele. In Frosini, G. / Polimeni, G. Eds. *Dante e il linguaggio.* Florenz: Accademia della Crusca, 83–90.

Convivio = Alighieri, D. *Convivio.* In Ed. von Fioravanti, G. / Giunta, C. / Quaglioni, D. / Villa, C. / Albanese, G. 2014. *Opere.* Bd. II. Mailand: Mondadori, 89–805.

Dante in den Akademievorträgen Benedetto Varchis (1543–1547)

Dessì Schmid, S. / Hafner, J. 2016. Die italienischen und französischen Akademien als Zentren frühneuzeitlicher höfischer Sprachdiskussion. In Balsamo, J. / Bleuler, A. Eds. *Les cours comme lieux de rencontre et d'élaboration des langues vernaculaires à la Renaissance (1480–1620).* Genf: Droz, 381–418.

DVE dt. = Alighieri, D. *De vulgari eloquentia.* Ed. von Klump, A. / Frings, M. 2007. Übers. von Frings, M. und Kramer, J. Stuttgart: ibidem.

DVE lat. = Alighieri, D. *De vulgari eloquentia.* In Ed. von Giunto, C. / Guglielmo, G. / Tavoni, M. 2011. *Opere.* Bd. I. Mailand: Mondadori, 1065–1547.

Gerok-Reiter, A. / Robert, J. 2022. Andere Ästhetik – Akte und Artefakte in der Vormoderne. Zum Forschungsprogramm des SFB 1391. In Gerok-Reiter, A. / Robert, J. / Bauer, M. / Pawlak, A. Eds. *Andere Ästhetik. Grundlagen – Fragen – Perspektiven.* Berlin / Boston: De Gruyter, 1–52.

Giovanardi, C. 2006. Storia dei linguaggi tecnici e scientifici nella Romania: italiano. In Ernst, G. / Glessgen, M.-D. / Schmitt, C. / Schweickard, W. Eds. *Romanische Sprachgeschichte.* Bd. II. Berlin / New York: De Gruyter Mouton, 2197–2211.

Hempfer, K. W. 1991. Intertextualität, Systemreferenz und Strukturwandel: die Pluralisierung des erotischen Diskurses in der italienischen und französischen Renaissance-Lyrik (Ariost, Bembo, Du Beilay, Ronsard). In Titzmann, M. / Jäger, G. Eds. *Modelle des literarischen Strukturwandels.* Tübingen: Max Niemeyer, 7–43.

Koch, P. / Oesterreicher, W. 2011. *Gesprochene Sprache in der Romania: Französisch, Italienisch, Spanisch.* Berlin: De Gruyter.

Kristeller, P. O. 1960. Der Gelehrte und sein Publikum im späten Mittelalter und der Renaissance. In Jauss, H. R. / Schaller, D. Eds. *Medium Aevum Vivum. Festschrift für Walther Bulst.* Heidelberg: Winter, 212–230.

Lezione seconda = Varchi, B. *Lezione seconda. Della maggioranza dell'arti e quali sia più nobile, la scultura o la pittura.* In Ed. von Bettoni, N. e Comp. 1834. *Opere di Benedetto Varchi con lettere di Gio. Batista Busini.* Mailand: Bettoni, 114–133.

Lezioni = Varchi, B. *Lezioni sul Dante e prose varie.* Ed. von Aiazzi, G./Arbib, L. Eds. 1841. Bd. 1. Florenz: Società Editrice delle Storie del Nardi e del Varchi.

Lindgren, U. 2012. Artes liberales. In Ueding, G. Ed. *Historisches Wörterbuch der Rhetorik.* Bd. I. Tübingen: Niemeyer, Sp. 1080–1109.

Maierù, A. 1993. Sull'epistemologia di Dante. In Boyde, P. / Russa, V. Eds. *Dante e la scienza.* Ravenna: Longo Editore, 157–172.

Mehltretter, F. 2009. *Kanonisierung und Medialität: Petrarcas Rime in der Frühzeit des Buchdrucks (1470–1687).* Münster: LIT.

Mehltretter, F. 2010. *Questione della lingua, questione dello stile.* Zur Diachronie von Pluralisierung und Autorität in der Frühneuzeitlichen Sprach- und Dichtungsreflexion. In Müller, J.-D. / Oesterreicher, W. / Vollhardt, F. Eds. *Pluralisierungen. Konzepte zur Erfassung der Frühen Neuzeit.* Berlin / New York: De Gruyter, 31–51.

Nimuendajú, C. 1952. *The Tukuna*. Ed. von Lowie, R. H., Übers. von Hohenthal W. D. Berkeley / Los Angeles: University of California Press.
Pirotti, U. 1970. Aristotelian Philosophy and the Popularization of Learning: Benedetto Varchi and Renaissance Aristotelianism. In Cochrane, E. Ed. *The Late Italian Renaissance*. London: Macmillan, 168–208.
Pirotti, U. 1971. *Benedetto Varchi e la cultura del suo tempo*. Florenz: Olschki.
Shah, M. 2019. The word of God: The epistemology of language in classical Islamic theological thought. In Yelle, R. A. / Handman, C. / Lehrich, C. I. Eds. *Language and Religion*. Boston / Berlin: De Gruyter, 158–192.
Varchi, B. 1555. *Dei sonetti di M. Benedetto Varchi. Parte prima*. Florenz.
Żywiczyński, P. 2019. *The Evolution of Language: Towards Gestural Hypotheses*. Berlin et al.: Peter Lang.

Franz Meier

Les phrases pseudo-clivées inversées dans la traduction scientifique dans l'Italie de la fin du 18ᵉ siècle

Abstract. In the 18th century, the translation of scientific texts played a fundamental role in the creation of scientific periodicals, which were mainly addressed to small groups of experts. This article focuses on the use of reversed pseudo-cleft sentences in the Italian translation of French scientific texts of the late 18th century. The aim is to determine, in a contrastive perspective, the frequency, form and function of this construction in the French and Italian scientific language of the time. The diachronic evolution of French and Italian reversed pseudo-cleft sentences has not been studied yet, contrary to the diffusion of cleft-sentences in Italian, which is often attributed to the dominant influence of French in the 18th century. The analysis is based on a corpus of translations published between 1770 and 1795 in Italian scientific periodicals and on a corpus of comparable untranslated Italian texts published in the same period and in the same periodicals.

Abstract. Au 18ᵉ siècle, la traduction de textes scientifiques joue un rôle fondamental dans la création de périodiques scientifiques qui s'adressent majoritairement à de petits groupes d'experts. Dans cet article, nous nous intéressons à l'emploi de phrases pseudo-clivées inversées dans la traduction italienne de textes scientifiques français de la fin du 18ᵉ siècle. L'objectif est de déterminer, dans une perspective contrastive, la fréquence, la forme et la fonction de cette construction dans les langues scientifiques française et italienne de l'époque. L'histoire des pseudo-clivées inversées en français et en italien n'a fait l'objet d'aucune étude empirique, contrairement aux phrases clivées dont la diffusion en italien est souvent attribuée à l'influence dominante du français au 18ᵉ siècle. L'analyse repose sur un corpus de traductions publiées entre 1770 et 1795 dans des périodiques scientifiques italiens et sur un corpus de comparaison de textes italiens non traduits publiés à la même période et dans les mêmes périodiques.

1. Introduction

Au siècle des Lumières, une partie importante de la communication scientifique se fait à travers de la presse périodique, qui constitue une réponse innovante à la nécessité de rassembler et de diffuser rapidement de nouveaux acquis dans la République des Lettres européenne (cf. Forner/Meier/Schwarze 2022). Ces périodiques sont d'emblée liés à la traduction, car ils sont publiés dans un contexte où le latin perd de son importance comme langue savante universelle au profit des différentes langues européennes. Durant la seconde moitié du 18ᵉ siècle, presse périodique et traduction scientifique s'influencent mutuellement pour remplacer l'ancien modèle de la revue érudite par celui d'une presse spécialisée consacrée exclusivement à des thématiques scientifiques et s'adressant majoritairement à de petits groupes d'experts (cf. Delpiano 2013). Selon Bret (2013), l'activité de traduction contribue significativement à cette spécialisation de la presse, car il devient possible de publier un nombre suffisant d'articles portant sur des thématiques très homogènes.

Dans la communauté scientifique italienne, les traductions du français sont particulièrement importantes, notamment parce que l'on attribue souvent au français une fonction de modèle stylistique (cf. Schwarze 2001). En effet, si la langue scientifique italienne est à l'époque encore très influencée par un style littéraire riche en subordonnées et en inversions, le français est fréquemment associé à la clarté et à la lisibilité. Ainsi, selon Altieri Biagi (1998), la traduction de textes scientifiques français influence la production de textes scientifiques italiens, notamment en ce qui a trait à la simplification du style. Cependant, il existe peu de travaux qui, d'un point de vue interlinguistique, portent sur la traduction de textes scientifiques français, ce à quoi nous nous intéressons ici.

Selon Aschenberg/Dessì Schmid (2017), les traductions peuvent contribuer à la diffusion d'innovations dans la langue cible. Ces innovations ne constituent pas exclusivement des interférences de la langue source (cf. Kranich/Becher/Höder 2011), mais proviennent aussi de la (dé)mobilisation de constructions déjà existantes dans la langue cible (cf. Frank-Job 2008). Il est généralement admis que le changement linguistique induit par la traduction est un « changement d'en haut » (Labov 1972), c'est-à-dire que les innovations sont d'abord employées par les locuteurs érudits avant de se généraliser à l'ensemble de la communauté linguistique.

Dans cet article, nous nous intéressons à l'usage de phrases pseudo-clivées inversées dans la traduction italienne de textes scientifiques français de la fin du 18ᵉ siècle. À notre connaissance, l'histoire des pseudo-clivées inversées en français et en italien n'a fait l'objet d'aucune étude empirique, contrairement aux phrases clivées dont la diffusion en italien est généralement attribuée à l'influence dominante du français au 18ᵉ siècle, bien que la construction soit déjà attestée de façon ponctuelle en ancien italien (cf. D'Achille/Proietti/Viviani 2005). Ainsi, l'objectif de cet article est de contribuer à une première description historique contrastive des pseudo-clivées inversées. Nous montrerons que les pseudo-clivées inversées italiennes jouent un rôle important en tant qu'équivalents dans la diffusion des phrases clivées dans la langue scientifique italienne de la fin du 18ᵉ siècle.

Notre analyse repose sur un corpus de 60 traductions publiées entre 1770 et 1795 dans sept périodiques scientifiques italiens et dont les textes sources proviennent de périodiques scientifiques français. Nous avons également constitué un corpus de comparaison de 30 textes italiens non traduits, publiés à la même période et dans les mêmes périodiques italiens. Tous les textes du corpus appartiennent au genre de la dissertation et du mémoire, précurseurs de l'article scientifique (cf. Altieri Biagi 1990).[1]

2. Les phrases pseudo-clivées inversées : aspects théoriques

En italien, les phrases pseudo-clivées inversées sont divisées en deux parties, à savoir une phrase matrice copulative contenant l'élément clivé et une phrase subordonnée constituant une phrase relative restrictive (De Cesare 2017 : 538–540) :

(1) Mio fratello   è   quello che ha la macchina
     [élément clivé copule] [phrase subordonnée]

Garassino (2014 : 56–61) propose une distinction formelle entre deux types de pseudo-clivées inversées selon la catégorie syntaxique du constituant clivé : d'une part, les pseudo-clivées inversées de type 1, dans lesquelles l'élément clivé peut prendre la forme d'un syntagme nominal, d'un syntagme prépositionnel, d'un syntagme adverbial ou d'un syntagme verbal fini ; d'autre part, les pseudo-clivées inversées de type 2, dans lesquelles seul le pronom démonstratif neutre *questo* peut être clivé (*questo è quello che mi piace di più*). La phrase subordonnée est introduite soit par les pronoms complexes *quello/quella che* ou *ciò che*, soit par des pronoms relatifs libres *chi, come, dove, perché* et *quando*. Il existe aussi des pseudo-clivées inversées suivant le modèle *La pragmatica è la cosa che mi piace di più* (cf. Garassino 2014 : 59) qui sont introduites par un syntagme nominal défini et dans laquelles un terme générique (*la cosa/il luogo/il modo/la persona/la ragione*) est modifié par une clause relative restrictive. Par ailleurs, on trouve aussi des pseudo-clivées inversées où il existe une relation hyperonymique entre l'élément clivé et le nom qui précède la phrase subordonnée, dont le sens est plus spécifique : *Il rosso è il colore che preferisco* (cf. Garassino 2014 : 59).[2]

---

[1] Les textes sources français et leurs traductions italiennes contiennent respectivement 166 400 mots et 157 300 mots. Les textes italiens non traduits contiennent 109 500 mots.

[2] Pour une présentation et une analyse détaillées des propriétés formelles des pseudo-clivées inversées, cf. aussi Roggia (2009) et De Cesare (2016).

Contrairement à l'italien, les pseudo-clivées inversées françaises ne sont pas identifiées dans les grammaires de référence,[3] surtout parce qu'elles sont généralement considérées comme un phénomène de la langue parlée (cf. Boxus 2006). Dans les pseudo-clivées inversées françaises, le sujet grammatical de la phrase matrice est exprimé par *ce* (cf. Apothéloz 2014), tandis qu'en italien, le sujet n'est pas réalisé :

(2) La liste des bouquins pour les examens, c'est ce que j'aimerais bien avoir.

Le terme *clivé* implique qu'une phrase monoclausale possède une variante biclausale équivalente (cf. Lambrecht 2001 : 463). Néanmoins, certaines clivées ne permettent pas de former de contrepartie non-clivée sans que ne soient apportées des adaptations. Nous ne considérons pas l'existence de contreparties non-clivées exactes comme un critère définitoire. Selon le contexte, des structures monoclausales sémantiquement équivalentes ne sont pas automatiquement équivalentes sur le plan pragmatique (cf. Krassenberg 2018 : 21–24).

D'un point de vue sémantique, les pseudo-clivées inversées sont des phrases copulatives spécificationnelles qui expriment une relation d'identité entre le référent du constituant clivé et le contenu propositionel de la phrase subordonnée (cf. Declerck 1984).[4] Sur le plan de la structure informationnelle, les pseudo-clivées inversées actualisent différentes configurations cognitives. Ainsi, les phrases matrice et subordonnée peuvent contenir soit des informations déjà connues, soit de nouvelles informations (cf. Delin/Oberlander 1995). Lirola (2006) constate toutefois des configurations préférentielles qui découlent de principes pragmatiques généraux : d'une part, la tendance à placer les informations connues avant les informations nouvelles (cf. Collins 1991 : 145) ; d'autre part, la tendance à placer les constituants syntaxiquement plus courts avant les constituants syntaxiquement plus longs (cf. Declerck 1984 : 280). Selon Garassino (2014 : 68), la forme du constituant clivé peut aussi influer sur la structure informationnelle dans la mesure où le clivage d'un pronom demande une progression allant de contenus connus à des contenus nouveaux, tandis que des éléments clivés non-pronmiaux permettent un éventail plus large de configurations.

---

[3] Pour les grammaires de référence italiennes, cf. par exemple Salvi (1991).
[4] Pour les différentes typologies de phrases copulatives, cf. Den Dikken (2006). Nous suivons ici la distinction entre les phrases spécificationnelles, où l'expression suivant la copule identifie un référent (*Luc est le père de Lucie*), et les phrases prédicationnelles, où elle dénote une propriété (*Luc est père*).

3. Fréquence

La présence des pseudo-clivées inversées est marginale dans les données analysées. Leur fréquence d'emploi est faible dans les textes italiens non traduits et nous n'en avons rencontré aucune occurrence dans les textes sources français.

	Textes source français		Textes italiens non traduits	
	N	*f*	N	*f*
Pseudo-clivées inversées	0	0	22	2,0

Tab. 1. Fréquence des pseudo-clivées inversées dans les textes sources français et les textes italiens non traduits (f = occurrences par 10 000 mots).

Compte tenu de ces résultats, il semble important d'inclure le paramètre des genres textuels dans la discussion sur la fréquence des pseudo-clivées inversées au 18e siècle. En ce sens, il ne faut pas exclure à priori un emploi plus fréquent de ces constructions dans d'autres genres qui ne sont pas publiés dans les périodiques scientifiques.

En italien contemporain, les pseudo-clivées inversées s'avèrent aussi extrêmement rares, en particulier dans la langue écrite (cf. Berretta 2002 ; Wehr 2016). Dans un corpus de quotidiens italiens publiées entre 2011 et 2012, Garassino (2014) mesure une fréquence de 4 phrases pseudo-clivées inversées par 100 000 mots, ce qui est cinq fois moins élevé que celle que nous avons relevée dans notre étude. On pourrait donc postuler un changement diachronique dans la mesure où la langue écrite du 18e siècle semble plus ouverte à l'emploi des pseudo-clivées inversées. Toutefois, étant donné le peu d'études sur le sujet, les données disponibles sont trop limitées pour qu'il soit possible de se prononcer globalement sur l'évolution des pseudo-clivées inversées dans l'histoire de l'italien. En français, le manque d'études diachroniques rend également impossible l'établissement d'un bilan de l'historique de la construction.

Malgré l'absence de pseudo-clivées inversées dans les textes sources français, la construction se rencontre près de deux fois plus souvent dans les traductions que dans les textes italiens non traduits. Cet emploi plus fréquent doit certes être considéré comme une conséquence directe du contact de langues à travers la traduction, mais pas comme un transfert interlinguistique de propriétés structurelles au sens d'un copiage du code (*code copying*) de la langue source[5] puisque la construction n'est pas attestée dans les textes français.

	Traductions		Textes italiens non traduits	
	N	*f*	N	*f*
Pseudo-clivées inversées	54	3,4	22	2,0

Tab. 2. Fréquence des pseudo-clivées inversées dans les traductions et les textes italiens non traduits (f = occurrences par 10 000 mots).

4. Forme

4.1 Textes non traduits

On note une large dominance des pseudo-clivées inversées de type 1 dans les textes italiens non traduits (21 occurrences sur 22, = 95,5 %).[6] Néanmoins, les données rendent compte de restrictions concernant la forme des éléments clivés. Ainsi, on relève 18 exemples, comme en (3), où le constituant clivé est réalisé par un syntagme nominal :

(3) **Questa luce, infiammazione, o fuoco**, che scappa dal corpo non elettrico per se, ma a cui è comunicata l'elettricità dal propriamente elettrico, **è ciò che si appella Fuoco Elettrico**. (Avelloni, 1771, *ROSF*[7])

En outre, on ne trouve que trois autres exemples dans lesquels les éléments clivés prennent la forme de syntagmes adverbiaux, d'ailleurs exclusivement réalisés par des adverbes spatiaux *quivi* et *qui*, comme en (4). Selon De Cesare/Garassino (2018 : 262–263), ces adverbes peuvent être interprétés comme des syntagmes nominaux qui ont des traits communs avec les pronoms, à savoir la possibilité d'être paraphrasés par des syntagmes prépositionnels lexicaux (*Qui* [= *in questo posto*] *si sta bene*), d'apparaitre comme élément nominal dans un syntagme prépositionnel (*Da qui si vede tutto*) ou de figurer comme argument du verbe (*Sono qui*). Ainsi, l'exemple (4) contient une pseudo-clivée inversée dont l'élément clivé est réalisé sous forme de syntagme nominal pronominal.

---

[5] Cf. l'approche du *code copying* proposée par Johanson (2002).
[6] La répartition relevée dans le corpus converge aussi avec l'italien contemporain, pour lequel Garassino (2014 : 63) constate aussi une dominance des pseudo-clivées inversées de type 1, tandis que celles de type 2 sont extrêment rares.
[7] ROSF = Raccolta di Opuscoli Fisico-Medici.

(4) Or **quì è dove** confesso di non comprendere la forza dell'illazione. (Litta, 1778, *OS*[8])

Outre ces exemples, on ne rencontre pas de pseudo-clivée inversée de type 1 dont l'élément clivé prend la forme d'un autre syntagme adverbial, d'un syntagme prépositionnel ou d'un syntagme verbal fini. Par ailleurs, on ne relève qu'un seul exemple (5) d'une pseudo-clivée inversée de type 2 ; le constituant clivé est alors réalisé par le pronom démonstratif neutre *questo*.

(5) la calce metallica altro non è che il ferro stesso del suo flogisto spogliato; dunque altro non accade al ferro in questa effervescenza, che lo spogliamento del suo flogisto: **questo è quello adunque, che ci somministra alla composizione dell'aria**. (Moreni, 1778, *OS*)

Dans les pseudo-clivées inversées relevées, la phrase subordonnée est surtout introduite par les pronoms complexes *ciò che*, comme en (3), ou *quello/quella che*, comme en (5), tandis que les exemples contenant des pronoms relatifs libres se limitent au clivage des adverbes spatiaux *quivi* et *quì*, où la phrase subordonnée est introduite par *dove*, comme en (4). Pour Roggia (2009 : 38), ces structures ont un statut ambigu puisqu'elles peuvent aussi être envisagées comme des phrases clivées qui actualisent des structures aujourd'hui peu usuelles où la copule et le constituant clivé sont inversés suivant le schéma *X è Che + Verbo*.[9] Par ailleurs, on ne trouve aucune pseudo-clivée inversée introduite par un syntagme nominal défini et dans laquelle un terme générique est modifié par la clause relative restrictive. De même, on ne trouve aucun exemple de relation hyperonymique entre l'élément clivé et le nom placé avant la phrase subordonnée.

4.2 Traductions

Dans les traductions comme dans les textes italiens non traduits, on observe une répartition inégale entre les deux types de pseudo-clivées inversées. Dans les deux cas, les pseudo-clivées inversées de type 1 dominent largement, même si l'écart entre les deux types est moins prononcé dans les traductions.

---

[8] OS = Opuscoli scelti.
[9] Dans les textes italiens non traduits, cette forme plus ancienne de la phrase clivée se trouve exclusivement lors du clivage des adverbes locaux et temporels comme *quì*, *quivi* et *allora* et prend la valeur d'une formule archaïsante (Meier à paraître).

	Type 1 % (N)	Type 2 % (N)	Total % (N)
Textes italiens non traduits	95,5 (21)	4,5 (1)	100 (22)
Traductions	68,5 (37)	31,5 (17)	100 (54)

Tab. 3. Fréquence des types de pseudo-clivées inversées dans les traductions et les textes italiens non traduits.

L'analyse des traductions montre que les pseudo-clivées inversées de type 1 remplacent souvent des phrases clivées françaises contenant des sujets clivés réalisés sous forme de syntagme (pro)nominal (23 occurrences), comme en (6). Le changement de la construction clivée ne mène pas à un changement de l'élément clivé, de sorte que la position syntaxique de la partie focalisée est conservée. En effet, le maintien de la focalisation de l'élément clivé constitue un critère d'identification central qui permet de distinguer les pseudo-clivées inversées de phrases copulatives prédicationnelles.[10]

(6) **C'est vraisemblablement le phlogistique extrait du sang, & concentré dans la liqueur séminale, qui** lui donne son activité sur les parties qui la renferment, & sur le germe qu'elle doit développer. (Senebier, 1776, *JP*[11])
Il flogisto estratto dal sangue, e concentrato nel liquor seminale è quello probabilmente che dà allo stesso liquore l'attività ch'egli ha sulle parti che lo racchiudono, e sul germe che dee sviluppare. (Senebier, 1776, *OS*)

Outre les phrases clivées, les pseudo-clivées inversées de type 1 remplacent d'autres phrases copulatives spécificationnelles dans lesquelles le constituant suivant la copule désigne un référent de discours focalisé (7 occurrences) :

(7) **M. Vicq-d'Azyr est celui qui** a le mieux distingué ces espèces de concrétions biliaires cristallines des calculs biliaires ordinaires. (Fourcroy, 1789, *ACHI*[12])
Il Sig VICQ-D'AZYR è quello che meglio ha distinto queste specie di concrezioni biliari cristalline dei calcoli biliari ordinarj. (Fourcroy, 1790, *AC*[13])

---

[10] À propos de la difficulté d'identification des phrases pseudo-clivées inversées, Garassino (2014 : 62) constate que « [f]rom a methodological point of view, a warning is necessary since RPCs [reverse pseudo-cleft sentences] are not easily recognizable in a written corpus. In particular, in Type 1 RPCs the absence of prosodic information sometimes makes it impossible to decide whether the initial XP bears a focus accent, which is the only feature distinguishing such structures from predicative copulative sentences ».

[11] JP = Journal de Physique.

[12] ACHI = Annales de Chimie.

[13] AC = Annali di Chimica.

On ne trouve qu'un seul exemple où la pseudo-clivée inversée est la traduction d'une pseudo-clivée française, c'est-à-dire que la pseudo-clivée inversée résulte de l'inversion de la suite des phrases subordonnée et matrice. Malgré ce changement, la focalisation demeure sur l'élément nominal clivé :

(8) Tout ce qui est au-dessus, est l'habitation des dieux; **ce qui est au-dessous est le séjour de la nature & de la discorde.** (Lande, 1789, *EJ*[14])
Quanto è sopra di essa è soggiorno degli iddj; **soggiorno della natura e della discordia è quello che sta sotto.** (Lande, 1789, *GSLA*[15])

Les données indiquent que les traductions peuvent contribuer à la diffusion de certains types de pseudo-clivées inversées qui sont inexistants dans les textes italiens non traduits. Ce constat concerne d'une part les pseudo-clivées inversées dans lesquelles un terme générique est modifié par une clause relative restrictive. Ainsi, on trouve deux exemples dans lesquels, comme en (9), le nom *la ragione* précède à la phrase subordonnée.

(9) **C'est en partie à cause de cela que** les vallées des pays primitifs sont toujours plus profondes que celles des pays secondaires. (Monnet, 1786, *JP*)
Questa in parte è la ragione, per cui le valli dei paesi primitivi son sempre più profonde, che quelle de' paesi secondarj. (Monnet, 1786, *OS*)

D'autre part, on rencontre un exemple où la phrase subordonnée est introduite par le pronom relatif libre *quando*.

(10) S'il est vrai qu'une controverse approche de sa décision, par la multiplication des faits qui la concernent, **c'est lorsque ces faits sont sans équivoque dans leurs conséquences.** (Luc, 1790, *JP*)
Se è vero che una controversia s'accosti alla sua decisione colla moltiplicazione de' fatti che la riguardano; **egli è quando questi fatti sono evidentemente nelle loro conseguenze.** (Luc, 1790, *BFE*[16])

Les pseudo-clivées inversées de type 2 résultent souvent de traductions de phrases clivées françaises dont le constituant clivé est occupé par le pronom clitique *ce* (14 occurrences). *Ce* entretient une relation anaphorique avec l'énoncé précédent et constitue principalement un objet clivé (10 occurrences), comme en (11). Dans ces cas, le recours à la pseudo-clivée inversée peut être motivé par le fait que, ni en français ni en italien, ces clivées ne permettent de former de contrepartie non-clivée sans que ne soient apportées des adaptations lexicales majeures (cf. Lambrecht 2001 : 463).

---

[14] EJ = L'Esprit des Journaux.
[15] GSLA = Giornale scientifico letterario e delle arti.
[16] BFE = Biblioteca fisica d'Europa.

(11) Ces différences entre ces deux airs doivent devenir plus considérables en soumettant aux mêmes expériences votre air inflammable huileux, & **c'est ce que je me propose de faire incessamment**. (Barbier, 1780, *JP*)
Queste differenze tra queste due arie debbono divenire più considerabili sottomettendo agli stessi sperimenti la vostr'aria infiammabile oleosa; **e quest'è ciò, che mi propongo di far quanto prima**. (Barbier, 1780, *OFSA*[17])

Dans deux cas, les pseudo-clivées inversées de type 2 remplacent des clivées cohésives contenant des éléments clivés qui sont le plus souvent des adverbes (cf. Wienen 2006). Par exemple en (12), la phrase matrice est constituée du connecteur grammaticalisé *c'est ainsi que* qui introduit une conséquence. Suivant Lahousse/Lamiroy (2015), l'adverbe modal *ainsi* est désémantisé et l'expression *c'est ainsi que* prend un sens consécutif plus abstrait qui n'est pas rendu par la traduction.

(12) **c'est ainsi qu'on voit tous les jours dans les cabinets d'histoire naturelle, les oiseaux, les insectes, les plantes**, &c. se décolorer si on les expose à la lumiere. (Dorthes, 1789, *ACHI*)
questo è quello che s'osserva continuamente ne' gabinetti di storia Naturale ove gli uccelli, gli insetti, c le piante ec. si scolorano quando vengono esposti alla luce. (Dorthes, 1789, *BFE*)

Enfin, en (13), la pseudo-clivée inversée de type 2 est la traduction d'une clivée inférentielle dont l'élément clivé est vide (*c'est que*). Ces clivées expriment une relation causale-implicative entre deux unités textuelles (cf. Atayan/Wienen 2014), ce qui est aussi souligné dans la pseudo-clivée inversée dont la phrase subordonnée est introduite par le pronom relatif libre *perchè*.

(13) **c'est que** le Pérou nord a beaucoup de gros volcans & que le Pérou sud n'en a pas même de petits que je sache. (Ducarla, 1782, *JP*)
Questo è perchè il Nord ha di molti e grandi vulcani, e 'l Perù Sud, per quanto è a mia cognizione, non ne ha nemmeno de' piccoli. (Ducarla, 1784, *OS*)

Les exemples (11), (12) et (13) montrent que les traducteurs ont recours aux pseudo-clivées inversées de type 2 pour éviter la traduction littérale de phrases clivées « informatives-présuppositionnelles » (clivées i-p). Dans ce type de clivées, l'élément clivé n'est ni focalisé ni présenté comme une nouvelle information, qui se trouve après la partie *c'est X* dans la phrase subordonnée (cf. Prince 1978).[18] La substitution fréquente des clivées i-p indique que les traducteurs les considèrent comme fortement marquées et peu

---

[17] OFSA = Osservazioni spettanti alla fisica, alla storia naturale ed alle arti.
[18] Pour une classification des types de phrases clivées, cf. Dufter (2009).

usuelles (cf. Meier à paraître). En ce sens, l'emploi que font les traducteurs des pseudo-clivées inversées de type 2 témoigne du faible degré de conventionnalité des clivées i-p à la fin du 18ᵉ siècle et confirme l'observation de Serianni (2006) selon qui ce type de clivée ne se répand qu'au 19ᵉ siècle.[19] La comparaison avec les textes italiens non traduits montre par ailleurs que le recours aux pseudo-clivées inversées de type 2 par les traducteurs est aussi fortement marqué dans la mesure où cette construction est presque inexistante dans les textes scientifiques non traduits.

5. Fonction

5.1 Textes non traduits

Les pseudo-clivées inversées de type 1 possèdent pour la plupart une structure informationnelle dans laquelle le constituant clivé contient des informations connues ou déductibles, alors que le contenu propositionel de la phrase subordonnée est entièrement ou partiellement nouveau (17 occurrences sur 22).[20] Ces pseudo-clivées inversées suivent alors le principe pragmatique général consistant à placer les informations connues avant les informations nouvelles (cf. Gundel 1988). Ces structures figurent pour la plupart au milieu d'un paragraphe (14 occurrences) et présentent une relation anaphorique entre l'élément clivé et le contenu propositionnel du même énoncé ou de celui qui précède. Par exemple, en (14), le pronom clivé *quai* renvoie à un référent introduit précédemment, à savoir *quai (voragini) vuoti* :

(14) Vaste voragini inoltre sono state osservate dall'Abate FORTIS nella Dalmazia (d). E **quai vuoti** non debbono aver lasciati i vulcani estinti; **quai non debbono esser quelli che** sono ampliati dai tuttora ardenti vulcani che da tanto tempo vomitano spesso grandissima quantità di materie? (Polidori, 1794, *AC*)

À trois reprises, ces pseudo-clivées inversées se trouvent au début d'un paragraphe. Les constituants clivés renvoient alors à un référent introduit au paragraphe précédent.

---

[19] Cette observation ne s'applique pas aux clivées inférentielles, qui sont déjà attestées en ancien italien (D'Achille/Proietti/Viviani 2005).
[20] Selon Garassino (2014), l'italien contemporain semble préférer une structure informationnelle dans laquelle le référent du constituant clivé est nouveau et le contenu propositionnel de la phrase subordonnée est entièrement ou partiellement nouveau.

(15) **Queste stesse particelle, o sia flogisto**, scosse, e staccate dalla massa del globo terrestre dall'azione delle centrali potenze, e da queste oltre la superficie della terra spinte, e disperse, **sono quelle che urtando le nostre fibre**, e penetrando addentro di nostri corpi, dettano in noi il sentimento del calore. Il qual calore se si riguarda l'origine, onde deriva, non impropriamente centrale si può dire. (Mazzi, 1784, *ROSF*)

On ne rencontre que peu de pseudo-clivées inversées de type 1 dont autant le constituant clivé que la phrase subordonnée contiennent des informations nouvelles (5 occurrences sur 22). Dans deux cas, les pseudo-clivées inversées se trouvent au début d'un paragraphe, comme en (16), où la construction suit la première phrase d'un paragraphe qui fournit un cadre temporel dans lequel s'insèrent les contenus d'un événement introduits dans la pseudo-clivée inversée :

(16) Erano le ore 23 e mezzo all'incirca quando con iscoppio violentissimo e fragoroso cadde il fulmine nel Campanile di quella Chiesa. **Varj globi di fuoco, dei pezzi di muro scagliati in diverse parti, un forte odore di fosforo, la rottura di molti vetri ec. fu ciò che quelle Monache appena caduto il fulmine osservarono.** (Landriani, 1780, *OS*)

Independamment de leur configuration informationnelle, les pseudo-clivées inversées jouent un rôle important dans le discours scientifique italien du 18e siècle. En tant que phrases copulatives spécificationnelles, elles constituent un dispositif permettant d'introduire dans la phrase subordonnée des définitions et des explications d'un référent qui est au centre de l'argumentation scientifique (cf. Declerck 1984 : 253). Ainsi, les pseudo-clivées inversées remplissent particulièrement la fonction sémiotique de représentation des textes scientifiques, notamment celle de la concrétisation des connaissances (cf. Roelcke 2010 : 24).

Selon Garassino (2014 : 71), les pseudo-clivées inversées de type 2 disposent d'une configuration cognitive fixe, à savoir une séquence allant d'informations connues à des informations nouvelles. Dans des positions textuelles médianes, le clivage du pronom démonstratif neutre permet de référer à une phrase introduite précédemment, voire à une section complète, et non seulement à un référent spécifique. En (17), nous observons un cas de référence anaphorique « imprécise » (Calude 2009) où le pronom démonstratif renvoie à la phrase précédente et signale l'introduction d'une conclusion résumant l'argumentation développée dans le passage textuel. En revanche, on ne rencontre aucune pseudo-clivée inversée qui apparait en début de texte, où ces constructions permettent d'introduire un topique à l'initale.[21]

---

[21] Cf. à ce propos aussi Givon (2002) qui, pour l'anglais, présente l'exemple suivant : *What we're going to talk about today is love.*

(17) la calce metallica altro non è che il ferro stesso del suo flogisto spogliato; dunque altro non accade al ferro in questa effervescenza, che lo spogliamento del suo flogisto: **questo è quello adunque, che** ci somministra alla composizione dell'aria. (Moreni, 1778, *OS*)

5.2 Traductions

L'analyse des traductions montre que les pseudo-clivées inversées de type 1 remplacent surtout des clivées *continuous-topic* (Gómez Gonzáles 2007), c'est-à-dire des phrases dont le constituant clivé est le sujet et qui établissent un référent déjà introduit dans le discours comme le topique de la clivée (26 occurrences sur 37). L'élément clivé fournit alors une information connue qui, en raison du clivage, est souvent présentée comme étant de nature contrastive, tandis que la partie suivante *c'est X* apporte des informations pour la plupart nouvelles (cf. Dufter 2009 : 100–101). En (18) par exemple, la valeur anaphorique du pronom clivé *elles* est soulignée en italien non seulement par la reprise nominale *queste considerazioni*, mais aussi par l'ajout de la particule emphatique *medesime*.

(18) **Ces considérations** avaient frappé depuis longtemps le sieur Loriot, mécanicien déjà connu par plusieurs découvertes dont l'utilité est avouée; et, **ce sont elles qui ont excité les recherches** dont on publie aujourd'hui le fruit. (Loriot, 1774, *MAB*[22])
Queste considerazioni avevano di lungo tempo fatta molta impressione nella mente del Sig. Loriot, Meccanico già celebre per molte e molte scoperte trovate utilissime; e **queste considerazioni medesime sono state quelle che hanno prodotto quei tentativi e quelle ricerche**, il frutto delle quali vien fatto pubblico adesso. (Loriot, 1775, *MT*[23])

Ces pseudo-clivées inversées rendent compte d'une configuration informationnelle que l'on observe aussi souvent dans les exemples de type 1 présents dans les textes italiens non traduits. Toutefois, on rencontre peu de pseudo-clivées inversées qui résultent de la traduction de phrases clivées dont le constituant clivé est présenté comme une nouvelle information, alors que le contenu suivant *c'est X* est connu (11 occurrences sur 37). Dans ces cas, les traductions diffusent un profil informationnel qui n'est pas attesté dans les textes italiens non traduits et qui, selon Garassino (2014 : 66), est très rare en italien contemporain.

---

[22] MAB = Mémoire sur une découverte dans l'art de batir.
[23] MT = (Nuovo) Magazzino Toscano.

(19) Cette force de cohérence, lorsque l'ouvrage a été séché par degrés jusqu'à une température de 25 à 30 degrés du thermomètre de. Réaumur, est d'autant plus grande, que l'argile avoit plus de ductilité lorsqu'elle étoit réduite en pâte, de sorte que l'une & l'autre de ces qualités doivent être confondues avec la ténacité de l'argile; mais cette ténacité est extrêmement variable; parmi les substances étrangères qui la modifient, **c'est le sable qui** la diminue le plus. (Arcet, 1791, *ACHI*)

Questa forza di coesione, quando il lavoro è stato diseccato gradatamente fino ad una temperatura di 25 a 30 gradi del Termometro Reaumuriano è tanto più grande, in quanto che l'argilla aveva più duttilità allorché era ridotta in pasta, di modo che una e l'altra di queste qualità doveano essere confuse colla tenacità dell'argilla, ma questa varia estremamente; fra le sostanze straniere che la modificano, **il sabbione è quello che la sminuisce di più**. (Arcet, 1791, *AC*)

Pour ce qui est des pseudo-clivées inversées de type 2, l'analyse montre que les traducteurs conservent toujours la structure informationnelle des clivées i-p françaises, c'est-à-dire que les informations connues sont placées avant les informations nouvelles. On observe également cette configuration cognitive dans la seule pseudo-clivée inversée de type 2 identifiée dans les textes italiens non traduits (cf. exemple 17). Il s'agit aussi de la seule structure informationnelle actualisée dans les exemples relevés par Garassino (2014). Il est intéressant de noter que l'auteur attribue justement la rareté des pseudo-clivées inversées de type 2 à l'emploi concurrentiel des clivées i-p, par exemple celui des clivées cohésives avec *per questo* comme élément clivé :

> [W]hy is the frequency of Type 2 RPCs so low in Italian? Although a proper answer to this question requires an analysis based on a parallel corpus, we could nonetheless speculate that the low frequency of Type 2 RPCs is inversely related to more successful competing structures. One of them could be Cleft sentences such as 'è per questo che sono venuto' […], which fulfil similar metalinguistic functions. (Garassino 2014 : 72)[24]

Les traductions indiquent plutôt qu'en italien de la fin du 18ᵉ siècle, les clivées i-p ne fonctionnent pas encore comme une construction alternative, mais qu'elles sont remplacées par des pseudo-clivées inversées de type 2. Comme le montre l'exemple (20), ces pseudo-clivées inversées remplissent

---

[24] Dans les textes italiens non traduits, les clivées introduites par *è per questo che* ne sont pas attestées. En revanche, dans les textes source francais, on rencontre trois clivées avec *pour cela*, dont deux sont traduites littéralement en italien et une est rendue par *perciò* : *c'est pour cela que j'ai préféré les mines de fer du genre de la pierre d'aigle* (Rouelle, 1773, *JMCP*) vs *è perciò ho io preferito le miniere di ferro del genere della pietra aquilina* (Rouelle, 1773, JMCP) (cf. Meier à paraître).

des fonctions pragmatiques semblables à celles des clivées i-p françaises : toutes deux servent à établir une référence anaphorique « imprécise » et, par la présentation de contenus nouveaux dans la phrase subordonnée, elles complètent ce qui a été décrit précédemment. Ainsi, pour un domaine fonctionnel similaire, le français et l'italien utilisent deux constructions différentes qui existent certes virtuellement dans l'autre langue, mais qui ne fonctionnent pas comme une ressource établie dans le domaine discursif de la langue scientifique.

(20) Le déchet qu'on éprouve en étuvant des blés, est nul pour le propriétaire qui le consomme; puisque cette farine prenant plus d'eau que celle d'un blé humide, il a plus de pain lorsqu'il la convertit en pâte; **c'est ce que connoît promptement un boulanger qui a acheté du blé étuvé**. Il ne tarde pas à demander ces blés de préférence à d'autres. (Fougeroux, 1786, *JP*)

La perdita, che si prova col porre il biade alla stufa, è nulla pel proprietario che le consuma; imperocchè questa farina prendendo più acqua che quella proveniente da un grano umido, fornisce più pane quando la converte in pasta; **questo è quello che immediatamente conosce un fornajo che ha comprato dei grani stati nella stufa**, e chiede sempre questi a preferenza degli altri. (Fougeroux, 1789, *BFE*)

En (20), la pseudo-clivée inversée de type 2 est alors une construction équivalente à une clivée i-p comme *Le donne hanno vinto, è questo che fa paura* (De Cesare 2017 : 545) qui, à la différence de l'italien du 18e siècle, constitue dans la langue contemporaine une structure non marquée. En ce sens, les résultats obtenus suggèrent des changements dynamiques dans le système des constructions clivées italiennes.

6. Conclusion

Bien qu'elles ne soient pas attestées dans les textes sources, les phrases pseudo-clivées inversées jouent un rôle important dans la traduction italienne de textes scientifiques français de la fin du 18e siècle. Elles servent de constructions alternatives à des structures syntaxiques qui sont fréquentes dans la langue scientifique française, mais qui sont peu usuelles dans les textes italiens non traduits. Cela vaut notamment pour les clivées *continous-topic* et plus encore pour les clivées i-p qui vont se généraliser ultérieurement, mais qui sont encore marquées et jugées peu standard à la fin du 18e siècle. En ce sens, les traductions du français transposent en italien un modèle de langue scientifique dans lequel l'emploi de phrases pseudo-clivées inversées est plus fréquent, ce qui est remarquable étant donné qu'en italien contemporain, l'emploi de cette construction est plutôt limité à la langue orale. En revanche, la comparaison avec les textes italiens non traduits indique peu de divergences formelles et fonctionnelles. Les différences concernent surtout l'emploi de structures informationnelles, qui sont plutôt rares en italien contemporain. Ainsi, le potentiel d'innovation qu'ont les traductions sur la construction de la phrase pseudo-clivée inversée semble limité, mais des études supplémentaires gagneraient tout de même à être menées afin que soit mieux connue la diachronie des phrases pseudo-clivées en italien.

Références

Altieri Biagi, M. L. 1990. *L'avventura della mente. Studi sulla lingua scientifica.* Napoli: Morano.

Altieri Biagi, M. L. 1998. *Fra lingua scientifica e lingua letteraria.* Pisa: Istituti editoriali e poligrafici internazionali.

Apothéloz, D. 2012. Pseudo-clivées et constructions apparentées. In Berrendonner, A. Ed. *Grammaire de la période.* Bern: Peter Lang, 207–232.

Aschenberg, H. / Dessì Schmid, S. 2017. Romanische Sprachgeschichte und Übersetzung – einige Überlegungen. In Aschenberg, H. / Dessì Schmid, S. Eds. *Romanische Sprachgeschichte und Übersetzung.* Heidelberg: Universitätsverlag Winter, 9–39.

Atayan, V. / Wienen, U. 2014. Inferential Cleft Constructions in Translation. French 'c'est que' in Political Texts. In De Cesare, A.-M. Ed. *Frequency, Form and Function of Cleft Constructions. Contrastive, Corpus-based Studies.* Berlin: De Gruyter, 345–376.

Berretta, M. 2002. 'Quello che voglio dire è che': le scisse da strutture topicalizzanti a connettivi testuali. In Beccaria, G. L. / Marello, C. Eds. *La parola al testo. Scritti per Bice Mortara Garavelli.* Torino: Edizioni dell'Orso, 15–31.

Boxus, M.-A. 2006. Considérations sur les constructions pseudo-clivées (en français, portugais et anglais). *Revista da Faculdade de Letras – Línguas e Literaturas, II Série* XXIII, 433–460.

Bret, P. 2013. 'Enrichir le magasin ou l'on prend journellement'. La presse savante et la traduction scientifique à la fin du XVIIIe siècle. In Pfeiffer, J. / Conforti, M. / Delpiano, P. Eds. *L'Europe des journaux savants (XVIIe–XVIIIe siècles). Communication et construction des savoirs, Archives Internationales d'Histoire des Sciences* 63 (170/171). Brepols: Turnhout, 359–382.

Calude, A. 2009. *Cleft Constructions in Spoken English.* Saarbrücken: Müller.

Collins, P. C. 1991. *Cleft and Pseudo-cleft Constructions in English.* London: Routledge.

D'Achille, P. / Proietti, D. / Viviani, A. 2005. La frase scissa in italiano: aspetti e problemi. In D'Achille, P. / Korzen, I. Eds. *Tipologia linguistica e società. Due giornate italo-danesi di studi linguistici (Roma, 27.–28.11.2003).* Firenze: Cesati, 249–279.

De Cesare, A.-M. 2016. Cleft Constructions in a Contrastive Perspective. Towards an Operational Taxonomy. In De Cesare, A.-M. Ed. *Frequency, Forms and Functions of Cleft Constructions in Romance and Germanic. Contrastive, Corpus-based Studies.* Berlin: De Gruyter Mouton, 9–48.

De Cesare, A.-M. 2017. Cleft Constructions. In Dufter A. / Stark, E. Eds. *Manual of Romance Morphosyntax and Syntax.* Berlin: De Gruyter, 537–568.

De Cesare, A.-M. / Garassino, D. 2018. Adverbial Cleft Sentences in Italian, French and English. A Comparative Perspective. In García, M. / Uth, M. Eds. *Focus Realization and Interpretation in Romance and Beyond.* Amsterdam: Benjamins, 255–285.

Declerck, R. 1984. The Pragmatics of It-clefts and Wh-clefts. *Lingua* 64, 251–289.

Delin, J. / Oberlander, J. R. 1996. The Function and Interpretation of Reverse Wh-clefts in Spoken Discourse. *Language and Speech* 39/2–3, 183–225.

Delpiano, P. 2013. Lire les sciences dans l'Italie du XVIIIe siècle. In Pfeiffer, J. / Conforti, M. / Delpiano, P. Eds. *L'Europe des journaux savants (XVIIe- XVIIIe siècles). Communication et construction des savoirs, Archives Internationales d'Histoire des Sciences* 63 (170/171). Brepols: Turnhout, 287–300.

Den Dikken, M. 2006. Specificational Copular Sentences and Pseudoclefts. In Everaert, M. / Riemsdijk, H. v. Eds. *The Blackwell Companion to Syntax* 4. Oxford: Blackwell, 292–409.

Dufter, A. 2009. Clefting and Discourse Organization: Comparing Germanic and Romance. In Dufter, A. / Jacob, D. Eds. *Focus and Background in Romance Languages.* Amsterdam: Benjamins, 83–121.

Forner, F. / Meier, F. / Schwarze, S. Eds. 2022. *I periodici settecenteschi come luogo di comunicazione dei saperi. Prospettive storiche, letterarie e linguistiche.* Berlin: Peter Lang.

Frank-Job, B. 2008. Schriftkultureller Ausbau des Französischen im 14. Jahrhundert: das Beispiel von Nicole Oresme. In Stark, E. / Schmidt-Riese, R. / Stoll, E. Eds. *Romanische Syntax im Wandel.* Tübingen: Narr, 585–600.

Garassino, D. 2014. Reverse Pseudo-Cleft Sentences in Italian and English: A Contrastive Analysis. In Korzen, I. / Ferrari, A. / De Cesare, A.-M. Eds. *Between Romance and Germanic: Language, Text, Cognition and Culture.* Bern: Peter Lang, 55–74.

Givon, T. 2002. *Syntax.* Amsterdam: Benjamins.

Gomez Gonzalez, M. 2007. 'It was you that told me that, wasn't it?' *It*-Clefts Revisited in Discourse. In Hannay M. / Steen G. J. Eds. *Structural-Functional Studies in English Grammar: In Honour of Lachlan Mackenzie.* Amsterdam: Benjamins, 103–139.

Gundel, J. K. 1988. Universals of Topic-Comment Structure. In Hammond, M. / Moravcsik, E. / Wirth, J. Eds. *Studies in Syntactic Typology.* Amsterdam: Benjamins, 209–242.

Johanson, L. 2002. Contact-Induced Change in a Code-Coying Framework. In Jones M. C. / Esch, E. Eds. *Language Change. The Interplay of Internal, External and Extra-Linguistic Factors*. Berlin: De Gruyter, 285–313.

Kranich, S. / Becher, V. / Höder, S. 2011. A Tentative Typology of Translation-induced Language Change. In Kranich, S. / Becher, V. / Steffen, H. / House, J. Eds. *Multilingual Discourse Production. Diachronic and Synchronic Perspectives*. Amsterdam: Benjamins, 11–43.

Labov, W. 1972. On the Mechanism of Language Change. In Gumperz, J. / Hymes, D. Eds. *Directions in Sociolinguistics*. New York: Holt, Rinehart and Winston, 512–538.

Lahousse, K. / Lamiroy, B. 2015. 'C'est ainsi que': grammaticalisation ou lexicalisation ou les deux à la fois? *Journal of French Language Studies First View* 27/2, 161–185.

Lambrecht, K. 2001. A Framework for the Analysis of Cleft Constructions. *Linguistics* 39, 463–516.

Lirola, M. M. 2006. An Approximation to the Communicative Values of Reversed-pseudo Cleft Sentences in Alan Paton's Novels. *Revista Virtual de Estudos da Linguagem* 4/6, 1–20.

Meier, F. à paraître. Les phrases clivées dans la langue scientifique italienne de la fin du 18ᵉ siècle : un cas de contact de langues à travers la traduction. In Neuß, A. / Peter, B. Eds. *Phénomènes du contact des langues et du plurilinguisme dans la Romania*. Berlin: Frank & Timme.

Prince, E. F. 1978. A Comparison of Wh-clefts and It-clefts in Discourse. *Language* 54, 883–906.

Roelcke, T. 2010. *Fachsprachen*. Berlin: Erich Schmidt Verlag.

Roggia, C. E. 2009. *Le frasi scisse in italiano. Struttura informativa e funzioni discorsive*. Genève: Slatkine.

Salvi, G. 1991. Le frasi copulative. In Renzi, L. / Salvi, G. Eds. *Grande grammatica italiana di consultazione* II. Bologna: il Mulino, 163–189.

Schwarze, S. 2001. L'apporto della traduzione alla scrittura scientifica italiana alle soglie fra Sette- e Ottocento. In Stella, A. / Lavezzi, G. Eds. *Esortazioni alle storie. Atti del convegno 'parlano un suon che attenta Europa ascolta': poeti, scienziati, cittadini nell'Ateneo pavese tra riforme e rivoluzione, Università di Pavia, 13-15 dicembre 2000*. Milano: Cisalpino, 527–542.

Serianni, L. 2006. *Grammatica italiana. Italiano comune e lingua letteraria*. Torino: UTET.

Wehr, B. 2016. Some Remarks on Different Classifications of Cleft Constructions and their Areal Distribution. In De Cesare, A.-M. / Garassino, D. Eds. *Current Issues in Italian, Romance and Germanic Non-canonical Word Orders. Syntax – Information Structure – Discourse Organization*. Frankfurt a. M.: Peter Lang, 147–179.

Biographies

Marina Albers studied Romance Philology at Ludwig Maximilian University (LMU) of Munich and passed her first state examination in French and Spanish in 2018. Since 2019, she has been a research assistant and doctoral candidate in the Class of Language at the Graduate School Language & Literature at LMU, where her dissertation focuses on Jesuit communication in the eighteenth-century Province of Paraguay. She is also a research assistant and lecturer at the LMU Institute of Romance Studies. Her research interests include language history, historical language contact (French and Spanish), discourse-traditional and epistolary linguistics and the so-called *primer español moderno*.

Vahram Atayan is the director of the French and Italien departments at the Institute for Translation and Interpreting at Heidelberg University. He obtained a Diploma in Physics from Yerevan State University in 1993, followed in 2001 by a Diploma in Translation Studies (French and Italian) from Saarland University. His doctoral thesis, completed in 2006, focused on macrostructures of argumentation in German, French and Italian, while his 2011 habilitation (also in Saarbrücken) was in Romance Linguistics and Translation Studies. His research interests include: linguistic theory of argumentation, text linguistics, languages for special purposes, corpus-based contrastive linguistics und translation studies. Atayan has also been the coordinator/director of three subsequent translation bibliographies (Romance-German *Saarbrücken Bibliography of Translations of Nonfictional Texts*, SÜB, Latin-German *Saarbrücken Bibliography of Translations of Nonfictional Texts – Latin*, SÜB-L, *Heidelberg Bibliography of Translations of Nonfictional Texts*, HÜB).

Katharina Fezer has been a research assistant in the project "Purism – Discourses and Practices of Linguistic Purity" within the Collaborative Research Center 1391 "Different Aesthetics" at the University of Tübingen since 2019. Prior to this, she studied German and Romance languages and literature in Freiburg im Breisgau, Stuttgart and Paris. The focus of her doctoral project is on private letters and the purism debate in the *siècle classique* and therefore on questions of historical sociolinguistics as well as corpus linguistics.

Biographies

Sebastian Lauschus studied Italian language and culture as well as history (B.A.) at the Humboldt University of Berlin and completed an M.A. in "European Languages: Structures and Use" at the Freie Universität of Berlin (with a focus on Romance languages). He is a research fellow at the Georg August University of Göttingen in the project "A fifteenth-century medico-botanical synonym list in Hebrew characters from central Italy", funded by the German Research Council (DFG). His research focuses on synchronic and diachronic aspects of Central and Southern Italian varieties, especially in relation to medieval and early modern times, as well as on medieval and early modern Judeo-Italian.

Laura Linzmeier is a research associate at the Department of Romance Studies (Italian and French) at the University of Regensburg. Her research activities include the study of minority languages and cultures in Sardinia, which has led to several fieldwork visits for her doctoral dissertation on Sassarese (a variety spoken in northwestern Sardinia). Currently, she is interested in the effects of ports, ships and waterways on the processes of maritime communication and in the functional literacy linked to maritime communities in France during the seventeenth and eighteenth centuries. Her research focuses on contact and (historical) sociolinguistics, minority languages and maritime communication. She is a co-organizer of the CITAS-funded research network MS ISLA (**M**editerranean **S**tudies on **I**sland **A**reas), also located at the University of Regensburg.

Franz Meier teaches French and Italian linguistics at the University of Augsburg. In April 2016, he received his PhD with a media and sociolinguistic study on the relevance of linguistic and textual norms in the language awareness of Francophone journalists in the Canadian province of Quebec. His current research is on the role of translations as a contact variety in the history of French and Italian. In his habilitation thesis, he studies the possible influence of Italian translations of French scientific texts on the syntactic development of Italian scientific language in the late eighteenth century. He is particularly interested in the interface of syntax, construction semantics and information structure.

Guido Mensching, PhD (1992) and habilitation (1997), both at the University of Cologne, held a professorship in Romance Linguistics at the Freie Universität of Berlin from 2000 to 2013. Since then, he has been Professor of Romance Linguistics at the Georg August University of Göttingen. He has published extensively on Romance medical terminology with a special focus on Judeo-Romance texts and on synonym literature, as well as on the syntax of the Romance languages. He is also a specialist in Sardinian.

Among his main publications are *Einführung in die sardische Sprache* (3rd ed. 2004), *La sinonimia delos nonbres delas medeçinas griegos e letynos e arauigos* (1994), and *Infinitive Constructions with Specified Subjects: A Syntactic Analysis of the Romance Languages* (2000). At the time being, he is one of the principal investigators in the project "A fifteenth-century medico-botanical synonym list in Hebrew characters from central Italy", funded by the German Research Council (DFG).

Daniele Moretti is a researcher in the DFG project "Heidelberg Bibliography of Translations". He obtained his B.A. in Translation and Communication Studies (English, German) in 2005 from IULM University in Milan, followed by a Diploma in Translation Studies (Italian, English) from Saarland University in 2009. From 2010–2013, he remained in Saarbrücken as a research assistant at the Chair of Romance Translation Studies at Saarland University, completing a Diploma in Translation Studies (French) there in 2012. Since 2013, he has been a research/teaching fellow at Heidelberg University.

Christine Paasch-Kaiser is a postdoctoral researcher at the Institute of Applied Linguistics and Translatology at Leipzig University. Her research areas include sociolinguistics, historical linguistics, translation didactics and machine translation. She has special interest in corpus linguistics, as well as law and language in the Middle Ages. On the latter, her research focuses more precisely on legal phraseological units in historical texts from the legal practice of the Normandy region.

Luca Refrigeri obtained a double M.A. degree in Modern Philology and Italian Studies in 2020 at both "La Sapienza" and Paris-Sorbonne University. Since September 2020, he has been a research fellow at the Georg August University of Göttingen within the project "A fifteenth-century medico-botanical synonym list in Hebrew characters from central Italy". Since June 2023, he has been employed for the *Lessico Etimologico Italiano* at Saarland University. His research interests include: Romance linguistics, in particular of medieval French, Occitan and Italian; Judeo-Romance linguistic varieties; and ecdotics, in particular with regard to medieval scientific texts.

Tabea Salzmann received her first degree in Hispanic Studies and Indology (M.A.) at the Martin Luther University Halle-Wittenberg, where she also wrote her dissertation (*summa cum laude*) in cooperation with the Hermann Paul School of Linguistics in Freiburg and the Université de Montréal. She worked as post-doctoral researcher at the IIA, UNAM, Mexico and at the University of Bremen, where she currently has her own research project,

Biographies

"Contact-Induced Language Change in the Portuguese of the *Estado da Índia*: the Indian Influence" (SA 3224/2-1), financed by the DFG. She has received various scholarships (two PhD scholarships, two (inter-)national post-doctoral scholarships, as well as foreign exchange scholarships) as well as an award for obtaining a DFG-funded project by the University of Bremen. She has published several books and peer reviewed articles, including her dissertation under the title *Language, Identity and Urban Space, the Language Use of Latin American Migrants*. Her corpus-based research focuses on language contact from both a synchronic and a diachronic perspective in Spanish and Portuguese, through the lenses of sociolinguistics, ecolinguistics, historical linguistics and text-pragmatic linguistics.

Frank Savelsberg studied Romance philology, Jewish studies and German philology at the University of Cologne and obtained his PhD in 2008 at the Freie Universität of Berlin. He is Senior Lecturer in Romance philology at the Georg August University of Göttingen and one of the principal investigators in the project "A fifteenth-century medico-botanical synonym list in Hebrew characters from central Italy", funded by the German Research Council (DFG). His PhD thesis focused on verbal obscenity in the work of the Spanish Baroque poet Francisco de Quevedo. His main interests in research and teaching are historical linguistics in general and Judeo-Romance languages and texts in particular.

Maria Selig holds the chair for Romance Linguistics at the University of Regensburg. She studied Romance philology, Medieval and Classical Latin in Würzburg, Rennes, Freiburg, and Munich. She received her PhD at the University of Freiburg in 1987 with a dissertation on Romance article development. In 1996, she was habilitated in Freiburg with a post-doctoral dissertation on the beginnings of Old Occitan writing traditions. From 1997 to 2003, she was a professor at the Humboldt University of Berlin. Since 2009, she has been a member of the Bavarian Academy of Sciences and Humanities. Her research concentrates on Vulgar Latin and Early Romance, language change and historical sociolinguistics. Since 2022, she has been responsible for an inter-academic research project on medieval expert cultures, knowledge networks and linguistic standardization (ALMA).

Martin Sinn studied French, Italian and German (first state examination) as well as literary and cultural theory (M.A.) at Eberhard Karl University of Tübingen, Paris-Sorbonne University, École Normale Supérieure de Lyon and Lumière University Lyon 2. Since 2020, he has been a research associate in the Collaborative Research Center 1391 "Different Aesthetics" at Eberhard Karl University of Tübingen, where he is working on Benedetto Varchi's linguistic theory and esthetics as part of the project "Purism – Discourses and Practices of Linguistic Purity".

Lorenzo Tomasin (Venice, 1975) is professor of Romance philology at the University of Lausanne and of History of the Italian language at the Scuola Normale Superiore of Pisa. His research focuses on the linguistic history of Venice; on linguistic contact in the Romance area during the Middle Ages and the early modern period; and on the history, problems and methods of Romance philology. He is a member of the Accademia della Crusca in Florence, and of the Accademia dell'Arcadia in Rome. His most recent books are: *Il caos e l'ordine. Le lingue romanze nella storia della cultura europea* (Turin, Einaudi 2019), and *Europa romanza. Sette storie linguistiche* (Turin, Einaudi, 2021).

Anne Weber is a researcher in the DFG Project "Heidelberg Bibliography of Translations". She completed her Diploma in Translation Studies (French, English) at Saarland University in 2008. From 2010–2015, she remained in Saarbrücken as a research assistant at the Chair of Romance Translation Studies at the same university, obtaining a Diploma in Translation Studies (Italian) there in 2012 and completing her PhD on the translation of German nominal compounds into and from French and Italian in 2016. From 2015–2017, she was a translator/senior translator in an ISP company, and since 2016 she has been a research/teaching fellow at Heidelberg University.

Gabriele Zanello is a researcher in Romance philology and linguistics at the University of Udine. After studies in Trieste and Vienna, he received his PhD in Ladin studies and multilingualism from the University of Udine. He is currently working on sermons and religious literature in Friulian in the eighteenth and nineteenth centuries, historical sources and literature of eastern Friuli, particularly works created in the climate of imperial multiculturalism, the plurilingual theater of the seventeenth century, the relationship between Friulian literature and music and Friulian translations over the centuries up to the present.